THE NEW ELITES OF TROPICAL AFRICA

THE NEW ELITES
OF TROPICAL AFRICA

STUDIES PRESENTED AND DISCUSSED
AT THE SIXTH INTERNATIONAL AFRICAN SEMINAR
AT THE UNIVERSITY OF IBADAN, NIGERIA, JULY 1964

Edited with an Introduction by
P. C. LLOYD

Foreword by
DARYLL FORDE
Director, International African Institute

Published for the
INTERNATIONAL AFRICAN INSTITUTE
by the
OXFORD UNIVERSITY PRESS
1966

Oxford University Press, Ely House, London W.1

GLASGOW NEW YORK TORONTO MELBOURNE WELLINGTON
CAPE TOWN SALISBURY IBADAN NAIROBI LUSAKA ADDIS ABABA
BOMBAY CALCUTTA MADRAS KARACHI LAHORE DACCA
KUALA LUMPUR HONG KONG

*Printed in Great Britain by Richard Clay (The Chaucer Press), Ltd.,
Bungay, Suffolk*

CONTENTS

Contents   vii

Contents vii

FOREWORD

This volume brings before a wider audience the studies presented and the trends of discussion at the International African Institute's Sixth Seminar on the New Elites of Tropical Africa, which was held at the University of Ibadan, Nigeria, in July 1964.

The eighteen papers, in English or French, each with a summary in the other language, deal with aspects of the emergence and development of modern elites in West, East, and Southern Africa. They provide data and present problems for study with regard to a wide range of social categories, from commercial farmers and women market traders to foremen and merchants, as well as administrators and managers in government and industry. Such features as the sharp contrasts with traditional patterns in style of life and aspirations, the development of class consciousness, and attitudes towards marriage and family life are analysed in the context of technical and economic change. A comprehensive introduction by Dr. P. C. Lloyd, based on the discussions at the seminar and his own studies in this field, provides a comparative review. It portrays the characteristics and variations of contemporary elites in Africa, their development in relation to educational advance, their part in traditional and modern associations, the evidence for achievement motivation, and the relationships between the elite and the uneducated. Future developments in African states will clearly be influenced by the composition and character of their elites, and the importance of reaching a deeper understanding of their emergence and of studying the trends of development make this collection of studies particularly relevant at the present time.

The International African Seminar programme as a whole has been made possible by generous grants from the Ford Foundation and we should like again to express our thanks for this assistance. Our thanks are also due to Dr. K. O. Dike, Vice-Chancellor of the University of Ibadan and Director of the Institute of African Studies, for receiving the Seminar, and to Dr. P. C. Lloyd, who devoted so much time and thought to it as Chairman and in editing this volume. We are also indebted to Mr. Michael Crowder, then Secretary of the Institute of African Studies, Mr. Elochukwu Amucheazi, Assistant Secretary, and other members of the staff who were responsible for the practical arrangements.

DARYLL FORDE

I. INTRODUCTION

THE STUDY OF THE ELITE

Throughout sub-Saharan Africa political power has been rapidly passing from the colonial rulers to members of indigenous national elites—men who are predominantly young, highly educated and comparatively wealthy. This process is being documented and analysed by the political scientist. We have descriptions of the rise of political parties, the stages in the contest for independence, the ideologies of the nationalist leaders. We know the biographies of the political leaders; but we still know very little about the social milieux to which these men belong—a category today described in the English-speaking territories as the elite but termed only a decade ago, the middle class. (In the French-speaking countries the term *évolué* has likewise suffered an eclipse.) It is nevertheless clear that future political developments in African states will be strongly influenced by the composition and characteristics of the elites, and the degree of their cohesiveness on internal rivalries.

Social research in Africa has been dominated by anthropologists interested more in community studies related to traditional societies than in the social categories increasingly relevant to the modern industrial and commercial towns. The migrant, adapting the norms and values of his village to those dictated by the urban environment, has attracted more attention than the secondary school and university educated youth increasingly divorced from his traditional culture. Studies of the new elite are also fraught with practical difficulties: its members are busy men and few in number, not readily available for interview; their lives are spent not in the open air but in offices, homes, and clubs; car-owners, their homes are often scattered across the town forming no recognizable territorial community. Thus, the I.N.C.I.D.I. (1956) conference on the middle class in developing territories and the U.N.E.S.C.O. (1956) symposium on African elites seem to have given little impetus to sociological studies in this field. So far, we have but few monographs devoted to an African elite (e.g. Kuper, 1965; Levine, 1965; Porter, 1963; Smythe and Smythe, 1960; Tardits, 1958); articles in sociological journals are more numerous, but tend to be somewhat limited to studies of family patterns and relationships and to political attitudes and aspirations.

The participants at the International African Institute's seminar on social class and elites in contemporary Africa felt themselves to be entering into an almost virgin field. They represented a wide range of sociological disciplines; all had lived for substantial periods in one or more African territories. Their several researches, illustrated in their contributions to the seminar papers, had been in limited fields and their studies of the elite were often marginal to their principal interests. Nevertheless, many of the participants had gained an intimate, if impressionistic, knowledge of the elite through living in the nation's capitals or teaching in their universities. From their contributions the participants endeavoured to synthesize a picture of the African elite.

This introduction to the papers presented at the seminar substantially follows the course of the discussions at the meetings. Its content reflects the regional interests of the participants, Thus, over half of them represented West African territories, both English-speaking and French-speaking—a bias which seems not unreasonable in view of the greater size and longer historical development of the elite in these states. Unfortunately no members of the seminar were able to speak with personal knowledge of the Congo, the French-speaking Central African states, or the Portuguese colonies. Northern Nigeria, too, presents a unique pattern of social stratification which was not discussed in the meetings.

At the outset it was decided that the term 'elite' could be appropriately used to denote those who were western-educated and wealthy, a lower limit of £250 ($700, C.F.A. 150,000) as an annual income being suggested. To label the category in this way was a matter of convenience and in no way prejudged later discussions of the aptness of the term when bearing in mind its accepted sociological connotations. The characteristics of an elite category do, however, vary widely from one nation of Africa to another—in size, levels of wealth, and antiquity. The first task of the seminar was therefore to spell out the major differences. Second, since our category was defined in terms of education, the seminar discussed the educational systems of African nations and in particular the degree to which the contemporary elite has been drawn from the masses (and not from an earlier elite, either western-educated or traditional) and whether it seemed likely to perpetuate itself. The third major topic for discussion was the participation of individual members of the elite in traditional or traditionalist associations—in their descent groups and in political offices in their home areas and in the new ethnic associations based in the towns; conversely, to what extent are the elite developing exclusive associations—and are such uniting it into a single group or dividing it into a series of parallel elites? The fourth topic concerned the cultural values of the elite and their achievement motivation; to what extent are these values derived respectively from indigenous and western society, and in the case of the latter how far can they be transmitted to the population at large? Are new values being transmitted to the rising generation through changed patterns of child rearing? In this field the paucity of data seemed paralleled by considerable uncertainty of the definition and usefulness of the concepts in common use. Finally, having re-viewed a wealth of data on the elites of various African nations, the seminar members reached the main theme of their discussions —the degree to which the elite (as loosely defined) is indeed an elite or a social class as these terms are understood by sociologists. Here again there is no unanimity in the use of these concepts, but members of the seminar stressed the various attributes which seemed pertinent in the African context. Thus, while with such imprecise concepts and with the complexity of the data it proved impossible to attach a neat label to the elite of each African nation, our discussions were invaluable to us in bringing out the principal variables which one would expect to be useful in constructing a model of the elite of any one country.

In the time available for the discussions it was clearly impossible to discuss all those topics which were of interest to participants. In particular, it is to be regretted that the seminar members were

unable to examine the ideologies of the contemporary elites—
négritude, the African personality, African socialism—placing
them in their social context. Nor did the seminar members discuss
in detail the attitudes of the elite to the western world; but here no
apologies are offered. The question of the alienation of the educated African or *évolué*, both from his traditional society and from
western society, has been amply discussed in the past two decades.
The dominant theme of our own seminar lay in exploring the
relationship between the new elites and the rest of the population
of their countries, and in so doing, to draw attention to some
hitherto neglected themes. It was the concluding hope of the participants that their efforts in this direction would prove fruitful to
others, as well as to themselves, in their subsequent studies of
African elites.

CHARACTERISTICS OF THE CONTEMPORARY ELITE

We defined as the elite those persons who were western-educated and wealthy to a high degree relative to the mass of the
population. A minimum annual income limit of £250 was suggested as a guide. But the size and characteristics of the elites of the
African states vary widely. To some extent these differences can
be correlated with variations in the pattern and speed of the
development of political independence, but this is not the whole
explanation.

Thus, the West African states have a long history of educational
experience. In both the former British and French colonial territories Africans gained early political training in their legislatures.
In the British territories, however, eventual independence was
foreseen soon after the end of the Second World War and the
higher education of Africans was promoted. Thus, Nigeria today
has nearly 2,000 lawyers in private practice and 600 indigenous
doctors; in the Eastern and Western Regions, as in Ghana, over
three-quarters of the senior posts in the civil service are held by
nationals. The same process did not take place in the French
colonial territories, where, even in the late 1950s, few Africans
held higher posts and many Frenchmen still held executive jobs

requiring only a secondary-school level of education (Berg, 1960). Elsewhere in Africa the road to independence has been followed much more rapidly and territories became self-governing with but a handful of university graduates—in Tanzania, for instance, there were probably less than a hundred of them in 1964. In such countries the elite includes a large proportion of trained primary-school teachers, secondary-school leavers, and the like, in contrast with some West African capitals with their hundreds of university-trained men and women.

Close estimates of numbers of elite members, using varying levels of education and wealth, are difficult to make for African states. We are, however, dealing with but a very small proportion of the total population. Thus Senegal, with a population of 3,000,000 has about fifty civil servants with a salary of over £2,400 per annum and another 275 earning between £1,200 and £2,400. The next lower category of civil servants earning over £850 per annum numbers 1,600. In private employment are 350 Senegalese with a mean income of £850 per annum (as against 1,600 expatriates in the same category). In Western Nigeria, if taxation figures are trustworthy, only $\frac{1}{2}$ per cent of the adult men earn above £500 per annum. In Zambia only 1,000 persons have twelve years of primary and secondary education, and 2·6 per cent of the adult men have eight or more years schooling—the equivalent of a full primary education. In Uganda only 5,000 men earn above £300 per annum. The Republic of South Africa, with a population of nearly 11,000,000 Africans, has only thirty African lawyers and 100 African doctors (with an annual increase of twelve to fifteen a year), and Rhodesia only five African doctors, four lawyers and a few administrative officers. Ethiopia has an intelligentsia of 1,000 university graduates, two-fifths trained in the United States and one-fifth in Britain.

The size of the elite category is minute compared with the total population. But these members are not dispersed throughout the country—they tend to be congregated in the national and regional capitals. Thus, half of Western Nigeria's senior civil servants are stationed in Ibadan, and the other territories and other occupational spheres, especially commerce, show a similar centralization.

In considering the degree to which the elite develops a self-consciousness of itself, or new values, the important variable is the size of the group in any one place. Thus, while Nigeria's university-trained elite probably number no more than that of Ghana (even though the former state has a total population five or six times that of the latter), numbers living in Lagos and Accra are perhaps comparable.

In the colonial territories the rapid growth of the elite is the product of the past fifteen years. Only with the imminence of independence was higher education stressed. Fourah Bay College in Freetown has a long history, but the remaining universities are of post-war foundation. In 1945 Nigeria had less than 150 students in British universities, and it was only in 1954 that there was a substantial intake of Nigerians in the Western Nigerian civil service. Today there are over 1,000 Nigerians in British universities and 4,000 in Nigerian universities. Mboya's spectacular 'air lift' of Kenyan students to the United States emphasized the urgency of the problem in this state. Everywhere primary and secondary schooling have increased at rapid rates, as shown in the later section.

Thus, the majority of the elite are young. For many of them, however, their education has been a protracted experience: they started primary school perhaps at the age of eight, leaving secondary school when past twenty; years of teaching or clerical work often intervened before admission to a university was secured. And thus the new graduate was often thirty years of age or more. If those who first gained a foothold on the elite ladder were comparatively old, their progress up its rungs has been rapid. The expansion of government and private business has created new posts at the top in excess of the number of expatriates who might move up into them. The expatriates have, in fact, been leaving the civil service, with early departures of those who found the political independence intolerable and a later drift of those who found the most senior policy-making posts closed to them and their promotion halted. Generous compensation has facilitated their resignations. Thus, it has been possible for Africans in the newly independent territories to reach the heights of permanent secretary or university professor within ten years of university graduation.

Occupations

The overwhelming majority of the elite of the independent African states are in bureaucratic employment. The colonial powers had composed a complex administrative structure on near-subsistence economies; government tended to control not only the public services but also many economic and social agencies, such as the Marketing Boards. African nationalist governments have taken over all these functions and expanded them in their efforts to increase economic production and to enlarge the social services. Agricultural extension work is fostered; government development corporations are linked with private enterprise in starting new plantations and factories.

The extension of secondary schooling has created a sudden demand for graduate teachers which few states can meet. Thus, in Nigeria at the present time only one-fifth of the teachers in secondary schools have a university degree (the figure is one-third in the Western Region); yet the majority of these are Nigerian. In the French-speaking West African states the number of university graduates is significantly smaller and, with independence, many of these have been recruited into the government administration, leaving the schools still largely staffed by expatriates. Thus, even the Senegal has only forty indigenous high-school teachers, and only 17 per cent of the staff of the University of Dakar are African (c.f. University of Ibadan 40 per cent). Independent states with more radical leanings tend perhaps to lose their expatriate civil servants at a faster rate, and they feel more strongly that policy-making posts should be filled by their own nationals. Unlike the civil servants, teachers are much more widely distributed through the provincial and district centres, especially in those states which have considerably increased their secondary-school education.

In the colonial period the private professions held great attraction for Africans; the successful were not insulted by being employed in ranks below those of expatriates with similar qualifications—the common allegation against the colonial civil service.

B

These professions are still popular. Most doctors are, however, now employed in the public service. Lawyers remain in private practice—a field which is already becoming nearly saturated in southern Nigeria; few seem attracted towards company or administrative law. Similarly, there are few independent accountants. As the qualifications for university entry, even to an African one, rise with the increased competition among holders of G.C.E. and similar certificates, the lower standards acceptable to legal training institutions help in maintaining the attraction of the profession.

Commerce and business have had little attraction hitherto for the educated African. Major enterprises have been either government-controlled—the Marketing Boards and public corporations —or expatriate import and export companies (such as the United Africa Company) and manufacturing industries. In the former, the African has risen rapidly to the top in an administrative capacity. In the independent states the expatriate firms have become more conscious of their public image and have recruited Africans to managerial posts, especially in personnel management and public relations or, in a few instances, to nominal directorship. When the civil service offers both security of employment and rapid promotion the expatriate-controlled business world seems to hold few attractions; but as the administrative ranks of the government become replete and as advancement slows up in the lower levels, with seniority as the main criterion for promotion, the prospects in the business world appear brighter. Even at a lower level much of the commerce of African states is in alien hands—the Lebanese of West Africa and the Indians of East and Central Africa. West Africa does, indeed, have a thriving indigenous trading community, but it is composed mainly of the less well educated. The university graduate rarely has any capital to invest in business, and is not likely to spend lean years building up his enterprise when the immediate rewards of salaried employment are so high. The principal exception to this pattern would seem to exist in South Africa, where, denied access to most public offices, the educated African does go into retail trading, transport ownership, and the like; one of the most prosperous of such businessmen was formerly a university lecturer.

Separated from their homes during long years of secondary and university education, most of the African elite have become divorced from the land, whatever rights they may continue to hold, in theory, in the property of their village or descent group. The Ivory Coast would appear exceptional in the number of its civil servants and politicians who have become landowners or absentee planters. In a rather different category are the Amhara aristocracy of Ethiopia, with their large estates worked by tenant labour. Investment in building land and house property is, however, one of the main outlets for savings, especially, for instance, in Nigeria or Ghana, where salaried men are able to obtain loans from government corporations. In the former a modern house might well yield a return of 15 per cent per annum of the cost of the building—an amount which well exceeds the mortgage repayment.

In few of the independent states is the military elite much in evidence in the social and political life. Armies are relatively small, and they are among the last organizations to be Africanized, for there seem to be few short cuts to a thorough military training. Here again Ethiopia seems to be one exception, with an army of 30,000 having over 1,000 men of the rank of major or above. The superior training of army officers and their seclusion from everyday political life does, however, insulate them from the envy and often the stigma of corruption attaching to the political and very newly rich elite, they, almost alone, could take power with clean hands (Gutteridge, 1962).

The final elite occupational category is that of the professional politician. In all the independent states the new legislators have been drawn overwhelmingly from the elite, with lawyers and secondary-school teachers well to the fore. Those attaining ministerial rank in governments tend to be among the better educated. The politicians have usually attained their educational qualifications, and hence elite membership, before becoming politically active, and certainly these qualifications are not rewards for political service. Yet, as political parties develop their organization down to village level, as the central party secretariat takes over some of the functions of the civil service, and as promotion to this secretariat from lower ranks in the party hierarchy is made on the basis of political loyalty, so does the party become an avenue of mobility into the elite. It is an avenue most likely to be utilized by those who have been frustrated, by lack of ability or finance, in educational advancement. Such development of party organization seems to be found in two contrasting situations. In Ghana, for instance, the original appeal of the C.P.P. was mainly to the 'verandah boys', the less-well-educated clerks and teachers; the better-educated elite was, in the 1960s, apathetic towards the party, and thus seen by the political leaders to be an opposed group. In Tanzania and Guinea the absence of a cadre of trained African administrative officers has prompted the development of party organs to fill the gap at the village and district levels.

Wealth and Style of Life

The salary structures of the independent African states remain as a colonial heritage. In most states a dual scale operated—one for the expatriate senior civil servant, adjusted to scales in the metropolitan country but carrying inducements and perquisites to make service in tropics more attractive; and the other for the African executive officers, set in relation to incomes from subsistence agriculture. Thus, in Nigeria before 1950 an African executive officer of considerable length of service, who reached the highest rank open to him in the junior civil service, would not earn as much as the recently graduated administrative officer. As Africans gradually entered the senior civil service, replacing the expatriates, they assumed the basic salaries and perquisites (if not the inducement allowance) attached to the posts. In the past decade the principle of equal pay between African and expatriate for equal qualifications has been strongly maintained. The shortage of expatriates willing to work in Africa has, however, resulted in higher salaries being offered—from which the African, too, has benefited. Public corporations, the teaching profession, and commercial firms have tended to adopt government salary scales; commercial firms have, however, tried to out-bid Government for the more able men; and, in Nigeria at least, the public corporations have tended to raise their salary scales far above those of Government—so that in the words of two members of the Morgan Commission 'it is indeed ironical that in the category of University Professors and High Court Judges can be found expatriates with more years of experience and comparable, if not superior, qualifications earning less than our indigenous Chief Executive Officers who have attained these posts mainly as a result of rapid Nigerianisation'. (Nigeria, 1964, p. 49.)

Reforms of recent years have tended to occlude the difference between senior and junior salary scales, making it possible for the executive officers to rise into the four-figure income category. But nothing has been done to reduce the difference between the poor farmer or unskilled labourer and the university graduate. Thus, in Western Nigeria the national income per head is £30 per annum; the farmer usually pays tax on an assessed income of £50; the unskilled labourer earns £75 a year and the most skilled artisan nearly £300. The holder of a West African School Certificate (gained on successfully completing five years of secondary schooling) will expect to start earning £240 as a clerk or teacher. The university graduate, however, commences at £750, with a ceiling at £3,000; in addition, he is given a loan to buy a car and a monthly allowance to run it; he may, if in the higher ranks, occupy a part-furnished government house, paying one-twelfth of his income (rent of a privately owned house would take between a quarter and a fifth of his income).

In other African states the salary scales are very similar; in Rhodesia, for instance, the African university graduate starts earning at £1,000 per annum. In Senegal the salary of secondary school-leavers seems much higher than in English-speaking West African territories.

The remuneration of politicians is equally high. Members of Parliament are often paid £1,000 per annum. For those who were, by training and occupation, teachers and clerks this sum represents a very considerable advance on their earlier incomes. Professionals, on the other hand, may still follow their careers and receive a dual income. Only for those appointed to Ministerial office does political life become a full-time occupation, and here salaries of £3,000 per annum are common. In at least one state it was argued that a minister could not be allowed to earn less than his civil service permanent secretary.

Again South Africa is an exception. Separate salary scales are here maintained for whites and Africans, so that the African university graduate commences only at £450 per annum rising to £900 per annum. Furthermore, in Johannesburg the mean income of the African household head is £250 per annum—a far higher figure than that prevailing in Lagos for instance (though this is, in fact, the income which the Morgan Commission recommended as the minimum necessary to keep the worker with a wife and one child above the 'Poverty Datum Line'). Thus, the relative affluence of the elite is a feature of the newly independent states.

With such incomes the members of the elite enjoy a style of life comparable with that of men of similar affluence in Western Europe; import duties on foreign food and status symbols (the car, radio and television, refrigerator) may be high, but income tax is usually low. Many fortunate men have been allocated the more commodious residences built originally for the expatriate officials. There is a lack of variety in furnishing styles, and the basic elements are copied from local expatriates or from those seen in the metropolitan country. The general uniformity of the housing and furnishing, and the emphasis placed on the more ostentatious status symbols, result in a fairly close correlation between income and style of living.

The Marginal and the Sub-elite

We have defined the elite in terms of possession of western education and wealth. This has the convenience of simplicity, but it tends to exclude certain categories of people who may well deserve the designation elite, when we use it in its sociological sense. Two of these categories, marginal to our own definition, seem worthy of mention here.

First, those holders of traditional political offices who are educated. In the ex-British territories of West Africa the offices of the earlier kingdoms were maintained under the policy of indirect rule. In Ghana and Nigeria, since the 1920s, these offices have often attracted men who have received substantial education;

each of these two states today has a lawyer among its traditional rulers. Second are the wealthy traders, who tend to be but ill-educated, and even on occasion self-taught, but who are able to afford most of the status symbols available to the elite proper. These two categories are numerically more important in West Africa than elsewhere on the continent.

A third category—that of the illiterate or poorly educated traditional chiefs—falls outside our own defined elite category. Such a person has a style of life which owes little to western influence; he is, perhaps through poverty, content to maintain the traditional symbols of his prestige.

Since we use the term elite to designate those with the high levels of education and wealth, we distinguish them from a sub-elite, the less well educated. The relationship between these two categories is an important one. In African states the sub-elite today consists of those with post-primary or some secondary schooling —the executive clerical grades, primary-school teachers, and artisans. Their numbers are difficult to abstract from the general totals of employed persons. Many members of the sub-elite are still striving to enter the elite, either through attainment of the appropriate educational qualifications or through political chan-nels; others are frustrated by their apparent failure and form a reservoir of political discontent.

It should be appreciated that through their close contact with the masses, both the marginal elite and the sub-elite may, in some contexts, be more significant as reference groups to the masses than are the elite of our present definition.

THE DEVELOPMENT OF ELITES

In the foregoing section we sketched in outline some of the characteristics of the modern elite, making no distinction between those men who were recent entrants, having been born into humble families, and those whose families had for a generation or more enjoyed elite status. In this context the distinction was not relevant. Yet we cannot study the role of the elite in contemporary society without placing it in relationship with other groups, and

especially the elite groups of an earlier period. Two earlier elites
are significant: the traditional elite of the political office-holders of
tribal societies and the earlier westernized elite.

The traditional elite still exists in most states, though often with
much diminished prestige. It differs from the modern elite which
we have been describing in that traditional chiefs and rulers are of
elite status only in their own ethnic area, town, or village. The
modern elite is a national elite, even though individual members
will be prominent members of their own local elites. How much
continuity exists between the traditional elite and the contemporary elite? Is there, for instance, an overlap in membership between
traditional and modern elites? Or if the two are distinct and separate, is there antagonism and conflict between the groups? To
what extent are the values of the two elites comparable; to what
extent do their political and economic interests coincide?

In West and South Africa western influence has a long history.
In what way did the early elites here differ from their modern
counterparts—in their relationship with the masses and with the
representatives of the Western nations? The same questions concerning the relationship of traditional to modern elites may be
raised in this context too.

Setting the modern elite in its historical context will enable us
to see and understand the conflicts which may exist within it.
These conflicts would seem to be of three types. First, the ethnic
differences: although we are describing a national elite, individual
members still retain strong ethnic allegiances; (in Nigerian hotel
registers one frequently sees the column 'Nationality' filled with
'Yoruba', 'Ibo', etc.). Certain ethnic groups which accepted education at an early date have maintained their advantages and fill a
disproportionate number of places in the elite—to the chagrin of
other ethnic groups. Second, the differences in generation: the
speed of political, social, and economic advance leads to marked
differences in attitude between generations. Young men not
understanding the political situation of the early colonial period
chide their elders for their feeble attacks on colonial rule, often
unfairly belittling these efforts. Young men with university
degrees find their promotion avenues blocked by older men with

lower educational qualifications. Third, a conflict between different functional groups within the elite. Politicians, perhaps less well educated than the civil servants, fall foul of the latter over methods of administration; the civil servants appear to the politicians to be inflexibly attached to the routines of the colonial period.

Let us examine some of these issues in different parts of Africa.

West Africa

Western trading contact with West Africa antedates the colonial period by at least two centuries. In this era it was the European who was in the weaker position. Coastal Africans became merchants, acting as intermediary between the European trader in his hulk or fort; they and their issue were often educated, and some held high government office—as Justice of the Peace or, in one case, Governor of the Coastal Settlements. The Brew family described by Margaret Priestley is a typical example. Such men retained strong links with their own ethnic groups. At the same time there was much intermarriage between coastal families of similar status. At any one time the numbers of members of such families who held elite positions was small; yet the whole family shared in the prestige of their leading figures. How far should the term elite here apply only to the wealthy and western-educated, how far to the whole family, the majority of whom were as poor as the masses? Again, western observers are apt to credit these Christian African gentlemen, resplendent in their wing collars and frock coats, with possession of most of the Victorian values; but how far is this justified? To what extent were education and dress adopted by these men only for the practical advantages they gave in their relations with the Europeans? To what extent, furthermore, did they become models for the masses; should one describe an entire family, or even the entire population of the coastal trading towns, as a reference group for the interior peoples? Such questions are difficult to answer today, let alone for a century ago.

A rather different situation evolved in Sierra Leone, where a settlement at Freetown of repatriated and freed slaves, having no ethnic links with the people of the interior, developed into a closed group—the Creoles—having a monopoly of elite offices and differentiating themselves from the interior peoples by an emphatic acceptance of western dress and manners. Members of this group settled also in the Gold Coast and Nigeria, intermarrying with local elites and becoming an inter-territorial elite. Intermediate between these types were the 'Brazilians', who returned from the country of their slavery to settle in Lagos and the coastal towns of Dahomey and Togo.

In the later colonial period of the twentieth century many of the offices attained earlier by the westernized elite were reoccupied by expatriate civil servants. The reaction of the elite to this narrowing range of administrative and political opportunities may be seen in the attraction of the independent professions and in their leadership of early nationalist movements. In this role they were frequently in conflict with the traditional elite of chiefs, who equally hoped to be heirs of the colonial powers. The descendants of these early elites have continued to receive such education to maintain them within the contemporary elite, but their numbers are now relatively small. Localized in the coastal towns, these men lost their political dominance as soon as parliaments were elected by the whole state. Nevertheless, individual members still hold high political office, and rivalry exists as in Ghana, Togo, and Sierra Leone between members of this early elite and the remainder of the larger modern elite.

South Africa

One is apt to forget that mission activity started in the southeast of the continent in the late eighteenth century, and that some of the leading schools for Africans were opened in the midnineteenth century. The relationship between these educated Africans and the European settlers was not, at this time, very dissimilar from that prevailing in West Africa. Early members of this elite, such as the western-oriented Jabavu, started newspapers for African readers. The African National Congress was formed in 1912, and the trade-union movement became, in South Africa, strong until events of the 1930s. Apartheid policies have, however, stunted the growth of the elite. Africans have no political rights—to vote or hold office—outside the Bantu states; jobs are reserved, residence is segregated. Instead of the predominance of a highly educated and wealthy national elite so frequently encountered in the independent states, one finds a set of distinct elites. The rural elite differs from the urban elite. An older mission-oriented elite still survives.

South Africa is a caste society; the African elite is a pariah elite with reference to the whites, even though individual members of the latter group cherish friendships with educated Africans. While the nationalist in the ex-colonial territories seeks in some contexts to revive traditional culture, the South African revolts against attempts to confine him to his traditional culture and to deny him the participation in western culture. Thus, while the South African elite does stress its own exclusiveness against the masses, it must also join with them to oppose Apartheid and white domination.

Central and East Africa

Western education came much later to Central and East Africa. In Zambia, for instance, it was not until the first decade of the present century that missionary endeavours really penetrated the country—as did the railway. The copperbelt developed from the 1930s. Thus, by 1950, the elite tended to consist of men with only primary school education, and it was not until later in this decade that men with higher qualifications began to predominate. Almost all the present elite attended the country's one secondary school—Munali College.

In East Africa one finds the same late development. Uganda, however, has some peculiar features. The Baganda, and especially the politically dominant groups, accepted education rapidly in the late nineteenth century, and members of the kingdom tended to dominate not only the national elite but also to provide the sub-elite of teachers and clerks in the remainder of the country. The heritable property rights in *mailo* land have, furthermore, ensured elite continuity, so that the educated Muganda is today likely to be a member also of the more traditionally oriented landowning

Baganda elite. This tends to intensify the conflict between different ethnic groups within the national elite.

In these countries the rapidity of the withdrawal of expatriate civil servants and the expansion of social services may produce vacant posts which cannot as yet be filled by Africans of similar qualifications. In as much as they are filled by men with lower qualifications, conflict will develop when the better-educated men enter the ranks below them. In Tanzania for instance, much of the work of administration at the local level is apparently carried out by the T.A.N.U. agents—men holding office by virtue of their political activity and loyalty. These men are likely to be threatened when the educational system has produced sufficient men to staff a regular bureaucracy.

Ethiopia

Ethiopia is in many respects quite unlike the remaining independent states of Africa. An absolute monarch remains in power with an entrenched traditional landholding elite of the Amhara aristocracy and the clergy. There is little mission activity—and relatively little primary education of any type. Few European-type associations exist. The modern elite here consists of three categories—the new nobility, the military leaders, and the intelligentsia—whose members are drawn both from the traditional aristocracy and from the commoners. The new nobility are salaried men, they live and dress in a western manner. But they are enmeshed in a pattern of patron–client relationships, and their own position depends largely on their favour with the Emperor; they are surrounded by retainers anxious for their own advancement. The large military officer group is in an equivalent position. As a result of their foreign contacts they are anxious to modernize the country. Yet within the army there is tension between the officers and the much lower paid N.C.O.s; and the civilian population is apt to view the army as a parasitic body. Among the university-trained intelligentsia there is a cleavage between those educated in the local university at Addis Ababa and those who have been overseas—the former being much more traditionalist in outlook. The conflict here seems greater than in West Africa, for instance, where an overseas education is much more prestigeous than the local equivalent, but seems to produce relatively fewer differences in values held.

THE EDUCATIONAL PROCESS

We have already seen that most of the well-paid employment opportunities in the African states exist in the bureaucratic systems of government or the large expatriate business enterprises. Rank at entry depends almost entirely on an educational qualification. Furthermore, since many of the jobs are of an administrative nature, it is not the content of education which is important but its standard. For many a young man his struggle to achieve ends with his entry to a university—the university will ensure that most of its students will graduate. Graduation is, of course, an achievement; but henceforth it becomes virtually an ascribed status, as promotion by seniority tends to prevail. Far fewer opportunities exist outside the bureaucratic systems than were found, for instance, in late-nineteenth-century western Europe. Thus, with the financial rewards of higher education being so lavish, the popular demand for secondary and university education is extraordinarily strong.

In this context, one cannot appreciate the characteristics of the modern elite without an understanding of the educational system by which they have gained their status. For it is this system which determines how open is recruitment to the elite; and it determines, in part, the degree of corporate feeling among the elite. The rapidity of educational expansion is correlated with the degree to which career aspirations are in accord with reality—the degree to which bitterness and frustration spread among substantial sections of the population.

The Colonial Period

The higher education policy of colonial governments was directed in general to providing a small cadre of executive officials for the bureaucracy. With the few notable exceptions, universities did not exist, and governments saw little need to provide scholarships for higher education overseas. The early elite provided such training for their children from their own resources. Secondary schools too were few in number. Some were government managed, others run by missionary bodies. In either case the schools were usually located in the capitals or principal towns; most were boarding schools. Those of the French colonial territories were overtly assimilationist—many indeed had the children both of African and settler European populations. In the British territories of East and Central Africa with settler populations segregated educational facilities existed. But although the principles of indirect rule and *association* (in contrast to *assimilation*) guided the colonial governments in their policies of developing indigenous political institutions, in the educational sphere their schools were run on the lines of the English boarding public school. The content of the curricula was almost entirely European—the staff knowing little about Africa. These schools divorced the youth from his local community during the most formative years of his life. They thus produced men who were elitist in outlook (Ajayi, 1963). And, because the secondary schools were so few, the elite of each territory tended to come from a very small number of establishments—for example, Munali College in Lusaka and the William Ponty School near Dakar.

Primary education was largely in the hands of missionary bodies. School fees were relatively low, particularly when the missions were trying to establish themselves, but their successes were not evenly distributed throughout the various territories (Foster, 1962). In some areas, where missions were founded at an early period, education quickly became popular, and these areas have continued to provide a relatively large proportion of the country's elite. In other cases one ethnic group seems to have responded more readily than its neighbour. The Tonga of Malawi, for instance, provided a large number of the elite of that country and of Zambia. The Scottish Presbyterian missions have a long history in the area—but this itself is the result of Tonga enthusiasm rather than its cause. Alternative explanations are that the Tonga lack prestigeful offices in their own society and are therefore obliged to look outside it for avenues of achievement, and here the universalistic contention of education is important.

Furthermore, the Tonga are a people lacking in marked self-identification and great traditions formed by refugees from the Ngoni slave raids.

In some areas, such as Buganda, the traditional elite fostered the missions and education as a means of enhancing their own superiority; in others, Northern Nigeria, for instance, they saw the missions as a threat to the traditional religious beliefs upholding their status, sending to the schools not their own sons but those of the slaves and servants, hoping perhaps that these youths might later be useful to them in a clerical capacity. In most societies, however, it was perhaps the under-privileged who, predicting the future importance of education, took advantage of the new opportunities for status advancement and sent their children to school.

With educational facilities on the scale prevalent in the colonial period it was fairly easy for school managers to waive or reduce the fees of the bright but indigent pupils. Furthermore, it was perhaps easier at this period for the boy who gained admission to the good secondary school to collect contributions towards his fees from a wide circle of relatives.

Education in the Independent States

With the promise and ultimate realization of self-government the independent states of Africa have embarked upon programmes of rapid educational expansion. They have argued that economic development will only be possible with a substantially literate population—education is thus seen as a necessary investment. Even though employment opportunities in industry may be relatively few, a literate farming community is necessary if agricultural techniques are to be improved. A counter-argument, that selective education of a few might yield higher returns, is not accepted. Furthermore, the newly elected politicians feel that they must reward their constituents with the social services they so eagerly seek.

More universities are needed to supply men for the expanding bureaucracies and to replace the retiring expatriates. For Nigeria, for instance, Sir Frederick Harbison estimated that the number of senior posts would almost treble between 1950 and 1970, and the Ashby Commission recommended a university population of 10,000 by the latter date; of this total only 20 per cent should be students in faculties of arts and 30 per cent should be in faculties of technology. Nigerian universities are expanding to meet the numerical target, but are still far from the distribution recommended. It is much more costly to build engineering laboratories and more difficult to recruit the appropriate staff than it is to teach history.

The rates of expansion have been phenomenal, though they still leave wide differences between states and regions. Eastern and Western Nigeria introduced free universal primary education in the mid 1950s; in the latter region in 1953 70 per cent of the children in some divisions were already attending school, in others only 20 per cent. In some of the provinces of Northern Nigeria the figure was as low as 2 per cent—and the Regional target is now only 25 per cent. In Ghana, too, the primary-school enrolment increased two and a half times in a decade. Similar rates of growth have occurred in secondary schools. In Ghana the enrolment increased threefold in a decade. In Western Nigeria the number of secondary schools rose from 59 in 1954 to 177 in 1961. Much of the development here was due to the enterprise of local communities, a grammar school being a symbol of prestige. Yet the maintenance of such schools fell to the Government, which, already spending over 40 per cent of its recurrent expenditure on education, has been obliged to put a brake on popular enthusiasm.

Nevertheless, it is still only a fortunate few who manage to reach secondary school. In no African state does the proportion exceed 2 per cent, though in some constituent regions this figure is exceeded. Western Nigeria probably has the highest rate of secondary (grammar) school attendance; but of 108,000 boys in primary class 6 in 1960, only 6,000 were in the bottom class of a grammar-school in 1961. The proportion of girls is, of course, lower. Nevertheless, this Region aims at sending 10 per cent of its primary school leavers to secondary grammar school and 50 per cent (instead of the present 32 per cent for boys) to secondary modern school.

Independence has occasioned much questioning of the type of education appropriate for contemporary Africa, but, so far, few changes from the colonial pattern have been made; some members of the seminar felt, in fact, that the educational systems were growing more like those of the metropolitan countries. It has been advocated that the curriculum of primary schools should be directed towards training the future farmers and villagers rather than providing an academic introduction to secondary education. But popular demand for the latter is insistent. Similarly, it is argued that the universities should train more people in vocational arts, or award a greater number of degrees of lower standards. But in the late 1940s, when the University Colleges of Ibadan and Gold Coast were being developed, such ideas were anathema to nationalist politicians. Only the best in Britain—the Oxbridge model—was good enough for Africa; no longer should one be fobbed off with colleges giving inferior qualifications with the argument that these were more suited to Africa's needs. (This was a sore point at this period when African graduates of the latter type of colleges were ranked below expatriates from the former.)

Recent years have seen the development of private fee-paying primary schools for the children of the elite; these have smaller classes and more highly trained staff than the state-aided schools, where the rapid expansion rates have inevitably reduced the calibre of the teachers. As the number of expatriates in these independent states increases and as more of them prefer to keep their children with them (Americans, in particular, keeping even their teenage children), so have expatriate bodies sought to provide schooling commensurate with that of the metropolitan country. Many of these have mixed African and expatriate staff and equally mixed classes of children. Fees tend to be high. The International Secondary School at Ibadan, managed under the auspices of the University's Institute of Education, charges £180 per annum for tuition and £200 per annum as boarding fees.

Social Mobility

The pattern of a state-aided and controlled educational system, in which entry to secondary schools is solely by competitive

c

examination, is a legacy of the colonial period. Loopholes certainly do exist for sons of the school governors and the like, but the more reputable schools are probably fairly rigid in their selection procedures. Yet the egalitarian principle of this system favours the children of the elite in Africa even more so than in Britain, for there is much greater disparity between the home conditions of the elite and those of the masses. As Barbara Lloyd indicates for Ibadan, elite child-rearing seems more directed towards individual achievement; elite children have more toys and books; they are mercilessly crammed by private tutors for two or three years before the secondary-school entrance examinations. The elite can also use their influence to gain admission to the better primary schools—those, for instance, attached to a teachers' training college. The most affluent and those not politically committed to patronizing the state schools can send their children to private schools.

The costs of secondary education frighten many poor boys from ever sitting for the entrance examinations. Others who pass are unable subsequently to find the fees. Most schools are still boarding. Thus, even in Western Nigeria, with its proliferation of schools in every sizeable town, only 7 per cent are for day boys only and 43 per cent take non-boarders. In this region the tutorial and boarding fees amount to about £75 per annum, whatever the quality of the school. In other states the fees seem commensurate. (In Ghana it has recently been announced that secondary-school fees are to be abolished.) Such a sum, in effect, penalizes the poor child, being beyond the means of his parents, while the education of the elite child is in fact subsidized by the State. Many scholarships exist, though the numbers tend not to increase in proportion with the rise in school attendance. One hears of their distribution with increasing frequency to the children of the wealthy and politically influential. Again the increasing number of secondary-school children tends to limit the range of kinsman which any one child can call upon for financial help.

These same principles tend to apply, *pari passu*, to entrance to African universities. Thus, although the fees payable in Nigerian universities are only one-eighth of the cost of the education provided (i.e. about £150–£200 per annum), many students who are offered admission are unable to find this sum. Far more entrants use their own savings to pay the fees for the first term or year and then live in insecurity, trying to collect just enough to prevent their expulsion. A large number of students are supported by scholarships, but their proportion, relative to the total student body, tends to fall as the number of university places rises.

One may examine the social mobility rates of the African states from two viewpoints. First, the present elite—or those well on the way to attaining this status—have been, and are still being, drawn quite substantially from the poor and ill-educated masses. Thus, over a third of the Yoruba university graduates living in Ibadan in 1962 had fathers with less than a complete primary education. In 1953, 27 per cent of the students of the University of Ghana had fathers who were farmers, 23 per cent professional fathers; two-thirds of the students had fathers in occupational groups which represented only 7 per cent of the total population (Johoda, 1954). Impressions of the University of Ibadan suggest a greater proportion from humble homes. In both countries the top elite endeavour to, and are in a large measure successful in sending their sons to overseas universities. Clignet and Foster (1964) calculate that a third of the students in Ghanaian secondary schools and two-thirds of those in the Ivory Coast had fathers without any education. In Ghana the children of the elite occupy a far higher proportion of the places in the two most prestigious secondary schools than in other schools. Comparable figures seem lacking in other African states, but would, if available, probably give the same picture.

On the other hand, one could examine (as no one seems yet to have done systematically) the attainments, in education and subsequent occupation, of the children of the elite parents. Most such parents hope that their children will attain at least the same status as themselves. The chances which children of educated parents have of entering secondary school are far greater than those of humble origin. Thus, Clignet and Foster (1964) estimate that in Ghana the children of professional men have over four times as good a chance of entering secondary school as those of clerks and teachers, fourteen times as those of farmers, and 140 times as those of semi- and unskilled workers. In the Ivory Coast the figures are over 4, 32, and 130. Foster (1963) estimates that, in Ghana, the son of a secondary-school-educated man has seventeen times, and the son of a university graduate, thirty-two times, as good a chance of secondary education as the son of an illiterate man. (In Great Britain, by comparison, over 60 per cent of the sons of men of professional or managerial status now enter secondary grammar schools, against only 10 per cent of the sons of semi- and unskilled men; 16 per cent of the sons of non-manual workers are entering university against only $2\frac{1}{2}$ per cent of the children of skilled manual workers and 1 per cent of semi- and unskilled workers [Little and Westergaard, 1964].)

The Effects of Rapid Educational Expansion

The rapid expansion of primary education has a number of immediate results. Standards set by employers rise; a primary school leaving certificate is no longer a passport to a clerical post —rather does it become the *sine qua non* of the lowest-paid urban job. As school-leavers drift to the town unemployment becomes a major problem, for the urban and industrial sector of the economy can hope to employ only a minority of these age cohorts. Those who do find work are frustrated in their expectations. Secondary school-leavers find that men who are only ten years senior to them in rank have but primary education; conflict between the education generations results (Foster, 1964). Even at the university level it is becoming difficult in some countries for graduates to find appropriate employment. In Nigeria, for instance, the estimated man-power needs are not always in accord with the number of posts that government revenues and overseas or local investment can in fact finance. There is ample scope for increasing the number of graduate secondary-school teachers (only a third being so qualified at present), but since the graduates would, at present scales, expect at least double the salaries of those whom they replace, the total costs of secondary education would be substantially increased.

THE ELITE IN TRADITIONAL AND MODERN ASSOCIATIONS

The modern elite of our study is, as we have seen, of recent growth. Many of its members have come from rural homes, born to non-literate parents. Of those of literate parentage many are the sons and daughters of an earlier local and provincial elite— the primary-school headmasters, government clerks, village catechists. Very few come from well-educated homes already divorced from the life of the masses; the West African creole and early elite families are the notable exception. But how far are the members of the modern elite participating in the traditional associations of their societies? How far are they withdrawing from them to participate instead in new and exclusive westernized associations? The wide disparity in incomes between the elite and the masses, with its correlated differences in living styles, produced a gap which is difficult to bridge. Yet bridged it must be if any feeling of national identity, so carefully being fostered by the elite, is to be maintained. The political elite rely on the support of the masses for their election. The elite as a whole relies for its own status on the popularly elected government. This particular problem is a transitory one. In a few years a larger proportion of the population of the African states will have received a substantial primary education; their incomes may still be low, but their values will no longer be those of traditional society. They will form a broad category linking the elite with the still illiterate masses. But the children of the present elite, growing up in the residential areas designed for colonial civil servants, will in turn be divorced from traditional society as their parents never were. Today the individual members of the elite enjoy the prestige accorded to the local boy who has made good; in the coming decades there may be a greater degree of conflict between frustrated literates and an entrenched elite.

Let us now examine some of the factors in the contemporary situation, looking in turn at the participation of the elite in the affairs of their kin, of their home towns, and of traditional political and religious associations.

Family and Kin

The elite are congregated in the national and provincial capitals of their states. Few opportunities exist for them to live close to the rural areas of their birth. But those who are from illiterate homes are frequently the only children who have attained elite status; their full siblings remain in the village, farming and living in the traditional manner. In some cases the successful man has been picked out by the local missionary as a bright lad and helped towards scholarships, in others the family could afford education for only one son. It is quite common to find among siblings of the first-generation member of the elite a range of occupations from farmer to clerk or petty trader.

Sentiments of family loyalty usually remain sufficiently strong for the successful son or daughter to feel obliged to help his junior kin. In societies where polygyny is prevalent and where women bear children throughout their productive years, it is not unusual for an elder sibling who has started in salaried employment to pay the school fees of those junior to him—it is perhaps the youngest who stand most to gain, the next most junior sibling having lost his chance of schooling before his elder brother is in a position to support him. Educated parents hope to give their children a good schooling. But here, too, the families, though large, are well spaced and the parents anticipate that while the burden of financing the training of their eldest children will fall on themselves, that of financing the junior children will be borne by the latter's elder siblings. Education is indeed seen as an investment—especially when the differences in salary between the secondary school-leaver and the graduate are so great, and the costs of university education so heavily subsidized. The young man who marries when he leaves university and who sends his children to the better among the state-aided primary schools finds that these children are relatively inexpensive to maintain for a decade. Savings and assurance schemes, which will spread the costs of children's education over their parents' early married years, are not yet popular. A young man is thought able to finance the schooling of junior siblings and cousins. And inasmuch as his savings are spent in this way, he is forced to look to his kin in his own time of need.

Again the elite are predominantly young; their parents are still alive and form a potent link with the rural areas, for few men will deny their parents. In societies with low life expectancy rates sickness and death are persistently feared, yet few of the elite as yet take out insurance policies. Their nearest kin are still, as in traditional society, their main protection against possible destitution.

There is undoubtedly a conflict between the desires of the elite, on the one hand to furnish their own homes and to educate their own children, and, on the other, their feelings of obligation towards near kin. But the latter are not denied, and many elite salary earners are giving substantial proportions of their salaries to their close relatives. The benefits of living away from the family compound are that one is freed from persistent demands from all and sundry; the preference is for a calculated expenditure on the most deserving causes. Furthermore, the solidarity of the family and descent group is hailed by many of the elite as one of the basic expressions of the 'African personality'; horror is expressed at the independence of and lack of contact between siblings in western society. Yet the degree of verbal emphasis placed on these traditional values may well be the result of their continually threatened erosion as societies become more urbanized, industrialized, and stratified.

In interpersonal relations it is not difficult to find situations of tension between illiterate or ill-educated parents and their elite children. The mission-dominated parents grieve at their children's lax attendances at church. Problems arise when parents and children visit each other. The illiterate mother is ill at ease—and probably frightened—in the all-electric kitchen of her daughter. When the elite family visits the rural home for the week-end it carries perhaps its beds and boiled water. Yet the prestige accorded to the parents in their own society is a sufficient reward for any inconvenience or sorrow suffered. In their small way they have striven for their children's achievement. They expect them to adopt the values and symbols of the elite. As de Graft-Johnson

describes in his paper, the recently arrived 'been-to' is expected
by his family to wear his woollen suit (hardly appropriate to the
Ghanaian climate) as an identification of success. The children take
these parental expectations seriously—especially when all the
savings of their family have been settled on them; mental illness
among students seems to derive more often from a failure (or
feared failure) to fulfil family expectations than from the increasing distance between their current and future styles of life and
those into which they were born.

Within the elite nuclear family the pattern of relationships
between husband and wife tends towards one of shared roles,
greater intimacy, and equality. Yet the patterns to be found in any
one part of Africa will vary widely according to the traditional
relationship and perhaps to the levels of education in ascendant
generations. (In Ibadan, for instance, it seems that the more conjugal relationship is associated with couples each having educated
parents: a more traditional relationship is found among those
couples with illiterate parents.) Furthermore, although the husband and wife may have received similar experiences in home
background and education, their expectations of the ideal marital
relationship may well differ. The husband is still tied very closely
to his own descent group; the wife is more divorced from hers,
and seeks greater fulfilment from her relationship with her
husband. The modern town provides employment opportunities
for the educated wife, and thus greater economic independence
from the husband; if this is not balanced by affection and a recognition of equality the marriage is in danger of breaking up.

Elite marriages are almost invariably the choice of the young
couples concerned. But if the parents are expected to acquiesce
they also expect that the traditional ceremonies shall be carried
out both at the period of betrothal and of the wedding. Bridewealth continues to be paid, although its social significance may
differ: today the sums may be very large, but they are often used
by the bride for furnishing her new home. Many a young man
establishes his rights over his future spouse by paying her school
fees.

With each higher level of education the proportion of men who take wives from ethnic groups other than their own seems to rise. With girls' education lagging so far behind that of boys, the chances of a well-educated youth finding an eligible (according to local rules of exogamy) and suitably trained wife from his own area are slight. Men who enter such mixed marriages are probably less likely to retain such close links with their home areas than those who have married within their own ethnic groups. The smaller the size of the elite, the greater, perhaps, is the proportion of mixed marriages; for as education, including that of women, expands, there will be a greater chance that the elite man will find a suitable spouse within his own area. Thus, half the Yoruba university graduates in Ibadan have wives from the same ethnic sub-group of the Yoruba as themselves. In contrast, the Zambian elite has a very high proportion of mixed marriages. (Such proportions are, of course, influenced by the size of the ethnic groups used in the calculations.)

Relations with the Home Community

The great majority of the elite are linked through their kin with the rural areas of their birth. They may also participate in the affairs of their community both directly, when visiting their homes, or indirectly through the branch of their ethnic association in the town where they reside. These associations are found throughout Africa, though they seem to be most strongly developed in some parts of West Africa and least developed in Southern Africa. Again, the scale of their membership varies widely. Some represent a single village, others a group of villages or clan or a modern administrative unit; some embrace a whole people—the Ibo State Union in Nigeria, for example. The associations at these different levels may be arranged hierarchically (as among the Ibo), so that membership of the village association is obligatory for participation at the higher levels; conversely, the associations at different levels may be autonomous.

Among those West African peoples, where these ethnic associations are most strongly developed, one finds that membership is virtually obligatory for all members of the group concerned, irrespective of education or status. Prestige is accorded to the elite; executive offices are given to the literate; but those who are eldest or who have lived longest in the town hold the presiding offices. For the poor and semi-literate these associations provide the main sources of recreation and of social security in the town. Even for the well-to-do, the security which they may provide against disaster can be quite considerable. The higher education of many members of the elite has been financed by their ethnic association.

The distribution and strength of these associations seem to be governed by three principal factors. First, they are most strongly developed where the home community is defined in terms of descent (i.e. all members of the village trace descent from a common ancestor) and where status is defined primarily in terms of age, sex, and lineage. Thus, a man who can return home after years in the urban areas and take his place as a lineage elder, claiming his rights to land and political office, is more likely to maintain his links with his home area and to plan to spend his retirement there.

Conversely, he is less likely to maintain such close links with the home community, where prestige is determined by political offices gained through a lifetime of service; where land rights may be forfeited by absence; where the returning migrant finds that men junior to him in age have surpassed him in rank or where status in a community is determined largely by a network of patron–client relationships.

Second, the ethnic associations seem most strongly developed where no other associations or services provide social security for the urban migrant. In West African towns the big employers of labour do not provide housing for their wage-earning staff, and their personnel departments are concerned only in the conditions of work and service within the factory or shop. Nothing here parallels the all-embracing functions of the Zambian copper companies, for instance, towards their workers.

Third, urban men will involve themselves in the affairs of their home community when there is money available, from local reserves or government grants, for rural development and when opportunities exist for manipulating its spending. The greater peasant wealth and the existence of local government councils distinguish West African societies from those elsewhere in Africa in this respect. Conversely, the lack of interest which the urban immigrant has in the town of his sojourn, his inability to influence policies affecting his livelihood and amenities, the lack of prestigious status for the elderly and retired stranger, will all turn his attentions towards his home community.

These factors affect all urban dwellers—both the elite and the wage-earning poor. An issue relating solely to the elite is the degree to which they feel a need to concern themselves with the affairs of their own ethnic and kin groups in the pursuit of higher positions. In parliamentary systems with adult suffrage the candidate for political office is frequently judged by what he has so far achieved for his community by his influence or his efforts. Hence participation in the ethnic association is advisable for the political aspirant. The candidate will also hope to aid his chances of success by ensuring the unanimous support of his own kin or descent group—thus contributing towards the solidarity of such groups when other modernizing factors are tending to disrupt them. Within the bureaucracies the upwardly mobile man may also try to exploit ethnic ties with his superiors in his drive for promotion.

But 'tribalism' has become a dirty word in the new African states—factions based on ethnic groups being seen as a threat to their independence and aspirations to unity. Thus, there may be a level at which it becomes a handicap to be identified too closely with one's ethnic groups or associations—a level at which it behoves one to assume overtly an ethnic neutrality.

It seems clear that in most African areas the members of the rural communities expect their elite sons to direct their efforts on their behalf, in obtaining local social services or jobs for their other children. The pressure will be greatest where the elite from any single community are few in number. Do the elite accept these expectations? Here we have much less knowledge. Most elites probably have among their members a small number who do not participate in home affairs, and their support of each other in this attitude enables them to evade the sanctions imposed on them by their home communities. On the other hand,

34 *Introduction*

participation may become an expectation of the elite themselves. An Ibo university student criticizing an unpopular politician offered as his final thrust, 'Why, he hasn't even built a house in his own home town.' The same standards of behaviour may not necessarily apply to both husband and wife. The seminar was told of a Dakar schoolmaster who, living on the school compound, took little part in the affairs of his ethnic group and suffered no reproach. Yet, because of the role of women in Moslem festivals, his wife was criticized for similar inactivity.

Elite Attitudes towards Traditional Institutions and Values

The attitudes taken by the contemporary elite towards traditional chieftancy, towards religion and witchcraft are diverse. Students in overseas universities tend to be less tolerant than they become after their return home. The early mission-dominated elite is perhaps more intolerant than the later elite with a more secular education; (though the elders of the earlier Ghanaian elite, typified by the late Dr. Danquah and Dr. Busia, have closer ties with chieftancy than the more radical C.P.P. leaders).

The policies of colonial powers and mission bodies together with the degree of urbanization and industrialization have all affected the persistence of traditional institutions and values into the present decade. Thus, elite attitudes towards chieftaincy are determined by the degree to which both colonial and independent governments have maintained the traditional offices and overtly endeavoured to preserve their roles. How far do the chiefs still represent their people? Are they still popularly chosen or are they imposed by Government? In those areas where the British colonial government have used indigenous chiefs in native administration —in the indirect rule territories—the traditional offices have often been filled by educated men who have reinterpreted their traditional roles to meet modern conditions. These men usually remain a local elite lacking any sense of nation-wide unity; but in some areas chiefs have formed associations for the protection of their own interests. (The Guinea chiefs' association of the late 1940s is a case in point; the houses of chiefs in some contemporary legislatures are another). In such instances are the chiefs in any way competing for power with the political leaders?

Whatever their attitude towards individual incumbents of these traditional offices or to their current political activities, the elite recognize the chiefs as symbols of local unity and of the historic past. At least they pay lip service to the institution. Although the Bamileke guerrilla fighters in the Cameroons captured many chiefs, few were harmed, although other prisoners were frequently killed; the soldiers hoped to reform the chiefs. In no independent state, however, does there seem to be any move to reinvest the chiefs with such political power as they held in pre-colonial days —such would be incompatible with national government. 'Preservation of the chieftaincy' seems but a subtle manner of ensuring its decay.

While traditional offices may tend to lapse, the traditional symbols of power are often assumed by the new political leaders. The most outstanding case is that of Nkrumah. At his installation as President of the Republic of Ghana the British symbols of the earlier parliament were replaced by those of Ghana—the Akan-type throne, the traditional sword instead of the orb and sceptre, and royal linguists acting as his escort. On a rather different plane, it was reported in the seminar that meetings of one Togolese political party always began with traditional prayers. In a wide variety of situations the symbols of the past are used to validate the leadership of the politicians of the contemporary elite.

The western-educated elite are almost invariably Christian— at least nominally so; even in Dakar the Christians predominate, although the Senegalese population is overwhelmingly Moslem. Their attitude towards traditional religious beliefs is, in its overt expression, largely determined by the official policies of the local churches. The differences here between the policies of the Roman Catholic and Protestant churches are quite marked (they may have quite a profound effect on the character of the elite itself—though little evidence on this point seems available). Roman Catholicism has recently become far more tolerant of traditional beliefs— though in Dahomey, for example, a traditional tolerance by local missionaries sometimes at variance with Rome, has existed for

several years. In such situations the expatriate priests usually
respect the traditional shrines, and the local elite converts are not
ashamed to participate in the annual rituals. Less tolerance is
usually shown in areas of Protestant dominance. A common situation here is the refusal of the existing chiefs to instal in a vacant
office a Christian who will not participate in all the usual rituals;
neither group will, for a time, modify its principles, though when
the chieftaincy is obviously being starved of its best candidates and
when the early religious fervour of the converted minority has
developed into the greater laxity of the Christian majority, a
middle way is usually found. Royal burials often involve the elite
in situations involving traditional rituals. Thus, when Oba Adele
of Lagos died (at the time of the seminar) a conflict developed
between the Moslem leaders and the senior members of the *osugbo*
cult over the form of burial—the late ruler being well-educated, a
Moslem and a participant in the traditional cults. The dispute
involved several well-known members of the Lagos elite.

In West Africa, in particular, there are many rumours of the
active participation of well known, and overtly highly westernized, elite political leaders in traditional or traditionalist secret
cults. Jahoda's paper in this volume discusses the beliefs in, and
uses of, witchcraft among educated Ghanaians, and his conclusions would seem valid for much of West Africa. Witchcraft can
be used not only to explain away one's own misfortunes but also
to incriminate one's opponents (see also Field, 1960). Thus,
President Houphouet-Boigny of the Ivory Coast explained the
suicide of the jailed President of the Supreme Court, a political
opponent, in terms of 'fetishism'—thus decrying its use but ad-
mitting its existence. The seminar was told of a wealthy Daho-
meyan trader who, from his economic activities, seemed to be
typical of early European capitalists; suddenly he sold his business,
using the money to attain a ritual office which gave him power in
his community of a very different kind.

In discussing the apparent gap between the elite and the masses
we might recapitulate an earlier statement that few of the modern
elite are landowners, and thus have little personal contact with
the peasantry in the work sphere. Customary land tenure usually

inhibits the personal acquisition of large agricultural estates, and the exceptions are often due to colonial policies. Thus, Buganda has its landowning elite with the subtle conversion of traditional rights into *mailo* freehold tenures. In the French West African territories, and especially the Ivory Coast and Togo, privately owned plantations developed and the landowning group has produced some of the leading politicians. But attempts at identification with the land are common, and government public-relations departments have endeavoured to show the leading politicians, hoe and cutlass in hand, working on their own small plots and ostensibly being 'men of the people'.

Modern Associations

In the modern African towns a plethora of new associations have developed, almost all having Western origins. Thus there are the various clubs attached to the churches; the major charities —Red Cross and Y.W.C.A.; the Boy Scouts and similar youth groups; Old Boys' associations of the leading schools; tennis and dancing and drinking clubs; political party branches and independent political groups; trades unions and professional associations; Rotary Clubs and Chambers of Commerce. It is easier to describe the social functions of these groups than to specify with any exactitude the degree of elite participation in them.

Few of these associations are exclusive by the terms of their constitution (though Accra's casino is open only to men with high incomes). Old Boys' and professional associations are obviously restricted. To some, such as the Lagos Island Club, membership is by election. Cases were cited in the seminar where the top elite had moved to a new club when the membership of their existing one was diluted with the sub-elite. In the charitable associations the office-holders are usually the wives of the leading elite men— ministers, the most senior civil servants, judges. In many cases the formal activities of the associations are limited. Thus the Old Boys' association meets once a year at the school for a dinner and speeches; but there may be quite a high degree of informal activity between individual members throughout the year. Other associations may meet more frequently, but be able, nevertheless, to

attract only a minimum number of members to any single meeting
—the remainder being busy at other meetings or, far more probably, with informal visiting. Among a small elite there must be
considerable overlapping in the membership of the various
associations.

These associations are widely used for mutual help and advancement; they serve to train the new elite in the expected behaviour,
the new norms being collectively defined by the existing members.
They are of especial importance here for the women, who are
frequently less well educated than their husbands, lack an overseas
training, and are ill equipped to provide the type of home enter-
tainment that accords with the husband's status. It was reported
from one country that the women in a charitable association would
discuss their husbands so that each woman would, on behalf of an
aggrieved wife, urge her own spouse to take action against the
errant husband; the association thus fulfils the role of the woman's
descent group.

Informal Networks

Little study has been made, unfortunately, of the informal
social networks of elite Africans. Impressions of one such West
African elite are that there is far more house-to-house visiting
than, for instance, in England. Yet there seem to be far fewer
purely social calls than among the expatriate population resident
in the same area. It seems likely that the informal network is more
important in the process of norm definition and diffusion among
the elite than is the formal association. It is almost certainly important in the diffusion of new norms and values to the mass of
the population. Jones, in his paper in this volume describes the
networks existing between some wealthy Tonga farmers, the
neighbouring European farmers, and the peasantry.

From a pilot study in Ibadan, a far more complex community,
it appears that the elite almost invariably chose their best friends
from among people similar in status. About half the friends came
from the informants' own ethnic sub-groups, though this proportion varied rather widely. A high proportion of the closest friends
both of husbands and wives were of persons known before

marriage—thus, the women gained few friends through their husbands, and vice versa. School and college were a most common origin of friendships. With the tendency towards intermarriage between educated families, and with the tracing of distant kinship links usual in tribal society, the links of descent and official relationship grow rapidly with the increasing size of the elite.

Unlike the western stereotype of the professional classes living anonymously in vast sprawling suburbs, the African elite, though dispersed through the modern housing areas, is thus knit together by a most complex network of relationships. They are relatively few in number, products of a few secondary schools working in a few, and in the case of the public services highly interrelated, bureaucratic structures, members of the same clubs and preferring social intercourse to the solitude of the home. As a result, most members are at least acquainted with one another.

Comparisons

For the topics raised in this section it is not very difficult to suggest variables which should prove useful in making comparisons between the elites of African countries. It is, however, almost impossible to submit generalizations which are true of all parts of the continent. Those suggested in this section are probably more appropriate to West Africa than elsewhere. At this point it may be useful to distinguish, in rather stark terms, the two apparently extreme situations—that of the elite of the West African states and that of the urban areas of South Africa.

In West Africa one stresses the links between the elite and their rural kin; the elite have cars, and the distances involved are not great (say up to 200 miles in most cases). In South Africa the elite are less affluent and distances are much greater. The West African is strongly bound to his home community by the ethnic association—an association almost completely absent in South Africa. The division of the population between 'red' (traditionalist) and 'school' that Mayer (1961) describes for East London has no parallel in West Africa, where the emphasis is continually on the compromise between the rural and urban values. Generally the

D

urban South African is committed to the town in a far stronger degree than are most West Africans.

ACHIEVEMENT MOTIVATION

In the previous section we have discussed some of the values held by the contemporary elite concerning kin relationships, attitudes towards traditional religion and chieftaincy. In each case one could, if one had the requisite data, scale the values of individual members or of particular elites along continua ranging from most traditional to most Western. In this section we shall discuss the overall value orientation or personality of the elite—a theme which the seminar discovered to be one of the most elusive, yet, at the same time, one of major importance.

The styles of the life of the emergent African elites are so different from those of the remainder of the population that one might expect the development of contrasting value systems or personalities, owing either to the experience of first-generation elite in their own lifetime or to the results of divergent patterns of child-rearing upon subsequent generations. The existence of such personality differences between the elite and the masses raises problems of social cohesion in the new states. It will be relevant too in our subsequent discussion of the concepts of social class and elite in the African context.

Furthermore, in these developing countries, with small western-educated elites and a vast illiterate peasantry, the task of ensuring economic advance rests almost solely upon this elite. Does the elite hold those values which are appropriate to a modern urban and industrial society? If it does not, it can hardly be expected to function adequately as the prime mover of change. If the relevant values are considered to be more the result of childhood learning in the home than of later educational processes we should expect to find that most of the values held by the elite are still traditional—the elite, in most cases, being a first-generation growth. Here one would ask whether this elite is nevertheless inculcating the appropriate values in its own children, so that it is the second and subsequent generations of elite which hold the new values (presuming always that the elite are in general able to guarantee elite status for their own offspring).

The questions we have posed here were reviewed by the seminar participants in the context of the psychological concept of achievement. In attempting to relate this concept to the African scene we are severely hampered by the comparative paucity of personality studies of African peoples in general, let alone the elite in particular. And with the field so wide open there is a danger that crude studies, lacking the rigorous methods necessary in such research, will produce results of poor reliability. But an even greater handicap is the ambiguity which still surrounds the achievement concept. In these circumstances we can offer little beyond a few illustrations of the relevance and application of the concept to the African data.

Weber's thesis showing the correlation between the Protestant ethic and the development of capitalism seems obviously pertinent in a period when social scientists are looking for the vital ingredients which will set the underdeveloped countries along the road to sustained growth. Interpreted in its more general sense, Weber's thesis was that the Protestant ethic is indispensable to capitalist development—and hence—it was the Protestant countries of Europe which experienced the industrial revolution of the eighteenth–nineteenth centuries. The Protestant ethic stresses man's individuality, his responsibility to God rather than his fellow men, his self-denial and asceticism. These are qualities which parallel the rationality which characterizes capitalism. The spirit of capitalism stresses planning, risk-taking, and, again, self-denial of immediate rewards in favour of reinvestment. Weber described these attitudes as being quite different from the spirit of acquisitiveness, which has existed among men at all times and in all countries; for him they were a peculiar product of western Europe in the beginning of the industrial era. It was a more specific interpretation of Weber's thesis that it was the teachings of the Reformation, and of Calvin in particular, which paved the way for capitalist development. Subsequently historians and theologians have found little to support this argument, and have even insisted that Calvinism had nothing to do with economic development in the seventeenth century. It should, perhaps, be noted here that while Weber equated Protestantism with capitalism, the empirical study in Baden, which in his own words started his thoughts on this issue showed that Protestants reached higher positions than Catholics in all spheres of activity—entrepreneurial, artistic, and political.

Weber's thesis is still widely discussed; those who accept it would argue that without the spirit of the Protestant ethic (as yet markedly absent in Africa among elite and masses alike) economic development will not get under way. It is a convenient thesis for those who wish to castigate the affluence and conspicuous consumption of the African elite and of the politicians in particular. But how far is this thesis relevant to Africa?

Economic development in Africa is largely state controlled, inspired, or aided. New industries are set up with a substantial foreign capital investment and technical knowledge. These industries tend to incorporate the more modern types of machinery. The individual African with capitalist leanings has the resources neither of money, management, nor technical skill to embark upon such enterprises. In the spheres in which he could use his resources he is priced out of the market by the competition of both local and overseas factories. Nigeria, for instance, has a large body of craftsmen working within guild systems; yet it does not seem economically feasible for any of these crafts to develop into factory industries. The qualities which fostered the development of industry in eighteenth-century Europe are perhaps not likely to be needed in twentieth-century Africa.

Weber's thesis has, however, been taken up by the American psychologist McClelland (1961), who endeavours to trace, through family structure and child socialization, the links between the Protestant ethic and capitalism. The Protestant ethic he redefines as 'need for achievement'—the competition with an internalized standard of excellence; need achievement is measured largely by the scoring of fantasies—in dreams, children's stories, art forms, etc. With Weber, McClelland identifies high need achievement with economic growth, and especially with entrepreneurial activity. However, his concept is not confined to capitalist or

Protestant societies of the Industrial Revolution. High need achievement can be traced in traditional African societies; it can be demonstrated, too, in contemporary Western societies, to account for their different rates of economic growth in recent years. (Although the internalized standard of excellence seems akin to the Protestant 'calling' in much of the literature using McClelland's concept, including his own, need achievement seems to become reduced to a general acquisitiveness. This perhaps results from the fallibility of scoring procedures. When a boy says that he has dreams of becoming rich is this a sign of acquisitiveness or of a 'calling'?—it is likely to be counted as need achievement.) Furthermore, McClelland stresses the importance of child socialization as the formative process of need achievement, and since child-rearing must precede adult activity, high need achievement scores are found at the very beginning of periods of economic expansion—they do not necessarily develop contemporaneously with them, and may even decline.

Thus, if one accepts McClelland's hypothesis one would expect that those African societies in which high scores for need achievement were registered would, other things being equal, be the most likely to develop economically in the coming years; and one would examine the child-rearing patterns of these societies, or of groups within them, to discover whether these are likely to produce high need achievement.

McClelland's concept of need achievement has the psychological advantage that tests can be scored so that differences between societies and between ethnic or occupational categories and social classes within societies can be simply quantified. When such differences confirm our stereotypes, such as that Jews have high need achievement, we are likely to be impressed. His own excursion into the African field will, however, mystify most anthropologists. He compares the degree of entrepreneurship said to occur in various traditional societies with their need for achievement shown in their folk tales. High on his list of high-need-achievement peoples are Yoruba; one might term them competitive or acquisitive, but the Protestant ethic is conspicuously absent. Slightly below the Yoruba rank the Masai. Near the bottom of the list of low-need-achievement scorers are the Kikuyu and the Chagga—usually regarded as two of the most go-ahead peoples of East Africa. With such a distribution among peoples that one knows one wonders what quality, if any, is being measured.

Yet McClelland's thesis may be very relevant for us in that he does accept that relatively high need achievement scores may be obtained from traditional societies. His use of the concept thus departs from the oft-cited dichotomy—status in traditional societies is ascriptive, industrial societies are achievement-oriented. From our ethnographic data we know that achievement of great wealth or of political office is possible in many traditional African societies. Political offices have often been confined to members of certain descent groups, and kingship is even more narrowly circumscribed; but competition for these offices can, however, be quite severe, and within the group of those eligible succession is an achievement. In many societies the gap between rich and poor farmer or trader has been a wide one, and here, too, great wealth is an achieved status. Such positions are, however, often thought to be the result of a benign 'fate' which largely predetermines one's future. Furthermore, they are usually the result of one's good standing in the eyes of one's fellows—for instance the chief who is elected by his lineage members or the trader whose business success depends as much on his personal popularity and generosity as on his assessment of market conditions. There seems to be little similarity between motivation for achievement of this type and Weber's Protestant ethic of Mc-Clelland's competition with an internalized standard of excellence.

Hagen (1962), an economist, follows McClelland but holds in addition that sustained economic development is set in motion by a bourgeoisie which has no access to political office (as in feudal Europe or Japan) and so intensifies its efforts in the only profitable field open to it. McClelland would rephrase this thesis so that any person with a high need achievement who is ineligible for political office will turn towards entrepreneurship. In many traditional African societies, however, the wealthy trader or farmer is not only eligible for but actively seeks political office; with success his energies are directed more to political affairs than to his economic enterprises. Throughout most of modern Africa, too, political offices are open to all and seem to attract many of the more ambitious men. Has there, moreover, been a greater development of African entrepreneurial activity in South Africa, where political achievement is denied? A merchant class, ineligible for political office, exists in the emirates of Northern Nigeria, but does not seem in the present century to have stimulated a greater rate of economic development than in the south of the country.

Several difficulties also arise in the measurement of aspirations for achievement in African conditions. First, it is difficult to design questions which are equally meaningful or relevant to both the illiterate peasant and to the graduate civil servant. Thus all Yoruba tend to state that they wish their children to reach the highest status possible. The educated father, with his knowledge of the educational system and his influence with headmasters, will pilot his son through all the intricate channels to success. The illiterate father may hope and pray, but is unable to make any more effective contribution towards getting his son into secondary school. Second, psychological tests are usually most conveniently carried out among secondary-school students, usually those of higher classes. These youths will have spent several years in boarding school, and a substantial proportion will have come from homes with educated or ambitious parents. Scores obtained for such persons may not bear much relationship with those which would be obtained from ill-educated adults were the difficulties of literacy and communication overcome.

Reisman (1950) divides men of industrial society into inner- and other-directed, while those of pre-industrial societies he terms traditional-directed. His inner-directed man has the values of Weber's Protestant; he is the entrepreneur. The other-directed man seeks public approval for his actions; he is akin to Whyte's 'organization man'. Reisman argues that whereas the inner-directed man was typical of the entrepreneur of the early Industrial Revolution, other-directedness is a growing feature of modern industrial, urban, and middle class society. Definitions of other-directedness bring it close to the concept of need for affiliation. McClelland makes use of both these concepts, appearing to use need for affiliation as the desire for personal friendships and other-directedness as responsiveness to public opinion. The former he describes as a concept not related to need achievement and not closely correlated with economic growth (save through an effect on the birth-rate). Other-directedness he sees as a feature of industrial societies and correlated with growth, though not directly linked with need achievement conceptually. To a psychologist need for achievement and need for affiliation are concepts not causally related, but perhaps complementary to each other. But inasmuch as they become identified respectively, in popular usage, with inner- and other-direction, or competition and co-operation, they appear as dichotomies.

While the Protestant ethic seems somewhat alien to Africa, the concept of affiliation seems, superficially at least, to be much more relevant. In traditional societies one sees the stress on affiliation in the education of children; in adulthood it is the man who becomes popular who succeeds. Could it be that the internationalized standard of excellence by which need achievement is defined is not seen in traditional societies in terms of individualism but of acceptance by the group?

Lipset (1961) has seen other-directedness as a feature of bureaucratized societies with rapid rates of social mobility—societies similar to those of modern African elites. The values of the contemporary Japanese middle class with a continued emphasis on loyalty as opposed to individualism may be more closely parallel to those of the African elite than those of the Puritans of Europe. Inasmuch as the African elite, in seeking new patterns of values, rely heavily on the approval of their status equals, they would seem to be demonstrating their other-directedness. The anxiety which they appear to feel in their new and somewhat insecure status in society also typifies, according to Reisman, the other-directed man. (And yet Lipset has pointed out that even the early Calvinists needed to confirm to the judgement of others of their group in order to enforce discipline among themselves.) For Lipset, other-direction is compatible with a motivation for competition and hard work, for it is by such that the successful move up the bureaucratic hierarchy.

A survey of the usage of the concepts of achievement and affiliation and their relevance to a study of the African elite leaves one rather bemused. Each concept seems to embrace a number of distinct characteristics which are not always distinguished in the literature and seem to be barely separable in psychological tests. Thus, achievement seems to embrace mere acquisitiveness, individual responsibility, innovation, an internalized standard of excellence (without specifying the qualities encompassed by the standard), and so on. What types of achievement motivation characterize African societies? Again we are not sure as to which of these characteristics might be the necessary concomitants of economic development of the type expected in African states— state and expatriate rather than indigenous private enterprise. And even if these questions are answered, shall we know how to inculcate these characteristics into the population or how to measure their incidence? At this stage the members of the seminar could do little beyond raising the issues for discussion.

Prestige Ranking

The ranking of occupations according to the prestige which they bestow upon their holder has proved a useful and oft-tried method of illuminating perceived patterns of social stratification and of discovering the general value orientation of the informants. One is safe in presuming that the most highly ranked occupations confer on their holders elite status—though not all possible occupations are, of course, listed in the tests. The testing procedures are fairly simple, and at first sight it would appear that the main problems encountered are statistical. Mitchell outlines several of these in his paper. What type of ranking should one use? While some occupations may be so specific as to be unknown to the informant, others—especially, in Africa, those of trader and farmer —may be insufficiently precise. However, a wide range in responses provides, as Mitchell shows, data for more intensive study of the ranking by various categories of persons. Again most tests are administered to adolescent schoolchildren, and one must wonder how far their answers accord with those which their illiterate parents might give. The occupations listed are mostly those of the modernized sector of the economy; traditional status, such as chief or father, are not considered as occupations.

In general, the results of the ranking exercise suggest that African schoolchildren attach the same prestige to certain occupations as do their counterparts in industrial societies. Foster notes a striking similarity between Ghanaian results and those from the United States and Japan. Marked differences in result between different African ethnic groups have not been shown in any published reports. Furthermore, it was stated in the seminar that little difference could be seen in Ghana in the rankings made by elite and non-elite informants.

But as with the concept of achievement we must ask—what is being measured by these tests? What are the components of prestige? Income is certainly an important one, for the occupations tend to be ranked in order of the remuneration that they command. Social responsibility is another component. As Mitchell shows, in colonial societies the ranking of occupations which are associated with governmental power is most variable; the high prestige of a regular and substantial wage is countered by the low prestige attaching to roles associated with political oppression. The importance of these components might be calculated by processes of factor analysis. Foster reports that the rankings given by Ghanaian informants corresponded far more closely to the presumed income level of occupations than did the ranking reported from Japan and the United States. The emphasis on income rather than on moral approval, suggested by this Ghanaian result, is significant in considering the role of the elite in the eyes of the masses.

Further qualifications must be made. High ranking of certain occupations need not necessarily mean that informants aspire to these; their own aspirations may be set at a much more realistic level. Furthermore, the ranking of occupations may not be an accurate predictor of behaviour in concrete situations; for, apart from the personal qualities of the actor involved, the various components contributing the prestige of his occupation may operate differently according to the context of the action.

Prestige ranking can throw valuable insights on informants'

perceptions of certain occupations, but it does not seem to bring us much nearer to understanding the motivations of the African elite.

ELITE OR SOCIAL CLASS?

A decade and more ago it was common to refer to the new African middle class; middle class because its members held professional and bureaucratic posts and were situated between the expatriate colonial officials and the mass of the population. Today, with western-educated Africans holding the reins of government, it is an elite of which we read—they are undoubtedly on top, with the expatriates occupying transient and peripheral positions. One feels that both terms were adopted by their users as means of referring, with more convenience than sociological exactitude, to an important category of persons. A recent writer who referred to the 'middle-class elite' seems to have tried to get the maximum of descriptive elements into his terminology!

How far is the terminology of social class and elites appropriate to that category which we have, hitherto, in this introduction loosely termed elite? The two terminologies are rarely used in conjunction with one another, even though they are not mutually exclusive—most writers confine themselves to either class or elite. Furthermore, the terms as sociologists use them have been developed in the analysis of western industrial societies, some salient characteristics of which are probably not being repeated in Africa. Neo-Marxists have coined 'the new class' to describe the upper stratum of the developing countries of communist Europe, for the classical Marxist division into bourgeoisie and proletariat is clearly inappropriate. It seems probable that the stratification of these developing communist countries has parallels in Africa, and it is unfortunate that its analysis has been bedevilled by political ideologies.

Any attempt simply to pin one or other of these terminological labels to the category of western-educated and wealthy Africans may well result in misleading usage of the terms or in falsification of our data. Again, the evidence that we have so far suggests that the dominant characteristics of this category are far from uniform from one African country to another, and the adoption of a single term to cover all situations would be an oversimplification. Our recourse, therefore, in this final section will be to outline some of the principal components of the terms class and elite, indicating those which seem most applicable to Africa. The writers of several of the papers in this volume have used and discussed the terms in the light of their own material.

Elite

The elite comprises the superior persons in society. For most sociologists their superiority is of a general character; few, today, would use the term, in Pareto's sense, of the top persons in each occupation or profession. It is this component which largely determines the colloquial use of the term elite (Nadel, 1956; Bottomore, 1964; and authors of studies in this volume). The elite, furthermore, are the superior group in an open society. Few would use the term of an upper-caste or an hereditary aristocracy. The concept of a 'circulation of elites' is still with us as implying the impermanence of elite status. Perhaps one could say that the more socially mobile a society is, the more appropriate is the use of the term 'elite' to designate its superior members. Here the use of the term in the African situation seems largely appropriate.

The most significant component of the concept elite defines the relationship with its counterpart—the masses. The elite influences the behaviour of the masses; it is an imitable body of persons. Influence is here distinguished from power and authority. The latter are associated with institutionalized relationships and structures, the former with non-structured relationships and with informal networks of communication. If we accept the hypothesis that an elite, to merit this designation, must influence the masses, we must seek both the degree to which this influence operates and the manner of its communication, neither is an easy task in any society.

The elite is the creator of new ideas and values. It operates in a sphere where, because of social change or rapid social mobility, appropriate norms for social relationships have not been clearly defined. It is an innovating body of persons (and, perhaps, a group of inner-directed men?). One might also describe the elite as a group which continually redefines the norms of society. But this component of the term is equally appropriate to an upper caste—say of Brahmin priests reinterpreting their scriptures. The emphasis on creation or redefinition of norms suggests that a stage will be reached when the norms are universally accepted and the elite will have ensured its own demise. However, this in turn would imply a static society, an unlikely event. Norms will always need redefinition and not necessarily by a new set of leaders.

This component of the elite seems most applicable to our African examples. The African elite is described as the mediator between western and traditional influences. Its individual members, born most probably into traditional homes, have to decide what to incorporate from the western industrial world, what to reject. The masses, furthermore, often look to them for leadership in these matters. The spheres of innovation have already been mentioned in this introduction, and are widely discussed elsewhere. In the domestic sphere we find that urbanization draws men away from their descent groups; new relationships have to be defined within the nuclear family and in occupational and neighbourhood groups. In the administrative sphere one sees the conflict between the idealized norms of bureaucracy and the systems of patronage which are more familiar to Africans. In the ideological sphere the African leaders are trying to create a new image for their countries and their people—one which will both transcend ethnic boundaries and give the African an identity comparable with and not dependent on that of the European. Thus, the concepts of *négritude*, the African personality, and African socialism are born. Each tries to stress elements which are to be Africa's contribution to human society—the most common being the corporate unity of the descent groups (in contrast to the atomization of western industrial society) and the lack of exploration of man by man and the concomitant class conflict. It seems to matter little to the proponents of these ideologies that the values they stress are those which economic development is most likely to assail; perhaps they are stressed because they are felt to be so vulnerable.

An elite is not only innovating; the values which it defines should be accepted by the masses—imitability is one of the components in its definition. Furthermore, it is the general values seen as being held by the elite which are exemplary, not any single specific traits. One would hesitate to term a wealthy category of persons an elite simply because their affluence is envied by the acquisitive members of the society. Nor should one use the term of persons whose values are copied merely as a means to an end— for instance, if one adopts certain behaviour in order to achieve political success. At this juncture we might recapitulate our earlier question: to what extent do the African masses admire the affluent members of their societies for their general value orientation or for their success as expressed in mere wealth?

An elite, of course, will not be completely imitable in those characteristics by which the concept is defined; if it were, it would cease to be a select category. Nor, on the other hand, should elite be defined in terms of characteristics which the masses are clearly incapable of copying. Thus, any characteristics related directly to the affluence of the elite would be clearly inappropriate in Africa where the gap in wealth between rich and poor is so great. Here one might ask how far the new urban patterns of marital relationships conceived by the elite are imitable by the masses in their rurally based descent groups? How far can concepts of 'African socialism' be understood by an illiterate? Are these values and ideologies restricted, in fact, to the urbanized and the affluent? And, if so, does our African elite, therefore, lack one of the essential components of the term 'elite'.

In this context of imitation our discussion broaches the allied field of reference group theory. Have modern African elites emerged as reference groups for the rest of the population—and if so what type of reference group? The term reference group (which may indicate a group of persons, an individual, or even a personal fantasy) embraces four types of situations in which the individual may refer to outside groups. The individual may adopt the values of a group in which he seeks membership—this being anticipatory socialization into the group; or he may take the values of the group as a model for his own behaviour without necessarily aiming at membership or identification. The individual may use the reference group simply to define his own position in society without making any value judgement of the group cited. Lastly, he may use a reference group in a negative manner, denying the values which it represents. Only in the second of the situations may a reference group, if acting as a model for the masses, be defined as an elite.

For theoretical analyses in this sphere we are severely hampered by our ignorance of the perceptions of the masses with reference to both their own position in society and that of the elite. What information we have tends to be impressionistic and perhaps un-representative, because the surveys carried out have so often been based on samples of adolescent literates.

Some sociologists feel that an elite should be a fairly cohesive and perhaps even a corporate group; others feel that the term may be applied to unrelated individuals. If the elite creates new norms these innovations are presumably made by relatively few persons. They become accepted by the wider group through the influence of the innovators over their peers; only through such acceptance do the innovations cease to be individual idiosyncracies. Studies of multiple roles and of informal networks help us to understand the diffusion within an elite of new values. Although such studies are lacking in Africa, our general impressions are of a small elite with a highly intricate network of relationships and numerous multiple roles. It seems reasonable, therefore, to ascribe a considerable degree of cohesiveness to modern African elites with regard to the definition and promulgation of new values.

By what channels of communication do the values of the elite permeate to the masses? Is the elite seen as a group, or do single individuals constitute the model? The first-generation members of the elite still have such close relationships with the masses through their kin ties and membership of ethnic associations that these relationships seem to be the obvious channels of diffusion of new values. One might, however, reverse the question and ask whether the masses see the elite as a group or whether they see only a collec-tion of affluent individuals, prominent among whom are some of their own kin. This question raises the issue of categorization. To

what extent can and do African languages describe the characteristics
of the new stratification? Can the masses adopt the vernacular words
available to them, or may they adopt European words in common
usage among the elite themselves? In the absence of suitable
terms definition of the new social categories is almost impossible.

A further component in the definition of an elite is the element
of unity or plurality among the elite. Since an elite implies
superiority, one cannot rank a plurality of elites heirarchically.
But there may exist a number of elite groups, each quasi-corporate
in itself, having its own network of interpersonal relationships
and, perhaps, serving as a reference group to a different section of
the people. Such a theoretical issue does not seem to arise in
Africa, and especially in the independant states. First, an entrepreneurial elite is largely absent. Second, while politics, the professions, and the bureaucracies may be held to constitute separate
occupational categories, they are manned by persons educated in
a few schools, and linked by the interpersonal networks already
described. One of the few divisions that may be prominent is that
between civil servants and politicians, where the latter are of inferior education to the former and have owed their success to
political acumen, loyalty, and personal qualities of leadership. In
South Africa where entrepreneurship seems more highly developed among the western educated, there seems to be relatively
little contact between the business and the intellectual communities.

Dominant among a plurality of elites is one often described as
the governing elite (or power or ruling elite), terms used to designate the decision makers (and distinguishing for example, between the political party leaders and the senior civil servants).
The governing elite may also embrace the leaders of business—a
category filled in Africa predominantly by expatriates. A governing elite tends to be a more highly corporate group. Yet it may
lack the components of innovation and imitability. It may even
be viewed with hostility by other elite groups or by the masses,
and in these circumstances the designation elite would seem to be
inappropriate.

Whether or not we apply the term elite in an African context will depend, first, on the components which we deem essential in defining the term. For some of the components arguments concerning the inclusion seem unnecessary; thus, since the African elites do tend to be close-knit groups, it matters little whether one insists on including this component in the definition. In the more important areas it is our lack of knowledge which causes difficulties; how far does any African elite possess a general value orientation which constitutes a model for the masses, capable of being imitated, at least part, by them? Nevertheless, whatever our answer to these questions, we have not exhausted the terminology of social stratification available to us, and we thus turn our attention to the components of the term 'class'.

Social Class

Sociologists may differ in the weight they attach to the components in the definition of elite; but they hold almost diametrically opposed notions of the definition of social class. One school, descended from Marx, sees classes as economic or political-interest groups largely hereditary in character and logically opposed to one another—a variant of the dichotomy between the 'haves' and the 'have-nots'. The emphasis is on the class conflict or struggle between the groups. The other school, typified by Warner, sees classes as status groups, hierarchically arranged, but not clearly divided one from another. Stress is placed on this continuum between classes and the possibility of individual social mobility between them. It is the functional relationships between the classes that is emphasized—conflict is not discussed. Although great differences in wealth exist between the upper and lower classes, these are held to be necessary, in a society where individual achievement is stressed, as a concomitant of rapid economic expansion. For this school the classes are defined by a series of status characteristics—income, house style, etc.—and by the assessments of informants of their own and of their neighbours' class position. The latter implies that class terminology is colloquially used. The possibility of its use in Africa is therefore limited. For not only are the masses ignorant of the class terminology but their perception of the division of their societies is

E

based more on ethnic groups or criteria of descent or age than on horizontal stratification by affluence. Educated persons who are aware of the terminology often use it in novel ways: senior civil servants have been described in conversation and in students' essays as the 'working class'—to distinguish them from 'lazy politicians', underemployed labourers, craftsmen, and farmers. As in our discussion of the term elite, we shall consider the components in the definition of class in the light of our African data.

Classes in the classic Marxist sense of property-owning and non-owning groups exist neither in traditional nor modern African society; land rights are still predominantly held by villages and descent groups. (Buganda with its private estates of *mailo* land is here an exception.) Industry is overwhelmingly owned and controlled either by state or by foreign companies, either singly or in combination. The wage-earner still clings to his land rights in his rural area. Thus, there are neither bourgeoisie nor proletariat in the strict sense of these words, even in the modern sector of the economy. On the other hand, since both the peasant economy and the pattern of industrial development of the independent African states are in a large measure controlled by the Government, either through the ministries or through public corporations, the separation which exists in western industrial states between direction in the economic and the political spheres does not here operate. Political leaders who control the economy in communist states have been described by Djilas (1957) as the 'new class'—a term which is becoming increasingly common. Dumont (1962) refers, in an African context, to 'une bourgeoisie de la fonction publique' (see also Fanon, 1963). One has the difficulty with these concepts in distinguishing between the political members of the class who formerly made the decisions and the salaried civil servants and managers in the bureaucracies who are close to and may strongly influence the decision-making process. In the African context one usually has the impression of quite close personal relationships between members of these two categories—they have been to the same schools, belong to the same modern associations. Furthermore, the bureaucrats are in a vulnerable position, having acceded to incomes and privileges initially designed for expatriate office-holders and far in excess of those enjoyed by the masses. These interests they may jealously guard, but their preservation lies in the hands of the politicians. Moreover, the privileged position of the elite is open in principle to all, and many aspire to it. A conflict of interest between the elite, on the one hand, and the peasantry and wage-earning townsmen, on the other, would be expressed only when it were demonstrated that the privileges of the elite impeded the development of the economy, and thus retarded the rise in the standards of living of the masses.

Classes tend to be hereditary groups. They will obviously be so when property owning is the basis of membership of the bourgeoisie. The educational system can facilitate or impede (and it is usually the latter) mobility between classes. In Africa, as we have seen earlier, the nature of the educational system, together with the great disparity in home conditions and parental attitudes to schooling, gives the elite parent a very good chance of ensuring that his children will enjoy the same status as himself. Thus, the well-educated and wealthy elite is tending to become a predominantly hereditary group; the proportion of future members who come from non-elite homes will depend on the increase in the size of the group—itself a function of the expansion of the economy. However, in Africa at present, the elite is characterized by the number of its members who have come from humble homes.

Consciousness of class membership is usually stressed as an important component of the concept of 'class'. We should, however, distinguish between class awareness and class consciousness —the latter implying consciousness of the special interests of the class and activity directed towards preserving these interests.

The degree of class awareness depends on the range of differences in wealth and styles of living between rich and poor, on the sharpness with which divisions may be drawn, and on the terms colloquially available to denote these divisions. In the advanced industrial nations, such as the United States, the range in wealth is wide, but no divisions are clearly marked, and the class terms— upper, middle, and lower—are most imprecise. In Africa also one has great variations in wealth. But it is probably easier to define limits to the elite. First, the use of the term 'elite' itself is spreading among Africans, and may well aid them in identifying the group. Second, in at least some countries a term such as 'senior service' denotes the holder of a post once reserved for expatriates and thus enjoying its privileges. So pervasive is the bureaucratization of the African countries that a man may be ranked by his salary grading, and this is regularly published in the staff lists. Thus, there are far fewer men whose place in the stratification is ambiguous. Third, by their affluence, their western education, and the small range of consumer goods available, the style of life of the elite is notably both internally homogenous to a high degree but also markedly contrasted with that of the masses. The members of the elite seem to choose their close friends from their status equals, even though most of them retain close ties of affection with their non-elite kin and many are active participants in the affairs of their home communities. Children of elite parents have a very different upbringing from those of the mass of the people; in many cases their perception of their privileged status is heightened by continual disparaging references to non-elite neighbours and their habits. (The sensitive expatriate teacher carefully avoids the term 'native', only to find his students using it of the non-literate peasantry.) These children frequently meet their non-elite kin on visits to their home town with their parents, but such visits are usually of short duration. Children of elite parents seem to prefer to marry those of similar parentage; the elites are to this extent tending to become endogamous groups.

Inhibiting the development of class awareness are the still powerful ethnic divisions, even within the elite. While education tends to reduce their intensity, the development of self-government (and hence the possibility of domination of one group by another) and the increasing reliance on patronage to secure career and professional advancement operate in a counter-direction. 'Tribalism' has tended to increase rather than decrease with independence. But the spirit of national unity which was evoked by the political leaders in their fight for self-government has not yet been forgotten. Indeed, in many states attempts are still made to strengthen loyalty to the new state by continued references to the neo-colonialist enemy without.

The privileges of the elite have already been cited. To what extent is the elite conscious of special interests and organized to maintain them? Those Africans who have struggled to attain an affluent Western style of life are not likely to relinquish these privileges soon after their acquisition. The associations of civil servants and similar organizations seek to protect the conditions of service of their members. Their strongest card is the need of governments for a loyal civil service to maintain stable administration. On the other hand, the elite fear the collapse of government and its substitution by anarchy. On issues involving civil liberties and the like, the protests of the elite are often strangely muted and ineffectual.

A most striking feature of the African scene is an ideology of classlessness in contemporary African society. The more Marxist-oriented politicians of French-speaking West Africa discuss their colonial and neo-colonial status in terms of exploitation but deny exploitation within their own societies. Some African leaders claim that their societies can pass from the tribal stage to that of socialism without experiencing the Marxist periods of conflict between antagonistic classes. The communalism of tribal life and the participation of the people in their local affairs in village meetings are taken as examples of the socialist spirit indigenous to Africa. The elite are portrayed as the leaders, not the exploiters, of their people (Grundy, 1964; Senghor, 1964).

Such an ideology, together with the lack of differentiation between the policies of rival parties (all promising a better life for their followers) and the desire of the established politicians to remain in office, favours the development of single-party systems. Political leaders then have a greater control of the means of propaganda, and the ideology of classlessness becomes more deeply entrenched. An ideology of non-equalitarian classlessness may be maintained in non-African societies, too; both the United States and Soviet Russia proclaim it; yet in the former classes as status groups, and in the latter the non-antagonistic classes of peasants and workers, are widely recognized. In Africa the colloquial use of class terms is virtually absent and the ideological constructs of the political leaders seem designed more for the elite, influenced by radical ideas in European universities, than for the masses.

Finally a social class can exist only in a system of classes. There can be no upper class without a lower class. In their homogenity, hereditary characteristics, and class consciousness, the classes should resemble one another. But if the African elite forms an upper class, where are the lower classes? The peasantry still thinks in terms of ethnic units, with descent and age as the main criteria of stratification and social divisions. The sub-elite of clerks, primary-school teachers, and skilled artisans are perhaps slightly less ethnically oriented, but actively aspire to elite membership. The urban labourer remains ethnically oriented, often relying on his ethnic association for his social security. Trades unions, which might otherwise protect his interests, are weakly developed, especially among the least skilled. In as much as this latter category of workers poses a threat to the politicians, it is as a mob rather than as an organized working-class party. One of the advantages of the term elite in describing the affluent western-educated African is that its counterpart, 'the masses', vaguely implies a lack of structure, or at least of dominant structures among the non-elite. This is certainly generally appropriate in the African context. In other respects, however, the components of the class concept seem more useful in describing the African elite. This seems especially so if we consider possible developments in the social stratification of African societies in the next few decades.

Most predictions of the future stratification of African societies depend on estimates of the rapidity of economic development. Let us presume that the rate of growth will be less than that hoped for by African politicians and more in line with present-day rates of overseas aid and investment and internal savings. The expansion of the bureaucracies experienced in the past decade will slow down considerably, and the present elite will be able to fill a high proportion of the vacant posts with their own children—especially if they continue to have large families. Competition within the elite for the higher posts will become more intense; the aspirations of the sub-elite will be less frequently rewarded. The frustrated among the elite and sub-elite will turn towards protest movements among the sub-elite and the masses, taking leadership positions. Such movements may adopt a socialist ideology of conflict, but much of their effectiveness will depend on the ability of their leaders to break free from the classic Marxist dogmas, largely unintelligible to African peasants and workers, and to reinterpret the basic principles of class conflict in an indigenous context.

In the present early years following the attainment of independence, the political leaders and the elite are reversed by their kin, and for their attainment of styles of life. The lavish presidential palaces are applauded, since they enable the new leaders to entertain the royalty and presidents of Western nations on terms of equality. But as the lot of the urban workers fails to improve while the affluence of the elite is easily maintained, respect is turning to hostility. The politicians, among the most conspicuously extravagant yet owing their positions to the votes of their constituents, are the first to be criticized. Widespread strikes in Nigeria in May and June 1964 arose over the Government's delay in publishing the report of the Morgan Commission's inquiry into wage structures; however, inept handling of the issue by the Government very quickly turned the demands for higher wages into a more general criticism of the affluence of the politicians and the elite; Government efforts to end the strike failed until the Government ostensibly made a substantial capitulation to the workers' demands. Such considerations apply with much less force to those states in which the elite live with less open extravagance. Bamako, capital of Mali, is noted among West African cities for its lack of cocktail parties. In Ghana leading politicians have been censured and cast out for their ostentation, though only to be rehabilitated at a later date; current propaganda includes a marked puritanical element as the Government tries to solve its balance-of-payments problems by restrictions on imports of consumer goods.

If the African elite becomes more hereditary, if hostility towards its privileged affluence increases, and if, as seems probable, the second and subsequent elite generations lose touch with the rural communities of their origin, cohesion within the elite will intensify. For such a group, the sociological term elite will then be inappropriate. On the other hand, continued backwardness of the masses would probably both inhibit the development of a class consciousness among them and also facilitate the maintenance of the classless ideology by the ruling groups.

Thus, while the term elite may be appropriate in describing the western-educated and wealthy men of some contemporary African societies, its relevance may be short lived. However, the terminology of class systems seems no more appropriate. In both sets of terms there are, however, components which are essential in any analysis of the stratification of African societies. Our search is for a deeper understanding of the so-called elite and the trends in its development—not merely for the most appropriate label.

BIBLIOGRAPHY

Note. The bibliography below, in common with those following some of the Special Studies, contains both works to which specific reference is made in the text and others which seem to the authors to be of special relevance to their topics. The literature devoted exclusively to the African elite is of very limited extent; a full bibliography of references to this elite would include not only most general works on contemporary African society but also a large proportion of the literature dealing, for instance, with urbanization, political development, and education.

Ajayi, J. F. Ade
    (1963) 'The development of Secondary Grammar School education in Nigeria', *Journal of the Historical Society of Nigeria*, vol. 2, no. 4, pp. 517–35
Balandier, G.
    (1955) *Sociologie des Brazzaville Noires*. Paris.
Banton, M.
    (1957) *West African City*. London.
Berg, Elliot
    (1960) 'The economic basis of political choice in French West Africa', *American Political Science Review*.
Bottomore, T. B.
    (1964) *Elites and Society*. London.
Bretton, Henry L.
    (1962) *Power and Stability in Nigeria*. New York.
Clignet, Remi P. and Foster, Philip.
    (1964) 'Potential elites in Ghana and the Ivory Coast: a preliminary comparison', *American Journal of Sociology*, vol. 70, pp. 349–62.

Coleman, James S.
(1958) *Nigeria: Background to Nationalism*. Berkeley. (Especially chapters 5 and 6.)
Djilas, Milovan
(1957) *The New Class*. London.
Dumont, René
(1962) *L'Afrique Noire est mal partie*. Paris.
Fallers, L. A.
(1959) 'Despotism, status culture and social mobility in an African kingdom', *Comparative Studies in Society and History*, vol. 2, pp. 11–32.
(1961) 'Ideology and culture in Uganda nationalism', *American Anthropologist*, vol. 63, pp. 677–86.
Fallers, L. A. (ed.)
(1964) *The King's Men*. London. (Especially chapters 2–4.)
Fanon, Franz
(1963) *The Damned* (transl. C. Farrington). Paris.
Field, M. J.
(1960) *Search for Security*. London.
Foster, Philip J.
(1962) 'Ethnicity and the schools in Ghana', *Comparative Education Review* pp. 127–35.
(1963) 'Secondary schooling and social mobility in a West African nation', *Sociology of Education*, vol. 37, pp. 150–71.
(1964) 'Secondary school leavers in Ghana: expectations and reality', *Harvard Educational Review*, vol. 34, pp. 537–58.
(1965) *Education and Social Change in Ghana*. London.
Fraenkel, Merran.
(1964) *Tribe and Class in Monrovia*. London. (Especially chapters 5 and 6.)
Friedmann, John
(1960) 'Intellectuals in developing societies', *Kylos*, vol. 13, pp. 513–44.
Garlick, Peter
(1959) *African Traders in Kumasi*. Legon, Ghana.
Geertz, Clifford (ed.)
(1963) *Old Societies and New States*. New York.
Goldthorpe, J. E.
(1955) 'An African elite: a sample survey of fifty-two former students of Makerere College in East Africa', *British Journal of Sociology*, vol. 6, pp. 31–47.
Grundy, Kenneth W.
(1964) 'The "class struggle" in Africa', *Journal of Modern African Studies* vol. 2, pp. 379–93.
Gutteridge, W.
(1962) *Armed Forces in New States*. London.
Hagen, Everett E.
(1962) *On the Theory of Social Change*. Homewood, Illinois.
Hellmann, E.
(1944) 'The development of social groupings among urban Africans in the Union of South Africa', *African Studies*.
Hodgkin, Thomas
(1956) *Nationalism in Colonial Africa*. London.
Hoselitz, B. F.
(1963) 'Entrepreneurship and traditional elites', *Explorations in Entrepreneurial History*, vol. 1, pp. 36–49.

INCIDI (International Institute of Differing Civilisations)
(1956) *Development of a Middle Class in Tropical and Sub-Tropical Countries.* Brussels.

Jahoda, Gustav
(1954) 'The social background of a West African student population', *British Journal of Sociology*, vol. 5, pp. 355–65, vol. 6, pp. 71–9.
(1961) *White Man.* London.

Kuper, Leo
(1965) *An African Bourgeoisie.* New Haven and London.

Levine, D. N.
(1965) *Wax and Gold: Tradition and Innovation in Ethiopian Culture.* Chicago.

Lipset, S. M.
(1961) 'A changing American character?' in Lipset, S. M. and Lowenthal, L. (eds.) *Character and Social Structure.* Glencoe, New York.
(1964) 'Research problems in the comparative analysis of mobility and development', *International Social Science Journal*, vol. 16, pp. 35–48.

Little, A. and Westergaard, J.
(1964) 'The trend of class differentials in educational opportunity in England and Wales', *British Journal of Sociology*, vol. 15, pp. 301–16.

Little, K. L.
(1957) 'The role of voluntary associations in West African urbanisation', *American Anthropologist*, vol. 59, pp. 579–96.

Lloyd, P. C.
(1962) 'Tribalism in Nigeria', in Dubb, A. A. (ed.) *The Multi-tribal Society* (proceedings of the 16th Conference of the Rhodes–Livingstone Institute). Lusaka.

Marris, Peter
(1961) *Family and Social Change in an African City.* London.

Mayer, Philip
(1961) *Townsmen or Tribesmen.* London.

McClelland, David C.
(1961) *The Achieving Society.* New York.

Mercier, Paul
(1954) 'Aspects des problèmes de stratification sociale dans l'ouest Africain', *Cahiers Internationaux de Sociologie*, vol. 16.

Nadel, S. F.
(1956) 'The concept of social elites', in UNESCO (1956) pp. 413–24.

Nigeria, Federal Republic of
(1964) *Report of the Commission on the Review of Wages, Salary and Conditions of Service of the Junior Employees of the Governments of the Federation and in Private Establishments 1963–4*, Lagos.

Omari, T. P.
(1960) 'Changing attitudes of Students in West African Society towards Marriage and Family Relationships', *British Journal of Sociology*, vol. 11, pp. 197–210.

Pauvert, J-C.
(1955) 'Le problème des classes sociales en Afrique Equatoriale', *Cahiers Internationaux de Sociologie*, vol. 19, pp. 76–91.

Peil, M.
(1965) 'Ghanaian University Students: the Broadening Base', *British Journal of Sociology*, vol. 16, pp. 19–28.

Porter, Arthur T.
(1963) *Creoledom.* London.

Reisman, David
(1950) *The Lonely Crowd*. New Haven.
Senghor, L. S.
(1964) *On African Socialism*. (Transl. and ed. Mercer Cook.) New York.
Smythe, H. H. and Smythe, M. M.
(1960) *The New Nigerian Elite*. Stanford, California.
Southall, A. W. (ed.)
(1961) *Social Change in Modern Africa*. London.
Tardits, C.
(1956) 'The notion of the elite and the urban social survey in Africa', in
UNESCO (1956) pp. 492–5.
(1958) *Porto-Novo: les nouvelles générations africaines entre leurs traditions et
l'occident*. Paris.
UNESCO
(1956) 'African elites', *International Social Science Bulletin*, vol. 8, pp. 413–98.
(1963) *The Development of Higher Education in Africa*. Paris.

Résumé français

INTRODUCTION

L'ÉTUDE DE L'ÉLITE

Dans toute l'Afrique sub-saharienne, le pouvoir politique a passé rapidement des gouverneurs coloniaux aux membres, dans l'ensemble jeunes et bien instruits, des nouvelles élites nationales. Pourtant, nous savons encore relativement peu de choses sur cette nouvelle catégorie de membres de la société. Les anthropologues sociaux ont eu tendance à concentrer leurs efforts sur les communautés rurales ou sur le choc que la vie urbaine inflige aux nouveaux immigrants. L'étude de l'élite soulève des difficultés d'ordre méthodologique: l'élite est peu nombreuse, ses activités publiques et privées ne sont pas soumises à la vue de tous, ce sont des hommes et femmes occupés, peu facilement disponibles pour être interrogés. Deux congrès importants sur les élites africaines ne semblent pas avoir stimulé des études approfondies; très peu de monographies consacrées à cette catégorie de personnes existent actuellement.

Les membres du séminaire sur les classes sociales et les élites dans l'Afrique contemporaine, organisé par l'Institut International Africain, eurent l'impression de pénétrer dans un territoire presque vierge; ils représentaient un vaste éventail de disciplines sociologiques, et avaient, personnellement, vécu pendant des périodes substantielles dans un ou plusieurs territoires africains. Dans la plupart des cas, leur connaissance de l'élite était due plus au fait qu'ils travaillèrent avec elle dans les bureaux du gouvernement et les universités, qu'à une étude directe.

Cette introduction aux communications soumises lors du séminaire suit d'une manière substantielle le cours de nos discussions au cours des réunions. Elle reflète également les connaissances et intérêts des participants, dont la moitié représentait les territoires de l'Afrique occidentale—proportion justifiée si l'on tient compte du développement plus prononcé des élites dans ces territoires, tant du point de vue de leur nombre actuel que de leur accroissement au cours des dernières décades.

Pour plus de facilité, il fut décidé dès le début, d'utiliser le terme 'élite' pour désigner ceux possédant une éducation occidentale et une certaine aisance—un revenu annuel de 250 livres étant proposé. Cette décision ne préjugea pas des discussions ultérieures en vue d'établir si cette catégorie constituait vraiment une élite ou une classe sociale, selon la terminologie sociologique en usage. Les caractéristiques de cette catégorie d'individus—du point de vue de leur nombre, de leur degré d'aisance et du développement historique—varient cependant très largement d'un territoire à l'autre, et la première tâche du séminaire fut de tracer des différences. Ensuite les participants discutèrent du système d'instruction scolaire qui produisit cette élite, en examinant à leur tour les types de mobilité sociale. Le troisième sujet traita du degré auquel ces élites continuent à participer aux associations traditionnelles ou traditionnalistes—en groupe de même descendance ou associations ethniques—et du degré de développement des associations à caractère exclusif. Quatrièmement le séminaire discuta de l'échelle des valeurs de l'élite et en particulier du thème de l'ambition de réussir, à quel point les valeurs de l'élite diffèrent de celles de ses parents et jusqu'à quel point ces nouvelles valeurs sont transmises à ses propres enfants ou aux masses. En dernier lieu, les membres du séminaire, à l'aide d'une vaste documentation descriptive discutèrent de l'applicabilité à la scène africaine des concepts sociologiques tels que ceux de classe sociale et élite. Les participants ne furent pas unanimes dans leurs définitions de ces concepts, mais ils définirent, au cours de leurs discussions, un certain nombre d'attributs de classe et de groupes d'élites. Les variations de caractéristiques de l'élite africaine ayant déjà été esquissées, une position fut atteinte d'où il serait possible d'établir un modèle du développement de l'élite dans n'importe quel territoire.

CARACTÉRISTIQUES DE L'ÉLITE CONTEMPORAINE

Les caractéristiques de l'élite contemporaine dans les états africains varient largement. On peut, jusqu'à un certain point, faire correspondre ces différences avec le développement de l'indépendance politique. Ainsi les territoires de l'Afrique occidentale, du Ghana et de la Nigéria qui accédèrent à l'indépendance après plusieurs années de préparation politique et culturelle, ont maintenant une très grande partie de leur population ayant fréquenté l'université et leurs services administratifs sont presque complètement composés de personnel indigène. Longtemps avant le 20ème siècle ces états furent soumis au contact européen et des africains ayant reçu une instruction supérieure eurent au 19ème siècle des postes importants dans les services publics. Là encore la richesse paysanne de ces pays a été employée pour financer l'instruction des étudiants particuliers. En comparaison l'élite des autres états africains est moins évoluée.

Il est difficile d'obtenir des chiffres exacts illustrant le nombre des élites contemporaines; pourtant, ces chiffres sont partout relativement peu élevés. Ainsi, le Sénégal, avec une population de trois millions d'habitants a 325 fonctionnaires dont le salaire annuel est supérieur à 1.250 livres. En Zambie, 2,6% seulement de la population a reçu une instruction primaire complète et 1.000 habitants seulement ont douze années ou plus de scolarité. Pourtant, ce nombre peu élevé d'élite est aggloméré dans les métropoles d'où il lui est possible de développer distinctivement un style de vie et une conscience de son propre groupe.

L'accroissement de l'élite est récent. Ce n'est qu'après 1945 qu'un grand nombre d'étudiants allèrent poursuivre leurs études dans les universités américaines et européennes; à l'exception du Fourah Bay College, les universités dans les territoires coloniaux datent de l'après-guerre. De même l'instruction primaire et secondaire s'est rapidement développée au cours de cette période. Il en résulte que la majeure partie de l'élite est composée d'êtres jeunes, encore que pour certains d'entre eux, l'instruction ait été une expérience prolongée, aux années de scolarité entrecoupées de périodes d'emploi. Beaucoup ont atteint la trentaine lorsqu'ils obtiennent leur diplôme. Ceux qui entrèrent jeunes dans l'administration et autres carrières accédèrent rapidement aux postes supérieurs au fur et à mesure que les européens les quittaient et que les services publics se développaient pour offrir un nombre accru d'emplois importants.

La majorité de l'élite dans les états africains est occupée dans la bureaucratie. Les gouvernements coloniaux avaient imposé une structure administrative complexe à des pays dont l'économie était au niveau de la subsistance et où les services publics et nombre d'organismes économiques, tels que les Offices de Contrôle étaient supervisés par l'état. L'instruction publique est également aidée et contrôlée par l'état, même lorsque celle-ci est nominalement aux mains d'agences privées ou de missionnaires. L'accroissement de l'instruction secondaire au cours de ces dernières années a été tel qu'une petite proportion seulement de professeurs sont diplômés d'université. Dans les nouveaux états indépendants les professeurs ont été attirés dans des fonctions politiquement plus importantes laissant les écoles recruter du personnel étranger pour leurs postes supérieurs. Le barreau et la médecine furent des professions très en faveur parmi l'élite au cours de la période coloniale, quand ses membres pouvaient exercer dans le secteur privé, loin des discriminations de rang et de salaire qui auraient existé dans l'Administration. De nos jours, les médecins ont tendance à être employés par l'état.

L'Africain instruit a jusqu'à présent été peu attiré par le commerce et les affaires. Les entreprises économiques majeures étaient aux mains des étrangers, et ces compagnies ont encore tendance à réserver leurs postes clés aux Européens expatriés dans ces pays; les Africains peuvent accéder à des positions élevées dans les services de relations avec le public ou l'organisation du personnel. Le diplômé supérieur africain n'a ni l'habileté technique ni le capital nécessaire pour créer sa propre entreprise. Il a peu d'encouragement à consacrer des années capitales à créer une affaire lorsque les récompenses d'un emploi de bureau sont à la fois immédiates et larges.

Au cours des longues années consacrées à son instruction secondaire et supérieure qui l'ont séparée de sa famille, la majorité de l'élite africaine, quels que soient les droits qu'elle continue d'avoir théoriquement sur les terres rurales dont sa descendance est originaire, s'est éloignée de son origine terrienne. Dans certains états de l'Afrique occidentale francophone et, dans une catégorie plus différente, en Ethiopie, l'élite possède ses propres plantations sur lesquelles travaille une main-d'oeuvre de louage. Ailleurs, dans les cités s'accroissant rapidement, investir dans la propriété foncière et immobilière est à la fois très en faveur et hautement rémunérateur.

La profession politique est l'une des catégories d'emploi finales pour l'élite. Dans la plupart des états, les nouveaux législateurs viennent des rangs de l'élite actuelle, les avocats et les professeurs étant au premier rang. Mais au fur et à mesure que les partis politiques développent leur organisation, l'accession au rang de l'élite est ouverte aux masses qui manquent d'instruction mais démontrent leur loyauté à leur parti et font preuve de qualités de chef.

L'échelle des salaires des états africains indépendants reste un héritage colonial. Bien qu'il soit maintenant facile de passer d'un emploi subalterne (auquel autrefois les Africains étaient largement confinés) à un poste supérieur (attribué autrefois aux Européens) la grande disparité entre les revenus de ces deux groupes persiste. Le salaire de début d'un diplômé supérieur (habituellement de 750 à 1000 livres par an) est souvent trois fois plus élevé que celui d'un jeune débutant ayant terminé avec succès cinq années d'instruction secondaire, et le salaire de ce dernier est trois fois supérieur à celui d'un manœuvre inexpérimenté. L'artisan qualifié ayant atteint son plafond ne gagne que le salaire initial du débutant ayant terminé son instruction secondaire; ce dernier ne peut jamais, à moins qu'il soit doué de qualités exceptionnelles ou qu'il poursuive ses études, atteindre le salaire initial dans l'échelle appliquée aux diplômés supérieurs. La différence entre les salaires de l'élite et le revenu de la masse est plus grande dans les états ayant récemment accédé à l'indépendance; elle est moindre en Afrique du Sud où d'une part les Africains instruits gagnent moins que les Européens effectuant un travail similaire, et d'autre part le manœuvre urbain et l'artisan ont un niveau de vie plus élevé que celui de leurs homologues dans les autres états africains.

Avec des revenus décrits plus haut, les membres de l'élite jouissent du même train de vie que des Européens occidentaux ayant une aisance correspondante. Des taxes élevées imposées sur les articles de luxe importés sont contrebalancées par des impôts sur le revenu relativement bas. Beaucoup parmi l'élite vivent dans des habitations construites à l'origine pour des Européens; les styles d'ameublement varient peu dans ces habitations. Dans ces circonstances, un rapport assez étroit existe entre le revenu et le train de vie, l'accent étant placé sur des signes de richesse ostentatoires.

L'élite a été définie, pour les raisons de facilité, en termes de richesse et d'éducation. Certaines catégories en marge doivent être mentionnées brièvement. Beaucoup de responsables politiques traditionnels, spécialement dans les anciennes colonies britanniques, sont bien instruits. D'autres individus sont de riches commerçants qui manquent d'instruction au sens propre. Dans chaque cas, leurs genres de vie et leur sens des valeurs sont plus proches de la tradition que de ceux de l'élite occidentalisée. Nous les appelons l'élite marginale. On peut aussi distinguer une sous-élite composée de personnel enseignant et d'employés de bureau, qui est moins instruite que l'élite elle-même. Beaucoup de membres de cette sous-élite aspirent à pénétrer dans les rangs de l'élite; d'autres se sentent frustrés et pourront former une réserve de mécontentement politique.

LE DÉVELOPPEMENT DE L'ÉLITE

Nous avons esquissé au paragraphe précédent certaines caractéristiques de l'élite contemporaine, ne faisant aucune distinction entre ceux de ses membres d'origine modeste et ceux dont les familles faisaient déjà partie de l'élite. Nous avons besoin d'étudier le rapport entre l'élite contemporaine et deux autres catégories: l'élite traditionnelle formée par les responsables politiques des sociétés tribales et l'élite déjà occidentalisée. Jusqu'à quel point les membres de l'élite contemporaine sont-ils issus de familles appartenant à l'élite traditionnelle ou antérieurement occidentalisée? Est-ce que les valeurs des membres de ces trois catégories sont compatibles? Jusqu'à quel point un conflit existe-t-il entre les membres de ces différentes élites? Nous pouvons résoudre ces questions seulement en examinant dans leur contexte historique les élites de chaque état.

On peut distinguer trois types de conflits. Premièrement un conflit entre des groupes ethniques dont les degrés d'instruction sont disproportionnés. Deuxièmement un conflit entre des générations d'élite différentes—par exemple lorsque les membres de l'élite contemporaine accusent leurs prédécesseurs d'une trop faible opposition au régime colonial. Troisièmement un conflit entre les différents groupes fonctionnels de l'élite, par exemple les fonctionnaires et politiciens.

Au 19ème siècle les rapports entre Européens et habitants de la côte occidentale d'Afrique donnèrent lieu au développement d'une élite indigène occidentalisée. La famille Brew, décrite par Margaret Priestley est un exemple typique d'une famille distinguée de la Côte d'Or. Cependant, bien que seuls quelques membres de cette famille assumèrent des fonctions élevées, le prestige qui en découla semble s'être étendu à toute la famille. Bien que vêtus ouvertement à l'européenne, leurs enfants fréquentent les écoles occidentales, ces membres intégrés aux résidents européens continuèrent à entretenir des liens étroits avec les groupes dont ils descendaient et avec leur parenté des villes de l'intérieur. Jusqu'à quel point les membres de l'élite ou leurs familles entières servent-ils d'exemple pour les masses? Les groupes créoles de Freetown et Lagos et les 'Brésiliens' de Lagos, Porto-Novo et Lomé font partie d'une catégorie plutôt différente. Les membres de ces groupes presque fermés acceptèrent les caractéristiques manifestes de la vie européenne afin de maintenir leur identité distincte de celle des masses tribales de l'intérieur. Dans chaque cas, les membres de

F

ces groupes d'élite originaux fournirent des employés de bureau aux services publics et la direction politique nationaliste initiale. Ils perdirent subséquemment leur suprématie lorsque des parlements furent élus par la nation entière.

Ailleurs en Afrique coloniale l'accroissement des élites ne commença pas avant qu'une bonne partie du 20ème siècle se soit écoulée. Ainsi, l'exploitation des mines de cuivre en Zambie eut lieu après 1920, une ou deux décades après le début effectif de l'activité missionnaire. Vers 1950 l'élite africaine de ces territoires se composait habituellement d'individus n'ayant reçu qu'une instruction primaire. Aujourd'hui, les niveaux d'instruction sont plus élevés, mais il n'est pas inusité que presque tous les membres de l'élite soient le produit d'une seule école secondaire. Comme le niveau d'instruction continue à s'élever rapidement, les nouveaux aspirants aux rangs de l'élite seront bien mieux qualifiés (du point de vue de diplômes universitaires) que ceux qui leur sont d'un rang supérieur dans les hiérarchies de l'administration.

On trouve dans deux états africains des situations particulières, dignes d'être mentionnées brièvement. En Afrique du Sud, l'activité des missions et l'établissement d'écoles produisirent au 19ème siècle une première élite. L'apartheid a néanmoins sclérosé le développement de ce groupe, lui déniant plusieurs droits politiques et économiques. Dans une telle société, basée sur le système de castes, l'élite africaine est obligée de s'associer aux masses pour résister à la domination blanche, tout en préservant simultanément une certaine exclusivité. En Ethiopie, nous avons la situation unique d'un monarque partageant le pouvoir avec une élite retranchée composée de l'aristocratie amharique et du clergé. Ici, l'occidentalisation est moindre que dans tout autre état africain. L'élite moderne, décrite plus loin par Levine, composée d'une nouvelle nobilité, des chefs militaires et de l'intelligentsia, maintient un mode de vie occidental tout en restant enlisée dans des rapports traditionnels de mécènes à bénéficiaires. On voit là un conflit relativement marqué entre ceux qui ont été instruits à l'étranger et les produits des écoles et universités locales qui conservent des vues plus traditionnelles.

LE PROCESSUS ÉDUCATIF

L'entrée dans les services de l'administration, les corporations publiques et grandes entreprises commerciales créées par les Européens dépend largement de la possession de qualifications scolaires appropriées. Les fonctions étant dans l'ensemble de nature administrative, c'est le niveau atteint plutôt que les matières étudiées au cours de la scolarité, qui est important. En dehors des emplois de bureau, il y a moins d'occasion d'emploi qu'il n'en existait, par exemple, dans les pays d'Europe occidentale lors de leur expansion économique à la fin du 19ème siècle. On peut apprécier dans ces circonstances, la force des revendications africaines non seulement en ce qui concerne l'instruction primaire mais aussi l'instruction secondaire et universitaire. Puisque l'élite contemporaine résulte du système éducatif, nous devons en examiner l'effet sur les types de mobilité sociale.

Au cours de la période coloniale, le manque de fonds nécessaires au développement des services éducatifs handicappèrent les gouvernements. Les missionnaires concevaient l'instruction primaire comme un moyen de conversion, mais on attachait peu d'importance à l'instruction supérieure: il semble que le but des directives gouvernementales ait été de placer dans les emplois administratifs supérieurs les élèves sortant en petit nombre des écoles supérieures. Les écoles secondaires étaient généralement situées dans les capitales; les programmes largement conçus sur les programmes européens. Bien que ces études ne fussent pas gratuites, il était relativement facile aux familles et relations du petit nombre d'élèves de trouver les fonds nécessaires, ou pour le personnel de la mission de renoncer aux frais de scolarité en faveur d'un élève particulièrement doué mais impécunieux.

Pour certaines raisons imparfaitement comprises, quelques groupes ethniques semblent avoir accepté l'instruction avec bien plus d'alacrité que d'autres; ces groupes ayant débuté plus tôt, ont eu tendance à maintenir leur supériorité jusqu'à l'heure actuelle. Dans certaines sociétés, l'élite traditionnelle vit dans l'instruction un moyen de maintenir sa propre supériorité et envoya ses enfants à l'école; dans d'autres sociétés, les premiers élèves provenaient

des masses, voire des groupes esclaves, les chefs traditionnels
considérant les missions et l'instruction comme une menace à
leurs propres rangs.

Les gouvernements des états récemment indépendants se sont
lancés dans un programme d'expansion de l'enseignement des
plus rapides, arguant que l'instruction des masses est une condition nécessaire au développement économique, et espérant le
soutien politique de leur électorat en satisfaisant ses aspirations.
L'instruction primaire universelle gratuite a été établie dans
certains territoires d'Afrique occidentale. Les écoles secondaires
ont triplé au Ghana, en Nigéria Occidentale au cours d'une
décade. Néanmoins, des différences marquées dans les facilités
éducatives existent à la fois entre les états et dans les états. De plus,
malgré l'expansion de l'instruction secondaire, la proportion
d'élèves qui en bénéficient demeure minime. La Nigéria occidentale a probablement la plus grande proportion d'élèves passant de
l'instruction primaire à l'instruction secondaire: cette proportion
n'était que de 6% en 1960–61.

La période coloniale a légué un système éducatif aidé et contrôlé par l'état, dans lequel l'entrée dans les écoles secondaires et
les universités dépend uniquement des résultats d'examens com-
pétitifs. Pourtant, en Afrique, la nature égalitaire du système
favorise les enfants de l'élite à un degré plus élevé que, par
exemple, en Europe, du fait que les différences entre les conditions
familiales de l'élite et celles de la masse sont beaucoup plus pro-
noncées. En outre, les membres de l'élite usent de leur influence
pour faire admettre leurs enfants dans les meilleures écoles primaires
de l'état, et de leurs moyens de fortune soit pour les placer dans
des écoles primaires privées ou pour financer des cours particuliers
pour leur faire passer l'examen d'entrée dans les écoles secondaires.
Ainsi, il est impossible aux parents nécessiteux de financer l'instruction secondaire de leurs enfants, tandis que les parents aisés
sont subventionnés. Des bourses existent, mais là encore, les
enfants de familles fortunées sont favorisés dans la concurrence
qu'elles suscitent.

On peut examiner à partir de deux points de vue les taux de
mobilité sociale en Afrique. Premièrement les membres de l'élite

contemporaine proviennent en grande partie des masses; une large proportion a des parents illettrés. De même, on s'aperçoit aujourd'hui dans les écoles secondaires que les élèves dont les parents ont reçu plus qu'une instruction primaire sont en minorité. Si les écoles et universités continuent à croître et à multiplier, les étudiants qui les fréquenteront seront immanquablement issus des masses, car les enfants de l'élite ne pourront pas remplir toutes les places disponibles.

Cependant, l'élite semble capable de satisfaire à un degré élevé son aspiration de voir ses enfants recevoir l'instruction qui assurera à leurs générations le rang d'élite. Ainsi, bien qu'un grand nombre de jeunes individus, de naissance très modeste, parviennent maintenant au rang de l'élite, les chances qu'un enfant d'un foyer semblable a d'obtenir une instruction universitaire sont immédiatement moindres que celles d'un enfant ayant des parents instruits.

Au cours des dix années écoulées, l'expansion de l'instruction dans les états africains a rehaussé les qualifications nécessaires pour entrer dans les différents bureaux de l'administration. L'aspirant à un emploi se sent frustré lorsque son degré d'instruction est jugé insuffisant pour le genre de travail qu'il demande. Pourtant le succès de quelques-uns entretient la croyance que les rangs de l'élite sont accessibles à tous.

LES ÉLITES DANS LES ASSOCIATIONS MODERNES ET TRADITIONNELLES

Le mode de vie de l'élite, qui découle des appointements qu'elle reçoit contraste d'une façon très marquée avec celui de la masse. Pourtant, comme nous l'avons déjà indiqué, une grande proportion de l'élite urbaine actuelle a une origine humble et rurale. Jusqu'à quel point ces hommes et femmes continuent-ils à participer aux associations traditionnelles, jusqu'à quel point s'en retirent-ils, formant au contraire des associations exclusives sur le modèle occidental, accentuant ainsi le sentiment d'être d'un corps organisé? La différence importante entre l'élite actuelle et la masse peut être momentanée, pendant que l'élite secondaire, composée de ceux ayant atteint un niveau d'instruction intermédiaire s'accroît et crée un pont entre les deux catégories. Pourtant, les enfants de l'élite actuelle (comme ceux de l'élite antérieure) élevés dans les familles instruites et fortunées, auront eu bien moins de contacts avec les régions rurales et les valeurs traditionnelles que leurs parents.

Dans la plupart des cas, l'occupation de l'élite nécessite une résidence dans les capitales provinciales et nationales, loin du lieu de naissance. Cependant, des rapports étroits avec la parenté continuent. Souvent un membre de l'élite est le seul parmi ses frères et sœurs à être bien instruit. Lorsqu'il réussit à obtenir un poste bien rémunéré, il est trop tard pour faire instruire ses frères cadets ou les enfants de ses frères aînés. Ce sentiment de responsabilité envers une parenté plus jeune augmente quand l'homme doit sa réussite à l'aide financière du vaste cercle de sa famille. L'incompatibilité entre une telle responsabilité et le désir de bien pourvoir aux besoins de ses propres enfants est partiellement évitée, les frais d'instruction commençant seulement à être un fardeau lorsque les enfants atteignent l'adolescence et qu'économiser en prévision de dépenses futures à l'aide d'une police d'assurance n'est pas en vogue; le diplômé qui jouit d'un salaire de plus de mille livres dix ans avant que ses enfants fréquentent l'école secondaire est considéré capable d'aider sa famille. Une telle dépense empêche encore plus de développer l'usage des économies et de s'assurer, et renforce ainsi la dépendance du membre de l'élite envers sa génération en cas de maladie ou de décès prématuré.

Il existe fréquemment une certaine tension entre les membres de l'élite et leur parenté illettrée. Chacun se sent mal à l'aise chez l'autre. Leurs valeurs ne coïncident plus; même des parents instruits, Chrétiens pratiquants et croyants souffrent de l'attitude plus séculaire de leurs enfants. Cependant, le prestige que la communauté accorde aux parents de celui qui a réussi est une récompense suffisante; en fait les parents attendent de leurs enfants qu'ils étalent ouvertement les signes de leur réussite—les costumes de laine, la grosse voiture. Les aspirations élevées des parents, jointe à la crainte d'échouer qu'a l'étudiant subventionné par sa famille entière conduisent régulièrement aux maladies mentales.

Il existe parmi les membres d'une famille de l'élite, un degré de rapprochement bien plus élevé que dans la société traditionnelle; pourtant le mari, pour des raisons données plus haut, reste très attaché à sa propre famille, peut-être même plus que sa femme qui peut même s'attendre à des rapports plus égalitaires que le mari n'est préparé à entretenir. Lorsque l'élite est restreinte, plus d'hommes trouveront des épouses hors de leur propre groupe ethnique et seront, en conséquence, plus séparés de leur famille. A mesure que l'élite s'étendra, la proportion des mariages dans le même groupe augmentera probablement, tendant ainsi à raffermir les loyautés locales.

Outre sa participation aux affaires de sa propre famille, un membre de l'élite peut également prendre une part active dans la vie politique de sa communauté d'origine grâce à la branche de son association ethnique. L'importance de ces associations varie— certaines sont des associations de village, d'autres englobent un groupe ethnique entier; leurs différentes échelles peuvent être ordonnées hiérarchiquement. Ces associations paraissent plus fortement développées en Afrique occidentale et moins en Afrique du Sud. Cette répartition semble correspondre à trois facteurs. Ces associations sont les plus importantes dans les régions où la situation d'un individu parmi sa communauté, dans laquelle il peut retourner après des années de résidence urbaine, dépend de son âge et de sa descendance. Elles seront fortement développées également là où les employeurs et agences du gouvernement offrent peu ou pas de sécurité sociale au citadin. Les associations ethniques seront vraisemblablement plus actives là où des fonds sont disponibles pour les agréments de la communauté (provenant de subventions gouvernementales ou de redevances locales) et qu'ils peuvent être alloués.

Il est attendu de tous ceux qui sont éligibles qu'ils s'associent à la branche locale d'une association ethnique; il en est de même pour l'élite et la pression pour qu'elle participe sera probablement plus forte lorsque son instruction lui donne des qualifications uniques parmi les membres. Celui qui refuse de s'associer ou de

contribuer aux fonds de l'association ruinera ses chances de
réaliser ses ambitions politiques dans sa région d'origine et pourra
même souffrir d'ostracisme lorsqu'il y retournera.

L'élite moderne adopte des attitudes diverses envers les fonctions politiques traditionnelles, les religions indigènes et la
sorcellerie. En général les étudiants fréquentant les universités
d'outre-mer font preuve de bien moins de tolérance qu'il n'en
démontreront plus tard lorsqu'ils seront revenus. Mais la situation
dans chaque territoire africain dépend largement des types de
gouvernement colonial et du prosélytisme des missions. D'habitude, l'élite soutient la chefferie traditionnelle qui symbolise
l'unité et le passé historique des peuples; cependant elle n'essaie
en rien de réinvestir les chefs avec les pouvoirs dont ils jouissaient,
même au cours de la période pré-coloniale. Comme les fonctions
traditionnelles deviennent des survivances archaïques, les signes
de l'autorité sont quelquefois assumés par les nouveaux chefs
politiques; le Ghana donne ici un exemple frappant. L'intolérance
des premiers convertis par les missions envers tout rituel traditionnel semble décliner tandis que les membres conservateurs
des cultes indigènes deviennent plus accommodants envers les
membres instruits de leurs sociétés. Ainsi les membres de l'élite
peuvent assumer des titres de chefferies et célébrer la plupart des
cérémonies traditionnelles.

Les tensions et l'insécurité de la vie moderne conduisent beaucoup d'Africains à maintenir les rites et pratiques traditionnelles.
Des rumeurs abondent au sujet de chefs ouvertement occidentalisés qui appartiendraient à des sectes secrètes. Les explications
concernant l'echec personnel sont, comme Jahoda le montre plus
loin, couchées en termes de sorcellerie.

Dans les villes modernes d'Afrique, une pléthore de nouvelles
associations, pour la plupart basées sur le modèle occidental, s'est
développée. Peu d'entre elles, aux termes de leur constitution,
sont exclusives dans le choix de leurs membres, mais beaucoup
attirent seulement l'élite. Les fonctions dans ces associations sont
souvent distribuées en tenant plus compte du rang qu'un individu
occupe dans la société que de ses capacités ou intérêts. Beaucoup
d'associations semblent avoir des réunions officielles peu fré-

quentes, bien que leurs membres peuvent avoir une plus grande fréquence de contacts spontanés. Les membres de l'élite ont tendance à appartenir à une variété d'associations et il y a ainsi un chevauchement considérable de sociétariat.

Ces associations servent non seulement à initier les membres nouvellement qualifiés dans l'élite au comportement de leur groupe (cette initiation a une importance spéciale pour les femmes qui sont d'habitude bien moins instruites que leurs maris) mais aussi à rendre l'élite consciente de son identité.

On possède peu de détails sur les rapports officieux qui existent entre les membres de l'élite. On en retire l'impression d'un nombreux échange de visites familières, dont peu sont purement mondaines. A la suite d'une petite enquête menée à Ibadan, il apparaît que les élites choisissent leurs amis personnels parmi ceux de rang similaire, bien que beaucoup d'amitiés remontent aux années scolaires ou d'université.

L'image que l'on se fait de l'élite est celle d'une petite collectivité vivant dans une cité moderne, dont les membres entretiennent des liens étroits, à tel point que chaque personne connaît au moins presque toutes les autres. Cependant, la plupart des membres de l'élite maintient également des rapports étroits avec les membres de leurs familles et les affaires de la communaté rurale dans laquelle ils naquirent. Une telle image de l'élite est plus vraie en Afrique de l'ouest où les liens ruraux restent les plus forts. A l'extrême opposé, nous avons la situation dans certaines parties d'Afrique du Sud où la population urbaine est divisée en deux groupes presque fermés, les 'rouges' et 'l'ecole', les premiers essayant de maintenir les valeurs tribales et le dernier les rejetant en faveur des nouvelles valeurs urbaines.

ACCOMPLISSEMENT

Dans les nouveaux états de l'Afrique moderne, la tâche de mener à bien les programmes de développement social et économique incombe aux élites. Mais est-ce que l'élite actuelle possède ces valeurs propres à la société urbaine et industrielle? Si elle les possède, en dérivent-elles des conditions familiales individuelles ou du processus éducatif? Si elle ne possède pas ces valeurs, sont-elles inculquées à ses enfants? Si l'élite possède des valeurs d'une différence très prononcée avec celles des masses, quel en sera l'effet sur la société? Ces questions sont importantes, cependant leur solution se heurte à l'imperfection des concepts qui nous viennent de l'étude de la société occidentale et le manque de renseignements applicables aux sociétés africaines, en présumant que ces concepts soient applicables. Notre examen de cette question repose sur le concept d'accomplissement.

La thèse de Weber faisant correspondre le développement du capitalisme avec le protestantisme semble pertinente à une époque où les sociologues recherchent un facteur nécessaire qui mettra les sociétés africaines sur le chemin d'un accroissement soutenu. La responsabilité individuelle, l'abnégation de soi et l'ascétisme de l'éthique protestante sont parallèles à la rationalité du capitalisme. Le protestant idéal de Weber ne ressemble en rien au membre opulent de l'élite dans l'Afrique moderne. Mais le développement économique moderne de l'Afrique provient plus de l'aide de l'état ou des entreprises étrangères dans lesquelles les qualités recherchées sont plus celles du bureaucrate que celles du capitaliste particulier.

McClelland a développé la thèse de Weber, déterminant le lien entre l'esprit protestant—qu'il appelle 'la nécessité d'accomplissement'—et le capitalisme à travers la structure de la famille et la socialisation de l'enfance. Une condition préalable à tout développement économique est une nécessité d'accomplissement ayant une courbe élevée. Il calcule les courbes de plusieurs sociétés africaines avec certains résultats inattendus. Cependant son insistance sur la possibilité de voir des campagnes d'accomplissement (achievement drives) dans les sociétés africaines, va à l'encontre de la dichotomie souvent citée—les sociétés tradition-nelles sont dominées par un statut attribué, les sociétés industrielles par un statut acquis. Un obstacle majeur à la mesure de la nécessité d'accomplissement dans les sociétés africaines réside dans la composition de tests psychologiques que l'on peut appliquer à tous les membres de la société et non simplement aux internes des classes supérieures de l'enseignement secondaire qui sont les moins susceptibles d'exemplifier les valeurs traditionnelles.

Reisman maintient que les individus dans une société industrielle sont divisés en deux types: l'intra-gouverné et l'extra-gouverné; le premier ressemble au protestant de Weber ou au capitaliste particulier; le dernier au membre de l'organisation de Whyte. L'extra-gouverné recherche l'approbation de ses semblables pour tous ses actes. Une parallèle étroite semble exister entre la direction extérieure et le concept psychologique du besoin d'affiliation. Ce concept semble bien plus applicable à l'Afrique où le succès, en devenant riche ou en jouissant d'une haute position politique, reflète vraisemblablement la bonne situation d'un individu aux yeux de sa communauté. Lipset a décrit la direction extérieure comme un trait des sociétés bureaucratiques. Dans la mesure où ces qualités semblent présentes dans la société traditionnelle africaine et semblent appropriées à la situation des élites modernes, nous pouvons peut-être en inférer que les valeurs tenues par l'élite sont appropriées pour leur tâche de développement national. Cependant la définition de ces concepts et notre manque de données privent notre problème de toute solution définitive.

Une méthode souvent utilisée dans la démonstration des attitudes envers différentes carrières, est celle du prestige qu'elles confèrent. Les processus sont passablement simples, bien que Mitchell, dans sa communication, souligne un certain nombre de difficultés. Les tests qui auraient été appliqués à l'Afrique suggèrent qu'en général les écoliers de ce pays attachent aux carrières le même prestige que ceux des sociétés industrielles. Une enquête montre que les cotes attribuées par les enfants Ghanaens se rapprochent plus du revenu supposé de ces occupations que le sont les cotes attribuées dans les autres pays. Là aussi la question 'Que mesure-t-on?' doit être posée. On doit distinguer entre le prestige accordé aux carrières jouissant d'une cote élevée et l'aspiration plus réaliste d'atteindre à une occupation ayant un rang moins élevé.

ÉLITE OU CLASSE SOCIALE?

Cette catégorie d'individus ayant reçu une éducation occidentale, que nous avons jusqu'ici appelée l'élite africaine était, il y a dix ans, communément désignée sous le nom de 'classe moyenne.' Aujourd'hui, le terme 'élite' est à la mode. Jusqu'à quel point cependant les terminologies d'élite et de classe, exposées par les sociologues occidentaux dans l'analyse de leurs propres sociétés industrielles, s'appliquent-elles ou éclairent-elles nos discussions sur le phénomène social africain? Ces deux termes, rarement utilisés conjointement, ne s'excluent pas mutuellement, car il n'y a pas de définition universellement acceptée. Dans cette section, notre tâche sera de définir certaines des principales composantes de chaque terme, en indiquant celles qui semblent le plus en rapport avec ou applicables à nos données.

Le terme 'élite' désigne les personnes d'une société qui sont, en un sens général, supérieures. De plus, la société doit être ouverte, afin de ne pas avoir à employer les termes de 'caste élevée' ou 'aristocratie héréditaire'. L'affinité entre les masses et l'élite s'aperçoit à ce que cette dernière a d'imitable ou par l'influence qu'elle exerce sur les masses. Cette affinité ne s'exprime pas en termes de 'pouvoir' ou d'autorité, étant plus associée aux rapports institutionalisés qu'aux structures irrégulières. Les idées et valeurs nouvelles dans une société sont innovées par l'élite qui agit dans des sphères où par suite de changements sociaux et de mobilité sociale rapide, les normes applicables n'ont pas été clairement définies. Toutes ces composantes semblent tout à fait applicables à notre élite africaine, si souvent décrite comme la médiatrice entre les systèmes de valeur traditionnels et les systèmes occidentaux. En étudiant les nouveaux rapports familiaux, en exposant les idéologies de négritude ou de personnalité africaine, la définition d'une élite semble convenir aux africains ayant reçu une éducation occidentale.

Mais l'élite n'innove pas seulement, les valeurs, surtout les valeurs morales, qu'elle détient devraient être adoptées par les masses. On ne saurait décrire comme étant une élite ces riches hommes d'affaires dont la seule fortune était admirée par les membres les plus âpres au gain de la société. On ne saurait non plus définir l'élite selon des caractéristiques que les masses sont tout à fait incapables de copier. Dans cet ordre d'idées, est-ce que l'africain rural peut imiter les genres d'affinités entre les membres d'une famille de l'élite? En discutant de ces questions nous arrivons sur le champ de la théorie du groupe de référence: est-ce que l'élite est un groupe auquel les masses se réfèrent? Et dans l'affirmative, quel type de groupe? Est-ce un groupe dans lequel l'individu particulier cherche à se faire admettre, un groupe qu'il utilise simplement pour définir sa position personnelle dans la société, un groupe dont il rejette les valeurs? Ici, nos réponses doivent être basées non sur nos propres études de l'élite mais sur celles des masses et leur perception du groupe en question, et en ce qui concerne l'Afrique les données manquent sur ce point.

Afin que les innovations soient acceptées, elles doivent se diffuser par l'entremise de l'élite, et c'est là que notre étude sur les associations et les réseaux familiers créés par l'élite devient importante. Nous avons l'impression que parmi l'élite africaine, les types uniformes d'un nouveau comportement social sont acceptés rapidement. Une fois passées dans les institutions de l'élite, quelles filières les innovations empruntent-elles pour parvenir aux masses? Les liens conservés individuellement par les membres de l'élite avec leurs familles et les communautés de l'intérieur semblent avoir une importance vitale; ces liens existent effectivement, bien que nous ne pouvons pas pour l'instant, évaluer exactement leur efficacité.

On définit dans plusieurs sociétés une pluralité d'élites. Cependant, l'élite africaine semble être un simple groupe dont les membres jouissent d'un mode de vie, d'occupations et de degrés d'instruction très similaires.

En considérant l'application du terme 'élite' au contexte africain, notre principale question concernera l'importance que nous attachons dans notre définition au caractère imitable de l'élite.

Les définitions sur la classe sociale varient plus largement que celles sur l'élite. L'école marxiste définit la classe d'après le rapport du droit de propriété et postule un conflit entre les classes. Une autre école est représentée par Lloyd Warner et ses disciples qui définissent les classes comme des groupes hiérarchisés selon le rang qu'ils occupent, n'étant pas clairement divisés entre eux et permettant une mobilité sociale. Selon la dernière école, le placement dans une classe est partiellement déterminé par l'appréciation subjective que les membres confèrent à leur propre rang et celui de leurs voisins dans la société. Devant l'absence d'une terminologie de classe d'un usage courant en Afrique, il est difficile de faire une réplique de ces méthodes.

La définition classique marxiste ne peut s'appliquer à l'Afrique où l'un des moyens de production majeurs—la terre—appartient aux masses et l'autre—l'industrie—est largement la propriété du gouvernement (élu par les masses) ou de compagnies étrangères. Il n'y a ainsi ni bourgeoisie ni prolétariat. D'autre part, les chefs politiques et les fonctionnaires d'un état africain exercent un contrôle bien plus ferme de l'économie de leur pays qu'il n'est habituellement observé dans les sociétés occidentales. Etant donné les rapports étroits qui existent d'habitude entre les politiciens, les fonctionnaires supérieurs et les administrateurs de corporations publiques, on peut dire que l'élite contrôle à la fois la vie économique et la vie politique du pays. L'élite est ainsi analogue à la 'classe nouvelle' de Djilas.

Les classes sont des groupes permanents de la société, mais comme la stratification sociale de la société africaine est en cours de développement rapide, nous ne pouvons dire quelles seront ses caractéristiques permanentes. Bien que le système éducatif des états africains semble conçu pour créer des sociétés ouvertes, son effet est, comme nous l'avons vu, plutôt contraire. Un ralentissement de l'expansion économique et du système éducatif résultera vraisemblablement en une élite devenant plutôt un groupe héréditaire.

Les individus sont conscients de la classe à laquelle ils appartiennent—mais on peut distinguer ici entre une simple reconnaissance des différences sociales et l'activité consciente consacrée à la préservation des intérêts particuliers de sa propre classe. L'élite africaine est certainement consciente de son opulence. De plus, il est probablement plus facile de délimiter l'élite en se référant aux échelles de salaires ou à la possession d'automobiles (une nécessité pour tout haut fonctionnaire). Les membres de l'élite agissent intensément les uns sur les autres et se marient entre eux. Cependant les divisions ethniques sont encore très puissantes.

Grâce à ses associations professionnelles et ses relations spéciales avec le gouvernement, l'élite réussit à maintenir dans la société la situation privilégiée qu'elle a hérité des européens de l'administration coloniale. Mais l'idéologie de l'élite est celle de l'absence de classe dans sa société. Son rôle de chef de file est accentué. L'union dans le combat pour l'indépendance n'est pas oubliée. Le développement d'un parti unique dans les états encourage une idéologie dans laquelle on dénie un conflit entre groupes à intérêts rivaux.

L'élite africaine peut seulement être une classe supérieure dans un système de classes—une classe ne peut exister seule. Mais les masses paysannes pensent encore à la division de la société en termes de groupes ethniques, descendance et générations. Les membres de la sous-élite urbaine, qui pourraient former un groupe opposé à l'élite, essaient encore d'en faire partie et de s'identifier à elle. L'un des avantages du terme 'élite' est que sa contrepartie—les masses—implique un manque de structure qui typifie la non-élite (excepté en termes traditionnels.)

A présent, en ce qui concerne l'Afrique, le terme élite semble peut-être le plus apte. Il s'accorde à la nature ouverte de la société et les rapports étroits qui existent entre les membres instruits et aisés et les masses. Ces caractéristiques pourront être maintenues aussi longtemps que le développement économique des états africains sera suffisamment rapide pour empêcher l'élite actuelle de placer ses propres enfants dans tous les nouveaux postes donnant accès au rang d'élite. Un développement plus lent fera de l'élite un groupe quasi-héréditaire. La frustration parmi la sous-élite qui se trouvera incapable d'accéder plus haut sera intensifiée et les particuliers pourront prendre la direction de mouvements politiques dirigés contre l'élite. Avec chaque nouvelle génération l'élite se scindera plus complètement des masses.

II. SPECIAL STUDIES

I. THE EMERGENCE OF AN ELITE:
A CASE STUDY OF A WEST COAST FAMILY

MARGARET PRIESTLEY

Originating in the circumstances of trade five centuries ago, European contact with West Africa has given rise to certain distinctive features. One of these was a special form of commercial settlement in a geographically limited area, the coast of modern Ghana, where most of the trading forts were built. In the neighbourhood of these forts, a working relationship was evolved with an indigenous society not as yet separated off by the colonial barrier. During the eighteenth century, there developed out of this situation a restricted degree of western education, among the beneficiaries of which were the mulatto children of local European traders. Such were the origins of the Brews. They stemmed on the father's side from an Irish merchant, Richard Brew, who spent thirty years in Fanti in the slave-trading days of the second half of the eighteenth century, establishing at Anomabu a considerable position for himself. Of his mulatto children, one, a son Henry, married into a Cape Coast family. From him can be traced several generations of educated male descendants in the Fanti coastal towns of Cape Coast and Anomabu. A study of the Brews thus throws light on the emergence of an educated elite on the west coast and is here presented as an illustration of some 'developmental trends' in its society.[1]

The main sources for this work are manuscript material in the Public Record Office in London and in the Ghana National Archives in Accra, printed material and the personal communications, mostly verbal, of elderly informants. Without the archives, however, it would not have been possible to present the work in

[1] Evans-Pritchard (1962), p. 54; Holloway (1963), p. 155; Priestley (1959).

G

its existing form, nor to distinguish in certain cases between nineteenth-century Brews who were called by the same Christian name, memory now being fragmentary and sometimes blurred. Inevitably, to trace several personal histories over such a long period of time means some unevenness in the facts that can be unearthed. Yet the body of material is still substantial and an analysis of it has been made extending over five generations from the later eighteenth to the early decades of the twentieth century, counting Henry, Richard Brew's son, as the first generation. It will be obvious that the Brew pedigree is being traced primarily through the males; the significance of this in relation to the Fanti matrilineal system will be commented upon later.[2]

The role of the Brews on the west coast during this period needs to be interpreted in the light of the changing structure resulting from European contact and the consequent variation in opportunities. In broad terms, it can be said that there were three main and overlapping phases of European organization. During the first, extending up to about 1830, the forts were primarily centres of trading administration. During the second, there was a gradual extension of British justice over the neighbouring coastal tribes for the purpose of establishing law and order, but without any assumption of territorial sovereignty outside the forts. During the third, the creation of the Gold Coast Colony in 1874 brought the coastal regions under the political control of Britain and clarified a hitherto anomalous position. By 1902 control had been extended inland to Ashanti and the Northern Territories. The development, therefore, on the British side was a gradual one from the limited function of trade in the later eighteenth century to full colonial power on the coast a hundred years later. The African corollary to this was a degree of participation in the European structure, diminishing as colonialism began to limit the range of possible openings.

Against this background, the Brews display a consistent trend of western education, varying in kind according to circumstances,

[2] I wish to record my appreciation of the assistance given in a number of ways by informants and also by Mrs. Miriam Dean in the process of working through manuscript material in the Ghana National Archives.

but in general following an ascending scale. Richard began the process in the second half of the eighteenth century by sending his mulatto sons to England, subsequent descendants being educated either in coastal mission schools or occasionally overseas. James Hutton Brew, for example, a fourth-generation descendant, spent several years of his youth in England, two of his nephews later being trained there as barristers. From the standpoint of Fanti society, the nineteenth-century Brews thus belonged to the category of 'scholars' much respected by the illiterate. What occupations did they follow accordingly? Three strands can be observed—trade, positions in the European organizational structure and the legal profession.[3]

It is not surprising, in view of their social origins, to find a succession of Brew merchants, although in changing conditions after Britain abolished the slave trade in 1807. A period of illicit slave dealing preceded the establishment of legitimate commerce and in this Sam Kanto Brew, grandson of Richard and described as a 'scholar', was active in the early part of the century. With the next generation came the age of legitimate trade, the export of palm oil and gold and the import of textiles and spirits. It was a younger son of Sam Kanto, Samuel Collins Brew, who achieved a notable position here both among European and African merchants, trading extensively through a firm of British shippers— one of the 'merchant princes' of the age, as he was called by a grandson. His sons and a nephew continued the long-standing mercantile tradition, even if in a more modest way, acting on occasion as commission agents for European firms in the later nineteenth century.[4]

Parallel with trade, there is evidence of continuous Brew participation in the European organizational structure. During the earliest phase, defined above as commercial, the first Henry Brew

---

[3] Letter to Richard Brew, dated 28 October 1768, T70/1536, pt. II (African Companies' Records, Public Record Office, London); Minutes of Meeting of Committee of Merchants, London, 22 December 1780, T70/145 (P.R.O.); Sampson (1937), pp. 90–95; Kimble (1963), pp. 87–88.

[4] Case references to the Brews in vols. 271/52, 284/52, 287/52, 315/52, 323/52, 413/52 (Records of the High Court, Cape Coast, Ghana National Archives); Duncan (1847), vol. I, p. 47; Bowdich (1819), p. 390; Casely Hayford (1903), p. 95; Kimble (1963), p. 4.

held the position of Linguist to the Governor of Cape Coast Castle, his native intermediary, that is to say, with the neighbouring chiefs and people. This role of bridging two cultures was to be repeated by the Brews during the next phase, the extension of British justice, when it was the literate coastal African who was often called upon to link British judicial methods with native law and custom. Hence a Brew became Interpreter to the Judicial Assessor's Court at Cape Coast in the 1840s, another—Clerk to the Anomabu Court in the next decade and, most important of all, the merchant Samuel Collins Brew was appointed a Justice of the Peace at Anomabu in the mid-century, a union in this case of trade and judicial function. Along with a small number of other leading Africans, Samuel Collins Brew held the same rank as Europeans on the coast, and did so for some twenty years, until his resignation at an advanced age in 1879. Towards the end of his service, he was receiving £200 a year, free quarters and a hammock allowance of £45 for a post now officially designated as District Commissioner.[5]

The last few years of his public career overlap with the third organizational phase, the political. With the growth of a colonial civil service staffed increasingly by Europeans, the opportunities for educated Africans became canalized to a much greater degree at the lower levels. The Brews reflect this narrowing of scope. Four brothers, great nephews of Samuel Collins Brew, held posts under the European administration during this time. Two of them, Samuel Henry and Ebenezer Annan Brew, were clearly men of ability and were among the small group of Africans who rose high in government service within the limits available to them. The former, educated at the Wesleyan High School in Cape Coast and a man of scholarly interests, entered the service as a Clerical Assistant in 1887 at a salary of £40 per annum; on the eve of the First World War he had advanced to be Native Chief Clerk in the Colonial Secretary's Office in Accra, being transferred from

---

[5] Acts of Council, Cape Coast Castle, 12 June 1792, T70/153; letter to Committee of Merchants, dated 12 March 1796, T70/33 (P.R.O.); S. C. Brew's letter of resignation, dated 22 November 1879; case and letter references to the Brews in 201/52, 202/52, 246/52, 323/52 (G.N.A.); *Gold Coast Blue Book*, 1875, p. 96; ibid., 1878, p. 100.

this post in 1914 to that of Chief Clerk in the Medical Department. When he retired on pension in 1920, he was receiving a salary of £360 per annum. His younger brother Ebenezer Annan, selected by the Administration for training in the Botanical Gardens in Jamaica, became a Garden Assistant at £50 per annum in the Agricultural Department on his return in 1901. Several years junior to Samuel Henry, he benefited in the post-war years from Governor Guggisberg's liberal policy of opening some of the more senior posts to Africans. By the time of his premature retirement in 1926, through ill-health, Ebenezer Annan had moved into the higher rungs of the Agricultural Department as African Assistant Superintendent at a salary of £500 per annum, the maximum for his grade being £780. It was not until 1942, however, that the trend of widening opportunities led once again to the situation which had prevailed under his great uncle in the previous century, of the appointment of Africans as District Commissioners.[6]

The last occupational trait to be noted relates to the legal profession. In part, this development arose out of the extension of British justice, the educated African now finding open to him a new semi-professional career, that of an attorney, whose services for a fee were available to clients. Although not as yet fully trained, the attorney's educational standing, knowledge of customary law and acquired experience of British judicial methods made him a prominent figure on the coast at a time when litigation was increasing. Of particular importance from the present point of view is James Hutton Brew, son of Samuel Collins Brew and licensed in 1864 as one of the first attorneys in the courts, where he practised until 1880. Professionally, the attorneys were followed in due course by qualified barristers, sent to England for their legal training and including in the early twentieth century two nephews of James Hutton Brew—J. E. Casely Hayford and William Ward Brew, both, like their uncle, distinguished in West African affairs. Casely Hayford and Ward

[6] Establishment Personal Files S. H. Brew and E. A. Brew, Accessions P3/1962 and P366/1962 (G.N.A.); *Gold Coast Blue Book*, 1901, p. 0.89; ibid., 1921, section 13; ibid., 1926–7, section 13; *Gold Coast Gazette*, 1898, p. 106; Kimble (1963), pp. 98–100, 105–9, 123, note 1.

Brew were of the same generation as the civil servants Samuel Henry and Ebenezer Annan, to whom they were second cousins. Thus can be seen two of the avenues open to the educated African by the 1920s, the independent profession of the law and lower-level appointments in government service.[7]

On the basis of the foregoing evidence, it would seem justifiable to place the Brews, throughout the period in question, in the category of a Western-educated elite, the 'marginal men' of their time. As such, they can be considered among the innovators of Fanti society, with values, attitudes, and ways of behaviour, non-traditional in origin, that were contributing to the growth of different religious, political, and social forms. One example of this is provided by their connexions with Methodism. It was Samuel Collins Brew's elder brother, Henry, who belonged to the Bible study group in Cape Coast responsible for the first arrival of the Wesleyan Methodists from England in the 1830s. Instances of Brew marriages by Wesleyan rites followed, and in later generations they held the positions of Catechist and Chapel Steward, memorial tablets to them being found in the Methodist Chapel in Cape Coast today. Similar support was given to new associations developing on the coast, for example, the Freemasons founded in Cape Coast in 1874, to which both Ebenezer Annan and William Ward Brew subsequently belonged.[8]

But there is no clearer illustration of innovating attitudes and behaviour than in the public careers of James Hutton Brew and his nephew Casely Hayford, extending over the sixty years 1870–1930. Here is revealed an expansion of horizon beyond narrow tribal confines with the idea of a Fanti Confederation, then of union with Ashanti and finally, in the 1920s, of West African unity—a changing vision accompanied by the development of new techniques, notably journalism and political deputations. Brew had actively participated in the Fanti Confederation scheme

[7] Letter to J. H. Brew, dated 30 May 1864, 202/52; case reference, 14 September 1880, 287/52 (G.N.A.); Sampson (1937), pp. 90–5; Kimble (1963), pp. 68–70.

[8] Case reference, 30 October et seq. 1865, 435/52 (G.N.A.); Hutchison (n.d.), pp. 54–5; obituary notice of E. A. Brew, *Gold Coast Farmer*, vol. I, no. 2, June 1932, p. 29 (Library of Ministry of Agriculture, Ghana); Southon (1934), pp. 24–36; Wolfson (1958), p. 15; Kimble (1963), p. 147; Ponsioen (1962), pp. 104–6; Goldthorpe (1961).

of 1868–73, by which the chiefs and educated elite attempted to create a stronger political unit. Its rejection by Britain and the introduction of colonial status in 1874 caused him to put forward the advanced aim of self-government, with the novel plan of an elected assembly representing all sections of society in the Colony. In order to achieve this, Brew urged that there should be a deputation to the Colonial Office. Unsuccessful, he continued the course of agitation after 1888 in London. His connexion there with the Ashanti Embassy of 1895, on the eve of the loss of independence, is an interesting example of broadening outlook; it associates him with the affairs of Fanti's historic inland antagonist at a time when even coastal towns found prolonged cooperation difficult. Still wider views were exemplified by Casely Hayford. A leading spirit behind the National Congress of British West Africa, also supported by his lawyer cousin William Ward Brew, and President of it from 1923 until 1930, Casely Hayford carried innovation on to the inter-territorial plane. The claim now advanced that the educated elite were natural leaders of society in the movement for political rights in West Africa marked a point of departure from the earlier association with traditional chiefdom.[9]

Analysis of the Brews has proceeded so far from the standpoint of a western culture group. Attention must now be directed to traditional society and the question of its acceptance of them as a new elite. On this point, it can be argued that the Brews illustrate the compatibility, in nineteenth-century Fanti, of western education and mixed racial origin with status and involvement in the traditional community. It is, perhaps, not irrelevant here to refer to their European forebear as himself the subject of a process of acculturation resulting, not from a brief appearance on the west coast, but from thirty years of life in Fanti in the non-colonial circumstances of the eighteenth century. The local 'wife' mentioned in his will, his knowledge of the vernacular and intervention in political disputes between Fanti and Ashanti all indicate a marked degree of integration. Of his descendants, it seems clear

[9] Sampson (1937), pp. 90–5; Casely Hayford (1903), pp. 173–7; Kimble (1963), passim.

that the first three generations had the necessary status in Cape Coast and Anomabu to make them useful to the European organization, co-operation with significant groups being a necessity in the pre-colonial era. The first Henry Brew, Linguist to the Governor of Cape Coast Castle under the African Company, held a post for which one requirement was sufficient local influence and standing to be an effective spokesman on behalf of the fort. His son, later an Interpreter to the Judicial Assessor's Court at Cape Coast, was a *penin* or elder—a senior member of a lineage, knowledgeable in customary law and associated with town government. Samuel Collins Brew, nephew of the above and Justice of the Peace, was also a *penin* of a coast town, Anomabu, and hence considered an appropriate person to be given an important British office. Further light is thrown on Samuel Collins in the local community by the fact that one of his many wives came from the stool family of Dunkwa, a small town about twenty miles inland in the Fanti state of Abura. It was this wife, Amba Opanwa, who was the mother of James Hutton Brew, born in 1844. To the latter's innovating role of journalist and reformer, then, must be added the traditional one of 'Prince Brew of Dunquah'.[10]

Comparing Brew of Dunkwa with his three aforementioned predecessors, one important point of difference is revealed—in his relations with the European structure. The changing circumstances of colonialism turned him into a critic rather than a co-operator; traditional rank was used here for the purpose of impressing upon the British that the Fanti chiefs and the educated elite were at one in their demands for reform. In the belief that this was not so, British official policy from the 1870s had placed emphasis on negotiation with the traditional authorities rather than with educated Africans, whom it regarded as an undesirable influence on affairs. Brew's reaction to this can be seen in his personal emphasis on the Dunkwa connexion and support of the growing Fanti cultural movement at the same time as his campaign for political change widened in method and objective, a meaning-

[10] Case references to the Brews in 246/52 and 258/52 (G.N.A.); Sampson, (1937), p. 91; Sarbah (1906), pp. 9 ff.; Priestley (1959).

ful combination of cultural trends. In 1878 he wrote to the Governor announcing that he had been placed on the stool of Dunkwa under the style and title of 'Prince Brew of Dunquah and Abracrampa', and on future occasions similarly referred to himself as a chief who held courts. His continued use of the title when in London after 1888 and during prolonged correspondence with the Colonial Office led to inquiries about its validity, the official reply from Cape Coast being that Brew had been appointed Chief of Dunkwa, but was not entitled to call himself Prince, as it had never had a King. The question of whether or not Brew was actually so appointed is somewhat perplexing, since the present Chief of Abura Dunkwa, who is of the same matrilineal family, says that Brew was the heir to the stool, but was in London when it became vacant and thus unable to succeed. For present purposes, the important point to observe is that Brew had a traditional status and made considerable use of it in his political career. In Abura Dunkwa today he is spoken of with pride by the Chief's family, who have in their possession an old Bible with dates of his birth and death and, among other papers, a family tree linking him through his mother with the stool. They add that their family corresponded with him in England for a time, but eventually lost touch; Prince Brew went there, they say, to become the first Gold Coast representative in Parliament.[11]

It is necessary, next, to give some consideration to the Brews in the context of the Fanti family. Basic to this was the matrilineal clan determining family and inheritance along the female line of descent from a common ancestress, corporate and not individual ownership of property being the rule. In his classic work *Fanti Customary Laws*, J. M. Sarbah pointed out, however, that within the European-influenced coast towns the idea of private property was beginning to emerge, the custom of disposing of it by will, in his opinion, being of 'modern growth'. From this, it can be argued that the elements of an individualistic approach to property in towns like Cape Coast would be likely to lead to conflict with

---

[11] Letter from the Acting Colonial Secretary, Accra to Prince Brew, dated 5 February 1879 (private papers of the Ohene of Abura Dunkwa); case reference, 16 December 1887, 296/52; Minute Paper dated 5 July 1895, Bd 19/1.S.C. (G.N.A.); Kimble (1963), pp. 259–60, 517–18.

the traditional concept of joint ownership and would affect, in due course, the family structure so closely bound up with the latter. The Brews would appear to illustrate such a trend. Legal records in the Ghana National Archives show that, in common with many others on the coast, they took part in frequent property litigation during the later nineteenth and early twentieth centuries. The material is extensive and complex; from a first analysis of it the following observations and lines of approach are submitted.[12]

A number of the court cases concerning the Brews involved the descendants of the Cape Coast family into which the first Henry had married in the later eighteenth century, subsequent generations being traceable back to this union. They arose over both the matrilineal family's 'ancestral property' and the 'self-acquired property' of the Brews, to which the matrilineal family ultimately asserted a right of possession. The disputes turned on questions of marriage, of 'domestic' (dependant) status within a family, and of relationship between branches of the lineage all relevant to inheritance, but often extremely hard to disentangle at the present distance of time. From a study of the evidence, certain points of significance nevertheless emerge. It becomes clear that throughout the nineteenth century the Brews were prominent in the community. They were in charge of substantial property in land and had their own domestics, Richard, son of the first Henry, for example, being described as 'a very rich man'. In part this property was ancestral and under corporate ownership, although there is some evidence of individualist action to be noted, as in the case, brought before an arbitration committee, in which a Brew was said to have made a sale without family consultation.[13]

Apart from ancestral land, there was also a large extent of self-acquired property near Cape Coast, first owned by the trader Sam Kanto Brew, the disposal of which throws interesting light on new trends and on the process of building up a Brew sub-lineage. At the death of Sam Kanto, it was inherited by his uterine

[12] Sarbah (1904), especially pp. 33, 42–43, 57–62, 96–97, 100–2.
[13] Case references to Brews in 305/52, 315/52, 320/52, 323/52, 324/52 (G.N.A.); Sarbah (1904), pp. 100 ff.

brother Richard and when Richard died in 1849, neither he nor his sister leaving issue, it could now be considered ancestral property in accordance with strict customary law. But it passed by testamentary disposition to his nephew, Sam Kanto's eldest son—inheritance, that is to say, along a male line of the Brews. Some sixty years later, the matrilineal family put forward a claim at law to this land, the eventual outcome of which was a private settlement to divide it between both sides of the family. Here is illuminated a point of considerable importance—the use of the will, whether in oral or ultimately written form, to transmit property within narrow limits of relationship, a practice which indicates the growing process of individual acquisition occasioned by forces of economic and social change. In this particular case, it was the matrilineal claims that ultimately gave rise to legal proceedings; on other occasions, the Brews themselves brought litigation to assert rights seemingly overlooked by testamentary disposition. One such instance was the written will of Samuel Collins Brew, in which he created a trust for the education of his youngest son and omitted the rest of his children from its benefits. Challenging this in 1881, after his father's death, James Hutton Brew used the argument that since this was the will of a native and not an Englishman, it could not exclude all members of his family save one, and he succeeded eventually in establishing himself as the administrator of his father's estate.[14]

Summing up the above evidence, it is suggested that within the traditional lineage system a 'Brew family' emerged displaying certain tendencies that reflect the influence of European culture on Fanti society. Among these was a more individualist strain in property attitudes and an emphasis on the male line of descent, status passing from father to son, associated with personal achievement and with attributes such as education. It is true, of course, that in Fanti patrilineal ties had always existed, both 'affectional and spiritual' and also formalized, in that sons belonged to the *asafo* or military company of their father, whose office they generally inherited, if suitably qualified. But it was the matrilineal

---

[14] Case and letter references to the Brews in 205/52, 287/52, 323/52, 324/52 (G.N.A.); Renner (1915), vol. I, pt. II, pp. 501, 802–4; Sarbah (1904), pp. 61–62.

unit that was the foundation of society and the structure around which property and collective rights and obligations revolved. To that extent, the Brew family differed from Sarbah's definition in that it was ultimately traceable, not to female but to male ancestry; it is clear that there was an awareness of a family of this kind with many European traits, although its existence in matrilineal society gave rise to an intermixture of patterns. European Christian names, for example, were used by the Brews over six generations, Richard, Henry and Samuel occurring with such frequency as to give rise to confusion; there are indications, too, of the development of a strong sense of family pride turning on male forebears. This can be seen in a letter written by Casely Hayford to his kinsmen in 1929, mentioning their 'notable ancestry', the 'family unity' and his late grandfather, Samuel Collins Brew; furthermore, when on a visit to England, he began to take steps to trace early Brew origins. A present-day link with the past is provided by two surviving grandchildren of Samuel Collins Brew, one aged eighty-four. Both can recall annual meetings of the elders at which they were told the family history and they recognize, although without knowing clear details, that there was a European ancestor. Descended from Samuel Collins Brew through sons, they undoubtedly think of themselves as members of their father's family.[15]

To a consideration of Brew social patterns the subject of marriage is also very relevant, although the information available is not as comprehensive as could be wished. A survey of it reveals that throughout the period under review, Brew marriages do not fall into any easily defined categories. During the first three-quarters of the nineteenth century, there were instances of domestics or family dependants being taken as wives; the children of such unions would then belong to the father's family. From about the 1840s onwards, as Methodism began to have effects, cases can be found of marriage by church rites. Sometimes a Brew contracted this type of marriage as well as one by customary law;

---

[15] Letter from Casely Hayford, dated 26 May 1929 (private papers of Mr. S. H. F. Brew, Freetown); personal communications; Christensen (1954), pp. 1–5, 97 ff.

in the former the wife took the name 'Mrs. Brew'. Some but not all wives were literate, the extension of education to women exerting an influence here; occupationally, they were often traders who assisted their husbands. This was particularly so with Samuel Collins Brew in his commercial activities along the coast. Two of his wives are known to have come from chiefly families; one has been mentioned already, the mother of James Hutton Brew. In terms of locality, the Brews were concentrated in the coastal region, mainly in Fanti, and only one branch of the family became established up country in Ashanti, through marriage in the early twentieth century with the daughter of a chief there. This branch stemmed from Albert Cruickshank Brew, uterine brother of James Hutton, both of whom are said to have been on friendly terms with the Asantehene. Among the coastal Brews there is an important trend to be observed, from the second half of the century, in the process of inter-marriage with other educated families, such as the Bannermans, the Fergusons and the Hayfords. Two instances especially should be noted—the marriage of Samuel Collins Brew's daughter, Mary, to the Reverend Degraft Hayford, one of their sons being J. E. Casely Hayford, and that of another daughter, Elizabeth, to Edmund Bannerman of Accra, a close friend of her brother, James Hutton Brew. By the second union, a family link was thus forged between two of the leading political figures of their time in Cape Coast and Accra.[16]

The emergence of an educated elite has been limited in this study to a defined area of the west coast and a particular family; there are many similar investigations that could be made. It has been shown that in Fanti coastal towns, the innovating behaviour of the new elite was consistent during the nineteenth century with the exercise of influence in the traditional community, although ultimately a weakening of the association between chiefs and intelligentsia took place. Viewed from the standpoint of the subsequent development of Ghana, it would seem a matter of no small consequence that roughly a hundred years ago there was a group of educated and intermarrying coastal families; it is an

---

[16] Case references to the Brews in 247/52, 278/52, 279/52, 287/52, 310/52, 315/52, 435/52 (G.N.A.); Sampson (1937), pp. 87 ff.; personal communications.

indication of the early appearance there of elements of change within society.

BIBLIOGRAPHY

Bowdich, T. E.
(1819) *Mission from Cape Coast Castle to Ashantee.* London.
Casely Hayford, J. E.
(1903) *Gold Coast Native Institutions.* London.
Christensen, J. B.
(1954) *Double Descent among the Fanti.* New Haven.
Duncan, J.
(1847) *Travels in Western Africa in 1845 and 1846.* London.
Evans-Pritchard, E. E.
(1962) *Essays in Social Anthropology.* London.
Goldthorpe, J. E.
(1961) 'Educated Africans: some conceptual and terminological problems', in Southall, A. W. (ed.) *Social Change in Modern Africa.* London. pp. 145–58.
Holloway, S. W. F.
(1963) 'Sociology and History', *History*, vol. 48, pp. 154–80.
Hutchison, C. F.
(n.d.) *Pen Pictures of Modern Africans and African Celebrities*, vol. 1.
Kimble, D.
(1963) *Political History of Ghana 1850–1928.* Oxford.
Ponsioen, J. A.
(1962) *Analysis of Social Change Reconsidered.* 'S-Gravenhage.
Priestley, M. A.
(1959) 'Richard Brew; an eighteenth century trader at Anomabu', *Transactions of the Historical Society of Ghana*, vol. 4, pt. I, pp. 29–46.
Renner, P. A.
(1915) *Cases in the Courts of the Gold Coast Colony and Nigeria.* London.
Sampson, M. J.
(1937) *Gold Coast Men of Affairs.* London.
Sarbah, J. M.
(1904) *Fanti Customary Laws.* London.
(1906) *Fanti National Constitution.* London.
Southon, A. E.
(1934) *Gold Coast Methodism, the First Hundred Years 1835–1935.* Cape Coast and London.
Wolfson, F.
(1958) *Pageant of Ghana.* London.

Résumé

L'ÉMERGENCE D'UNE ÉLITE: L'ÉTUDE D'UNE FAMILLE DE LA CÔTE OCCIDENTALE

Le premier commerce entre les Européens et l'Afrique Occidentale donna naissance à une forme particulière d'établissement commerciale dans et autour des forts construits sur la côte de ce qui est maintenent le Ghana. Un dégré restreint d'éducation occidentale développa de cette situation, dont il y avait parmi les bénéficiaires les enfants métis des commerçants éuropéens. Une telle famille, les Brew, existe dans la région des Fanti depuis le 18ème siècle; ils montrent l'émergence d'une élite instruite dans un milieu de conditions changeantes pendant plus d'un siècle. On remarque trois phases principales et qui se recouvrent dans l'organisation éuropéenne pendant cette époque— la phase commerciale, la phase judiciaire avec l'étendue de législation sous le régime anglais, la phase politique avec l'établissement de la 'Gold Coast Colony' en 1874. Pendant ces diverses phases on trouve les Brew, qui exerçaient les fonctions de commerçant, qui occupaient les offices dans la structure éuropéenne d'organisation, qui suivent la profession légale. Dans le second cas, ils arrivèrent au comble, au milieu du 19ème siècle quand Samuel Collins Brew fut nommé Magistrat, plus tard 'District Commissioner'. L'entrée des Brew dans le service du Gouvernement au début du 20ème siècle montre que l'étendue des opportunités pour les Africains est devenue de plus en plus étroite à cause du développement d'un service colonial.

Comme une élite instruite occidentale on peut les considérer parmi les innovateurs de la société Fanti qui présentaient les valeurs, les attitudes, les modes de comportement qui n'étaient pas d'origine traditionnelles. Ils avaient par exemple, des liens avec les premiers Méthodistes de la Côte, faisaient partie de nouvelles sociétés telles que les Francs Maçons, se lanceaient dans la politique. Ce dernier fair est illustré par les carrières de James Hutton Brew et son neveu J. E. Casely Hayford. On y voit un élargissement de perspective au dela des limites étroites de la tribu pour comprendre des groupes politiques plus larges, de nature réprésentative et autonome, qui se termine dans l'idée de l'Afrique Occidentale.

Le développement de nouvelles techniques de journalisme et des délégations au 'Colonial Office' accompagna ces idées. En ce qui concerne les Brew par rapport à une société traditionnelle, on peut constater qu'ils montrent la compatibilité, parmi les Fanti du

19ème siècle, de l'éducation occidentale et le métissage avec l'acquisition de statut.

Les trois premières générations de la famille Brew avaient de l'autorité et du préstige dans la région; il y en avait deux qui étaient 'penins' ou conseillers dans les villes de la Côte et un qui se maria avec une fille de la famille royale ('stool-family'), de la petite ville de Dunkwa en Fanti. De ce mariage fut né James Hutton Brew, dont le rôle innovateur de journaliste et réformateur doit être considéré comme parallèle à son rôle traditionnel de 'Prince Brew of Dunkwa'—titre qu'il adopta et employa considérablement dans sa carrière politique. Aujourd'hui, à Abura Dunkwa, on est très fier de se souvenir de Prince Brew, quoique la 'stool-family' perdit tout contact avec lui pendant les dernières années de sa vie, qu'il passa à Londres.

Il faut aussi considérer les Brew dans le cadre de la famille Fanti et ses liens avec le systeme matrilinéaire qui établissait la famille et l'héritage en ligne féminine, la propriété étant commune et non pas individuelle. On a signalé, cependant, quelque conception de propriété privée et sa disposition par testament qui commençait à apparaître dans les villes de la Côte subies à l'influence européenne. Il paraît que les Brew démontraient le tendance conséquente de conflit entre les conceptions de propriété individuelle et propriété collective et leurs effets sur la structure de la famille. D'après une analyse des Archives légales dans Archives Nationales de Ghana, on peut faire certaines observations préliminaires. Il paraît y avoir des disputes entre les Brew et les descendants de la famille de Cape Coast à qui le fils métis de Richard Brew s'était apparenté par mariage, à cause de la propriété familiale de la famille matrilinéaire, aussi bien que la propriété personnelle acquise par les Brew. Ces disputes portent dans une certaine mesure, sur les questions de mariage et de parenté entre les branches du lignage—questions qui sont actuellement extrêmement difficile à resoudre. Elles témoignent, cependant, d'une attitude individuelle à la propriété qui démontre de nouvelles forces économiques et sociales. Prenons, par exemple, le cas d'un domaine considérable acquis par un des commerçants de la famille Brew au 19ème siècle. Ce domaine, disposé par testament en ligne masculine, fut le sujet d'un procès, beaucoup plus tard, quand les descendants de la famille Brew matrilinéaire prétendèrent le droit de possession selon le droit de coutume. Le testament de Samuel Collins Brew donna naissance, de la même façon, à un procès initié par son fils, parceque le père avait exclu tous ses enfants sauf un de ses bénéfices.

En présence de ces deux procès, on peut constater que la disposition de propriété dans les limites étroites de la parenté était liée avec l'émergence d'une différente espèce de famille dans le lignage, qui rende plus importante la ligne masculine de descendance et qui souligne le passage de statut de père en fils selon les attributs personnels, tels que l'éducation. On peut pousser plus loin cette thèse en remarquant que le nom de Brew passe de père en fils depuis 7 générations et que la fierté de la 'famille Brew' dépende des ancêtres masculins.

En ce qui concerne le mariage, sujet qui porte sur les attitudes sociales, l'évidence est variée et difficile à classifier. Il y a des mariages selon le droit de coutume, selon les rites méthodistes, aux femmes instruites, aussi bien qu' aux femmes illetrées qui faisaient souvent le commerce, assistées par leurs maris. Les mariages des Brew furent, pour la plupart, contractés dans la région littorale, malgré l'établissement d'une branche de la famille à l'intérieure, en Ashanti. Il faut observer la tendance importante, dès la seconde moitié du 19ème siècle, d'intermariage entre les Brew et de semblables familles de la Côte, par exemple, les Bannerman, les Ferguson, les Hayford.

La présence, un siècle auparavant, d'une élite, quoique petite, de familles instruites qui se mariaient entre elles, semblerait une indication de la croissance de diverses structures sociales et du développement conséquent du Ghana. On se demande dans quelle mesure elle se rapportait à l'affaiblissement de l'association entre les chefs et les intellectuels qui apparaissait pendant les premières années du 20ème siècle.

H

II. THE EVOLUTION OF ELITES IN GHANA

K. E. DE GRAFT-JOHNSON

History was for centuries concerned with the fortunes and misfortunes of the upper classes and elite groups. Despite the modern correction to this past tendency, interest in elite groups has by no means waned. Indeed, over the past decade there has been increasing interest in the character, composition, and functions of social classes and elite groups. All over the world, owing largely to economic factors, but more especially to the severe shake-up of social systems that the Second World War occasioned, the question of social classes and elites and their role in reshaping new social structures has become very pertinent.

That this special interest should now be focused on Africa is inevitable. Here in less than two decades a social and political revolution has taken place on a dimension seldom paralleled in history. How has the traditional social structure stood up to these changes, what new groups have emerged, what are their characteristics, and what part do they play in this period of immense social transformation? This paper attempts in a preliminary way to answer some of these questions with respect to Ghana.

The immediate problem that confronts one is whether the traditional concepts such as class, status and elite are adequate or suitable for application in an African context. As they have often been used in the analyses of European and American societies, these concepts have acquired shades of meaning, not to speak of emotional connotations, which bedevil the task of the social scientist attempting an objective analysis. This is a familiar problem. As Professor S. M. Lipset observes (1964, p. xix): 'It is important to recognize that one of the most important methods of macroscopic social science is the method of the dialogue. By looking at the same problem from different theoretical perspectives, we increase knowledge about social processes. It should be clear in dealing with studies of complex systems that, no matter how rigorous the methodology employed, in elaborating or presenting a thesis that involves inter-relating variables such as national values, class, personality and the like, most social scientists are still engaged basically in presenting an argument which they then "validate" by showing that there is more supporting than contradictory evidence available.'

It is in this spirit that this paper is presented, as a brief argument in favour of a certain approach to the analysis of certain functional groups, in the hope that it will aid our understanding of the current, somewhat fluid social structure of Ghana.

To return to the problem of concepts, it seems to me more meaningful to speak of elites rather than social classes in Ghana. As the term has been used by Marx and Weber, social class refers primarily to economic differentiation of groups. Such a method of differentiation, and the income and occupational indices used to analyse social classes, would have to be greatly modified to be applied to the traditional system of stratification in pre-colonial Ghana. In tribal social structures, where the division of labour is not advanced and a capitalist–industrial class manifest, other criteria may be more relevant. I shall avoid some of the arguments that have been going on about the appropriate terms to describe the various 'ruling', 'prominent', or 'influential' social groups by referring to them simply as 'elites' and describing their characteristics.

Lasswell (1962, p. 13) defines the elite as 'those who get the most of what there is to get'. More specifically he refers to those who have the most of certain values classified under deference, income, and safety. As safety is often inversely correlated with great deference and high income—a point Lasswell himself makes —it would seem paradoxical to include it as an index for determining the elite, although it ranks high as a value. Lasswell's elite group is an aggregate of those with the most power and influence and is consistent with elites in pluralistic societies. On the other hand, others like Mosca (1939, p. 50) see elites as necessarily cohesive groups. The assumption upon which this analysis is based is that there is a group, or groups, of people who by virtue of their status and role (whether this be ascribed or achieved), determine to a marked extent the character of the social structure. More specifically their influence may be exercised in such a way as to help maintain the existing social structure and attendant mores, or they may act as innovators or reformers or rebels and help alter the character of the social structure (Pareto, 1963, chs. 11–13). Elites, then, according to my use of terms, must be functional groups within a social system.

Dahl (1958) has warned against the assumption of a ruling elite in any society and has suggested three conditions which must be fulfilled before we assume the existence of a ruling elite. These are:

1. That the elite be a well-defined group.
2. That there be a fair sample of cases involving key political decisions in which the preferences of the hypothetical ruling elite run counter to those of any other likely group that might be suggested, and
3. That in such cases, the preferences of the elite regularly prevail.

I find these conditions too rigid. The dynamic relationship between rulers and ruled is seldom a one-way process. The preferences of the elite itself are often tempered by what they consider necessary to keep them in power. Dahl's approach also tends to place greater emphasis on elites as status groups rather than as dynamic functional groups. Pareto's approach to elites, contrasting conservative rentiers with progressive speculators, would seem more relevant. Dahl was, of course, referring specifically to *ruling* elites. In Pareto's broader conception an elite group need not necessarily be in power, although it has power.

As applied to Ghana, where a deliberate and crucial experiment with the social structure is taking place, the elite must be seen in functional terms, i.e. in terms of the part they play in preserving or reshaping the social structure. Looked at this way, there emerges not one but several elite groups. The elite in more settled communities, or in communities with monolithic political structures, will tend to be cohesive, even if recruited from different segments of the society. Even where such elite groups are structurally opposed, they will co-exist in some kind of equilibrium. In Ghana the elites are not yet integrated, nor are they necessarily opposed. Their composition and functions reflect a society in transition whose values, old and new, have yet to be synthesized.

We are here dealing with an essentially fluid situation, and an analysis is more meaningful if we take an historical view of the situation.

In pre-colonial Ghana there had existed a number of independent or semi-independent tribal states, many linked by linguistic, religious, and other cultural ties. Although the political structure varied somewhat from tribe to tribe, each such unit had certain characteristics in common with the others. Over each tribal state there was a chief (or priest with high sanctions). Such positions of power and prestige were based on ascription with a limited measure of achievement. All these societies were operated on a kin-oriented basis. There were few positions in them that were not ascribed to a particular clan or lineage. Often in rural relations it was the sub-lineage or extended family that counted, and the individual was subsumed within such a unit. Land, the principal source of wealth and status, was owned in the name of the tribe by the chief, or in the name of the lineage and extended families by the elected heads of these units. Avenues to power and wealth in these societies were closely tied up with the traditional, largely ascribed, roles and statuses. In consequence, the chiefs or sub-chiefs formed a category which accumulated power, social status, wealth and prestige. None the less, the range between rich and poor, apart from a few powerful chiefs, was not very great. Chiefs and clan or lineage heads were supposed to hold their positions in a fiduciary capacity and had obligations to use the wealth at their disposal for the welfare of the entire group.

In such traditional, kinship-oriented societies the emergence of social classes in the Marxian sense was somewhat restricted. Status rather than class was the basis of snobbery. Prior to the abolition of the slave trade, the category of domestic slaves, and 'panyarred' servants could be said to form a separate class. But even here inter-marriages between the master or his sons and the daughters of the slaves were permitted and sometimes actually encouraged. In certain circumstances the issue of such unions succeeded as heirs to the family property or position.

Contrary to what was thought by earlier writers, the structure of tribal society was not feudal in the normal sense with a complex of synallagmatic relationships. Among the Akan, in particular, every person (apart from the domestics) was an *odehye* (an heir). Slavery was clearly recognized as a misfortune of war or poverty.

From 1844 ,when the notorious Bond was signed between the chiefs of southern Ghana and the British, the social structure began to change By the turn of the century most of what is now Ghana had become a British colony. The system of indirect rule which the British established permitted a gradual transformation. As the years went by, the British Administration consolidated its power and took on more and new functions which deprived the chiefs of much of their power, wealth, influence and prestige. Although the transformation was slowly spun out, it was none the less traumatic in its effects.

The chief lost his power to wage war, to inflict capital punishment, to adjudicate in serious criminal and civil cases. He became, in the new administrative machinery, little better than a second-class administrator who was used to interpret British policy to his people and to secure their loyalty. Christianity came in as a new and prestigious religion of the new ruling white elite to undermine the chief's traditional religious role and his ritual sanctions.

Thus, the indices of power, influence and prestige which were concentrated around the status of chief and lineage-head became diversified and truncated.

The British, up to the time of independence, became a kind of upper caste or super-prestige group. As an alien elite they determined to a considerable extent the new character of the social structure. For contact with the British not only introduced new structures, and new institutions, but also led to a re-orientation of social values, of mores and attitudes.

Below the British caste, a new African elite gradually emerged. These were those who had had access to British and European schools in Ghana and overseas. Most of these were initially children of the chiefs and clan elders, and the wealthy traders.

Outwardly, at any rate, they fashioned their life according to the stereotype of the west as they perceived it. The group was small and was concentrated at Cape Coast and Accra, later spreading to other larger towns. By the 1920s it was estimated that there were about 100 graduates and professional Africans in Ghana. Few of these had entered the civil service, the majority were lawyers and some were doctors.

This group of educated Africans came to be referred to as the *intelligentsia* (although the term is now less frequently used). What were the characteristics of this group? They were mostly in occupations which enabled them to live well. In many instances they had access to family wealth. They affected a European style of dress, tended to keep to a nuclear family, were almost all Christian, and were invariably town-dwellers.

Many writers have remarked on the marginality of the intelligentsia. Thus Dr. Gail Kelly (1959, p. 87), referring to the near caricature of Victorianism often displayed by the group in the early decades of this century, suggests that it is a consequence of 'transfrontal culture learning', that many members of the intelligentsia had either not been to Europe or had seen only a segment of it, and in consequence were attempting to build up a subculture based upon an unrepresentative and highly biased glimpse of it. Stonequist makes a point about the unsettled and ambivalent position of such groups of people. 'The missionary made man is the curse of the coast, and you find him in European clothes and without. . . . The pagans despise him, the whites hate him, still he thinks enough of himself to keep him comfortable. His conceit is marvellous.' More unfavourable references can be cited. Rattray (1923) and Apter (1963, pp. 145–7) have both referred to the 'unfortunate' intelligentsia. Joyce Cary's *Mister Johnson* is well known.

Yet it must be clear that these descriptions are exaggerated. Few of the intelligentsia were completely alienated or detribalized. Indeed, many played prominent roles in their extended families, and in public life in their home towns. Some, like Sarbah, Casely Hayford, Sekyi, and Danquah, devoted time and energy to a study of native institutions and folklore. Although they were few in numbers, or because of it, their prestige was very high, and they became an inspiration to many an ambitious young man. Envy and jealousy were naturally ingredients in the attitudes of the non-elite to them. This, of course, is a universal phenomenon. The attitude of the British towards them was also understandable, for while they copied western ways and played about with western ideas, they none the less articulated grievances against the British. From 1871, when the Fante Confederacy was formed, and 1897, when the Gold Coast Aborigines' Rights Protection Society was founded, their protest against many measures by the British remained persistent and often developed into organized if short-lived movements. It is they who spear-headed the movement to nationhood (Shils, 1963, p. 195).

By the end of the Second World War the number of college and university graduates totalled several hundred. Differentiation had entered into the category of intelligentsia and more secondary elite symbols had developed. To be called *'obroni'* (white man) was a term of praise. To have had part of one's education in Europe or America, or even merely to have visited carried the prestige label 'been-to'. To live in a bungalow (however small) in the European residential area carried prestige. A senior civil service post was designated a 'European appointment' and was rated high. Eating European dishes frequently was prestigeful, so was inviting Europeans to your home.

Behind all these symbols and practices was more than mere imitation. The notion of racial inferiority often plagued and irritated the intelligentsia. Their response to western culture was partly, therefore, an attempt to prove ability to absorb the best that the west could offer. At the same time self-interest during the colonial period dictated a pro-western orientation. Despite the criticism of British writers and administrators, they favoured the more western-oriented intelligentsia.

The sub-culture of the intelligentsia must be viewed also as a function of role expectations of the non-elite. Not to conform to certain social expectations and use certain elite symbols was to lose face with friends and relatives. The newly arrived 'been-to' was often expected by his relatives to wear woollen suits, at any rate for some time after his arrival. As the standard of living rose, he was expected to own a car, a refrigerator, a radiogram, etc.

The diminution of the power and functions of the chiefs and the rise of the intelligentsia coincided, and the two elites struggled for power, each claiming to be the true spokesman of the people. In this, the British Administration invariably supported the more conservative and predominantly illiterate chiefs.

The end of the Second World War ushered in a new era in Africa. For the first time protest against colonialism and all that it stood for became articulate, organized, and pervasive. This became possible partly because of a growing middle class of educated or literate Africans. The nature and momentum of the African revolution and the stress on nationalism necessitated an adjustment in orientation of the intelligentsia. As many sought to lead the liberation movements in their countries, they felt the need to identify more closely with the rank and file of their people. Anti-colonial and anti-British slogans compelled a measure of disengagement from the British way of life. The search for a new cultural identity was to lead to the popularization of such concepts as *négritude* and the African personality.

The intelligentsia by now could be broken up into two classes. There were the lower-middle classes—clerks, school teachers, store-keepers, etc.—and the more prestigious lawyers, doctors, senior civil servants, and the rising class of business managers. This upper-middle class, who will now be identified more specifically as the intelligentsia, though small, was fast accumulating status symbols. During the past decade or more their ranks have swollen fast with the withdrawal of British and expatriate officers and personnel and the creation of many new posts attendant upon independence. The bureaucratic structure in which most of them operated determined to a large extent their public image. And this was largely based on the image of the British bureaucrat. The result was further alienation between the intelligentsia and the people. The intelligentsia was consistently confronted with ambivalent roles.

In the struggle for independence three groups made a bid for leadership. The chiefs, who through treaties or conquest had lost their powers to the British, sought, unsuccessfully, to regain some of their lost powers and functions. They had long been by-passed in the race because the people had identified them with certain unfavourable symbols: (*a*) The chiefs had become 'stooges' of the British, and had sometimes sought British support against their own subjects. (*b*) Too many chiefs were illiterate or had little education. (*c*) The chiefs were considered backward or conservative and not progressive enough to assume leadership in a modern state. (*d*) The taboos and ritual restrictions on chiefs often hampered them in their attempt to compete for leadership. (*e*) The public had come to prefer achieved to ascribed roles.

The intelligentsia, more openly recruited, had most of the prestige symbols. They were comparatively wealthy, and they had useful intellectual and professional skills. They naturally considered themselves heirs to the colonial government. But a reaction against them had been building up. Overtly, at any rate, they appeared to the people too detribalized, too westernized, too individualistic, too snobbish and arrogant, and out of touch with the masses. The fear that they might easily constitute themselves into an upper class was often voiced.

When Dr. Nkrumah broke away from the predominantly intellectual United Gold Coast Convention and founded his own Convention People's Party in 1949, it could be said that it represented a symbolic break with the intelligentsia as an incipient class. The new category that came into prominence and won power is difficult to typify. They were mostly lower-middle class (I use these terms loosely)—clerks, school teachers, trades unionists, farmers' representatives, store-keepers. These, as a group more closely identified with the aspirations of the common people, came quickly into prominence. Today they are firmly in power. In a sense this was a class struggle fought largely through the medium of the ballot-box. The picture is blurred if one thinks of the groups in terms of personnel. It is in orientation, in attitudes, in function that this new group of the mass party is distinguished from the other two.

What I have sought to do is to describe briefly the development of three types of elite, each representing predominantly certain social values in the society, values which are not yet integrated. Consequently, Ghana so far has a divided elite. 'A divided elite is a collection of persons coming from different social origins and drawing their personal power from different sources; it is the antithesis of a ruling class, for the simple reason that it is not a class' (Marshall, 1964, pp. 132–3).

These three groups, chiefs, intelligentsia, and the new political elite, represent respectively traditional culture and values, pro-western culture and values, and an attempt to marry the two. These are, of course, generalizations. Just as there are liberals in conservative parties and millionaires in socialist parties, so there is overlapping personnel between these three groups. In terms of function and orientation the groups are distinguishable.

The relative power and importance of the elites are factors which underlie any analysis of the present Ghanaian social structure. Obsolescent as the institution of chieftainship may seem, it has residual power in representing a well-validated source of legitimacy, tying the community to its locale under the chief. The intelligentsia represent a source of skills, intellectual and professional, indispensable to the purposes of a new and progressive nation. The political elite represent the hopes and aspirations of the 'common man'. They seek, by political direction, to create a new society. Of the three elites, the chiefs are now the least powerful, and the political elite the most powerful.

Despite this attempt to describe the elite in terms of their function, the fact must not be overlooked that elites must also have high status. A study by the writer to assess prestige and status ranking of various occupations and public posts in Ghana yielded a weird result. Chiefs were usually ranked lower than the intelligentsia and the politicians, although they were never ranked low. On the other hand, considerable ambivalence was reflected in comparative ranking of the intelligentsia and the politicians. This is not surprising, for the struggle between the elites has also meant a struggle between statuses. Many posts in the civil service, and in public affairs, have been up-graded or down-graded, salary scales have been revised, new posts with new schedules have been created. Some of the respondents were clearly confused, or did not know what some of the posts entailed. Inconclusive as the study was, it revealed a state of status anomy symptomatic of a society undergoing rapid transformation. The problem may be regarded as a case of 'multidimensional stratification' stemming from the characteristics of a divided elite. It implies 'the co-existence in one society of two or more systems of stratification, based on different principles or interests'. Marshall (ibid., p. 127) argues that this is a consequence of division of labour in an advanced or advancing society.

In an earlier reference Marshall has argued that a divided elite is not a class. In the orthodox Marxian sense, of a dominant economic group that gradually dominates all other sectors of the social structure, a social class must be integrated and cohesive. In this sense there is no ruling social class in Ghana. But there is a ruling political elite.

The question which naturally arises is whether the ruling elite will transform itself into a ruling class. Alternatively, the question could be whether the multidimensional strata described above would become 'multibonded', and the different groups merge into one, forming a broad-based class. At this point one can only speak of possible trends.

The factors that will eventually determine the form of the social structure will be partly economic, partly educational, and partly ideological.

Politically, Ghana is committed to a one-party state with a trend towards the total mobilization of the population for the task of transforming the society into a modern socialist state. Consequently, power will tend to be concentrated in the hands of the political hierarchy for effective direction. At the same time socialist and centralized régimes tend to develop large bureaucratic structures for implementing national and nationalized schemes. An expanding and diversified educational programme will be necessary to support the schemes. This latter process will depend upon the development of the economy to sustain the initial expense and will in turn speed up the development of the economy. If the economy should fail to sustain, and be sustained in turn by, an open educational system, recruitment to the ranks of the elite will be closed or limited and the development of an open society will be difficult.

BIBLIOGRAPHY

Apter, D.
(1963) *Ghana in Transition.* New York.
Dahl, R. A.
(1958) 'A critique of the ruling elite model', *American Political Science Review*, vol. 52, pp. 463–9.
Kelly, G. M.
(1959) *The Ghanaian Intelligentsia.* (Unpublished Ph.D. thesis, University of Chicago.)
Lasswell, H.
(1962)*Politics: Who Gets What, When, How.* World Publishing Co., NewYork.
Lipset, S. M.
(1964) 'Introduction' to Marshall, T. H., *Class, Citizenship and Social Development.* New York.
Marshall, T. H.
(1964) *Class, Citizenship and Social Development.* New York.
Mosca, G.
(1939) *The Ruling Class.* New York.
Pareto, V.
(1963) *A Treatise on General Sociology.* New York. vols. 3 and 4.
Rattray, R. S.
(1923) *Ashanti.* London (Edition of 1955).
Shils, E.
(1963) 'The intellectuals in the political development of the New States', in Kautsky, J. H., *Political Change in Under-developed Countries.* London and New York.

Résumé

L'ÉVOLUTION DE L'ÉLITE AU GHANA

L'intérêt envers l'étude des élites s'est dirigé au cours des récentes années vers l'Afrique à cause du rôle que ces groupes jouent dans le remaniement des nouvelles structures sociales. On peut comprendre les changements sociaux rapides en cours sur le continent africain qui mènent à de nouvelles formes sociales, ainsi que certaines prédictions à leur sujet si l'on concentre son attention sur les groupes de l'élite. Le concept des élites et des classes sociales, tel qu'on l'applique à l'Afrique doit nécessairement être modifié, car les structures sociales des sociétés africaines n'offrent pas la possibilité de donner à ces systèmes la même signification. Au stage du développement actuel, le terme 'classe sociale' au sens Marxien et Weberien est fallacieux car la division de la main d'œuvre dans de telles sociétés n'est pas avancée et la structure sociale traditionnelle en rend difficile l'usage comme base de différentiation sociale nette.

Il est plus simple de trier les différents groupes sociaux 'gouvernant', 'prééminent' ou 'influent' et leur donner l'étiquette d'élites, mais il n'est pas nécessaire de concevoir ces élites comme élites dirigeantes.

Un rapprochement historique en ce qui concerne de telles élites au Ghana semble approprié à cause des changements rapides qui ont lieu. Au Ghana pré-colonial les signes du pouvoir, de richesse et de prestige étaient concentrés dans les positions traditionnelles élevées des chefs et anciens du clan, mais une nette structure de classe ne se développa pas car le système de famille étendue empêcha la croissance des distances sociales. Au cours de la période coloniale la présence britannique dérangea cette structure. Les Britanniques devinrent en un sens la classe supérieure, ou caste qui se greffa sur ce système. Par le même procédé, de nouvelles voies vers l'instruction, la richesse et le prestige, furent ouvertes à ceux qui par l'entremise des écoles missionnaires et du commerce furent à même de prendre des postes dans l'enseignement, l'administration et le commerce. Ceci représenta des débouchés envers le rang dans la société et le prestige en dehors de la hiérarchie traditionnelle. Il en résulta d'une part une diminution du prestige et des pouvoirs des chefs et la croissance d'autre part d'une nouvelle classe moyenne, appelée parfois l'intelligentsia. Dans la lutte pour l'existence qui suivit la seconde guerre mondiale, un troisième groupe se manifesta: la nouvelle élite politique rejetant à la fois l'orientation traditionnelle et en un certain sens vieillissante des chefs qui s'étaient subordonnés au système colonial et l'intelligentsia qui bien que critiquant le système colonial n'en façonna pas moins son mode de vie sur le modèle occidental. Ce modèle articule l'état d'esprit du peuple et constitue la conduite des masses.

On peut donc distinguer trois groupes élites fonctionnels au Ghana. Les chefs, maintenant plus faibles, légitiment leur rôle dans la coutume et la tradition. L'intelligentsia représente largement la compétance professionnelle et les talents modernes. L'élite politique réclame sa raison d'être dans l'appui des masses. Des signes indiquent que ces élites deviendront, en bon temps, 'multi-liées'. La question si ces élites formeront le noyau d'une classe nouvelle ou non dépend du succès de la révolution socialiste.

III. MASSES ET ÉLITES EN AFRIQUE NOIRE: LE CAS DU TOGO

F. N'SOUGAN AGBLEMAGNON

La notion de classe est l'une des plus difficiles à cerner par l'analyse sociologique. Mais ce n'est pas la première fois qu'elle retient notre attention. Déjà en 1954–55, sous le titre: 'Masses et élites', nous avions donné, surtout dans les cercles étudiants africains de Paris, une série de conférences. Nous avions en 1955, fait à la Sorbonne, un exposé sur le problème de la 'définition de la classe sociale'. Récemment, dans une communication au Centre International de Prospective à Paris, dans le cadre d'une étude collective publiée depuis aux Presses Universitaires sous le titre de: 'Conflits de Générations', nous avons abordé le problème du 'Transfert des responsabilités' dans les sociétés africaines. Enfin, il y a quelques jours à Paris, au Club de l'Association des Femmes Françaises Diplômées, nous avons fait un exposé sur le 'Statut de la Femme Africaine' aujourd'hui, thème qui, comme on le voit, a un rapport évident avec le problème général de la stratification sociale et des redéfinitions des catégories sociales dans l'Afrique contemporaine. Aussi nous permettra-t-on de laisser de côté toutes les questions de définitions qui seraient, à juste titre, considérées comme une propédeutique indispensable à la présente étude. Qu'on nous permette donc de ne pas revenir sur les distinctions et les professions de foi qu'il faut faire à propos des notions de classe, de caste, de clan, et d'aborder en quelque sorte le problème de la différenciation sociale dans l'Afrique moderne, immédiatement, sans plus tarder.

Mais, si nous nous épargnons cette analyse théorique par simple économie de temps—puisque le nombre de pages qui nous est accordé est fort limité par rapport à l'ampleur du sujet—nous ne pouvons nous empêcher toutefois de faire certaines remarques préliminaires. Tout d'abord, il semble incontestable—et ceci en contradiction avec certaines théories classiques sur la classe sociale—qu'à l'heure actuelle, nous devons admettre que si le phénomène de 'lutte de classes' ne se manifeste pas encore dans les sociétés africaines avec l'acuité qu'il revêt dans d'autres sociétés et sous d'autres cieux, si la lutte des classes ne se manifeste pas encore dans les sociétés africaines telle qu'elle s'est manifestée historiquement dans les sociétés industrielles à partir des 18ème et 19ème siècles en Europe Occidentale, c'est un fait que nous observons en Afrique, même dans un contexte encore non industrialisé des phénomènes qui témoignent de l'apparition de classes, qui sont des signes avant-coureurs de la constitution de veritables classes sociales. En effet, à côté d'une prolétariat qui s'offre aux yeux et dont tout le monde constate d'emblée la présence dans les villes africaines, on est aussi de plus en plus d'accord à parler de l'existence d'une véritable bourgeoisie. Bien que nous n'ayons pas encore dans le domaine africaniste le plaisir d'avoir une étude sociologique pertinente sur les caractéristiques, le statut et le rôle de cette bourgeoisie comme le regretté Professeur Frazier l'avait fait pour les Noirs Américains dans son livre célèbre 'Bourgeoisie Noire', nous devons donc admettre qu'il existe aujourd'hui dans cette Afrique en transition, un groupe que l'on peut *grosso modo*, classer sous l'étiquette de bourgeoisie, bien que cette bourgeoisie ne se définisse pas exactement par les mêmes critères historiques, par les mêmes manifestations sociologiques que les bourgeoisies des pays industrialisés d'Europe Occidentale ou d'Amérique.

Une des difficultés du problème est de savoir: comment définir ces groupements nouveaux? Comment par exemple à l'aide d'un certain *revenu*, on peut caractériser une classe et dénombrer ses membres? Et d'autre part, comment sur la base du *degré d'instruction* on peut dénombrer toutes les personnes qu'il faudrait ranger dans cette catégorie? Si nous considérons l'éducation, il semble difficile de s'arrêter à 'l'éducation secondaire' pour une simple raison pratique parce que cette 'éducation secondaire' n'existe que depuis peu de temps dans certains pays d'Afrique. Même au Togo, où nous avons notre champ privilégié d'observation, l'éducation secondaire n'a connu un véritable développement qu'aux environs de 1950. De plus, beaucoup de personnes occupant des fonctions élevées et bien rétribuées n'ont pas bénéficié d'une telle formation.

I

Quant à ce qui concerne le revenu de 250 livres, il y aurait une difficulté matérielle de savoir quelles sont les personnes qui se classent dans cette catégorie, puisque nous n'avons pas toujours une déclaration régulière et rigoureuse des revenus comme c'est souvent le cas dans les pays d'Europe Occidentale.

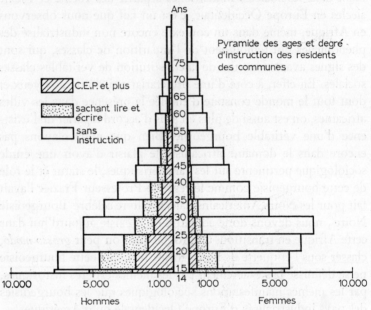

Recensement Général de la Population du Togo, 1958–1960 5ᵉ fasicule, p. 41.

Cette petite mise au point étant faite, il importe maintenant de souligner un fait nouveau: c'est le statut et le rôle de l'Africain moderne possédant soit une certaine instruction soit une certaine richesse. Car, s'il est vrai que dans les sociétés africaines traditionnelles, d'une part la notion de richesse était plûtôt conçue sous l'angle du prestige, d'autre part la richesse acquise n'était pas capitalisée au sens moderne, mais était considérée comme une sorte de propriété collective, gérée par un individu qui s'employait dès que l'occasion se présentait pour en faire bénéficier les autres par une série de réseaux de redistribution, instituant ainsi une sorte de sécurité sociale collective, il semble qu'il en soit de plus en plus autrement. En effet, aujourd'hui, dans ces sociétés, le riche est considéré en tant que riche et son statut social est très valorisé. Nous assistons donc à la définition ou à la constitution sous nos yeux de nouvelles catégories sociales. Sans compter les couches les plus favorisées qui naturellement en tirent la plus grande partie de leur prestige, la notion d'argent devient le thème habituel de discussion et de valorisation de l'individu à ses propres yeux et aux yeux de son groupe, même dans les couches les moins défavorisées de la société. Ce fait a été abondamment illustré par une enquête que nous avions faite au niveau des couches sociales flottantes dans un camp de travail en 1960 à Tsévié, à 35 kms de Lomé. Nous avions étudié un groupe de jeunes travailleurs que l'on voulait réadapter aux travaux agricoles. Nos questions portaient non seulement sur les attitudes concernant le travail proprement dit, concernant la discipline dans le camp de travail, concernant le jugement qu'ils portaient sur eux-mêmes dans la situation présente et le jugement qu'ils croient que leur entourage et leur famille portaient sur eux, concernant leur autobiographie d'avenir, mais également sur les raisons principales qui les avaient déterminées à accepter à venir dans ce camp, puis à y persévérer malgré la vie très difficile qu'ils y menaient. Presque la totalité des réponses de nos 120 sujets concernaient directement l'argent. Ce n'est d'ailleurs pas le seul groupe où l'argent soit placé au sommet de l'échelle des valuations et au premier rang des préoccupations. En Afrique aujourd'hui, et comme le dit un vieux diction, l'argent ouvre toutes les portes (cf. Geld öffnet alle Türe). Mais il serait difficile de faire dans le cadre de cette brève étude, une énumération de toutes les nouvelles catégories. Car si certaines d'entre elles sont déjà bien repérables, d'autres sont simplement en gestation. Il faut encore attendre la forme qu'elles prendront. Nous réservons une analyse plus détaillée d'une telle question dans un travail en cours. Contentons-nous pour l'instant de dire qu'il y a, à côté des couches économiquement plus favorisées constituées par le riche *planteur*, le riche *commerçant*, le riche et puissant *propriétaire foncier* des terrains à bâtir dans la capitale et aux abords immédiats de la capitale, nous avons d'autres catégories comme les *professions libérales*, les *hauts fonctionnaires*, les *députés* et le *personnel parlementaire*, les *membres de l'appareil gouvernemental et diplomatique*: les nouvelles catégories constituant la nouvelle bourgeoisie issue des fonctions politiques. Il y a ainsi des secteurs privilégiés où se recrutent les nouvelles catégories: soit à partir des professions libérales, soit des fonctions politiques.

Quant aux nouvelles relations qui s'instaurent entre ces nouveaux groupes et les anciennes associations traditionnelles, il faut souligner le fait que la richesse et l'instruction tendent à conférer un leadership de fait à ceux qui les possèdent. Ce leadership de fait s'exprime non seulement au sein des associations nouvelles, mais aussi dans la structure même des relations entre parents, entre l'homme 'arrivé' ou riche de la ville et les parents plus pauvres restés à la campagne, se manifestant quelquefois à l'intérieur même du ménage. C'est un fait bien connu que dans la région de la côte Ouest-Atlantique qui s'étend depuis le Ghana jusqu'en Nigéria en passant par le Togo et le Dahomey, les femmes dites 'revendeuses' occupent souvent une position économique plus forte que celle de leur mari. Et ceci a des incidences non seulement sur les rapports interpersonnels mais comporte souvent des incidences politiques. Enfin lorsque nous observons un peu les choses de plus près, on voit qu'il y a une certaine tendance à se constituer ce que nous pourrions appeler des mariages entre catégories semblables. A Lomé, il circule une phrase qu'on prête à une famille bien connue, qui lorsque l'on venait demander la main d'une de ses filles demandait au prétendant 'est-ce que vous consommez du beurre à table? Est-ce que vous prenez le café le matin?' En d'autres termes, est-ce que vous avez un revenu élevé? Est-ce que vous vivez à l'européenne? Cette boutade pour aussi lapidaire qu'elle soit aide à pénétrer semble-t-il la nouvelle mentalité de la nouvelle classe qui se développe. Pour étayer ces faits nous prendrons quelques exemples. Commençons par le rôle de l'instruction. L'instruction, venons-nous de dire, constitue, la clef d'un leadership de fait dans la société nouvelle. Ceci a été merveilleusement illustré par nos récentes enquêtes au Togo au niveau des associations nouvelles. Nous avions étudié 25 associations, ainsi que tous les partis politiques et tous les syndicats. Nous avons en effet essayé de voir comment se manifestait ce leadership de fait, comment est né ce qu'on pourrait appeler le Comité directeur ou, si l'on préfère, le bureau de ces associations, le bureau de ces syndicats, le bureau des partis politiques, reflétant ce phénomène nouveau. Partout et presque sans exception, nous avons constaté que le bureau de toutes ces associations, que le bureau de tous ces syndicats, que le bureau de tous ces partis politiques était tenu par des membres provenant de certaines fractions seulement de la population et ayant reçu au moins un certain niveau d'instruction. Certes ce ne sont pas toujours des bacheliers, ce ne sont même pas des gens qui ont tous fait des études secondaires, mais le fait est que l'instruction dans tous les cas, confère à l'individu une sorte de technicité nouvelle, une sorte de savoir-faire indéfinissable, auxquels les gens de son milieu attachent une extrême importance.

Considérons maintenant le rôle de l'argent dans le nouveau processus de différenciation sociale. Evoquons d'abord un cas typique de relation ambiguë que nous avons observé en 1960 au Togo. Il s'agit de la position de fonctionnaires plus instruits mais économiquement plus faibles du fait qu'ils sont locataires chez leurs subordonnés; nous avions ainsi observé cliniquement le cas d'un chef de service qui était logé par l'un de ses subordonnés, qui devait donner à son subordonné une partie importante de sa paye du mois, ce qui faisait finalement que son subordonné finissait par avoir un revenu plus important que le sien. Si nous citons cet exemple c'est pour montrer comment ces processus dans certains cas peuvent créer des relations d'une certaine complexité et induire des types nouveaux de rapport, entretenant toute une dialectique remaniée de la stratification telle qu'elle s'opère sur le plan de la seule instruction. D'autre part on assiste à une certaine prolétarisation du lettré par rapport aux propriétaires fonciers. Quant à cette classe de propriétaires fonciers et de commerçants, elle a toujours occupée avec celle des planteurs une place toute spéciale dans la société togolaise. Les riches planteurs de Palimé ont pu manifester à plusieurs reprises leur indépendance même sur le plan politique à cause précisément de cette position privilégiée. Les propriétaires fonciers de Lomé, qui n'hésitent pas à spéculer sur les terrains à bâtir, ont en effet acquis une sorte d'autorité de fait essentiellement à cause de ces propriétés. C'est dire qu'à travers ce remodelage se dégage déjà une certaine stratification. La manière dont cette nouvelle bourgeoisie foncière et cette catégorie issue des professions commerciales entendent leur rôle a une grande importance et pèse déjà dans la vie sociale, économique et politique.

C'est ainsi qu'au niveau de la lutte contre le système colonial plusieurs propriétaires terriens dont de Souza avaient dans une certaine mesure prêté de l'argent au parti politique; le problème serait aussi de savoir aujourd'hui comment dans une certaine mesure un certain type de relations se développe entre cette bourgeoisie issue des professions commerciales et la bourgeoisie issue de la propriété foncière, dans le nouveau contexte. Enfin il faut souligner un autre cas qui traduit le rôle de plus en plus grand accordé à l'argent quelquefois au détriment de l'instruction. Ainsi il n'est pas rare d'entendre à propos de personnes ayant fait beaucoup d'études mais qui ne gagnent pas toujours proportionnellement aux études faites, ces réflexions désabusées de leurs amis moins instruits mais plus riches: 's'il faut faire tant d'études pour gagner ce que vous gagnez je crois moi que j'ai bien fait de ne pas faire mes études en Europe, d'être resté ici en Afrique'. Notons enfin une réaction typique à la fois de défense et de rattrapage que cela entraîne chez certains petits fonctionnaires. Ceux-ci, qui sont par ailleurs en lutte avec les propriétaires fonciers qui sont leurs logeurs à la ville, ont tendance de plus en plus à s'approprier les terres paysannes qu'ils achètent à bas prix avec leur maigre salaire afin de devenir eux-mêmes de puissants propriétaires fonciers et planteurs. Tous ces exemples que nous avons ainsi donnés assez rapidement—puisque nous n'avons pas le temps ni la place d'entrer dans le détail de l'analyse—montrent que tout un processus de remaniement est actuellement en œuvre au sein de cette société, et que ce serait se tromper que de s'arrêter à la surface de l'évolution sociale. Bien au contraire plusieurs phénomènes qui n'ont été induits pour certains que depuis le siècle dernier, pour d'autres que depuis peu seulement, sont déjà en train de transformer, de bouleverser la physionomie des sociétés africaines traditionnelles et en particulier de la société togolaise.

Summary

MASSES AND ELITES IN BLACK AFRICA: THE TOGOLESE EXAMPLE

The status of the individual in Togolese society tends more and more to be conditioned by two new, essential factors: education and wealth. These two factors confer upon their owners a *de facto* leadership in the new society. Our investigations in Togo, in 1960, into twenty-five new associations, political parties, trades unions, and a group of young workers all confirmed this fact.

On the other hand, if the liberal professions, political functions, plantation and landed property ownership constitute, at the present time, the determining elements of the new social structure and all its forms of stratification, the development of an intellectual proletariat can already be observed, and there are significant reactions which bear witness to a certain class consciousness.

In certain categories, like that of the 'little man' who has suffered the rough shock of speculation by urban landowners, a typical reaction of compensation, recovery, or adjustment has arisen, reflected in the craving to take over land owned by the peasants.

If therefore education and wealth constitute the new criteria for valuation and prestige, the priority of wealth over education must be emphasized.

IV. THE SOCIAL CHARACTERISTICS OF AN EMERGENT ELITE IN HARARE

M. B. LUKHERO

This paper is concerned with Harare, one of the five African townships on the outskirts of Salisbury. It has a population of well over 50,000. Under the Land Apportionment Act of 1930, Harare, like the four other townships, is an African residential area—that is, no European can reside in the township. Likewise no African can reside in Salisbury proper, which is reserved exclusively for Europeans.

The purpose of this paper is to show how an African elite in Harare is becoming distinguished from the ordinary people of the community.

EDUCATION AND THE ELITE GROUP

In (Southern) Rhodesia Africans have been drawn into the western economy through their labour. Once Africans were drawn into the western economy the social system in which they were absorbed offered them an opportunity for higher standards of living as an incentive in the competition for prestige and rank. Naturally most of them who were drawn into commercial and industrial enterprises at the early stages of contact became un-skilled labourers. Later, some of the Africans who had received education from the Mission schools were able to fill posts as teachers, messenger-interpreters, evangelists, and foremen in industry. This rise in status was accompanied by better accom-modation, higher wages, better food; better treatment, too, was generally accorded to them by their European masters.

In Southern Rhodesia as early as 1899, when the rule of the country was under the B.S.A. Company, the Company's interest in education was reflected in an Ordinance. Though this law was mainly concerned with European education, it nevertheless set conditions in terms of which Mission-managed African schools could qualify for a grant. The first grants made in 1901 to three schools enrolling 265 Africans totalled £133.

The report of the 1951–52 Commission, of which Dr. Alexander Kerr was chairman, is quoted by the Judges Report to the effect that it fully recognized the awakening of African education. In the war years the Missions, fully occupied with the demand for schools in rural areas, could not cope with that in the towns as well. As a result of this growth of demand, African education was placed under a separate Native Education Department instead of being administered by the Native Development Department. Later it passed to the Chief Native Commissioner, and the Kerr Commission found it, together with agriculture, engineering, and native labour, in the Native Affairs Department. Here it remained until 1956, when Native Education was withdrawn from Native Affairs to be separately administered.

The African elite group originates in this growth of African education. Today increasing numbers of Africans have acquired higher education and earn big wages, occupy better accommodation and enjoy a higher standard of living than the majority of the African population.

Harare township itself has ten schools extending from Sub. A to Form II. Of these, two are run by the Roman Catholic Church, one by the Salvation Army, while the remainder, including the school going up to Form II, are run by the Government. The 1959 Annual Report by the Director of the Native Affairs Department (the latest available report) shows that there were 3,441 male children and 3,080 female children attending primary and lower secondary schools. The following table shows the vast difference between the numbers receiving secondary and primary education. Only 1 per cent of the population, according to the table, goes beyond Standard 6. In 1964 there were only twenty-three African students from Rhodesia reading degree courses at the University in Salisbury.

Africans residing in Harare are becoming more and more education-conscious, and they are struggling to increase the educational attainments of their children and themselves. Every year too there has been a large number of children of school

Proportion of the Population over 16 by Standard of Education Attained
(1958)

Standard of education attained	Africans born in S.R.			Africans born outside S.R.					
	Males	Fem.	Total	Males	Fem.	Total			
	%	%	%	%	%	%	%	%	%
No schooling	26	29	27	70	74	70	51	41	48
Under Standard I	5	5	5	6	5	6	5	5	5
Standard I	8	11	9	7	7	7	8	10	8
Standard II	11	14	12	6	4	6	8	11	9
Standard III	15	14	15	5	4	5	9	12	10
Standard IV	12	11	12	3	3	3	7	9	8
Standard V	9	7	8	2	1	2	5	5	5
Standard VI	11	7	10	1	1	1	6	6	6
Over Standard VI	3	2	2	(a)	1	(a)	1	1	1
	100	100	100	100	100	100	100	100	100

(a) less than 0·5.

age from rural areas trying to find places in Harare schools. This is because of better educational facilities in Harare as compared with rural areas, where in most cases the upper limit is Standard III.

A significant manifestation of the interest in education is the way in which African parents in the township came together to form a Community school to accommodate the children who were over-age, or who had failed at Government schools. This idea was conceived by an African politician and educationalist and a University graduate of good standing. The parents must sacrifice considerably to enable their children to go to Community schools, since fees are higher than those at the Government schools. The idea of the Community school is now spreading to other African townships as well as to other main Rhodesian urban areas. The people in the townships have come to realize that education is essential, because it leads to better-paid jobs and higher status. To show how high a value is placed on education I quote the following case history:

Mr. B. was born in the early twenties in a rural area. His parents had no education. He did manual jobs while he was studying privately. Through private studies he managed to get a scholarship to go to a University and on his return he is said to have been congratulated by his former employer because he had gained a degree. He is now holding a high teaching post with a four-figure salary and has bought a *mҙambarara* (big American car). Before he got his degree he had lived in Harare African township, but he has now moved to an upper class white residential area. His living style is that of a European. He uses knife and fork and possesses modern furniture and a television set. He has bought his wife a car which she uses to take the children to school. He mixes mainly with people of upper class and of University education. He is paid visits by his close kinsmen and he goes to visit them in the rural area. He usually drinks at his house and only rarely at one of the European hotels in the city.

This case history clearly shows the value placed on education by the African people and its prestige in the community as a whole.

HOUSING DIFFERENCES IN HARARE

The residents of Harare are both uneducated and educated Africans. It is a Municipal township in which they pay rent every month. The maintenance of the township is met by the Municipality out of funds which are partly derived from African beer sales and the rent paid to the City Council. It has clinics, recreation halls, sports grounds for football, a tennis court, and a modern swimming pool. The African people living in Harare are drawn from various ethnic groups of Southern Rhodesia itself, Zambia, Malawi, and Portuguese East Africa. They are employed in various commercial firms, and their occupations range from unskilled labourers to white-collar and professional workers.

The township is said to have started at Magaba ('Tins'), so-called because around 1924 the Africans lived in corrugated-iron huts put up by themselves. These huts no longer exist, as Indian-owned shops have been built where they once stood. About 1932 the first section called 'Old Bricks' was established mainly for single men, probably because the labour force then was mobile and came mainly from the northern territories without wives. Today it is occupied by both married men and their families and by single men, most of whom are poorly educated. In 1935 a section designed for married men with their families was built, and in 1937 'Ma-Joburg', another section catering for small families, was built. In 1939 a section called 'New Location' was built, followed in 1953 by a section of much bigger four-roomed

houses called 'National' after the building contractors who con-
structed the houses. To these was added another section in 1954,
called 'Runyararo' (quietness), of houses with the same number
of rooms. It was in the area adjacent to this that the Government
erected houses of a type better than any of those in the other
sections I have mentioned. These houses were built originally for
the Polish war refugees and are called 'Beatrice Cottages'. They
were later taken over by the Salisbury City Council in 1958 and
let to an African elite group. As the number of Africans with
higher education increased, more and more of the better-type
houses were built by the City Council to accommodate them.
Men such as teachers no longer wanted to live in the 'Old Bricks',
'Ma-Joburg', and 'New Location' sections, for with the latrines
and bathrooms in these sections being communal they thought
they were not good enough for men such as themselves.

Some unmarried teachers, because of their profession, were
accommodated in those sections normally reserved for married
couples, particularly in 'Ma-Joburg'. A move was made in 1963
by both the Housing and Education Departments to move all the
unmarried teachers, but this was met by strong opposition from
the teachers, who argued that it was degrading and that the new
arrangement would not allow them facilities to prepare their
classroom work. This state of affairs led to some of them becoming illegal lodgers in Harare township or Highfields township,
instead of their going to live in hostels where they would have to
share rooms with illiterates.

When the Government built hostels for unmarried teachers in
Highfields these teachers objected to their being known as
'teachers' hostels', so they are now called 'teachers' flats'. Each
block is named after a well known educated African with high
standing in the community—for example, 'Jabavu flats', 'Chitepo
flats'. The reason for this dislike of the word 'hostel' is because of
the association with the hostels in Harare, which accommodate
poorly educated manual labourers.

Members of the elite tend to move into exclusive residential
areas. While some, such as Mr. A and Mr. C, have moved into
exclusive areas in the African townships, others are able to move

into certain European areas, such as the University campus, where Mr. B is residing because of his occupation. Indeed, residence patterns express the status differences in Harare African township very clearly, as has been shown in the brief history of the township.

The African elite group of Harare township has, as I have described, shown resentment at sharing rooms with the poorly educated manual labourers. They have also shown the dislike of residing in a section of Harare township which they have considered to be occupied by less-educated people who do not belong to their social class. The following case history shows this:

Mr. A., who was born in 1923 in a tribal area, started teaching after he had passed Standard VI. Since he was not happy with the salary, he started studying privately for a G.C.E. which he later passed. He won a study-tour grant to visit Europe. On his return, he gave up teaching to take up a job as a sales representative for a large European-owned firm that offered him a higher salary. Before he resigned from his teaching position he mixed with many people and he frequented all the beer gardens. When he took the new job he changed accommodation and withdrew himself from the friends he had mixed with earlier, as he considered that they did not belong to his social class. He moved house because he said his previous house was near a trading centre, near the main road, and therefore too noisy. Instead of drinking in the ordinary beer gardens in the African township he now goes to drink in those European hotels which have opened their doors to well-dressed and well-behaved Africans. He sometimes buys his liquor to drink at his house. The house which he now occupies is well furnished with modern furniture and television. Processed oats are seen in his kitchen. He eats with knife and fork. When he visits the ordinary beer gardens he declines to drink when offered a beer and he only nods his head when someone he thinks to be beneath him greets him. He has a big car and wears suits. His friends are those doing jobs that pay them well, men who have high education and own cars. He is one of the relatively few people driving *mʒambarara*. He is known as *shoko-shoko* or *mboʒha*[1] and *anopureya disenti*.[2]

Competition for various types of accommodation in Harare township is based mainly on two factors: (i) men with large families try to move to sections where houses with more rooms are available such as in the sections of 'National' and 'Runyararo'; (ii) the elite group, because of their educational qualifications, the jobs they do, their higher salaries, the style of their life based on

[1] *Shoko-shoko* or *mboʒha*—a well-to-do person who has spent money but is not necessarily educated.
[2] *Anopureya disenti*—one who 'plays decent', not because of money alone but because of his good education.

European standards, are impelled to look for accommodation in Beatrice Cottages and the area called 'Special Housing Area', which are houses formerly occupied by Municipal European employees.

The following case history shows how education particularly is a feature of the elite group:

Mr. C. was born in the late 'twenties and went to school where he passed Standard VI. He did his G.C.E. and is doing second year B.A. degree course through private studies. He lived in Harare African township when he was employed in a professional capacity in a firm of publishers. When because of his efficiency he was promoted to a senior post he moved to a residential area which was formerly for war refugees. He later found this residential area to be no longer for the '*disenti*' and, when another former European residential area was opened to middle class Africans he moved in there. He said he wanted to live in a quiet area, an area with neighbours of good education, holding good jobs and with whom he could share modern ideas. He lives a European life; his wife has a professional job with a good salary. He is a widely travelled man and is a member of several bodies including the Scholarship Committee. His close kinsmen pay him visits but they have commented that they do not see much of him. They complain that when they visit him in Salisbury he cannot find time to be with them, which to them is a European way of doing things. The residential area in which he now lives is composed of African graduates from well-known Universities and some of whose wives are from countries other than Africa.

The most important distinction between the elite and the non-elite is education. The very small number of highly educated Africans immediately puts a limit on the number of people who are considered by the African community to belong to the elite. The three case histories demonstrate this. Even so, education, although necessary, is not sufficient to distinguish the elite from the rest of the community. It seems that the elite section of the community has always tried to preserve its exclusiveness by constantly moving into new districts. Messrs. A, B, and C have done this, and it is interesting to note that the teachers who cannot afford to do this insist on their hostel being differentiated from those occupied by illiterate or poorly educated people.

WEALTH

The elite also differ from the non-elite in the wealth of its members. All three persons cited in the case histories own one or two cars, expensive furniture, television sets, and other items associated with a European style of living. This alone is not enough. An elite needs money, but with money alone without education he will not be admitted into the company of the elite. A businessman, for example, was not invited to a social function organized by a member of the elite group, although he is rich and lives among the elite. Another example is of a gentleman in business with a fleet of buses. Although he lives in a large modern house worth over £5,000 and drives a *mẓambarara*, he is not accepted among the elite group. He is only known as a *shoko-shoko* or *mboẓha*.

STYLE OF LIFE

The members of the elite also differ from the non-elite in their style of life. The persons in all three case histories live as Europeans. They all eat with knife and fork rather than with fingers, and their diet includes European foodstuffs such as processed oats. They wear suits and they know what kind of clothes to wear and at what time of the day or year to wear them. A member of the non-elite, though he might be very rich, lives differently from the elite. He eats with his fingers and the main food in his family is *sadẓa* (solid porridge). The non-elite speak Shona among themselves, while the elites tend to speak English when they meet. A radio in a house of an elite is played quietly, while in the house of a non-elite it is played at full blast to show off his wealth to neighbours and passers-by.

DIFFERENCES IN SOCIAL NETWORK

From the case material presented in this paper it seems that the members of the elite groups also have different social networks. They appear to have left behind their former friends in favour of other people occupying a similar position in society. Mr A now only nods when he is greeted by former friends, and declines to drink in municipal beer halls. Mr. C finds it difficult to sit down and talk with his kinsfolk, as he used to do before he moved into the elite group, and this is true in other cases also. For instance, a Mr. D is married to a highly educated foreign woman who, when they were having lunch, told her husband to tell his mother, who had just arrived from the country, to wait in the kitchen until they had finished eating.

Rather than drink in beer halls with their friends, they now prefer to drink in European hotels in town or in their houses. They do not join football clubs which are organized on tribal lines.

All the men in the case studies presented have educated wives, and they, too, have generally little contact with the wives of the non-elite. The wives of Messrs. A, B, and C can all drive cars, and two of them have cars of their own. They rank among the few highly educated women in Harare township. The wife of Mr. A is a teacher at a Government school in the township. She commands high respect in the Harare community. The wife of Mr. B has been trained in advanced domestic science at a University in the United States where her husband graduated. She drives her own car, which she uses to transport her children to school. Her children hob-nob with children of other races at the University College campus where they have accommodation. The wife of Mr. C is also highly educated. She has her own car, which she drives to her place of employment, where she works as a state-registered nurse. When we look at the non-elite the situation is different because kinship ties are still very important to them and they do not cut off existing friendships. One very popular member of the community is an example of this. Although he has lived in town for many years and is a very prosperous person in many respects, he still has many contacts with his kinsmen. Though he lives in town, he is a member of the Tribal Council in his tribal area outside the town. When kinsmen come to pay him a visit he eats together with them.

This is not the case with the elite. When Mr. A was visited by his wife's brother, who has never been to school, at supper the wife's brother was called into the kitchen where his food was put, while he, Mr. A, and his wife ate together at the table. The following day the wife's brother had breakfast in the kitchen, while Mr. A and his wife had theirs together. The wife's brother said he would stay a week with them in Harare, but after only two days' stay he cut his visit short and returned to the rural area. Mr. A himself said that when he went to his wife's village during a holiday he and his wife found it necessary to take some eggs, sugar, tea, and other foodstuffs with them, from which the wife of Mr. A could prepare meals for themselves, because they found the food in the village distasteful. Both Mr. and Mrs. A said the kinsmen remarked in a joking manner: 'You are not our kinsmen now, but you are Europeans.'

Mr. B, who lives in a European upper-class area, had the following experience. One day his sister's son came to pay him a visit unexpectedly. His wife had gone to fetch the children from school when the visiting kinsman arrived. On her return she found Mr. B's sister's son at the house. After greeting him she asked why he did not write or send a word to say he was coming. Mr. B also asked a similar question after he had inquired about the health of people at home. After a few days' stay the visitor returned back to the rural area. When later Mr. B went to see his father, who was reported to be unwell, he was told by his father that Mr. B's sister's son complained about the welcome he had been given at Mr. B's house.

These two case histories clearly show the position in which the elite are placing themselves and how, in this situation, they resent the tribal way of doing things. They welcome their kinsmen to their homes, but not to eat together with them, and they remonstrate with their kinsmen for not sending word to say they are coming to pay a visit. Obviously this is not a traditional African practice, and it makes the less well-educated people feel they are not welcome at the homes of their educated kinsmen.

POLITICAL ACTIVITIES

Members of the elite group tend not to be political leaders. Although they participate in politics, they are not entirely committed to politics. They talk of being politicians and boast that they know a good deal about politics; but luxury is deeply rooted in their lives.

One young well-educated man who belonged to a certain political party was asked to become an organizer in the Tribal Trust Land area; he told the President of the party that he had not finished the 'medical treatment' from his doctor. He later produced a doctor's certificate to the effect that he needed a complete medical check-up, but when the President wanted to send a representative to a Far Eastern country this sick person volunteered to go.

Another very interesting case is that of a newly graduated young man from University who, when asked by a friend whether,

K

now that he had graduated, he was going to take up active politics, said, 'Why did I go to a University if I wanted that life, I am going to swim in money and life.'

The rest of the African population does not see the elite as political figures, although they may belong to political parties. Two of the three cases in this paper are members of political parties, but they are not looked upon as very important figures.

CONCLUSION

The object of this paper has been to illustrate the way in which a very small group of Africans in Rhodesia with relatively high educational qualifications and living according to westernized standards are marking themselves off from the rest of the African population who do not possess these characteristics. There may, however, be some who are wealthy but are not counted among the elite, since the possession of the educational qualifications is an essential characteristic of this group.

As educational opportunities expand, the general level of education of the African population will rise, and this rise is likely to be fairly rapid. The present-day elite, whose position of prestige is based on their relative educational advantage over the rest of the African population, is likely to be replaced in a short time by a new elite now beginning to come out of the universities. Among these will be some who have higher degrees, and they are likely to constitute a superior elite.

This presupposes that educational attainments alone will remain the distinguishing characteristic of the African elite in Harare. While they do, there is likely to be a high rate of circulation of elites as younger people have more opportunities of advanced education than their predecessors had. But no doubt in time, as in other countries, the advantages and privileges which the elite group now possesses will tend to become limited to the families of the elite, thereby giving them initial advantages over the less privileged in the struggle for status prestige. The current rapid circulation of the elite will then slow down and social stratification in Harare will have assumed the form of a class structure.

BIBLIOGRAPHY

Central African Statistical Office
(1958) *Second Report of the Salisbury African Demographic Survey 1958*. Salisbury.
Goldthorpe, J. E.
(1961) 'Educated Africans: some conceptual and terminological problems', in Southall, A. (Ed.) *Social Change in Modern Africa*. London.
Judges Report
(1962) *Report on Southern Rhodesia Education*.
Lukhero, M. B.
(1962) 'Tribalism in voluntary associations', in *Proceedings of the 16th Conference of the Rhodes–Livingstone Institute*, Lusaka.
Mitchell, J. C.
(1956) 'The African middle classes in British Central Africa', in I.N.C.I.D.I., *The Development of a Middle Class in Tropical and Sub-Tropical Countries*. Brussels.
Mitchell, J. C.
(1960) 'White-collar workers and supervisors in a plural society', *Civilisations*, x, pp. 293–306.
Mitchell, J. C. and Epstein, A. L.
(1959) 'Occupational prestige and social status among urban Africans in Northern Rhodesia', *Africa*, xxix, pp. 22–40.
Parker, Franklin
(1962) 'Government entry into multitribal education in N. Rhodesia', in *Proceedings of the 16th Conference of the Rhodes–Livingstone Institute*, Lusaka.
Schwab, W. B.
(1961) 'Social stratification in Gwelo', in Southall, A. (Ed.) *Social Change in Modern Africa*. London.

Résumé

LES CARACTÉRISTIQUES SOCIALES D'UNE ÉLITE QUI EMÉRGE AU HARARE

Parmi la population africaine de la Rhodésie du Sud la revendication pour l'instruction augmente, alors que seulement 10 pour cent des enfants d'âge scolaire parviennent au stage final de l'éducation primaire, et seulement 1 pour cent continuent au delà de l'instruction primaire. Il n'y avait en 1964 que 23 étudiants rhodésiens africains à l'université de Salisbury. L'élite composée d'individus relativement bien instruits est extrêmement restreinte.

Les différences de rang sont plutôt précisément en corrélation avec les quartiers résidentiels de la ville africaine de Salisbury, tel que le quartier d'Harare. Il existe un mouvement continuel de la classe aisée et instruite vers les plus récentes banlieues: les professeurs par exemple s'offensent de voir leurs domiciles englobés dans la même catégorie que ceux des ouvriers manuels—'les appartements' sont différenciés des 'foyers'.

Non seulement l'élite ayant reçu une instruction supérieure vit à l'écart de la masse urbaine de la population africaine, mais son mode de vie est ouvertement occidental. Elle tend à éviter tout rapport dans les édifices publics avec ceux moins bien instruits; elle voit relativement peu sa parenté rurale; son engagement dans les affaires de sa communauté natale a tendance à être minime. La plupart ont des épouses bien instruites et ces dernières ont également peu de rapports avec les femmes du commun. On peut faire une nette distinction entre les hommes et femmes bien instruits qui maintiennent leurs distances d'avec la masse, et les hommes d'affaires riches, mais moins instruits. Les premiers n'ont que peu de rapports réciproques avec ces derniers.

V. ATTITUDES TOWARDS MARRIAGE AND THE FAMILY AMONG EDUCATED YOUNG SIERRA LEONEANS

KENNETH LITTLE

INTRODUCTION

Apparently, one of the characteristic features of the new West African elite is its attitude towards matrimony and matrimonial relationships.

Writers who have studied this matter include, *inter alios*, Baker (1957), Bird (1958, 1964), Crabtree (1950), Jahoda (1958, 1959), and Tardits (1958), and they seem to be agreed on certain conclusions. They suggest, for instance, that monogamy is regarded as a mark of higher social status; that in addition to exercising personal choice educated[1] Africans want a companionate form of marriage; that they are taking over the notion of romantic love, etc.

Granting that this outlook on marriage is widely expressed, how far is it associated with a particular social class? Also, to what extent are such attitudes consistent with European models of the family as a self-contained institution based upon the conjugal relationship?

With a view to throwing more light upon this situation, a questionnaire was drawn up and was distributed in April 1961 in Freetown, Sierra Leone, with the help of social-welfare workers and of college and school teachers[2] among groups of college students, boys and girls in the senior forms of secondary schools,

[1] 'Educated' is used specifically to denote individuals with a post-primary education; 'literate' to denote individuals whose education finished in a primary school.

[2] In this connexion I have to thank principally Professor Arthur Porter of the University College of Sierra Leone; Mrs. Gershon Collier, Headmistress of the Freetown Secondary School for Girls; and Mrs. Amelia Davies and Miss Rosalind Garber (now Mrs. Ford), of the Department of Social Welfare, Sierra Leone Government.

and other young girls who had already left school. Since, in Freetown, the Creole population of the former Colony is generally much more westernized than the people who originate up-country, it was intended to compare the attitudes of numbers of Creoles and non-Creole young men and women. Unfortunately, most of the forms completed by the Creole males were lost and in the end samples consisted basically of 7 Creole and 54 non-Creole young

Table 1

	Males		Females	
	Creoles	Non-Creoles	Creoles	Non-Creoles
	N=7	N=54	N=84	N=49
Age				
Mean	23·7	24·8	18·9	18·4
S.D.	4·4	3·9	6·0	1·6
Religion		%	%	%
Christian	n*=7	88	100	91·8†
Moslem	—	12	—	8·2
Standard of Education				
Previous Ed.	Primary and Secondary schools or colleges		Primary or secondary school or convents	
Actual level	Teacher Training College First Year		Secondary Schools (Plus 5 Creoles and 1 Non-Creole working)	
		%	%	%
Fathers literate	n*=5	28	94	75
Mothers literate	n*=5	n*=1	94	69
	N=7	N=52	N=84	N=47
Number of Fathers' wives				
Mean	1	4·9	1	1·2
S.D.		4·6		0·8
	—	N=52	N=80	N=47
Father's Occupation				
		%	%	%
Farmer		59	—	12
Clerk		—	16	—
Trader		—	—	33
Miscellaneous		41	84	55

* These figures represent the actual numbers of answers, as the sample was too small to draw any percentage.

† Creoles: 9·4% of Christian R.C. Non-Creoles: 40% of Christian R.C.

men and 84 Creole and 49 non-Creole young women. The non-Creole males gave their tribes respectively as: Mende 26; Temne 12; Sherbro 5; Fula 4, and some Kono, Susu, Gallinas, etc. The non-Creole females gave their tribes respectively as: Mende 22; Yoruba (Western Nigeria) 5; Sherbro 4; and Mandingo, Ibo (Eastern Nigeria), etc. Particulars of age, education, and education of parents are provided in Table 1. The Creole male sample is omitted from subsequent tables, but account is taken in the discussion of the responses of this group.

In the first section the comparison referred to is made in terms of the replies given respectively by the Creole and the non-Creole groups. A further comparison is made in the second section of the African group as a whole with the responses of a British group to a similar set of questions.

THE AFRICAN GROUP

Table 2 summarizes replies as to the best age at which to get married, the number of children wanted, and whether the number of children ought to be regulated (Questions 1, 9, and 10).

Table 2

	Males	Females	
	Non-Creoles	Creoles	Non-Creoles
	N=51	N=84	N=46
Best age at which to get married:			
Mean	23·8	23·5	24·0
S.D.	3·9	2·9	1·4
	N=51	N=72	N=39
Number of children wanted:			
Mean	*	4·3	4·13
S.D.	—	1·5	1·4
	N=54	N=79	N=41
Number ought to be regulated:	%	%	%
	46·3	75·5	46·3

* The mean is not reliable as 23 of the respondents answered the question by as many as God wants' or 'as many as possible'.

Another question (Q. 3) asked respondents what qualities they specially look for in a prospective husband or wife. The percentages shown in Table 3 indicate the number of times particular qualities were mentioned, proportionate to the size of the sample.

Further questions (Qs. 2 and 4) asked respondents to say if parents or relatives or the question of education, religion, or tribe were likely to influence their choice of a spouse. Table 4 summarizes in percentage terms the replies given in the affirmative.

Table 3

	Males	Females	
	Non-Creoles N=54	Creoles N=84	Non-Creoles N=43
	%	%	%
Handsome	—	21·2	41·9
Beautiful	40·7	—	—
Intelligent	18·5	12·9	11·7
Loving	27·8	29·2	14·2
Housewifely and domestic	35·2	—	—
Good manners and behaviour	27·8	18·8	25·6
Educated	—	30·6	30·2
Faithful	—	8·2	9·3
Respectable, kind, considerate	—	5·9	11·3

Table 4

	Males	Females	
	Non-Creoles N=54	Creoles N=82	Non-Creoles N=48
	%	%	%
Parents or relatives	59·3	52·6	70·8
Education	61·1	82·9	81·3
Religion	74·1	79·3	81·3
Tribe	46·3	68·3	62·5

The next questions (Qs. 5 and 6) asked respondents to say how they would expect to be treated by the girl/man they married and what obligations they would have towards their spouses. The percentages shown in Tables 5 and 6 indicate respectively the number of particular expectations and obligations mentioned, proportionate to the size of the sample.

The next questions (Qs. 7 and 8) asked respondents what their attitude would be in the event of a serious 'palaver' between their relatives and their spouse, and whether after marriage they would

Table 5

	Males	Females	
	Non-Creoles N=53	Creoles N=56	Non-Creoles N=42
	%	%	%
Respect	35·8	18·4	23·8
Love	28·3	28·9	23·8
Obeyed	24·5	—	—
Given all necessities	—	15·8	16·7
Behave faithfully	—	2·5	14·3
Treat kindly	—	18·4	28·6
Treat as a sister	—	18·4	9·5
Treat as a lady	—	2·6	14·3
To be trusted and treated as a partner	—	9·2	3·5

Table 6

	Males	Females	
	Non-Creoles N=51	Creoles N=75	Non-Creoles N=38
	%	%	%
Financial obligations	45·0	—	—
Take care of her/him	23·5	5·3	13·2
Share sorrows, and points of view	17·7	—	—
Make him/her happy	23·5	8·0	23·7
Love	—	16·0	26·3
Obey	—	26·7	36·8
Respect	—	18·8	26·3
As housewife and cook	—	32·0	28·9
Be faithful and loyal	—	21·3	15·8
Help him	—	10·6	7·9

prefer to live with relatives or separately with their spouse in a house or compound of their own. All the Creole men and 92·3 per cent of the non-Creole men said that they would prefer to live on their own. In the case of the women, all the Creole girls and all the non-Creole said that they would prefer to live on their own. The percentages shown in Table 7 summarize responses to the former question.

In the next question (Q. 11), respondents were asked to say if a girl should have a career of her own after she marries. Of the Creole males 57·1 per cent and of the non-Creole males 50 per cent (including two respondents who qualified their answers)

Table 7

	Males Non-Creoles N=53	Females Creoles N=83	Females Non-Creoles N=31
	%	%	%
Try and settle, palaver	22·6	31·3	54·8
Find the cause first	22·6	3·6	3·2
Talk to wife/husband	—	—	12·9
Talk with relatives	—	12·1	12·9
Call in someone else	18·9	2·4	12·9
Favour spouse	5·7	—	16·1
Favour relatives	1·9	—	—
Be impartial	26·4	14·5	19·4

replied in the affirmative. Of the females 76·5 per cent of the Creoles (including four who qualified their answers) and 52·3 per cent of the non-Creoles replied in the affirmative.

Respondents were also asked (Q. 12) how, in the event of their replies being in the affirmative, a woman can combine her duties as a wife and a mother with a career. The main ways, in which both Creole and non-Creole men thought this combination might be possible, would be to have a nurse at home (2 answers out of 4 and 34·5 per cent respectively). Creole men also thought that the children might be placed in a nursery (2 answers out of 4) and non-Creole men mentioned in addition to nursery (11·5 per cent), servants (30·8 per cent), relatives (19·2 per cent); 23·1 per cent of the non-Creole men repeat the question and say that their wife would have to combine both her career and her duties at home. Among the women, Creoles mentioned mainly 'nurses' (25·9 per cent) and servants (25·9 per cent), nurseries (12·1 per cent); 24 per cent thought that they might combine both work and house-duties, by cooking in the evening, for example; one said that the husband might help. Non-Creoles mentioned mainly servants (42·1 per cent), nurses (31·7 per cent), nurseries (21·1 per cent); 21 per cent thought that they would combine both work and duties, by working in the evening; 21 per cent thought that they could work at home as a dressmaker, for instance; one mentioned that the husband could help.

The respondents were also asked what career they would like their children to follow (Q. 13). Of the non-Creole males, 13

Table 8

| | Males | | Females | | | |
| | Non-Creoles | | Creoles | | Non-Creoles | |
	Boys N=42	Girls N=42	Boys N=48	Girls N=48	Boys N=31	Girls N=31
	%	%	%	%	%	%
Doctor	50·0	35·7	72·9	22·9	51·6	16·1
Lawyer	14·3	9·5	23·9	—	29·1	—
Farmer	7·2	—	—	—	6·4	—
Politician	7·2	—	—	—	—	—
Engineer	19·1	—	39·9	—	19·4	—
Teacher	19·1	54·8	6·3	87·5	3·2	29·1
Priest	—	—	4·1	—	6·4	—
Nun	—	9·5	—	—	—	—
Mechanic	—	—	6·3	—	12·9	—
Nurse	—	30·9	—	52·1	—	38·7
Secretary and radiographer	—	—	—	—	—	12·8

said that they would like their children to choose themselves their career; 22 of the non-Creole females and 18 of the Creole females made the same reply. The percentages in Table 8 indicate the number of times particular careers were mentioned, relative to the size of the sample.

In the next question (Q. 14) male respondents were asked if they felt entitled to marry more than one wife. Of the small sample of Creoles 85·7 per cent answered 'No' and 14·3 per cent 'Yes' to the question, while of the non-Creole men 66·7 per cent answered 'No' and 31·5 per cent 'Yes'. Of the last mentioned, only one respondent said, in answer to a supplementary question (Q. 15), that he would be prepared to make an additional marriage without his wife's consent.

The women were also asked their attitudes (Q. 14), and of the Creoles only two respondents (2·4 per cent) and of the non-Creoles only three respondents (6·7 per cent) said that they would be willing for their husbands to take additional wives; one of them mentioned that the second wife would do the house-work while she could work outside. Among the majority who answered in the negative to the question and gave reasons why they objected to this idea, 35·3 per cent said that they would be jealous and 22·3 per cent that it would be against religion for their husbands to have more than one wife. In addition, the women were asked how they thought they would react to their husbands taking a second wife (Q. 15). The percentages shown in Table 9 indicate their responses proportionate to the size of the sample.

Table 9

	Creoles N=69	Non-Creoles N=40
	%	%
Leave husband	32·5	48·9
Take husband to court and/or divorce him	20·0	10·9
Ask husband to send other woman away	14·4	44·0
Inform a priest	4·8	13·3
Inform relatives	8·4	4·4

The next question (Q. 16) asked the men if they would be agreeable to their wives having male friends and the women if they would expect to have male friends after they have married. This question was answered in the affirmative by 6 out of the 7 Creoles and by 31 out of the 53 non-Creole men (58·5 per cent) who answered it. Of these 31 non-Creole men, however, 19 indicated that their agreement would depend upon how 'friendship' was defined, while 2 out of the Creoles make the same reply. Of the women, 42·1 per cent of the Creole sample and 32·6 per cent of the non-Creole sample indicate that they would expect to have male friends. In addition, 2 Creole girls thought that male friendship was a possibility.

In the next question (Q. 17) respondents were asked if they consider it an advantage or a disadvantage for a wife to be as well educated as her husband. Among the males, a number of the Creoles and 71·7 per cent of the non-Creoles considered it an advantage. Among the females, 80·9 per cent of the Creoles and 86·2 per cent of the non-Creoles considered it an advantage. Three Creole girls were uncertain of the answer; both groups of men and women seemed to be agreed that for the wife to be as well educated as the husband would lead to better understanding (non-Creole men, 41·5 per cent; non-Creole women, 24·0 per cent) and be economically beneficial (non-Creole men, 18·9 per cent; non-Creole women, 24·0 per cent). Creole women also thought that it would be beneficial from the point of view of society (20·6 per cent) if they are able to discuss matters intelligently and their husbands were not ashamed of them.

With very few exceptions both groups of men and women also expected to share common interests with their spouses (Q. 18). Non-Creole men apparently thought that they would find these common interests mainly in dancing (22·9 per cent) and sports (22·9 per cent). They also mentioned films (14·6 per cent), games (12·5 per cent), and music (8·3 per cent). Creole girls mentioned mainly 'discussion' (25·9 per cent) and also referred to sport (8·6 per cent) and to the family (7·4 per cent). Non-Creole girls referred mainly to dancing and films (both 14·8 per cent) and also mentioned family, social activities, and walking (all 11·1 per cent).

Summary and Discussion

The questions asked respondents were concerned broadly with four particular aspects of marriage and family life:

(a) the factors likely to influence the choice of a spouse;
(b) a person's expectations of his/her own conjugal role and that of his/her spouse, including the question of personal and sexual freedom;
(c) prospective relationships with kinsfolk and affinal relatives;
(d) the ideal size of family.

In addition, information was sought about the best age at which to get married and about occupational ambitions for children.

Allowing for the small size of the Creole male sample, the following facts may be deduced from the broad pattern of the answers. Both Creoles and non-Creoles, male and female alike, are agreed that the best age for a man or woman to get married is twenty-three or twenty-four. Non-Creole men looked for girls who were beautiful, housewifely and domestic, loving and well-mannered. Both Creole and non-Creole girls looked principally for (well-)educated spouses. In addition, they wanted their prospective husbands to be well-mannered and loving. Non-Creole girls attached importance also to fidelity.

The principal factor likely to influence a person's choice of a spouse seemed to be religion, although both groups of girls laid an equal amount of stress upon education. The non-Creole girls also emphasized the influence of parents and relatives; apparently the tribe is considered less important, although both Creole and non-Creole girls paid more attention to it than did the men.

Non-Creole men expect respect and love and obedience, in that order, from their prospective wives. While considering that their own main obligation is financial, they also feel that they should share their wives' point of view and make them happy. They were completely divided over the idea of wives having a career and somewhat ambiguous in their attitudes towards relationships outside monogamous marriage. Thus, although a proportion of the sample were willing apparently for the women they married to have male friends (61 per cent, including 35·6 per cent who were dubious about this idea), about one-third of the sample felt that they were themselves entitled to have more than one wife.

The women expect a prospective husband to love, respect, and treat them with kindness and to provide them with all the (economic) necessities of married life, roughly in that order. They consider that their own main obligations are domestic (e.g., to keep house, cook and look after husband's clothes), but they also emphasize that a wife owes her husband obedience, respect, love, and loyalty. The Creole girls evidently feel more strongly than the non-Creole girls that married women should have a career, the non-Creole girls being about as divided about this question as the non-Creole men. Although about a third of the women, Creole and non-Creole alike, expect to have male friends, having in mind a platonic relationship, it is quite clear that most of them are strongly opposed to polygamy. Rather more than half of them say that they would either leave their husband or start legal proceedings in the event of his taking a second wife.

Another strong reaction which, in this case, the women share with the men is against the idea of living with relatives in the same house. In the same connexion it is perhaps significant that in reply to the open-ended question about how respondents would behave in the event of a serious domestic quarrel the main interest expressed was in settling the dispute. About one-third of each sample (excluding the Creole men) said that they would be impartial, and only two respondents declared that they would side with their own relatives.

Towards the idea of regulating the size of the family, there is a statistically significant difference between the attitudes of the Creole and non-Creole girls, the latter being more strongly opposed. Something of their attitude is reflected in the response of the non-Creole men ('as many as God wants ... as many as possible') to the question of how many children they want.

What emerges from these data is that overall both Creole and non-Creole young men and women regard marriage as a companionate relationship. The wife is to accept her husband's leadership (stressed more in non-Creole than in Creole attitudes) and is to play her accustomed role as a housewife and mother. The man is to be the main provider, and marriage is to be a true union of husband and wife, as well as an economic partnership. This is emphasized both by the general agreement on the advantages of wives being as well educated as their husbands and by the general expectation of husbands and wives sharing common interests. Apparently the girls (particularly the non-Creoles) are rather more swayed by the older associations (e.g. kinsfolk and tribe) than are the men, but both sexes evidently consider that a modern outlook and training is more significant for marriage than any other factor. The fact that there was relative agreement with the idea of wives having careers of their own may be interpreted in a variety of ways. It may represent the idealized view (which some of the men evidently share) of women as 'free' and independent partners. Alternatively, the idea may be favoured on account of the extra money brought into the house through a wife working, thereby increasing the household's standard of living. In this connexion, the fact that a large proportion of the respondents, Creole and non-Creole alike, look forward to their children becoming doctors seems to show some interest in social status. Other relatively well-paid professional occupations frequently mentioned were nurse, teacher, lawyer, and engineer.

AFRICAN AND BRITISH STUDENTS

We turn now to the total sample, and from the data available it would appear that a fairly large proportion of the respondents have been brought up in homes in which the influence of western education is strong. Thus, among the Creoles, 94 per cent and among the non-Creoles about 33 per cent had literate parents; in both samples the percentage of literate parents of girls was much higher than it was for the parents of boys. In any case, through their experiences in schools and colleges, Creole and non-Creole respondents alike must have assimilated western ideas and values. Not only do the majority of them profess Christianity, but a proportion are boarders at Roman Catholic convents. This being the case, the general nature of the responses is not surprising. The question that arises, however, is how closely do these attitudes approximate notions of the family and of matrimonial relationships as held at the present time in Western Europe?

The latter problem was approached by treating the Creoles and non-Creoles as a single African sample and comparing their responses to a broadly similar questionnaire given to a sample of British students at Edinburgh University. The latter sample consisted of 67 male and 109 female students drawn from a first-year class in psychology.

As Table 10 indicates, the British young men and women, particularly the girls, are further advanced in education than the Africans. On the other hand, although the two groups also differ somewhat in age, a high proportion of both samples profess to be Christian. There are therefore some broad similarities between the two groups, and Table 11 summarizes replies as to the best age at which to get married; the number of children wanted, and whether the number of children ought to be regulated (Qs. 1, 9, and 10).

Question 3 asked respondents what qualities they specially look for in a prospective husband or wife. The percentages shown in Table 12 indicate the number of times particular qualities were mentioned, proportionate to the size of the sample.

Further questions (Qs. 2 and 4) asked respondents to say if parents or relatives or the question of education, religion, tribe,

Table 10

		African students		British students	
		Males N=61	Females N=133	Males N=67	Females N-109
		%	%	%	%
Age	Mean	24·69	18·57	21·18	20·28
	S.D.	3·94	2·05	2·97	1·63
Standard of Education		Teacher Training College	Secondary School	University	University
Religion:					
Protestant		64·0	75·5	82·2	90·0
Roman Catholic		24·6	17·6	8·9	6·3
Moslem		11·4	6·9	—	—
No religious affiliation, or not stated		—	—	8·9	3·6

Table 11

	African students		British students	
	Males N=57	Females N=130	Males N=52	Females N=85
Best age at which to get married:	%	%	%	%
Mean	23·79	23·74	25·98	23·93
S.D.	3·75	1·59	4·85	2·03
	N=34	N=113	N=63	N=102
Number of children wanted:				
Mean*	4·44	4·26	3·05	3·70
S.D.	1·72	1·55	0·89	1·23
	N=61	N=120	N=66	N=109
The number ought to be regulated	37·7	64·2	89·4	78·0

* This mean is not reliable, as 26 respondents out of 61 said that they will have 'as many children as God wanted'.

or nationality were likely to influence their choice of a spouse. Table 13 summarizes in percentage terms the replies given in the affirmative.

The next questions (Qs. 5 and 6) asked respondents to say how they would expect to be treated by the girl/man they married, and what obligations they would have towards their spouses. The percentages shown in Tables 14 and 15 indicate respectively the number of particular expectations and obligations mentioned, proportionate to the size of the sample.

L

Table 12

| | African students | | British students | |
	Males N=61	Females N=133	Males N=67	Females N=109
	%	%	%	%
Beautiful	36·1	—	39·0	—
Handsome	—	25·2	—	6·4
Intelligent	16·4	12·6	51·0	30·3
Loving	26·2	19·5	21·0	16·5
Educated	—	27·7	—	—
Good manners	26·2	17·6	—	—
Housewife and cook	31·2	—	16·4	—
Kind and gentle	—	15·7	—	43·1
Considerate, under- standing, generous	—	7·6	13·4	53·2
Sense of humour	—	—	27·0	55·0

Table 13

| | African students | | British students | |
	Males N=61	Females N=126	Males N=67	Females N=109
	%	%	%	%
Parents	61·0	42·9	24·7*	53·0†
	N=61	N=131	N=67	N107
Education	62·3	74·8	64·2	76·7
Religion	72·1	78·1	67·7	81·3
Tribe or Nationality	47·5	62·3	49·3‡	76·7§

* Including 4·5% mentioning that it would be an 'indirect influence'.

† Including 17% mentioning that it would be an 'indirect influence'.

‡ Including 6% mentioning that they would not like 'a coloured person' as a spouse

§ Including 4·7% mentioning 'not a coloured person'.

The next questions (Qs. 7 and 8) asked respondents what their attitude would be in the event of a serious quarrel between their relatives and their spouse and whether, after marriage, they would prefer to live with relatives or separately with their spouse, in a house or compound of their own. 93·2 per cent of the African males and 93 per cent of the African females want to live on their own; all the British, whether males or females, want to live on their own. The percentages shown in Table 16 summarize responses to the former question.

Table 14

	African students		British students	
	Males N=59	Females N=118	Males N=64	Females N=107
	%	%	%	%
Respected	33·9	18·0	21·9	34·6
Loved	28·8	25·2	39·1	29·0
Obeyed	27·1	—	7·8	—
Be faithful	6·8	—	26·6	—
Be given all material necessity	—	16·6	—	—
Respect man's career	8·5	—	17·2	—
Treated as an equal and (or) a partner	—	20·6	—	54·2
With consideration, ideas respected	—	—	—	38·3
Husband, head of family	—	—	—	28·0

Table 15

	African students		British students	
	Males N=57	Females N=113	Males N=66	Females N=106
	%	%	%	%
Financial obligations	43·9	—	56·1	—
Take care of her/him	24·6	6·2	13·6	20·8
Make her happy	22·8	—	12·1	—
Obey him	—	26·9	—	6·6
Respect him	—	20·8	—	10·4
Love her/him	—	19·2	27·3	18·9
Be faithful	—	16·9	27·3	47·2
Be a housewife and a cook	—	26·2	—	48·1
Share sorrows, under- standing	17·6	—	12·2	—
Help him	—	10·0	—	17·0

In the next question (Q. 11) respondents were asked to say if a girl should have a career of her own after she marries. Of the African males, 48·8 per cent (including 3·3 per cent who qualified their answers: 'if no children') and of the British males, 18 per cent replied in the affirmative; 49·4 per cent of the British males said that their wife would work only if there were no children; if their work did not interfere with family life, or if money was needed. Of the African females, 68·6 per cent said 'Yes' and 8·8 per cent said that it would depend on the circumstances. Of the

Table 16

| | African students | | British students | |
	Males N=59	Females N=114	Males N=66	Females N=107
	%	%	%	%
Calm parties; reconcile them	25·4	20·5	20·9	31·8
Find the cause of the quarrel	22·03	4·6	6·0	—
Depends on the situation	—	—	16·4	6·5
Be impartial	25·4	15·2	9·0	—
Be on spouse's side	6·8	4·5	61·2	81·3
Keep on good terms with relatives	—	3·03	—	3·7
Call someone to settle it	16·9	4·5	—	—

British females, 13·9 per cent replied in the affirmative and 74·2 per cent would say 'Yes', only if there was no children, if their career would not interfere with their duties as a wife and a mother or if money was needed.

Respondents were also asked (Q. 12) how, in the event of their reply being in the affirmative, a woman can combine the duties as a wife and a mother with her career. African males and females repeated the question and said that they would combine career and house-work (20·7 and 30 per cent respectively). British males and females thought mainly that a career for the wife would not be possible with young children (70·4 and 43·6 per cent respectively for males and females). However, African males and females referred to a 'nurse' (37·9 and 38·6 per cent), to nurseries (17·2 and 16·9 per cent) and to servants (27·6 and 40 per cent) and relatives (17·2 and 9·2 per cent); in addition, 9·2 per cent of African females mentioned a part-time job. Among the British, 70·4 per cent of the males said again that it would not be possible for the wife to work if they had children; however, 37·1 per cent suggested a part-time job or some work which can be done at home; a few mentioned a nanny, a maid, or put the children in a nursery (all 3·7 per cent). Of the British females, 43·6 per cent thought it would not be possible to work with children, at least when they are young; 15·4 per cent would like to work, provided career does not interfere with their duties as a wife or a mother. Part-time work seems again to be the main solution (34·6 per cent), or a maid (9 per cent), a nanny (2·6 per cent), or a nursery (1·3 per cent); 3·8 per cent thought that the husband could help, and 6·4 per cent would try to combine both activities by cooking and looking after the house in the evening.

The respondents were also asked what careers they would like their children to follow (Q. 13). The percentages in Table 17

Table 17

	African students				British students			
	Males		Females		Males		Females	
	Boys	Girls	Boys	Girls	Boys	Girls	Boys	Girls
	N=61		N=119		N=63		N=109	
	%	%	%	%	%	%	%	%
Doctors	50·0	31·3	57·7	18·9	9·5	—	14·1	2·8
Nurses	—	33·3	—	48·0	—	9·5	—	6·5
Teachers	42·0	56·3	—	63·5	9·5	11·1	3·7	11·2
Engineers	22·9	—	33·0	—	—	—	—	—
Lawyers	16·7	—	27·1	—	—	—	—	—
Ministers of church	14·6	—	—	—	4·7	—	—	—
Farmers	27·0	—	—	—	—	—	—	—
Profession	—	—	—	—	9·5	—	13·1	7·5
University level	—	—	—	—	—	—	11·2	12·1

indicate the number of times particular careers were mentioned, relative to the size of the sample. But while the African males and females made direct answers, apart from 21·3 per cent of the males and 32 per cent of the females who said that their children would decide themselves what they want to do, the British group mainly left the choice of a career to their children (respectively 61·9 and 66·8 per cent for the males and females).

In the next question (Q. 14) Africans were asked if they felt entitled to marry more than one wife and the British males if they felt entitled to have women friends after they are married. This question was also more directly answered by the Africans, as the British were not sure about the meaning of the word 'friend'. Of the African males, 70·5 per cent answered 'No', and 29·5 per cent 'Yes': only one respondent said that he would be prepared to make additional marriage without his wife's consent. Among the British males, 19·7 per cent said 'No', 21·2 per cent 'Yes', and 59·1 per cent qualified their answers by 'if real friends' ... 'if friends of the wife' ... 'if platonic relationships'.

The females were also asked their attitudes (Q. 14), and the African females were not agreeable to their husbands having additional wives (95·7 per cent); only 4·3 per cent said 'Yes'. Of the British females, 24·3 per cent answered that they would be agreeable to their husbands having women friends; 12·2 per cent said 'No', but they mainly qualified their answers, an affirmative one depending on the kind of friendship it would be.

The next question (Q. 16) asked the men if they would be agreeable to their wife having male friends after they are married. This question was answered in the affirmative by 25·4 per cent of the African males and 18·2 per cent of the British males; 35·6 per cent of the Africans and 59·1 per cent of the British men said that their agreement would depend upon how 'friendship' was defined; 39 per cent of the African and 24 per cent of the British males said 'No'. Of the women, 38·1 per cent of the African and 26 per cent of the British answered in the affirmative. However, the African females gave mainly negative answers (60·3 per cent), and only seven out of the 126 (5·5 per cent) said that their answers would depend upon the definition of the word 'friendship'. Of the British females, 10·2 per cent only said 'No', but 67·6 per cent said that their agreement would depend on the kind of friendship it would be.

In the next question (Q. 17) respondents were asked if they considered it an advantage for a wife to be as well educated as her husband. Among the males, 74·6 per cent of the African and 75·8 per cent of the British considered it an advantage. Of the females, 81·3 per cent of the African and 89 per cent of the British considered it an advantage. Both groups of men and women seemed to think that for a wife to be as well educated as her husband would lead to better understanding (African males 45·8 per cent; African females 14 per cent; British males 25·8 per cent; British females 22·9 per cent) and it would help with the education of the children (African males 16·9 per cent; African females 11·2 per cent; British males 9·1 per cent; British females 14·7 per cent). African males and females mentioned that it would be economically beneficial (respectively 11·9 per cent and 15·9 per cent). The British respondents said also that a similar level of education between husband and wife would allow them to 'discuss' together and be an intellectual companion for each other (24·2 and 34·9 per cent respectively for males and females). Of the British males, 22·7 per cent, and of the females, 28 per cent mentioned also that they would have the same interests and feel equal (19·7 and 24·8 per cent).

Among those who mentioned that a same level of education would be a disadvantage (African males 22 per cent; females 14 per cent; British males 10·6 per cent; females 3·7 per cent), 13·6 per cent of the African males explained their answer by saying that the wife would not respect the husband or would not obey him (3·5 per cent) or would be too free (5·1 per cent). The African females gave the same reasons: lack of obedience (6·5 per cent) and of respect (5·6 per cent); they also mentioned that spouses would quarrel more often, the wife being able to argue (1·9 per cent). The British did not give any reasons for their negative answers; they only mentioned that intelligence was more important than education. Of the British males, 7·6 per cent, and of the females, 2·8 per cent said that it was both an advantage and a disadvantage, and 12·1 per cent of the males and 3·7 per cent of the females said that it was an advantage but not essential for the wife to be as well educated as her husband.

Both groups of women and men expected to share common interests with their spouses (Q. 18). African males thought that they would enjoy sport together (24·5 per cent), go to dance (22·6 per cent); they also mentioned films (13·2 per cent) and games (13·2 per cent). The African females mentioned mainly 'discussion' (26·7 per cent). The British group referred mainly to sports (28·8 per cent for the males; 37·6 per cent for the females), music (18·2 and 25·7 per cent), home and gardening (16·7 and 10·1 per cent), family (19·7 and 14·7 per cent), and theatre (18·2 and 14·3 per cent). Of this last group, 7·6 per cent of the males and 7·3 per cent of the females mentioned that they would not like to share all interests.

Summary and Discussion

In respect of the best age at which to get married, both groups are more or less in agreement, although the British males would postpone matrimony for two years longer than would the male Africans. Both samples of young men look for girls who are 'beautiful', but the British students apparently attach more importance than the Africans to 'intelligence'. Again, while both groups expect a prospective wife to be loving, the Africans look for domestic qualities and good manners and the British students for a sense of humour. The last-mentioned quality is also mentioned by the British girls—more frequently than any other attribute—and they also stress kindness and gentleness. Apparently, in contrast, although the African girls also want their husbands to be kind, gentle, and loving, they lay a lot of stress on good looks and education. The British girls emphasize their desire to be respected and treated as a partner and an equal as well as loved. For both samples of men, love and respect seem to be rather important, but whereas the British attach more importance to fidelity than to obedience, the Africans exactly reverse this order. Both male groups are broadly in agreement over how they would treat a wife. They stress their financial obligations, and the British students, both males and females, stress fidelity and loyalty. Whereas, however, both the African and the British girls emphasize their domestic obligations, the former group attaches more importance to the idea of obeying and respecting a husband than do the British girls.

The African group as a whole was much readier to contemplate the idea of married women working than were either the British men or women. It might appear, however, from the answers given that the negative reaction of the latter was conditioned more by the anticipated difficulty of providing care for the children while the mother was absent than by any other factor.

Similarly, in view of the ambiguity of the term 'friend', it is impossible adequately to compare attitudes to the idea of a husband's or a wife's relationship with a member of the opposite sex. Excepting that nearly a third of the African males apparently felt entitled to marry more than one wife, if they wished, what mainly emerges from responses to these particular questions is the wider meaning that the term 'friend' apparently had for the British men and women.

Evidently the desire for a home of their own is very strong among both British students and Africans. In the case, however, of the African group this apparent separation from relatives is not correlated with an equally strong allegiance to the spouse's point of view in opposition to them. Thus, relative to the number of responses given, only 6·8 per cent of the African men and 4·5 per cent of the women said that they would take their spouse's side. This is in contrast to 61·2 per cent of the British men and 81·3 per cent of the British women.

It may also be noted from Table 4 that in considering their choice of a spouse the British men and women attribute less influence to parents than do the African group. Africans and British are broadly in agreement over the significance of educational, religious, and tribal/national factors.

Although the statistical mean that indicates the number of children wanted is not representative of the whole sample of African men (as a large proportion of them answered by 'as many as God wants'), on the average the Africans hope for a slightly larger number of children, and they are also somewhat less disposed than the British men and women to regulate the size of the family.

CONCLUSIONS

Summarizing the data discussed, the present findings seem to confirm that in Freetown the attitude of educated young people towards marriage is strongly 'western'. Excepting that non-Creoles, more particularly girls, have a slightly more traditional idea of the marital role, the general outlook of Creoles and non-Creoles is virtually identical and bears on the whole very little resemblance to indigenous notions of marriage and family relationships. In other words, what appears to be crucial in this regard is not ethnic origin, but the fact that most of the individuals concerned have been educated to a relatively advanced level (by African standards) as well as being closely in touch with Christian institutions.

It is equally significant that the ideas of the Africans approximate closely European ideals of marriage as represented by a broadly comparable sample of British students. The only real difference is that the solidarity of husband and wife as a conjugal group is apparently less marked in the African case. Like the British students, the Africans expect man and wife to co-operate on a companionate basis, but they lay less stress on equality of status and on the importance of the spouses having intellectual and temperamental qualities in common.

BIBLIOGRAPHY

Baker, Tanya
   (1957) *Women's Elites in Western Nigeria*. (Unpublished MS, Department of Social Anthropology, University of Edinburgh.)
Bird, Mary
   (1958) *Social Change in Kinship and Marriage among the Yoruba of Western Nigeria*. (Unpublished Ph.D. thesis, University of Edinburgh.)
   (1964) 'Urbanisation, family and marriage in Western Nigeria', in *Centre of African Studies Proceedings*, Edinburgh.
Crabtree, A. I.
   (1950) *Marriage and Family Life among the Educated Africans in the Urban Areas of the Gold Coast*. (Unpublished M.Sc. thesis, University of London.)
Jahoda, Gustav
   (1958) 'Boys' images of marriage partners and girls' self-images in Ghana', *Sociologus*, vol. 8, pp. 155–69.
   (1959) 'Love, marriage, and social change: letters to the advice column of a West African newspaper', *Africa*, vol. 29, pp. 177–90.
Tardits, Claude
   (1958) *Porto Novo: les nouvelles générations africaines entre leurs traditions et l'occident*. The Hague.

Résumé

ATTITUDES ADOPTÉES EN SIERRA LEONE, PAR LA JEUNESSE INSTRUITE À L'ÉGARD DU MARIAGE ET DE LA FAMILLE

Les attitudes qu'adopte à l'égard du mariage et des relations conjugales l'élite d'Afrique Occidentale, sont elles représentatives d'une classe sociale particulière et sont elles comparables aux modèles européens de la famille?

Un questionnaire fut distribué dans des écoles secondaires de Freetown—Sierra Leone—parmi les élèves des classes terminales, afin de comparer les attitudes des Créoles, plus occidentalisés, et celles des Non-Créoles, originaires de l'intérieur du pays.

Créoles et Non-Créoles des deux sexes pensent que l'âge ideal pour se marier est 23 ou 24 ans. Les hommes Non-Créoles veulent des jeunes filles belles, bien élevées et bonnes femmes d'intérieur. Les jeunes filles, Créoles ou non, veulent des maris qui aient de l'éducation, soient bien élevés et aimants; les jeunes filles Non-Créoles attachent également de l'importance à la beauté et la fidélité. Religion et éducation influent sur le choix du conjoint. Les Non-Créoles mâles attendent respect surtout, amour et obéissance de la part de leur femme; leur principal devoir est d'ordre financier; la moitié des hommes accepterait que leur femme travaille et qu'elle ait des amis masculins et un tiers se sent libre d'avoir plusieurs épouses.

Les femmes attendent de leurs époux amour (les Créoles surtout), respect et d'être traitées avec gentillesse (les Non-Créoles surtout); leurs obligations sont d'abord domestiques; elles doivent aussi à leur mari obéissance (les Non-Créoles surtout), respect amour et loyauté. Les Créoles surtout pensent qu'une femme doit avoir un métier. Un tiers environ veut avoir des amis masculins (en pensant à des relations platoniques); la plupart sont fermement opposées à la polygamie.

Hommes et femmes sont contre la cohabitation avec leurs parents; dans le cas d'une querelle entre un des conjoints et les parents de l'autre ils seraient impartiaux.

Les jeunes filles Non-Créoles sont plus fermement opposées à la régulation des naissances que les Créoles; leur attitude est illustrée par celle des hommes Non-Créoles qui accepteront autant d'enfants que Dieu leur en enverra.

Un bon niveau d'éducation permet aux femmes de partager avec leur mari le même genre d'intérêts et aussi d'apporter un supplément d'argent donnant lieu à un niveau de vie plus élevé; cet intérêt pour le statut social est aussi révélé par le fait que Créoles et Non-Créoles veulent que leurs enfants soient docteurs, infirmières, notaires. . . .

La comparaison de l'échantillon africain à un échantillon d'étudiants d'université britannique montre que les Britanniques veulent se marier deux ans plus tard. Les hommes attachent plus d'importance à l'intelligence qu'à la beauté de leur future femme;

ils la veulent aimante mais préfèrent aux qualités domestiques un sens de l'humour, qui est aussi la première qualité réclamée par les étudiantes, ainsi que la fidélité; elles veulent être traitées en égales, respectées et aimées. Les étudiants mâles attachent plus d'importance à l'amour qu'au respect et à la fidélité qu'à l'obéissance de leur femme, que les Africains; ils mettent l'accent sur leurs obligations financières et les jeunes filles sur leurs obligations domestiques.

Les Britanniques s'opposent plus à ce que la femme travaille, à cause des enfants. Il est impossible de comparer les attitudes des deux groupes à propos des relations des conjoints avec des membres de l'autre sexe à cause de l'ambiguité du terme 'ami'. En cas de querelle entre l'un des conjoints avec les parents de l'autre les Britanniques soutiendraient plus leur conjoint que ne le feraient les Africains.

Africains et Britanniques s'accordent sur les influences respectives de l'éducation, de la religion et de la tribu ou nationalité sur le choix d'un conjoint mais l'influence des parents est moins grande pour les Britanniques. Les Africains veulent un peu plus d'enfants et sont moins disposés à réglementer la taille de la famille. Les deux groupes considèrent que l'éducation de la femme est un avantage et conduit à une meilleure compréhension des conjoints.

Une même éducation, chrétienne le plus souvent, fait assimiler aux Créoles et Non-Créoles les valeurs occidentales. La solidarité du couple est moins marquée chez les Africains et les Britanniques insistent plus sur l'égalité et les qualités intellectuelles communes aux époux.

VI. EDUCATION AND FAMILY LIFE IN THE DEVELOPMENT OF CLASS IDENTIFICATION AMONG THE YORUBA

BARBARA B. LLOYD

Class consciousness as known in Europe and America is not an outstanding feature of contemporary life in Western Nigeria. A cultivated feeling of classlessness may indeed be necessary to ensure government stability in the present situation of marked contrasts in wealth and privilege.[1] Despite apparent adult disregard of class differences, a study of the child-rearing methods employed by well-educated Yoruba mothers indicates the emergence in the next generation of a fairly homogeneous group more distinct from their countrymen than their own educated parents, who had themselves been recruited rather widely from the population. The home and family life, the schools and educational opportunities, as well as the attitudes and values which the elite parent offers his offspring to assure him a bright future, will most probably produce adults quite different in experience, training, and motivation from the majority of their contemporaries. The contrast is heightened here by emphasis on the comparison of Yoruba home life in a traditional quarter of Ibadan with that of the well-educated professional group.[2,3] The sizeable middle

[1] See P. C. Lloyd, *infra*, p. 328 ff.

[2] The research reported here was carried out between November 1961 and June 1963 and supported by Grant M-4865 of the National Institute of Mental Health to the University of Chicago, Dr. R. A. LeVine, chief investigator, and by the Ford Foundation through grants to the Universities of Chicago and Ibadan. Miss V. Damis and Mrs. O. Akinkugbe gave valuable service in conducting the structured interviews. Drs. P. Rosenblatt, Leigh M. Triandis, and Mr. A. Chalmers offered helpful criticisms of early versions of the paper.

[3] Most of the data presented in the paper are drawn from structured interviews concerning maternal attitudes towards family, marriage, and the raising of children carried out among sixty Yoruba mothers of five-year-olds. The thirty educated mothers were selected from a large number replying to a questionnaire designed to recruit educated women, those of secondary schooling or its equivalent, with children aged zero to three years for a study of physical growth. A traditional quarter of Ibadan had been surveyed before the medical study began,

category of petty officialdom and small businessmen is largely ignored.

FAMILY AND HOME LIFE

Children of the educated elite are taller, heavier, healthier,[4] and begin schooling earlier and with more skills than the products of illiterate or traditional Yoruba homes. These are the most obvious results of superior housing, diet, medical care—in fact, of privilege. Of interest in this analysis are the social and psychological aspects of home and family life which set these children apart from their peers and which make the Nigerian situation unusual.

More so, perhaps, than in industrial nations, the educated Nigerian seeks his career in the professions or in the governmental bureaucracy. Unlike western middle-class suburban-dwelling children, however, these youngsters are not ignorant of their fathers' occupations. Due in part to the residental patterns set down during the colonial era, officers are housed near their work. Thus, today's Nigerian university staff live on the university grounds, senior government officials in residence areas near their offices, graduate teachers on their school compounds, and even among private lawyers it is common for the family to live on the first floor of a two-story building which houses the father's chambers on the ground floor. The children may go to school by car, together with their parents, who leave home for work at the same time in the morning, and in the early afternoon return together for dinner. On Sundays a busy father sometimes takes the children with him when he goes to work in his office for a few hours in the afternoon. Thus, elite children become familiar

---

and it was thus possible to select children for the growth study and mothers of five-year-olds from our own census data. It was not possible to select at random mothers of five-year-olds from the larger samples, as it was scarcely possible to fill the quotas of each group. Throughout the educated mothers are referred to as either the elite or educated group, while those from the traditional quarter are referred to as uneducated, illiterate, or traditional.

[4] The medical data is supplied by Dr. M. D. Janes of the Institute of Child Health, University of Ibadan, and is based upon the larger samples of elite and traditional children described in footnote 3.

with the work of government officials, lawyers, professors, and teachers, and through observation learn the requirements of the roles they may expect one day to perform.

The pressure to provide funds to educate her siblings and later her own children sends educated Yoruba mothers to work in great numbers. Only a very few wives of top-level civil servants and politicians can afford the luxury of staying at home.[5] The majority, who have been trained as nurses and teachers, carry on their professional activities, despite the demanding hours required. Unlike the illiterate or semi-educated women who trade and can set their own hours and locations, often taking the baby along with them, the educated woman is a slave to hours, which, as one nurse assured me, must have been devised for unmarried nursing sisters resident at the hospital. Yet, difficulties notwithstanding, 88 per cent of the Nigerian, Western Region, government nursing staff is married.

The employment of teenage, primary-school educated, nurse-girls, and the profusion and popularity of nursery schools are the immediate consequences of mothers working away from home at least six hours of the day. Unlike the traditional Yoruba family, which lives in a lineage-based compound housing fathers, sons, wives, and children, the elite nuclear family lives in employer-provided quarters isolated from relatives, or in modern houses in the newer residential parts of Ibadan. When relatives live with the elite family they are often children pursuing an education.[6] In the majority of homes adult kinsmen, particularly grandparents, are frequent visitors, but are not often permanent guests. This is marked in Ibadan, which recruits professional people throughout the region. In the absence of relatives to mind their small children, working mothers employ young unmarried girls, who come to Ibadan from the provinces after primary schooling. Mothers who feel uneasy about leaving their children of three years or more

---

[5] Twenty-four of the thirty educated mothers were in full-time employment at the time of the interview.

[6] Twenty-seven permanent visitors were reported by elite mothers. Two-thirds of these were children and adolescent relatives, as well as three young adults and six adults of the grandparental generation, one a grandfather staying with the family until father returned from overseas duty.

with these semi-educated girls, or who wish to provide a more stimulating environment, send their offspring to nursery schools.

A surprising feature of educated families is their large size. While educated women in other parts of the world have tended to limit the number of children they bear, elite families of four are modal in this sample, and completed families of six children are common in Ibadan.[7] Thus, without further recruitment from outside its own ranks, the educated elite may well, if children reach the educational standard of their parents, double in a generation.

The large family with an ample supply of brothers and sisters is a boon to the elite child, who must often find his playmates among his siblings. Not only is the elite nuclear family isolated in a social sense from relatives, but it is also physically isolated. Typical of this isolation are the government housing areas, where homes are surrounded by large gardens. Children walking just a few houses from home along the tarred roads which cut through these areas risk the hazards of fast cars, as there are no pavements. In their concern for safety, parents may restrict children to their own gardens or those of the adjoining houses.

Children who live in the more densely settled parts of Ibadan, rather than in the spaciously laid out reservations, face another kind of isolation. In town, parents take pains to see that their children play only with other children from 'good homes', and they point out that children learn bad habits easily by imitation. Thus, naughty, stubborn, rude, obscene, and dirty children must be avoided. Rules are strictly enforced, and some children are even restricted to their family apartments and veranda on the first floor, if the children on the ground floor of the building in which they live are not thought suitable companions. Though it is often maintained by the educated Yoruba that social class is a Western concept with limited applicability in Africa, it does appear that

[7] Though families reported here are not complete, one can compare the mean of 4·7 children reported by educated mothers and 3·2 reported by traditional women. Though educated women tend to marry later it is difficult to determine whether the difference in numbers of children is a reflection of differential survival or of the six-year mean difference in age of mothers. Considerations are further complicated by the generally unreliable nature of illiterate women's memory of dates.

elite children are made aware of social differences which some might describe as class distinctive.

Life is not dreary for the elite child, despite parental rules for choosing playmates. Though neighbours may be unavailable, there are siblings and the children of family friends. Children often attend and play host at elaborate birthday parties. They are taken along to play with the children when parents visit their friends. Parents take care to see that their children learn manners appropriate for these occasions, i.e. to say thank you, sit quietly when necessary, and not to ask for too many things.

A child reared in a traditional family compound would find such social life strange and unfamiliar. All the compound children play together and are expected to get along well with one another. A mother who tried to choose her child's companions would be considered unsociable and rude. The compound child is seldom alone and is thought to be odd or preoccupied with spirit friends when seeking solitude; the elite child, however, is actively encouraged by his parents to learn to play by himself. Elite mothers believe solitary play gives a child time to think, to learn skills such as drawing or painting, and perhaps, most importantly, from a mother's point of view, it teaches him not to fret when there is no one about who can play with him.

The family car offers ease of movement and tempers the isolation of the nuclear family. Parents frequently visit friends in Ibadan, go to Lagos to shop or see people, and usually maintain active ties with their home towns. Residential mobility is also a feature of elite family life. Since occupation and dwelling are linked, and it is common for children to be born in the years when a father is becoming established, children move about frequently in their early years. One-fifth of the elite five-year-olds were born in England while both parents were studying. Frequently the child born abroad is boarded in a foster home until studies are completed. Children of civil servants often live with their parents outside Ibadan before starting school, but once their education has begun parents try to ensure continuity. This may necessitate children living with relatives in Ibadan, staying at boarding schools, or for mother and children, occasionally even

M

father and children, to remain in Ibadan while the other parent is on transfer in another part of the country. Naturally permanent posts in Ibadan are sought. Though a traditional father might be employed outside Ibadan, his wives and their children would usually remain in his compound. Thus, compound children of five may have travelled no more than a mile or two from home.

Changes in home life and ways of raising children are apparent to most Nigerians. Uneducated mothers reported these changes mainly in terms of child health, and some spoke of the modern world as that of the hospital. Among educated mothers, the most frequently noted change is that in the atmosphere of the home. Of course, some educated women are themselves from educated homes, and these people are less often struck with modern innovations. Even when the overall change is only slight, from the stiffness of a Victorian, mission-patterned home, to current relaxed family life, educated mothers believe that today's children are more at ease with their fathers than they had been.[8] The transition from the traditional home in the parental generation to that of the current elite group is more sharply marked, and mothers mention the greater physical amenities now available to them. The modern educated father is reported to actively seek a warm, friendly relationship with his children; he plays ball with them, reads to them, and if need be, while living abroad, will help to feed and look after them. Generally, this attitude is not achieved by completely giving in to children's whims. Educated parents still expect children to be obedient, e.g. to fetch something when sent, but consideration is given to what the children are doing at the time they are summoned, and if the parent's request can be delayed children may be allowed to complete their activity.

Elite children still receive spankings and even beatings, though discipline is less harsh than in the traditional family. A few educated mothers have even mentioned that, contrary to traditional practice, their husbands refuse to spank the children, and thus they must be the strict parent in the family. Mothers take care

---

[8] Nineteen out of thirty reports of elite women include mention of changes of patterns discipline or the approachability of fathers, factors described by the phrase 'atmosphere in the home'.

to see that their servants never use physical punishments in their absence, but wait instead until the parents return to report any misdeeds of the children. Visiting grandparents would be allowed to discipline children, but it seems an almost universal complaint that they only spoil their grandchildren.

SCHOOLS AND EDUCATIONAL OPPORTUNITY

Membership in the elite is currently determined primarily by education. Entry into the governmental and educational bureaucracies, in which the majority of educated people find employment, is relatively open to those with the essential academic qualifications. As rank is largely determined by education at the time of entry, promotion is mainly by seniority. Though private business and the independent professions of law and medicine offer greater opportunity for non-academic abilities and the manipulation of influence, fewer positions are as yet established in these spheres. Generally the elite are not extensive land or factory owners, though they may have some rent-producing residential property. Thus, an elite child's principal inheritance is the education which his parents can provide.

Familiar with Nigerian educational institutions, elite mothers see their task as taking an interest in their children's schooling, giving help when necessary, and continuously offering support and encouragement. To improve their children's creative and intellectual capacities, parents are prepared to spend as much as their financial means permit in order to provide teachers, books, toys, and recreation. Mothers take special care to answer children's questions, since the belief is widespread that ignoring questions from children stifles their curiosity. Though academic achievement is the chief concern of an elite family, a majority of children will be taught additional skills. Some mothers mentioned plans for music lessons, others reported that older children were involved in the Scouting movement, while a number of mothers hoped their children could have swimming lessons.

To the young child in an elite home, going to school is often seen as a privilege to be won, especially where both parents and older siblings leave home together each morning. Though 4·2 years is the mean entrance age, one mother reported that a daughter began nursery school eight months after her second birthday. It is not unusual for children over three years to attend regularly. The nurseries may be attached to a private, fee-paying primary school, be part of a demonstration school attached to a Teacher Training College, or informally organized in the home of a trained Nigerian teacher or expatriate wife. A majority of the children attending nursery schools come from the homes of the elite, but a number of expatriate children are also enrolled, often affording Nigerian children additional opportunity to learn English—beyond that acquired listening to parents who converse with ease in both English and Yoruba.

Parents often teach their children numbers and the alphabet, even though they attend nursery school. A large number of elite children are registered in private, fee-paying schools, often with mixed classes of expatriate and Nigerian children. The Western Region provides free primary schools, and children from educated homes do attend them, either of necessity (with four to six children, a number of whom may be enrolled in secondary schools, fees mount up) or from genuinely democratic sentiment; but parents strive to provide additional training. Classes in state primary schools are larger, the teachers less thoroughly trained, and the curriculum narrow, as supplementary educational materials are expensive, and in short supply. In educated homes tutors are frequently employed to give two-hour lessons in the house each weekday afternoon, or parents themselves may regularly coach their offspring. With few exceptions, one parent, usually the mother, checks each child's homework daily. Though many parents believe they should not make corrections, they will give additional work in areas in which the child is weak, thus helping him to correct his own mistakes.

By contrast, traditional families send their children to school only when they are six or seven years old, and then with little preparation. They attend nearby state schools, to which they walk each morning. Even in the absence of fees, it may be difficult for parents to provide the requisite books and uniforms. Almost all boys attend school, though in a poor Moslem home there are still doubts about sending girls to school. Parents can offer little assistance with school work; sometimes they do manage to provide money for lessons, but most often tutoring, if any, would come from older children living in the compound.

In all homes primary school performance is a major concern. The competitive process of secondary school entrance selection sharpens this interest. No secondary education is free, though the older schools offer scholarships which are awarded on the basis of test performance, apparently without consideration of family means. Despite the formidable barrier of nearly one hundred pounds a year expenses for fees, board, books, and uniforms, there are more applicants than places in better boarding grammar schools. The well-established schools, the state-managed colleges, and older mission or church grammar schools recruit the brightest students, or rather those with the best performance on the common entrance examinations tests, largely based on primary school subject achievement. Though fees vary little, the quality of education is not constant, in part reflecting the finances available to a school. While Government Colleges may receive several hundred pounds a year to spend on school libraries, independent schools often have less than fifty pounds. Educated parents are acutely aware of these differences and do everything possible to ensure their children places in the best schools. Children are sometimes specifically coached for the common entrance examinations.

For many years a very small group of Yoruba children have been sent to Public Schools in England. Whether the opening of the International School at the University of Ibadan (with its close ties to Prince Charles's school, Gordonstoun in Scotland) will reduce the flow remains to be seen. From the press announcements that the son of the Western Region's Premier will be the first Nigerian to attend Eton, one may judge that the famous English Public Schools are still attractive to the elite.

University education for their offspring is the goal of most elite parents, and two-thirds of the mothers interviewed stated it explicitly, while the others mentioned professions requiring extensive study. Though such aspirations at first seem high, they become readily understandable in the light of the salary scale automatically offered to the graduate and the rapid increase in secondary education throughout the Western Region. Unemployment, already common among persons of primary and secondary modern education, is beginning to affect grammar school products as well. A university degree thus becomes necessary to assure occupational success.

Sentiment is strong for allowing children to follow their own inclinations and abilities in the particular career they choose. There appears to be little occupational prejudice, though great emphasis is given to the level of education sought for one's children. Medicine, the most popular choice, was mentioned by eight mothers, three of whom were reporting their children's own preference. Mothers' ambitions for their daughters seem as high as for sons. One mother expressed, with feministic fervour, the wish for her daughter to qualify as a physician, while another hoped a daughter might follow her father's medical career, as their son had already indicated that his interests lay elsewhere.

Uneducated mothers have difficulty verbalizing their educational and occupational aspirations for their children. They appear quite unaware of the expanding educational opportunities available in Nigeria. Most mothers say only that they want their children to be good people and to get an unspecified 'higher qualification'. When pressed, they would often reply that they wanted their children to attend a secondary school or go overseas to England for further study. These are unrealistic aims in terms of family resources, though for an exceptional child an entire compound might manage to provide financial support. Only two traditional mothers were explicit in mentioning a university education. On the vocational side, nursing or office work are seen along with medicine and law as occupations which would afford their children, and themselves, indirectly, a good life.

Unclear in their view of the educational system, illiterate mothers are at a loss to know how to help their offspring succeed academically. When questioned, about half say that they would pray to God and make certain to get the medicine necessary to ensure success, though a number do mention verbally encouraging their children, buying them books, but also praying for success.

Prayer may seem an odd approach to education, but in fact, traditional parents have little else to give their children. Lacking capital for extensive trading or the educational qualifications to obtain well-paid employment, they are unable to finance costly education. They must be satisfied if their children can attend primary school and may hope to be able to finance an apprenticeship or secondary modern school. In addition, some Moslem parents provide lessons in the Koran, while others hope to arrange lessons in useful crafts, such as sewing and raffia weaving. Unfortunately, the careful primary school training provided by elite parents ensures that the Government's limited financial assistance for secondary education in the form of subsidies and scholarships goes primarily to the elite child rather than to the most needy, those from uneducated homes.

VALUES, ATTITUDES, AND MOTIVATION

The first section described the patterns of home life among the Yoruba elite and contrasted them with the traditional compound. In the second the techniques employed by elite parents seeking privileged status for their children through education were considered. Throughout, parental attitudes and values were set forth descriptively without any attempt to relate them to theories of child development.

A general feature of elite family life which emerges is that, despite the pursuit of professional careers by mothers, as well as by fathers, a very strong desire for children, and a deep concern for their children's intellectual growth and achievement, exists. This aspect of the elite family will be considered more fully in the discussion of motivational systems.

Training in the areas of dependence, aggression, and sexuality are all important in any consideration of personality development. However, the most relevant social motive for our discussion of class and social change is, no doubt, achievement. Thus, the analysis of motivational systems among children from elite and traditional homes is limited to achievement, and focuses, in the absence of measures of the children's motive strength, on the familial antecedents known to produce differences in motive strength.

David McClelland's work dominates current thought on achievement motivation. He has sought to explain the modern technological and economic transformation (described by Max Weber as the Protestant Revolution, when analysing the change from faith in the Catholic Church to reliance on oneself for evidence of salvation) in terms of changes in the motivational systems of individuals. Modern capitalistic, entrepreneurial behaviour is interpreted by McClelland as dependent upon a strong need achievement; i.e. expression of an internal drive and emotional concern with success in competition with some inner standard of excellence. A great deal of research has been concerned with the fundamental problem of assessing achievement need using various projective techniques (McClelland *et al.*, 1953) and from behavioural indices (McClelland *et al.*, 1958).

Of primary interest here are studies seeking the familial and social structural antecedents of the achievement motive. Two aspects of the socialization process—training in achievement and in independence—have proved to be important in a number of studies (Rosen, 1962; Winterbottom, 1958). Direct reward for trying to succeed, guidance and encouragement in solving problems, and maintaining high standards, as well as reward for successful efforts and punishment for failure, are achievement training factors related to strong need achievement. Training in self-reliance and independence, with demand optimally occurring about eight years of age, are held to benefit achievement motivation by strengthening the tendency to persist in the pursuit of excellence on one's own. In an attempt to reconcile certain inconsistencies in efforts to relate independence training and achievement, Argyle and Robinson (1962) have suggested that the process be viewed more generally as a form of identification which results in the learning and internalization of parental demands for achievement. Thus, both overprotective and unsuccessful parents, themselves poor models, would serve as producers of low-achievement motivation in their offspring.

At a structural level, studies of western class differences support findings from individual difference studies. Middle class, as well as certain highly mobile ethnic groups, appear to produce strong achievement motivation through placing stress upon self-reliance, autonomy and reward for achievement, and punishment for failure (Rosen and d'Andrade, 1959; Rosen, 1961). Further, the values of middle-class mothers stress individual rather than group obligations, the possibility of manipulating the world to their advantage and the necessity of present sacrifice to obtain future goals (Strodtbeck, 1958). Finally, there is evidence that a more egalitarian power structure within the family, where a father allows his sons autonomy, is also conducive to heightened achievement motivation. Before proceeding to look at elite and traditional child-training practices in respect of these dimensions, it is especially interesting in the context of the seminar to examine the empirical evidence supporting the assertion that greater achievement motivation produces greater social mobility (Crockett, 1962).

A review of the preceding sections indicates that life in the elite home approximates, in many respects, to the high-achievement-producing western middle-class home. The stress on learning to amuse oneself, and the importance given to children's own inclinations in the choice of career, are evidence of maternal concern for self-reliance and independence. The traditional authoritarian Yoruba father disappears too in the educated family. Life seems geared to standards of excellence, with children's academic performance the central issue in many families. Long-range goals are evident in parental orientation to a university career and, more immediately, qualifying examinations. Belief in the ability to control one's fate also flourishes in elite homes where health is managed with medical advice and necessary qualifications gained through planning and the resources to procure any aid which is necessary.

By contrast, uneducated mothers find they must often resort to prayer as the only method available for problem solving. Compound children are treated as a family group, with little stress on individual development. Whereas in western society we expect sibling rivalry to occur, traditional Yoruba expect that only children, or the children of a man's sole wife, will feel unhappy that they have no half-brothers and sisters. It is a form of childish abuse to mention that another has no half-siblings.[9] The uneducated may have long-range goals, but as these wishes do not take the form of articulable educational or occupational standards or aims, it is doubtful whether they are learned by their children. Also it is unlikely that uneducated women can serve as effective, successful, modern models for children growing up in a society where education is a prime determinant of status.

A reliable difference in the reward pattern of the two groups emerges from the interviews.[10] In answer to the question, 'What do you do when your five-year-old brings home a good report or will in future, if he's not yet at school?', almost all (29/30) elite mothers report either praising the child or giving him a tangible reward, with half employing both methods. The dominant traditional response (20/30) is to thank God or feel happy, though the remaining ten mothers do mention praising the child or giving him something. The response of praying to thank God for success is consistent with uneducated mothers' views of God as the source of academic achievement. The theme expressing personal satisfaction repeats the notion of an occupational choice designed to ensure the mother future comfort also.

Punishment for academic failure does not present clear-cut differences between the groups or strong evidence to support the hypothesis that high-achievement mothers punish failure more. Among elite mothers, five found it inconceivable that their children should fail to do well. The remaining twenty-five mothers made seventeen replies, which could be classed as punitive—scolding, depriving of privilege, or using physical punishment. Some mothers made more than one reply, and these, though not classifiable as punishment, include encouraging to do better, correcting errors, and seeking the cause of failure, and are probably related to achievement. Among uneducated mothers, nineteen reported using punitive measures when their children performed poorly

[9] Uneducated women report favouring polygamy in order to spare their children this abuse.

[10] Significant at $<0\cdot005$ using Fisher's exact test (Finney, *et al.*, 1963).

and five reported offering encouragement either alone or with punishment.

A measure of concern with achievement and maternal involvement in it may be drawn from reported ages of, and maternal efforts towards, walking and talking. The difficulties illiterate women face in estimating time should be taken into account. The sample of elite children for whom we have mothers' direct observations is twenty-four, as six babies were living with English foster mothers when these events occurred. The mean age, among elite children, was 12·3 months for walking and 14·3 for saying a few words.[11] Though only fourteen elite mothers reported encouraging their children to walk, the other ten report a mean age of 11·5, and thus, perhaps the child learned to walk prior to maternal expectation and, consequently, no help was thought necessary. Half the educated mothers report deliberately talking to their babies to encourage speech. Children from traditional homes are reported to say a few words at 15·1 months and walk at a mean age of 17·1 months. Two-thirds of these mothers report doing nothing to encourage walking, though a few mention supplying pushcarts for their children to play with, using magical methods, or allowing other children to teach the baby. Only six uneducated women reported deliberately encouraging the child to talk, and this difference is significant in the expected direction.[12] One can only speculate on why compound children walk so much later. Some mothers did report deliberately not encouraging their children's development as a means to delay renewed marital relations and pregnancy. Carrying on the back may interfere with children's practice in walking.

Though the evidence for stronger achievement motivation among elite children presented here is by no means conclusive, it is all in the expected direction. Examining the evidence presented throughout, it seems reasonable to conclude that the children

[11] Cattell's report of mothers' estimates of a few spoken words at 11 months and Shirley's observations placing the date at about 60 weeks offers some encouragement as to the validity of the mothers' reports despite the known difficulties in defining a 'few spoken words'.
[12] Significant at the 0·025 level using Fisher's exact test.

reared in educated homes will be different in experience, training, and motivation from those raised in a traditional Yoruba home. The orientation and practices of elite mothers are similar to those of achievement-producing western middle-class mothers. But a troublesome question remains—and that concerns the motivational system of the elite parents themselves. Judging from both educated mothers' own comments and a comparison of the two forms of home life presented here, many aspects of the contemporary elite family are new to Yoruba society. How, then, were these elite parents, presumably high-achievement people, produced?

One place to search for an answer may lie in examining the extent to which individuals were traditionally encouraged to compete with and be concerned with inner standards of excellence.

In most towns Yoruba men could distinguish themselves in political–military and economic affairs. However, with the exception of Ibadan, which developed from a war camp, some proportion of political power, titles, was usually inherited through a man's lineage. Even in royal lineages, however, succession was not assured by primogeniture, and a man still had to contest for positions with other family members. To gain titles which were unrestricted to particular lineages, men had to win popular support as well as demonstrate prowess. Though success in trade depended upon personal skills, such as knowing when to buy and how to arrange credit, western notions of cut-throat competition and underselling are alien. To draw business, traders depended upon their personal attractiveness as well as on any economic advantage they might offer their customers. Thus, men actively competed for wealth, status, and prestige, but skill in trade, war, and politics alone did not guarantee fulfilment of their aims. Success depended to a considerable degree on their interpersonal capacities in attracting business or in gaining group support, and usually, too, the backing of one's family. Thus, traditional society provided scope for individual incentive and achievement—the title and wealth belong to the man who gained it—though it was seen to reflect also on his supporters and kin, and in a sense to depend upon them. Failure was tempered by belief in a personal destiny (*ipin ori*) determined before birth, but human responsibility through character (similar to the Protestant concept of salvation) left ample scope for individual achievement.

While strong achievement motivation may not be new among the Yoruba, it would seem that the traditional form was fused with what is often referred to as an affiliative motive. Certainly the desire for competitive success, perhaps with an internal standard of excellence, existed in traditional society, though its attainment was dependent upon the ability to manage a quasi-dependence on other people as well as on individual skills in manipulating the material world. Notions of achievement, independence, and affiliation may need to be recombined and greater stress placed on the social forms of achievement in order to explain the traditional means to achieve and the dimensions of traditional achievement motivation.

If one accepts the idea that training in childhood lays the foundation for adult motivation, one expects that traditional methods of training for achievement will emphasize affiliation. Our observations support this conjecture. Children living in a compound are expected to get along with everyone, in contrast to the somewhat isolative elite childhood. Goals for traditional children are presented in social form, 'to make mother happy', or to provide for her. Whether this desire to please others and gain their affection can be internalized lies beyond the scope of this paper. One may reasonably conclude, however, that life in the elite home is probably producing children with an achievement motive new to Yoruba society. Without overstating the case, or rushing to predict tremendous technological and economic changes when the present generation of elite children come of age, certain changes may be considered.

The decision of the Nigerian Government to raise the required retirement age in the civil service from 55 to 65 may be related to elite affiliative patterns. With postponed retirement, elite parents will be able to finance the education of almost all their children. Thus, the new generation will not be called upon to educate their young siblings, as their own parents are required to do. Whether more distant relatives will benefit, or whether the situation will reinforce the more individualistic less affiliative, achievement training of the nuclear family cannot be predicted with certainty, though it would appear to reduce the conflict traditional child training with stresses on affiliation and achievement might engender.

A remaining point which might be raised against the assertion that children of the educated elite will, when their generation reaches maturity, constitute a distinct social group, perhaps a class, concerns the samples from which mothers were interviewed. Admittedly, the samples of mothers whose responses are presented here come from extreme sections of Yoruba society, and the middle group of clerks, prosperous traders, and primary school teachers has been omitted. This selection was deliberate, designed to highlight differences and discover trends, not to serve as a representative sample of contemporary Nigerian society. The uneducated group is treated as a baseline for change, while the educated elite are viewed as furnishing models for aspiring Nigerians. However, the current salary structure separates the middle group sharply from the university graduates and professionals, thus making an elite style of life, distinctive and difficult for the partially educated group to attain.

One final question concerns the need to stress the privilege of the educated group in view of the high mobility of Nigerian society and particularly in the light of the Western Region Government's attempts to provide greater educational opportunity for all, i.e. free primary schooling and a vastly extended programme of secondary education. Though planners often intend that greater state support will foster more universal access to education, studies in England indicate that since secondary-school fees were abolished the proportion of students from working-class origins has risen only slightly, and may be counterbalanced by decreasing opportunities for mobility outside of education as the occupational sphere places greater stress on the qualifications for entry (Little and Westergaard, 1964). Besides, there is ample evidence of the permanence of early learning. Thus, even where children of less-privileged background succeed in gaining the necessary educational qualifications, they may discover that the attitudes, values, and motives of the elite group still set them apart.

BIBLIOGRAPHY

Argyle, M., and Robinson, P.
    (1962) 'Two origins of Achievement Motivation.' *British Journal of Social & Clinical Psychology*, vol. 1, 2, pp. 107–20.
Carmichael, L. (ed.)
    (1954) *Manual of Child Psychology* (2nd Edition), New York.
Crockett, H. J.
    (1962) 'The achievement motive and differential occupational mobility in the United States.' *American Sociological Review*, vol. 27, pp. 191–204.
Finney, D. J., Latsha, R., Bennett, B. M., and Hsu, P.
    (1963) *Tables for testing significance in a 2 × 2 contingency table.* Cambridge.
Idowu, E. B.
    (1962) *Olodumare, God in Yoruba Belief.* London.
Little, A., and Westergaard, J.
    (1964) 'The trend of class differentials in educational opportunity in England and Wales.' *British Journal of Sociology*, vol. 15, pp. 301–16.
McClelland, D. C., Atkinson, J. W., Clark, R. A., and Lowell, E. L.
    (1953) *The Achievement Motive.* New York.
McClelland, D. C., Baldwin, A. L., Bronfenbrenner, U., and Strodtbeck, F. L.
    (1958) *Talent and Society.* New York.
Rosen, B. C.
    (1961) 'Family Structure and achievement motivation.' *American Sociological Review*, vol. 26, pp. 203–11.
    (1962) 'Socialization and achievement motivation in Brazil.' *American Sociological Review*, vol. 27, pp. 611–24.
Rosen, B. C., and d'Andrade, R.
    (1959) 'The psychosicial origins of achievement motivation.' *Sociometry*, vol. 22, pp. 185–218.
Strodtbeck, F. L.
    (1958) 'Jewish and Italian immigration and subsequent status mobility', in McClelland *et al. Talent and Society.*
Winterbottom, Marian R,
    (1958) 'The relation of need achievement to learning experiences in independence and mastery', in Atkinson, J. W. (ed.) *Motives in Fantasy, action and society.* Princeton.

Résumé

L'ENSEIGNEMENT ET LA VIE DE FAMILLE PAR RAPPORT AU DÉVELOPPEMENT DE CONSCIENCE DE CLASSE PARMI LES YORUBA

Quoiqu'il y a, en générale, une absence de conscience de classe dans la vie sociale actuelle au Nigéria Occidentale, des interviews des mères instruites Yoruba soutiennent l'hypothèse que dans une génération un groupe se dégagera, distinctif par ses attitudes, ses valeurs, ses motifs d'action.

L'examen de la vie familiale et domestique indique que les modèles traditionnels, où plusieurs femmes habitent la concession ('compound') familiale, organisées selon les principes d'âge et de durée de mariage, ont été remplacées, dans le cas de l'élite instruite, par les familles monogamiques, physiquement mobiles, mais isolées. Quoique la plupart des femmes instruites travaillent comme professeurs ou infirmières, laissant leurs enfants sous la garde des bonnes d'enfants adoléscentes et semi-instruites, les familles sont grandes, avec une moyenne de 4 enfants. Par contraste à l'enfant grégaire de la concession, l'enfant de l'élite est isolé. Il assiste souvent aux parties et on lui enseigne, avec soin, la politesse, mais il doit apprendre, au même temps, à jouer tout seul, ou avec ses frères et ses soeurs quand il n'y a pas de camarades convenables. Le père sévère de la concession traditionnelle dont le salon était un lieu sacré a été remplacé par le père élite qui cherche les rélations amicales avec ses enfants. Les mères élites, quoiqu'elles ne sont plus sévères avec leurs enfants, disent toujours qu'elles exigent l'obéissance, en considérant, au même temps, les propres intérêts de l'enfant.

L'enseignement dans les familles instruites suit de très près le même modèle. Puisque l'élite est déterminée, dans une grande mesure, par l'enseignement, les parents ont de très hautes aspirations pour leurs enfants, désirant, pour la plupart, qu'ils fassent l'université. Les enfants peuvent choisir leurs propres carrières et professions, mais on laisse très peu au hasard. Quoique l'enseignement élémentaire est gratuit dans la région, il y a toujours un grand nombre de concurrents pour les places dans les meilleures écoles secondaires et les parents de l'élite s'intéressent beaucoup au progrès de leurs enfants. Ils emploient souvent les précepteurs pendant les dernières années de l'enseignement élémentaire, pour préparer les enfants au concours d'entrée à l'école secondaire, et depuis le début des cours élémentaires, quelqu'un, très souvent la mère, surveille les devoirs. D'autre part, les enfants des mères illetrées, confuses elles-mêmes par le système d'enseignement, ne vont pas à l'école, même à l'âge obligatoire de 6 ans. La plupart des enfants de l'élite vont à l'école maternelle dès l'âge de 3 ans. Or, bien que le Gouvernement tâche de plus en plus de fournir les opportunités d'enseignement, les enfants des familles instruites peuvent mieux en profiter.

Une étude très brève de la théorie psychologique contemporaine de la nature des changements technologiques et les motifs d'accomplissement souligne l'importance du développement de l'indépendance, d'après les modèles qui ont réussi dans un milieu où on estime les rélations familiales égalitaires, et la résponsabilité pour son propre destin. De ses notions occidentales qui accentuent les pouvoirs et les motifs d'action individuels se détachent les modèles d'accomplissement de la tradition Yoruba, qui soulignent l'importance de l'attrait personnel et de la capacité de s'entendre avec les autres, aussi bien que de la pénétration commerciale et de la prouesse militaire. Un bréf résumé de l'étude de la vie domestique élite et traditionnelle suggère que les enfants des familles instruites jouissent d'une mode de vie qui promettrait des buts élevés d'accomplissement – système différent de motifs d'action de ce qu'on inculque dans la concession familiale où le 'moi' est soumis au groupe selon les principes, nettement définies, de supériorité.

N

VII. PARENTÉ ET CLASSE SOCIALE À PORTO-NOVO

CLAUDE TARDITS

Les faits rapportés ici proviennent d'une enquête fait en 1955 au Dahomey, à Porto-Novo. Son objectif était d'analyser la situation économique et sociale des élites africaines modernes dans cette cité.[1] Il est donc possible que les changements intervenus depuis, en particulier l'accession du pays à l'indépendance, aient modifié les rapports entre les éléments de la population que nous avions étudiés quelques années plus tôt et accentué les différenciations repérées à cette époque.

Avant d'aller plus avant, précisons un point de langage qui relève en même temps de la méthode. L'usage du terme 'élite', pour commode qu'il puisse être, nous paraît contestable; il implique en effet que les critères d'excellence attribués par définition à ceux que le terme désigne ne puissent être l'objet de contestations. Il est difficile d'en être assuré. Le terme, en outre, ne permet guère de déterminer facilement et avec précision un univers de population (Tardits, 1956). Dans l'étude, il a servi à désigner la fraction lettrée, masculine ou féminine, de la population; le critère de sélection retenu a été l'achèvement du cycle scolaire primaire, qu'il ait été ou non sanctionné par l'obtention du certificat d'études. La scolarisation est en effet la condition de toutes les différenciations importantes; seule, elle donne accès aux activités professionnelles modernes, procure des revenus plus stables et souvent plus élevés que les activités traditionnelles, rend possible un changement de mode d'existence et permet de participer activement à la vie politique. La conversion à l'islam ou au christianisme, si elle n'est pas associée à une fréquentation de l'école, n'ouvre pas de possibilité de cet ordre. Il existait évidem-

---

[1] Les résultats de ces recherches, conduites sous l'égide de l'U.N.E.S.C.O., ont été publiés dans Tardits (1958).

ment des cas limites, tel celui du commerçant riche, influent et cependant illettré. Dans la perspective adoptée, celle d'étudier la situation des éléments les plus scolarisés, il était sans intérêt d'élargir les critères de sélection.

L'enquête a fait ressortir que la persistance des liens traditionnels entre la fraction lettrée de la population et le milieu non évolué était l'un des traits saillants de la situation. Qu'ils aient été acceptés avec faveur ou défaveur, ces liens constituaient une limite aux effets des différenciations sociales réelles qui se manifestaient dans les occupations, le niveau des revenus, les modes d'existence et la participation à la vie publique. Malgré les avantages dont bénéficiait la population scolarisée et la réalité des différences sociales, il ne nous est pas apparu possible d'avancer que cette fraction était déjà constituée en une classe sociale distincte.

Entendons par classes sociales des catégories sociales distinctes, différenciées simultanément par les occupations, les revenus, les modes de consommation, l'usage de symboles particuliers affirmant le rang social des membres, le recours éventuel à des idéologies particulières et justificatrices et, quels que soient les caractères de différenciation retenus par la société, des catégories suffisamment stables et fermées pour que la mobilité sociale n'estompe pas et ne finisse pas par éliminer les différences.

Les liens traditionnels ne sont sans doute pas les seuls facteurs limitant les processus de différenciation: la situation coloniale marquée par la domination de l'élément étranger français suscitait une opposition, dissimulée ou manifeste, plus ou moins consciente des modalités selon lesquelles elle s'exprimait, de nature à limiter dans la société africaine l'apparition de différences qui l'auraient divisée contre elle-même et à inciter ses membres à réaffirmer ce qui pouvait les identifier à leur culture. Le attitudes des éléments chrétiens vis-à-vis des grands rituels animistes en seraient sans doute un exemple. Ce n'est toutefois pas les rapports entre Africains et Européens que nous nous proposons d'examiner ici mais quelques-unes des relations entre éléments lettrés et illettrés dans la vie sociale. Cette option ne préjuge pas le poids respectif de chacun de ces groupes de facteurs.

Nous donnerons d'abord une brève description des deux fractions de la population qui nous intéressent. Les témoignages historiques le permettant, nous y ajouterons quelques observations faites au 19ème siècle, qui donnent un aperçu de la façon dont s'est constituée la société porto-novienne.

La cité de Porto-Novo est relativement ancienne; l'agglomération se serait développée vraisemblablement au 16ème ou au 17ème siècle, lorsqu'un groupe de lignages d'origine adja vint s'installer sur la lagune, au lieu actuel de Porto-Novo et y aurait supplanté des éléments yoruba déjà fixés. Ces émigrants, appelés les Gun, s'établissent alors sur le pourtour de la lagune et dans l'arrière-pays immédiat où ils vivent de l'agriculture, la pêche et la chasse. Les premières relations avec les Européens sont attestées au 18ème siècle où le nom de Porto-Novo apparaît sur les cartes. La ville a joué un rôle dans le trafic négrier qui n'y a cependant jamais atteint le même volume qu'à Ouidah et, au début du siècle dernier, Adams (1823, p. 77) pouvait écrire: 'Porto-Novo seemed to me the most populous town (Benin excepted) of any that I have visited in Africa and contains probably from seven to ten thousand inhabitants.' Le même auteur relate la présence sur les marchés de produits venant d'Europe, d'Amérique et même d'Asie. A la fin du siècle, l'huile de palme est devenue l'objet principal du négoce porto-novien.

Pendant le 18ème et le 19ème siècle, de nouvelles migrations se sont produites: des familles yoruba et un petit nombre d'éléments dits 'Créoles' ou 'Brésiliens' sont venus s'installer dans la ville. Ces derniers sont les descendants de captifs achetés dans les ports même de la côte, quelques décennies plus tôt, transportés en Amérique et qui, libérés par des moyens divers, sont revenus dans le pays d'où leurs ancêtres et parfois eux-mêmes étaient partis; à ceux-ci paraissent s'être mêlés quelques éléments métis locaux. Cette société est organisée, en ce qui concerne les Gun et les Yoruba, en patrilignages de taille variée et, pour les 'Brésiliens', en grandes familles étendues à caractère patriarcal. Les nouveaux émigrants se sont juxtaposés à la société rurale gun; ils sont quelquefois artisans, plus souvent intermédiaires et commerçants. L'activité des Yoruba est orientée vers l'intérieur du pays; quant aux 'Brésiliens', ils se livrent à tous les commerces pratiqués sur la côte et servent souvent de truchement entre les souverains africains et les trafiquants et navigateurs étrangers.

La structure sociale est, au 19ème siècle, fort complexe; il y a d'une part une stratification des rapports entre lignages due au fait que les fonctions politiques sont investies dans les groupes gun et que les lignages yoruba et les familles brésiliennes détiennent néanmoins des pouvoirs et des influences liés à leur richesse, leur industrie et le réseau de leurs relations avec l'extérieur. Ces rapports entre groupes dont l'unité repose fondamentalement sur des liens de caractère parental se compliquent par l'existence, à l'intérieur de chacun d'eux, d'une hiérarchie fondée sur les fonctions et l'âge et par la présence d'une population de condition servile alimentée par la guerre ou le trafic des captifs. Ces éléments venaient grossir l'effectif des segments lignagers dans lesquels ils étaient plus ou moins incorporés; leur situation dans les lignages interférait avec leur condition d'origine. Il apparaît difficile de dire, sans une étude particulière vraisemblablement impossible aujourd'hui, si au 19ème siècle les facteurs qui définissent le statut des individus et corollairement la structure de la société relèvent de façon prépondérante de l'appartenance réelle ou fictive à un lignage ou de leur condition d'origine. Ce sont d'ailleurs là des questions qui touchent à la stratification sociale dans de nombreuses sociétés africaines anciennes.

Les effets de la politique coloniale vont donc, dès la fin du 19ème siècle, s'exercer sur un milieu depuis longtemps affecté par l'économie de marché. Après l'établissement du protectorat de 1882 et de la colonie du Bénin de 1893, la vie économique va se diversifier de façon accélérée. Le commerce local africain se développe avec l'augmentation du volume global des échanges; le nombre et la variété des artisans—maçons, charpentiers, tailleurs, couturiers et un peu plus tard mécaniciens, électriciens, transporteurs—va croître; les maisons de commerce et les petites entreprises artisanales à direction européenne vont offrir du travail à une population d'employés et même d'ouvriers tandis que la création des services publics entraîne l'apparition de tout un corps de fonctionnaires. Ces transformations se font avec beaucoup de souplesse, la minorité brésilienne fournissant immédiatement à la colonisation ses premiers agents.

Au moment de l'enquête, la population de la ville est évaluée à 30.000 habitants dont les Gun représentent à peu près les deux-tiers, les Yoruba le troisième; les Brésiliens et les ethnies originaires de l'intérieur, la plupart du temps employés de commerce et fonctionnaires, ne dépassent pas quelques centaines d'individus. La plus grande partie de la population est à peu près illettrée. Le recensement fait pour déterminer avec précision l'effectif de la population scolarisée et pour établir l'échantillon fournit un chiffre de 963 personnes, hommes et femmes, ayant reçu une éducation du niveau égal ou supérieur au certificat d'études.[2] Ce chiffre, rapporté à la population adulte active, en représentait très approximativement le dixième. La situation 'minoritaire' de l'élément lettré est rendue manifeste; cette indication globale ne fait toutefois pas apparaître leur répartition spatiale. En effet, la scolarisation ne s'est pas, chez les Gun et les Yoruba, développée uniformément dans les lignages et n'atteint pas en même temps tous les membres d'une même génération. Elle est inégalement développée entre les sexes; un comptage dans un lignage gun par exemple révèle que 68 pour cent des hommes contre 18 pour cent des femmes ont fréquenté l'école. En outre, il arrive qu'au sein d'une même famille un garçon sur deux ait reçu une formation scolaire ou que, par suite d'une scolarisation inégale, un enfant sur trois ou quatre soit en mesure d'accéder à la condition enviée de fonctionnaire. La différence sociale que la scolarisation va entraîner à l'âge adulte sera portée au coeur même d'un groupe de parenté: au niveau des frères.

Les effets de cette scolarisation limitée se lisent directement dans la répartition des professions. L'élément illettré s'adonne aux activités traditionnelles: pêche et agriculture pour les hommes, commerce local ou régional pour les femmes. L'artisanat traditionnel est tantôt féminin—poterie, teinturerie—tantôt masculin

---

[2] A ce chiffre s'ajouterait évidemment celui des fonctionnaires africains étrangers à la ville. Il exclut les éléments récemment scolarisés beaucoup plus nombreux qui n'avaient pas atteint leur majorité, n'étaient pas inscrits sur les listes électorales et ne participaient pas à la vie politique.

—forge; il groupe la plus grande partie de la population analphabète. Les artisanats modernes—construction, vêtement—recrutent leurs effectifs en partie dans la population illettrée, bien qu'ils ne puissent alors se qualifier professionnellement, mais surtout chez ceux dont la scolarisation n'a pas été suffisante pour prétendre à des emplois où l'on doive tenir quelques écritures.

La répartition des professions dans l'échantillon établi pour l'enquête révèle une toute autre orientation. Les activités africaines privées y sont distinguées des activités privées dites mixtes où les Africains ont des emplois subalternes et où la direction est européenne. La distinction se justifie par le fait que les Africains du secteur privé mixte échappent, au moins immédiatement, aux aléas de l'entreprise privée et bénéficient d'une sécurite proche de celle des fonctionnaires des services publics.

Distribution des professions dans la population de l'échantillon

	Hommes		Femmes	
	N	%	N	%
Secteur privé africain:				
Artisans	44	13	16	10
Commerçants	60	17	29	19
Divers	6	2	6	5
Ménagères	—	—	40	26
Total	110	32	91	62
Secteur privé mixte:				
Maîtres d'enseignement privé	11	3	10	7
Employés de commerce	51	15	—	—
Divers	2	—	—	—
Total	64	18	10	7
Secteur public:				
Fonctionnaires	173	50	50	33
Total	347	100	151	100

Le tableau fait ressortir la concentration professionnelle des hommes dans le secteur privé mixte et le secteur public; les femmes, pour des raisons qui tiennent aux traditions des entreprises ou aux règlements, ne jouissent pas des mêmes facilités d'accès que les hommes à ces secteurs.

Aux différences d'occupation en correspondent d'autres sur le plan des revenus. Les données dont nous disposons pour la population illettrée sont sur ce point insuffisantes, fragmentaires, indirectes ou même nulles. D'après la classification fiscale et les observations que l'on peut faire, ses revenus ne dépassent guère quelques milliers de francs mensuels et ne sont pas réguliers. Quelques commerçants semblent toutefois avoir bâti des fortunes importantes mais elles sont trop rares pour affecter la répartition générale des revenus.

Les revenus du personnel africain des entreprises commerciales et industrielles mixtes et des services publics rapportés ci-dessous se situent, pour la grande majorité, au-dessus du montant des revenus du reste de la population.

Répartition des revenus du personnel africain des secteurs privé et public

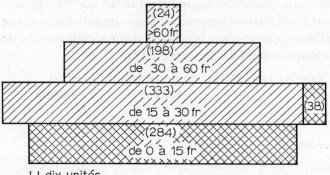

 dix unités

Les revenus s'entendent en milliers de francs CFA

▨ salariés africains secteur privé   ▧ fonctionnaires africains secteur public

Les différences dans les occupations et les revenus, qui se traduisent ensuite dans la consommation et le mode de vie, n'ont pas échappé à la perception commune. On distingue, dans la société gun, le *gletanu*, l'homme des champs, de l'*akawe*, le scribe fonctionnaire ou employé. Les deux termes ne recouvrent pas la gamme des occupations que nous venons d'énumérer mais ils en indiquent les deux pôles: le cultivateur analphabète et le bureaucrate préparé par l'école. En enregistrant cette situation dans la langue et l'imagerie, la population a montré sa sensibilité à l'existence de deux types qui symbolisent toute l'actualité des différences sociales.

Envisageons maintenant la situation des éléments lettrés dans le groupe familial et lignager dont ils sont issus et qui reste composé d'éléments en majorité illettrés. Les données proviennent pour l'essentiel du sondage d'opinion fait dans l'échantillon. L'intérêt attaché aux variations des réactions nous a fait préférer un procédé d'enquête extensive à la collecte d'observations directes mais limitées.

Un fait retiendra initialement l'attention: les deux tiers des ménages lettrés vivent dans la 'concession' du lignage du mari, c'est-à-dire dans une résidence partagée par plusieurs générations de parents proches. Les effets des règles résidentielles sur les systèmes de droits qui ordonnent les rapports au sein des groupes ont été assez souvent analysés pour qu'il soit inutile d'en souligner l'effet conservateur. L'ambition des jeunes gens de disposer d'une résidence séparée montre combien ils sont conscients des multiples conséquences sociales de cette situation.

Les chiffres relatifs à la composition des ménages révèlent des différences d'éducation entre mari et femme: 231 hommes sur les 294 de l'échantillon sont mariés avec des femmes illettrées. Celles-ci préservent les liens avec leur lignage d'origine où elles pourront toujours retourner en cas de divorce ou de veuvage, Elles acceptent également plus facilement la série des obligations qui incombent à une femme mariée vis-à-vis des parents de son mari avec lesquels elle réside. Qu'on en juge par cette description que donne une femme:

> Je salue à genoux mon beau-père, ma belle-mère, les oncles, les tantes, les frères et soeurs aînés de mon mari. Je ne m'agenouille pas devant les frères et soeurs cadets mais leur dois le respect. Je rends service à toute ma belle-famille: je fais les courses, les travaux du ménage, je puise de l'eau pour tous, je vais au marché, j'écrase le piment. Quand je prépare un repas, j'offre de temps en temps une portion de la nourriture que j'ai cuite à une tante, un oncle, un frère de mon mari, ma belle-mère, mon beau-père.

Enfin; elles s'accomodent mieux que les femmes scolarisées de la polygamie des hommes. Dans l'échantillon, 40 pour cent des hommes ont des foyers polygynes. Les obligations de l'homme à l'égard de ses beaux-parents se trouvent ainsi multipliées par le nombre de ses femmes. La situation matrimoniale actuelle tend à maintenir, pour près de la moitié de la population masculine lettrée et mariée, les relations traditionnelles d'entraide à l'égard des alliés. Elles consisteront, entre autres, à prendre part à toutes les manifestations cérémonielles qui auront lieu dans la parenté proche des épouses.

Cette disparité dans l'éducation des époux tient évidemment à l'écart entre les taux de scolarisation des garçons et des filles mais aussi au fait que les hommes préfèrent souvent des femmes illettrées qui ont moins d'exigences que les autres et ne font pas obstacle à de nouvelles unions; par contre, l'enquête révèle la préférence des femmes pour la monogamie.

Dans les rapports domestiques, les relations entre hommes et femmes conservent encore souvent un aspect traditionnel: plus du tiers des femmes gardent leurs gains grâce auxquels elles s'habillent, elles et leurs enfants et aident éventuellement leur famille d'origine, autonomie et précaution qu'éclairent sans doute ces propos d'une femme:

> Avoir un budget commun, c'est avoir confiance dans le mari; avec des maris dont on n'est jamais sûre qu'ils ne deviendront pas polygames, comment avoir confiance?

D'autres données attestent le souci qu'ont les générations lettrées de maintenir les rapports traditionnels. C'est ainsi que les chefs de lignages sont toujours élus et que les relations d'autorité sont, au moins formellement, respectées. On le voit lors des mariages: alors qu'une partie des unions sont contractées sans versement d'une dot qui obère les ressources des futurs conjoints, le consentement des familles a été donné dans 93 pour cent des cas. Ceci peut évidemment indiquer qu'il s'agit de mariages arrangés par les familles autant que d'unions auxquelles l'agrément des parents a été donné ultérieurement. Le fait n'en témoigne pas moins du respect que l'on manifeste à l'égard de la famille.

Traditionnellement, les différends et les violations de règles qui se produisaient dans un lignage relevaient de son autorité, leur sanction ayant souvent un aspect religieux. L'ordalie n'est plus pratiquée que dans des milieux très traditionnels mais, bien qu'un appareil judiciaire étatique fonctionne depuis plusieurs décennies, l'opinion reste en majorité favorable à un règlement par le lignage de différends tels que les vols, qui pourraient être l'objet de plain tes devant les tribunaux: 92 pour cent des hommes de l'échantillon se montrent favorables à cette solution lorsqu'il s'agit de désaccord en matière de biens et 88 pour cent pour sanctionner des faits tels qu'insultes ou vols. Les tribunaux ne sont saisis que des affaires qu'un factionnalisme interne ne permet pas de résoudre. Le traditionalisme se manifeste également sur le plan religieux. Les rites de naissance traditionnels ont été universellement conservés dans les milieux islamisés et christianisés. Ils sont suivis des cérémonies musulmanes et chrétiennes par lesquelles les enfants acquièrent la religion de leurs parents si ceux-ci le désirent. 'Un enfant qui n'a pas passé par ces cérémonies, entend-on dire, n'a pas de famille.' Les observations sur les décès intéressent plus particulièrement les lignages gun ou animistes et chrétiens vivent ensemble. Les parents et les alliés lettrés et illettrés assistent aux funérailles en milieu animiste et participent toujours aux dépenses qu'entraînent les cérémonies. Nous avons pu observer l'exécution d'un double cérémonial funéraire dans une famille gun où le mort s'était converti peu avant son décès. Les absents manquent rarement de faire parvenir leur contribution financière. Parmi les chrétiens, 68 pour cent ont déclaré avoir assisté au dernier rituel funéraire et avoir remis de l'argent; 19 pour cent envoyé de l'argent sans y être allé; 12 pour cent ne pas y avoir pris part du tout. Les cérémonies coûteuses et longues sont l'objet de critiques; néanmoins la fraction lettrée de la population ne s'y dérobe que rarement, tout en manifestant le désir de voir réduire sa participation à des gestes symboliques.

Nous allons maintenant examiner quelques faits très différents des précédents; il s'agit des fonctions qu'ont été amené à remplir les lignages dans la vie politique moderne. Ils servent en effet de réseau à l'action politique et électorale et ceci n'a été possible que parce qu'ils ont conservé leur unité. Un lignage de quelques centaines et parfois quelques milliers de personnes constitue en effet un groupe d'électeurs représentant environ la moitié de son effectif total. Si aucun factionnalisme ne s'est développé dans le lignage, ses membres voteront vraisemblablement de façon identique: l'appui du chef de lignage ou des personnalités influentes qu'il comprend, en particulier des prêtres de *vodun*, paraît décisif pour obtenir les votes de l'ensemble. L'unité du lignage se traduit par l'uniformité de ses réactions politiques et la technique électorale a consisté, depuis la mise en place d'institutions représentatives, à obtenir et conserver l'appui des éléments écoutés des groupes de parenté.

Cette situation ne se comprend clairement qu'en raison du rapport numérique entre la fraction lettrée, qui seule peut briguer les faveurs électorales de la population, et les dizaines de milliers d'illettrés qui constituent la masse des électeurs; en dehors de celle-ci il n'y a donc pas d'électorat sur lequel puisse s'appuyer la fraction lettrée, ce qui pourrait la dispenser de maintenir certaines formes de solidarité. Elle est en effet trop peu nombreuse et même trop dispersée territorialement—puisque la plupart de ses éléments continuent de vivre dans les 'concessions' anciennes—pour constituer une base politique autonome.

La contrepartie de l'appui politique ainsi fourni se trouvera dans les interventions que fonctionnaires et élus peuvent faire en faveur de leurs électeurs: tantôt ils procurent une facilité administrative sur le plan scolaire ou économique—prêt, aide technique—tantôt ils interviennent pour obtenir qu'une loi ne soit pas appliquée trop rigoureusement. Cette solidarité était très importante dans le contexte colonial où le pouvoir politique et administratif restait très largement aux mains de l'étranger.

Dans l'ensemble des données que nous avons indiquées, toutes les relations n'ont pas la même importance. Une série de rapports ont été préservés. Lettrés et illettrés acceptent le maintien de la hiérarchie traditionnelle. La tolérance religieuse est un des aspects les plus frappants de la vie à Porto-Novo. La présence de chrétiens à des rites animistes comme celle d'animistes à des cérémonies chrétiennes peut, dans certains cas, relever de l'ambiguïté des attitudes religieuses ou des synchrétismes individuels mais, à vrai dire, l'exclusivisme religieux aboutirait à des conflits entre générations et éventuellement entre frères au sein des groupes. Il n'est pas excessif de dire que le respect des rites a une fonction conciliatrice, manifeste explicitement l'unité du lignage et, au delà, affirme qu'une certaine identification avec la culture traditionnelle est encore reconnue. Cette situation tient fondamentalement au fait que la majorité de l'effectif des lignages est à peine lettrée et qu'approximativement la moitié de la population gun avait été convertie. Conversions et alphabétisation ne se recouvrent pas.

C'est sans doute moins le rapport numérique qui est intéressant ici, car la tolérance bénéficie aussi bien à des fractions minoritaires qu'aux autres, que la dissociation entre la vie traditionnelle et la vie moderne. L'autorité du lignage et les pratiques traditionnelles n'affectent pas les domaines où sont conférés aux lettrés les éléments de leur statut social: occupations, gains, promotions, affectations. L'autorité traditionnelle ne peut donc constituer une menace pour les différences acquises par l'élément lettré. Il reste les obligations les plus lourdes, celles qui sont fondées sur la tradition—réunions et contributions lors des naissances, des mariages et des deuils—et l'ensemble des interventions requises de ceux que leur situation favorise. C'est dans ces obligations que s'exprime en termes concrets la solidarité des éléments lettrés et illettrés du lignage. Les réactions d'hostilité qui se dessinent parfois ne traduisent que l'impatience. Ni l'éthique traditionnelle impliquée dans la pratique des liens de solidarité, ni les préceptes de l'islam ou du christianisme ne peuvent aisément servir de fondement à un rejet de ces liens.

On peut considérer que le maintien de telles relations tient à deux ordres de faits plus généraux que nous avons évoqués; le premier, c'est la persistance des grandes unités résidentielles constituées par les segments patrilignagers augmentés des épouses. La fraction lettrée, diluée dans sa communauté d'origine, a vu se maintenir un cadre où les sollicitations traditionnelles sont restées quotidiennes. Nous avons indiqué comment l'évolution qui s'est produite au 20ème siècle s'est articulée sans cassure sur celle du 19ème. Le second ordre de faits tient aux effectifs respectifs des groupes en présence qui, dans le contexte politique de l'époque, ne permettait pas aux éléments lettrés la rupture avec le milieu traditionnel. Dans ce contexte, les liens de parenté, support de tout le système d'obligations traditionnelles, ont évidemment constitué un frein à l'approfondissement des différences sociales et il nous paraît fondé de dire que, dans les rapports entre

Africains, la parenté a limité le développement de classes sociales. Ce facteur est intervenu concurremment avec la pression exercée par la puissance coloniale. La situation que nous avons connue s'est considérablement modifiée. L'opposition à une souveraineté étrangère ne peut plus guère constituer une limite aux différenciations intérieures, du moins sous sa forme coloniale. Les solidarités traditionnelles constituent-elles maintenant les seuls liens rapprochant encore les fractions lettrée et illettrée de la population ? Si, comme nous le prétendions, ces solidarités dépendent de la persistance des liens résidentiels et de la condition minoritaire des éléments scolarisés, s'amenuisent-elles au point de disparaître puisque les jeunes ménages tendent de plus en plus à créer des foyers indépendants et que la scolarisation continue de se développer? Formulons la question en termes à la fois plus schématiques et plus généraux: les changements actuels tendent-ils à constituer une société différenciée en classes sociales entre lesquelles les différences seraient d'autant plus profondes qu'elles reposeraient, au moins pendant plusieurs décennies, sur un fait aussi capital que la scolarisation ou bien d'autres modalités de développement peuvent-elles être envisagées? Les enquêtes conduites ailleurs peuvent peut-être, par voie d'analogie, fournir des éléments de réponse à cette question.

BIBLIOGRAPHY

Adams, Ch. J.
   (1823) *Remarks on the Country extending from Cape Palmas to the River Congo.* London.
Akindélé, A. et Aguessy, C.
   (1953) *Contribution à l'étude de l'histoire de l'ancien royaume de Porto-Novo.* Mémoires de l'Institut Français d'Afrique Noire, no. 25, Dakar.
Balandier, G.
   (1949) 'Evolution, évolués.' *France Outre-Mer*, 243, décembre.
Geay, J.
   (1924) 'Origines, formation et histoire du royaume de Porto-Novo.' *Bulletin du Comité d'Etudes Historiques et Scientifiques d'A.O.F.*, VII, 4.
Goldthorpe, J. E.
   (1955) 'An African elite.' *The British Journal of Sociology*, VI, 1.

Pauvert, J. C.
(1953) 'Le problème des classes sociales en AEF.' *Cahiers Internationaux de Sociologie*, XIX.
Tardits, C.
(1956) 'La notion d'élite et l'enquête en milieu urbain africain.' *Bulletin International des Sciences Sociales*, VIII.
(1958) *Porto-Novo. Les nouvelles générations africaines entre leurs traditions et l'occident.* Paris.
Verger, P.
(1953) 'Influence du Brésil au golfe du Benin, les Afro-americains.' *Mémoires de l'Institut Français d'Afrique Noire*, no. 27, Dakar.

Summary

KINSHIP AND SOCIAL CLASS IN PORTO NOVO

The paper deals with the relations between the educated and the non-educated sections of the population of Porto Novo, Dahomey. Education is regarded as the most important differentiating social factor today. The Gun, farmers settled in Porto Novo since the sixteenth century, represent two-thirds of the population, and half are Christian converts. To these should be added the Yoruba, mostly merchants and Moslems, who came in the eighteenth and nineteenth centuries. Finally, there are small numbers of 'Creoles' or 'Brazilians', whose ancestors came from America in the nineteenth century. They are all educated and either Christians or Moslems. The Gun and the Yoruba are organized in large patrilineages, the Creoles in extended families. More boys than girls are educated, and in some families one boy in two is educated. The literate population is in a small minority.

Most of the educated work in public services or in private businesses under European management. Their income is regular and higher than that of the rest of the population, and this is reflected in the differing patterns of expenditure of the salaried employee (*akawe*) and the farmer (*gletanu*).

The majority of households in which the husband is literate live in the compound of the man's founding lineage; in these households the majority of women have never been to school; 40 per cent of households are polygenous. Relations between spouses follow the traditional pattern; the women keep what they earn. The authority of the lineage chiefs is still respected; differences are resolved within the kin group. Christians contribute financially to traditional ceremonies, and there is wide religious tolerance.

The small educated elite are politically dependent on the support of the illiterate population, who make up the great mass of the electorate and who in turn benefit from the political influence of the elite.

The solidarity between the different elements is thus seen on many levels and expresses itself in the framework of lineage groupings.

The kinship ties, which the residential community tends to maintain, hinder the development of class relationships among a minority which cannot dissociate itself from the illiterate majority.

VIII. SOCIAL ASPIRATIONS, MAGIC AND WITCHCRAFT IN GHANA: A SOCIAL PSYCHOLOGICAL INTERPRETATION

GUSTAV JAHODA

Some years ago a controversy arose about the psychological effects of rapid social change. It was set off by an article claiming that an increase in the general level of anxiety may be inferred from a spread of new witch-finding cults (Ward, 1956). This view was strongly criticized, both on the grounds that it is impracticable to draw up an emotional balance sheet and also that to regard social change as leading to anomie is tantamount to making an unjustified value judgement (Goody, 1957). It is not proposed to enter this controversy directly, but merely to dispute the definition of anomie attributed to Durkheim, namely 'normlessness'. In fact, as may be seen from the quotation below, Durkheim (1951, p. 253) used the term to denote not just the absence of rules in general, but a state of society where there are no effective rules defining realistic life-goals.

> The limits are unknown between the possible and the impossible, what is just and what is unjust, legitimate claims and hopes and those which are immoderate. Consequently, there is no restraint upon aspirations. If the disturbance is profound, it affects even the principles controlling the distribution of men among various occupations... At the very moment when traditional rules have lost their authority, the richer prizes offered these appetites stimulates them and makes them more exigent and impatient of control. The state of de-regulation or anomy is thus further heightened by passions being less disciplined, precisely when they need more disciplining.

By and large, this passage presages with remarkable closeness the situation in many of the new African states, and an attempt will be made to elaborate its implications and suggest some of the causal processes at work.

Investigations in Ghana yield a picture of vocational aspirations closely resembling that reported by Schwab (1961) for Gwelo, where about two-thirds to three-quarters of parents

o

questioned about their children, and of young people themselves, aspired to professional or at least white-collar jobs. In terms of existing or even potential occupational outlets this is entirely unrealistic. Apart from this global aspect, little if any account is taken of individual differences in life-chances which are glaringly obvious to the outsider. In Ghana the evidence indicates that the chances of social mobility tend to be a combined function of parental literacy and father's occupational level (Jahoda, 1954).[1] In analyses of the vocational aspirations of adolescents according to these variables no significant differences in aspiration levels were discerned.

One feature of Schwab's presentation merits special notice: he felt able to treat occupational aspirations as a direct measure of the relative prestige of occupations. Without denying this in the given circumstances, it should be pointed out that such an equation would be completely inappropriate in a society like Britain, where both adolescents and their parents tend to choose jobs which are well within actual reach (Carter, 1962; Veness, 1962). These striking differences are not elucidated by references to greater 'fluidity in the social system', a phrase used by Schwab; the nature of the social system has to be examined in more detail.

SOCIAL STATUS IN GHANA

At the outset it is desirable to distinguish between 'status' and 'class'. Weber's classical definition of the latter refers to life-chances as determined by differential access to economic power, within a given economic order (Gerth and Mills, 1947). Weber made it clear that 'class' in this sense bears only a tenuous relationship to psychological characteristics; the shared 'class situation' involves merely a common economic interest, which may or may not lead to mutual identification and concerted action. Hence the

[1] Particularly in the past, these factors were in turn associated with birth place, in terms of educational opportunity. For example, if one arbitrarily defines the literary elite as the thirty-four Ghanaian-born contributors to the volume *Voices of Ghana*, one can trace their origins as follows: twenty-two were born on the coast, fourteen of these in the relatively short strip between Winneba and Sekondi. Thus some 5 per cent of the 1931 population produced over 40 per cent of the literary elite; the reason is no doubt that this represents the catchment area for Cape Coast, an educational centre since the eighteenth century.

question as to whether the notion of 'class' is applicable will not be pursued.

A related, but distinct, concept put forward by Weber is that of 'status', which is closely linked with values and behaviour. It is thus pertinent to ask how far the attributes of status postulated, and found, in Western societies hold in Ghana, and perhaps other parts of Africa. Weber proposed the four criteria set out below, which will be considered in turn.

(*a*) prestige ranking;
(*b*) distinctive style of life;
(*c*) restriction of informal social intercourse to own status level;
(*d*) high degree of status endogamy.

Prestige Rankings

Comments on this must be prefaced by the observation that there are, of course, two overlapping prestige hierarchies, traditional and modern. The former remains operative to some extent within the tribal communities; it still means something if one says about a person that he is the son of a chief, or the descendant of a slave. However, the traditional hierarchy is well on the way to becoming a mere survival as far as effective aspirations are concerned. Within the urban/literate section of the population the determinants of social prestige are essentially the same as those in the West, namely occupation, education, and wealth; and this applies even to the relative standing of different types of occupation (Mitchell and Epstein, 1959).

Distinctive Style of Life

The most obvious and highly visible attributes of different status levels can be seen in material possessions: housing, cars or bicycles, radiograms or gramophones, and generally the presence or absence of certain durable goods (Jahoda, 1961/2; University of Edinburgh Economic Research Unit, 1962).

Other more subtle, yet at least equally important features include variations in habits, manners, and speech (e.g. the occasional use of English). Without going into details, it can be stated emphatically that styles of life, however defined, do vary according to status.

Restrictions of Informal Social Intercourse to Own Status Level

While it is very likely that the relative frequency of informal social interaction may be somewhat greater *within* than *between* status levels, there are as yet few conventional barriers of the kind existing in Western industrialized societies. The sense of loyalty to both tribe and kin, as well as the feelings of dependence on these, remain sufficiently strong to ensure the persistence of frequent personal contacts (e.g. visits, joint participation in rituals) among people of widely disparate status levels. An additional factor will be mentioned under the next heading.

High Degree of Status Endogamy

There are several reasons why this fails to hold in Ghana. First, the traditional mode of selecting a spouse tends to militate against status endogamy. Young people may dislike it, but where family pressures are fully exerted few are prepared to rebel (Jahoda, 1959; Omari, 1960). Second, although an increasing proportion of families would not object to their son's preference for an educated girl, there are as yet not enough to go around. Lastly, and this links up with (c) above, it would appear that the prestige rankings of occupations below the professional level apply to a limited extent to women's activities, such as trading or crafts. Thus, it is an accepted practice for wives of clerks or teachers, even if they have had some schooling, to trade in the market side by side with illiterate mammies, on terms of social intimacy (Christensen, 1961). This has a two-fold bearing on the present argument: on the one hand, the lack of congruence on the prestige scale of male and female occupations means that women's status is less easy to define, which leaves one important element in the whole system of stratification relatively open; on a concrete plane, it indicates another broad area of informal contact linking people of contrasting status levels.

In general, one may conclude that while in Britain all four of

Weber's criteria apply to a large extent, this is true of only two in Ghana (Glass, 1954). For this the label 'semi-open status system' will be employed.

THE STATUS SYSTEM AND FORMATION OF ASPIRATIONS

At this stage it becomes possible to venture upon a comparative analysis of the patterns of aspiration in Britain and Ghana. In neither are aspirations noticeably governed by any rational calculus of life-chances; extensive research in Britain (Jahoda, 1952; Carter, 1962) and more informal exploration in Ghana indicates that in both informal social influences, operating within the broader context of a 'success ideology', are the predominant factors.

In Britain these influences emanate from people within the adolescents' social circle, i.e. parents and friends, uncles, aunts, and neighbours. In semi- or unskilled working-class families nearly all these models will belong to a relatively narrow band of the occupational range. Owing to the force of restrictions on informal social intercourse, and status endogamy, the perceived social distance between the offspring of such families and professional men like lawyers or doctors is too great for them to entertain aspirations of becoming like these. The mental map of society in such a milieu tends to be restricted to a small segment, and social mobility is conceived in the main as 'getting a trade'. Moreover, a positive sentiment of attachment to one's own status group is not uncommon, with a corresponding disdain for 'toffee-nosed pen pushers' (Jahoda, 1953). Thus the closed status system sets definite limits to aspirations and is an effective shield against the impact of the success ideology. Where the latter does break through, unrealistic aspirations are more likely to take such forms as wanting to be a star footballer, or pop singer, than to be directed towards the professions.

In Ghana, with its semi-open status system, the position is totally different. A majority of the parental generation are either illiterate or have had only limited schooling. Many of them are apt to regret their own 'backwardness', hoping that their educated offspring will have a better future. Their social perspective is distorted in a manner opposite to that of British lower-working-class parents: it is foreshortened, so that given education, it seems only a short step to the higher ranges of professional and administrative jobs. This is not merely a matter of 'ignorance', but stems from the fact that the exceptional opportunities have resulted in individuals from such a background rising meteorically to professional status. Such cases, selectively perceived, stand in the foreground of their awareness, notwithstanding the more sober truth that many more who move up come from families which are already literate.

Probably even more important than this slender experiential basis for great expectations is one of the salient characteristics of the semi-open status system: those who move in the social scale remain tied to those who stay behind (even where the tie is mainly one-sided) by common membership of kin, or perhaps merely tribe. This renders the 'big man' accessible, frequently in practice, always at least in sentiment. The psychological barrier which is such a pronounced feature of Western status systems tends to be weak or absent. Hence young people find their models generally not within their immediate social circle, but among those who have 'made good'. When discussing their aspirations with middle-school boys they were apt to refer to an 'uncle' who was a doctor or lawyer, and whom they may or may not have met; on inquiry it often turned out that this 'uncle' was a distant member of either parent's lineage. It is noteworthy that the social ascent of their models was sometimes delayed well into maturity, which may help to account for the fact that people are able to cling to the hope of a favourable change in their status long after it seems, in the eyes of an outside observer, to have become entirely illusory.

The factors stressed here are those that appear to be specially potent in Ghana, owing to the great expansion of opportunities since 1951. They are reinforced by others, which make an independent contribution. Thus, while education is rightly seen as the key to status and affluence, there is relatively little awareness of the possibility of personal limitations. There is also a remarkable faith of the Samuel Smiles type that if you try hard enough you are bound to get on, but this is subject to some qualifications, which will now be considered.

MAGIC AND WITCHCRAFT IN RELATION TO SOCIAL ASPIRATION AND MOBILITY

Mary Kingsley wrote about West Africa 'Charms are made for every occupation and desire in life . . .' The use of magic for the purpose of personal advancement, especially the acquisition of wealth by trading, is obviously nothing new. There is wide agreement that the spread of education has done little to reduce the prevalence of supernatural beliefs of this kind in Africa. In Ghana, on the basis of personal observation, one is impressed by the pervasiveness of such beliefs throughout society, up to and including university students. Studies of the clientele of supernatural practitioners indicate that it includes a substantial proportion of literates (Brokensha, 1962; Field, 1960; Jahoda, 1961b); and a detailed survey of some 500 adult students revealed that only about 5 per cent of this select sub-group of literates appeared to be entirely free from magical or witchcraft beliefs. There is thus good evidence for regarding such beliefs as a continuing part of the cultural ethos[2] (Jahoda, 1961a).

It is therefore only to be expected that would-be social climbers avail themselves of such means in an effort to overcome the numerous obstacles that stand in their way. The objectives they seek may be classified into three types: (*a*) an increase in personal effectiveness; (*b*) influencing in their favour a person in authority; (*c*) magical action involving physical objects. Illustrations will be cited from the two most common spheres, i.e. examinations and the work situation: (*a*) charms for superlative powers of learning, or the ability to produce work of such excellence that superiors will single the person out for promotion; (*b*) examiners to be made to mark the candidate's papers in a suitable manner, or the creation of 'love' on the part of the boss—failing that, his removal by higher authority; (*c*) magical pre-view of the examination paper,

[2] There is, of course, no suggestion that magical or other 'superstitious' beliefs cannot be found among contemporary Europeans; available evidence indicates, however, that their incidence is of a very much lower order of magnitude.

or money to be channelled into the right pocket. All this is best described as *instrumental* magic, since personal relationships are at most indirectly involved.

In view of the frequent emphasis on witch-finding cults in this general context, it should be pointed out that this type of magic is mainly provided by several other types of agents and institutions. At the lowest level it can be bought at market stalls; this is where schoolchildren usually go. Some herbalists and similar individual practitioners, especially in urban areas, have adapted themselves to the requirements and expectations of a literate clientele; although the charm 'for promotion' may be the same as it was in Mary Kingsley's time, it is more in keeping with the self-image of an educated man to receive it from the 'Director of "X" Herbal Laboratory' or a specialist in 'Super-science' than from a traditional practitioner. There are also a number of so-called, 'independent churches', whose activities overlap with those of new-style healers and also of the shrines. Their tenets, apart from the usual blend of indigenous beliefs and Christianity, have a substantial component of occult elements derived from the West and Far East. Some of these 'churches' seem to cater very largely for the needs of aspiring literates, judging both by the composition of the membership and the kind of help for which they appeal.

Instrumental magic, on which the discussion has focused so far, can hardly be taken as index of anxiety or malaise. It is sometimes suggested that such practices are socially dysfunctional, because they serve as a substitute for effort. Close observation of a number of individual cases offers no support for this view. One illustrative case may be quoted: a middle-aged routine clerk acquired a 'talisman' to get him through examinations; but this entailed no slackening of effort, and most nights he studied with the aid of a correspondence course.[3] The magical devices of type (*a*) are in fact a close equivalent of 'nerve-foods' and pep-drugs in the West. Some psychological gain may perhaps be derived from all of them,

[3] Survey results indicate that between one-quarter and one-half of adult-class students take such courses; the higher the level of schooling reached before a person had to leave school without a formal qualification, the greater the chances of private studies being pursued.

in so far as they engender confidence and sustain morale in a struggle against what are often heavy odds.

The clerk whose case has been cited failed his examination repeatedly, and ascribed this to the machinations of his enemies. The 'talisman' was thus also intended as a measure of protection, though it turned out not to be 'strong' enough. This is a characteristic kind of response to failure, technically known as 'extrapunitive', whereby the responsibility is shifted on to external agents. Field (1960) states that it is almost universal in Ghana, and the survey of adult students (Jahoda, 1961/2) confirms the prevalence of ideas which are an essential ingredient of this pattern: about half the respondents felt that their relatives would be jealous of their success, and another statement couched in more general terms ('Witchcraft is often used because of envy or jealousy of the success of others') was endorsed by more than three-quarters of the sample. The implications must be examined in relation to two types of outcome, namely those who fail and those who succeed; 'success' and 'failure', it must be remembered, are, of course, relative to an individual's aspirations.

In a situation where social aspirations tend to be excessively ambitious, some experience of failure is inevitable for a majority. A socially recognized means of escaping self-blame may thus be beneficial and help to ensure the continued effective functioning of the personality. It may be held that Field's results are to some extent at variance with such an interpretation; for while she found, as would be expected on the present view, that the largest single cause of supplicants attending the shrines were complaints of 'unprosperity', the more detailed descriptions of cases show that many of the people were suffering pain and misery. However, the supplicants constitute a self-selected element of the population, and those able to shrug off their failure as being the fault of others are less likely to spend the time and money required to go to a shrine or other institution.

The potential danger, paradoxically, is far greater for those who actually succeed, owing to a number of complex and interlocking causes. For a start, it is evident that people within their social circle have good reasons for being envious. Both the socially mobile actor and his real or imagined enemies share the set of beliefs about envy leading to witchcraft or other forms of hostility; he knows that people do sometimes go to irresponsible magical practitioners and ask for a rival to be killed, and spurious confirmation is, of course, not uncommon. All this can create a predisposition to experience what may range all the way from a slight feeling of unease to frankly pathological fear and distrust.

It is useful to distinguish at this stage between the universalistic and particularistic spheres. In the former, typified by the field of employment, a defence mechanism may be brought into operation. This is a notion which may be described as 'immanent justice': if you are in the right, and your conscience is clear, then evil forces can do you no harm. If the actor is convinced that the rules of the bureaucratic game can be kept distinct from those in other areas of life, and are just in their context, then he is able to ignore threats from his fellows.

The position is quite different in particularistic relationships, where social mobility almost invariably creates a certain amount of intra- as well as inter-personal conflict. In addition to the element of pure envy and hate (real or imaginary) directed against the man who has left others behind, there are the claims made on the kinsman with greater status and wealth. These may be very onerous (e.g. unlimited hospitality) and sometimes altogether irreconcilable with the new status (marriage to an illiterate cross-cousin). There is no ready escape from such dilemmas, because the actor generally acknowledges, at least to some extent, the legitimacy of traditional obligations; being unable to fulfil them adequately induces guilt, and this increases the likelihood of diffuse anxiety or explicit fears of supernatural reprisals. The whole process occurs in the context of the semi-open status system, which does not sanction the severance of social relations with members of one's kin, which is a solution in western societies when conflict arises.

It is perhaps necessary to guard against a possible misinterpretation of the above analysis. There is no intention to suggest that social mobility invariably entails acute fears of witchcraft and sorcery; but in the prevailing climate of belief the rivalries, conflicts, and stresses that are always involved to some extent are not only seen to take on a supernatural colouring, but to be reinforced by the expectations generated owing to these beliefs. Normally resilient people can learn to live with this and achieve an accommodation; but a minority incur a serious risk of mental breakdown, and there are indications that some of the ablest are liable to succumb. It thus becomes an important question what factors, other than constitutional predisposition, may be regarded as affecting a person's vulnerability to these undesirable by-products of social mobility.

CHILD-REARING ANTECEDENTS

Meagre as they are, all the available strands of evidence point to modes of child-rearing as a key variable. There is first of all the problem of envy, which has been sadly neglected by recent psychology.[4] In anthropological literature envy is taken for granted as a basic human sentiment,[5] though little attempt seems to have been made to investigate variations in the extent to which envy affects the nature and quality of social interaction in different societies. In Ghana envy appears to be attributed to small infants, who are said to be jealous of their forthcoming sibling before he is even born. It is likely, therefore, that this notion is implanted at a very early age. At any rate, the study of adolescents at school shows that they have adopted the adult attitudes; two examples will be quoted of spontaneous expressions, typical of many, given by middle-school pupils who had been asked to write an essay about their ambitions in life:

... if people see that you are going higher, they always hate you; sometimes they make gang and kill you at once.
... when they saw that you are going too high they hated you and perish you from the earth or make juju so that you may be mad.

---

[4] A conspicuous exception is Freud, who regarded it as the source of a sense of social justice.
[5] For instance Evans-Pritchard (1950, p. 100) wrote that the Zande 'is well aware that others take pleasure in his troubles and are displeased at his good fortune. He knows that if he rises in social position his inferiors will be jealous of his authority. . . .'

Within the traditional community control of the child's behaviour was not only strict but enforced to a large extent by
threats of supernatural sanctions (Kaye, 1962). Respect for elders
and obligations to kin were also inculcated at that stage of development. There are strong grounds for holding that cultural elements
learned in the course of emotionally charged situations in early
childhood are liable to be particularly resistant to later modification. A certain amount of support for this view can be adduced
from the study of adult students: the extent of supernatural beliefs
to which an individual subscribed correlated more highly with
type of home background (literate versus illiterate father) than
with level of education reached; thus, for the group as a whole
longer education failed, in this particular sphere, to counteract
effectively the results of early indoctrination.

In view of these converging pointers towards the decisive
importance of early learning in these areas, it is relevant to note
that in the same survey it was also found that some three-quarters
of the respondents declared their intention to bring up their own
children in a freer atmosphere. In a subsequent small but more
intensive study of literate and illiterate families in the neighbourhood of Accra an even more significant trend was uncovered: not
only seventeen out of twenty-five literate parents, but as many as
eleven out of twenty illiterate ones explicitly stated that they had
changed, or intended to change, the training of their children
away from the manner in which they themselves had been brought
up. In both categories the justifications, briefly illustrated below,
were closely similar:

I was intimidated a lot during my childhood. I lacked self-confidence. I
am training my children to have self-confidence and try things for themselves.
I was brought up by a relative and looked upon as a servant. I was always
under constant fear, but trained to be obedient and respectful. My children
are brought up under my own care. There is no master–servant feeling.
I don't punish my children as much as I used to be punished. I try to encourage my children to think for themselves and not just to behave according to commands as our fathers wanted us to behave.

From the context in which this kind of statement was made, it
does not seem that the new attitudes to child-rearing were the

direct outcome of a deliberate reckoning as to what would be required in a mobile society. Parents may have been broadly aware of this, but the major factor appears to have been a re-valuation of their own childhood experiences in the light of their adult life-situation; they often felt that their training had been inappropriate, and determined to bring up their children differently. It should be noted that this is independent of the empirical question, on which there is no evidence, as to whether traditionally trained children are in fact relatively deficient in self-confidence and capacity for independent action.

However, one indirect consequence of considerable importance is likely to follow the changes in child-rearing patterns: with decreasing emphasis on rigid conformity and subordination to elders, there will be less need to resort to threats of supernatural sanctions. This set of beliefs is thereby likely to be weakened at the crucial point of transmission.

If the general interpretation presented here is at least broadly justified, then the very changes in social values and norms that first rendered a rise in social status hazardous will in due course have the effect of reducing the risk of conflict and maladjustment. In terms of Durkheim's conceptual framework, people will increasingly acquire a more realistic 'knowledge of the possible', and thus be less liable to suffer frustration; in the evaluative sphere it is to be expected that the legitimacy of social mobility will become more and more widely acknowledged, so that the successful will have less reason to fear the hostility of those they have left behind. At the same time the persistence of the semi-open status system acts as a brake on these changes, and it would be rash to attempt a prediction of the eventual outcome.

BIBLIOGRAPHY

Brokensha, D. (ed.)
   (1962) *Volta Resettlement*, Legon, Ghana: Dept. of Sociology.
Carter, M. P.
   (1962) *Home, School and Work*, Oxford; Pergamon.
Christensen, J. B.
   (1961) 'Marketing and exchange in a West African tribe.' *South Western Journal of Anthropology*, vol. 17, 124–39.

Durkheim, E.
  (1951) *Suicide*, Glencoe, Ill.: The Free Press.
Evans-Pritchard, E. E.
  (1950) *Witchcraft, Oracles and Magic among the Azande*, London: O.U.P.
Field, M. J.
  (1960) *Search for Security*, London: Faber, 1960.
Gerth, H. H. and C. Wright Mills.
  (1947) *From Max Weber*, London: Kegan Paul.
Glass, D. V. (ed.)
  (1954) *Social Mobility in Britain*, London: Kegan Paul.
Goody, J.
  (1957) 'Anomie in Ashanti?' *Africa*, vol. 27, pp. 356–63.
Jahoda, G.
  (1952) 'Job attitudes and job choice among secondary modern school leavers.'
    Occupational Psychology, vol. 26, pp. 125–40; 206–24.
  (1953) 'Social class attitudes and levels of occupational aspiration in secondary
    modern school leavers.' *British Journal of Psychology*, vol. 44, pp. 95–107.
  (1954/5) 'The social background of a West African student population.'
    British Journal of Sociology, vols. 5 and 6, pp. 355–65, 71–79.
  (1959) 'Love, marriage and social change', *Africa*, vol. 29, pp. 177–90.
  (1961a) 'Magic, witchcraft and literacy.' *Lumen Vitae*, pp. 137–44.
  (1961b) 'Traditional healers and other institutions concerned with mental ill-
    ness in Ghana.' *International Journal of Social Psychiatry*, vol. 7, pp. 245–68.
  (1961/2) 'Aspects of westernization.' *British Journal of Sociology*, vols. 12 and
    13, pp. 375–86, 43–56.
Kaye, Barrington
  (1962) *Bringing up Children in Ghana*. London: Allen & Unwin.
Mitchell, J. Clyde, and A. L. Epstein
  (1959) 'Occupational prestige and social status among urban Africans in
    Northern Rhodesia.' *Africa*, vol. 29, pp. 22–40.
Omari, T. P.
  (1960) Changing attitudes of students in West African Society toward marriage
    and family relationships, *British Journal of Sociology*, vol. 11, pp. 197–210.
Schwab, W. B.
  (1961) 'Social Stratification in Gwelo', in A. Southall (ed.): *Social Change in
    Modern Africa*, London: O.U.P.
Veness, T.
  (1962) *School Leavers*, London: Methuen.
Ward, B. E.
  (1956) Some observations on religious cults in Ashanti, *Africa*, vol. 26, pp.
    47–60.
University of Edinburgh Economic Research Unit
  (1962) *Survey of Food Expenditure by Middle Income Households in Accra, 1962*,
    Ghana Study Paper No. 1, Edinburgh: Dept. of Political Economy.
  (1958) *Voices of Ghana*, Accra: The Government Printer.

Résumé

LES ASPIRATIONS SOCIALES, LA MAGIE, LA SORCELLERIE AU GHANA: UNE INTERPRÉTATION SOCIO-PSYCHOLOGIQUE

La conception Durkheimienne de l'anomie comme un état de société où il n'y a pas de règles effectives pour définer les buts réalistiques de la vie est caractéristique de plusieurs problèmes importants dans les nouveaux états de l'Afrique. Les enquêtes indiquent que les aspirations vocationnelles ont une tendance d'être irréalistiques avec peu de conscience de vraies opportunités de la vie. On peut comprendre cela sous les termes de la nature du système de rang social, analysé avec référence spécifique au Ghana.

Weber a distingué 4 critères principales de rang;

(a) rang de prestige
(b) mode distinctive de vie
(c) restriction des relations sociales informelles au propre niveau de rang de soi-même
(d) Haut degré d'endogamie de rang.

Tandis que tous les 4 critères s'appliquent à un pays comme la Grande Bretagne, il n'y a que (a) et (b) qui sont justes au Ghana; il faut, donc, employer le terme 'semi-open status-system'. Ces divergences servent à expliquer le contraste entre les formes des aspirations dans les deux sociétés. En Grande Bretagne il y a des barrières psychologiques qui tendent à restreindre les aspirations de ceux qui appartiennent à un rang bas dans l'hiérarchie à une bande assez étroite dans le domaine des métiers; au Ghana l'absence comparative de telles barrières à cause de la continuité des liens de parenté à travers les niveaux de rang tende à obscurcir la conscience des obstacles qui s'opposent à la mobilité sociale. L'enseignement est justement consideré comme la clé au rang et à la richesse, mais on ne s'est pas suffisament rendu compte des délimitations personnelles possibles.

Dans une telle situation il n'est pas inattendu, en présence de la grande prévalence des croyances surnaturelles, qu'on aurait recours au moyens magiques pour l'avancement social. Les buts désirés comprennent un surcroît d'efficacité personnelle, le pouvoir d'exercer une influence, avantageuse à soi-même, sur les personnes d'autorité. On peut appeler cette espèce de magie la magie instrumentale, traitée d'habitude, par les intermédiaires autres que les cultes, souvent discutés, qui trouvent les sorcières.

Il est quelques fois suggeré que de tels usages ont un mauvais effet sur les fonctions de la société, parce qu'ils remplacent les efforts personnels; le peu d'évidence présenté indique que cette thèse est d'une validité incertaine et que quelques avantages psychologiques de second rang pourraient être obtenues par un surcroît de confiance. Quand la magie n'est pas efficace, la réponse caractéristique est de rendre coupables les agences externes. Quand les aspirations sociales sont trop ambitieuses, une expérience de faillite est inévitable et un moyen, accepté par la société, de s'échapper de la condamnation de soi-même pourrait être salutaire.

Le danger potential est, dans une certaine mesure, plus sérieux pour ceux qui réusissent sur le plan social à cause des croyances à l'envie qui mènent à la sorcellerie ou à d'autres formes d'hostilité. Les résultats pourraient être divers—d'une légère malaise jusqu'à une peur pathologique dans les cas extrêmes. Dans le sphère universel il paraît y avoir des méchanismes efficaces de défense, mais il n'y en a pas dans le sphère particulier. Les parents réclament des droits qui sont reconnus par une personne d'une mobilité sociale, mais qui sont quelques fois irréconciliables avec le nouveau rang. Dans un système semi-ouvert de rang il n'y a pas de moyen de s'échapper facilement d'un tel dilemme. Il s'agit d'un conflit intra- aussi bien qu'inter-personnel. Il faut insister que la plupart des gens d'une mobilité sociale apprennent à s'adapter à cette situation et il n'y a que ceux qui sont vulnérables pour d'autres raisons qui risquent une débacle.

Il y a des indications que la base de tout le problème est dans l'éducation des enfants. On inculque très tôt une disposition d'attendre l'envie; et le recours à la sanction surnaturelle pour le contrôle du comportement produit des croyances qui sont profondément enracinées et difficiles à changer plus tard.

En présence de ces faits, l'évidence que l'éducation des enfants est en train d'être modifiée est très importante, puisque cela pourrait avoir des résultats d'une grande portée. Les croyances surnaturelles pourraient probablement devenir moins fortes au point critique de transmission, rendrant moins dangereuse la mobilité sociale au point de vue psychologique. Sous les termes de Durkheim les buts de vie pourraient être plus réalistiquement délimités avec une fréquence réduite des expériences de faillite. Les limites de ce procès seront fixées cependant, tant qu'il y aura un 'semiopen status system'.

IX. AFRICAN ELITES IN INDUSTRIAL
BUREAUCRACY

C. KUMALO

INTRODUCTION

The purpose of this paper is to describe the status-role adjustment
of twenty-seven Africans who, in 1961, had been appointed to
Executive and Managerial posts in private industry in the city of
Kampala, Uganda. These Africans represent 'the new elite' in the
history of industrial bureaucracy in Kampala. For, until the last
few years of the last decade, the two occupational ranks had been
staffed almost exclusively with non-African personnel, viz.
Europeans and Asians. The primary interest, therefore, is in the
adjustment of these Africans to an industrial bureaucracy which is
alien both in its structure and functioning and in the racio–ethnic
composition of its 'traditional' personnel.

In view of the latter aspect of alienness, it is necessary to include
here data on contacts and relationships between the new African
bureaucrats and the 'traditional' Euro-Asian bureaucrats during
and outside office hours. And, in view of the former aspect of
alienness, it is necessary to include data on the extent to which
these African bureaucrats share the kinds of individualistic values
generally associated with private enterprise, as distinct from the
collectivistic values generally associated with socialist enterprise,
at the ideological level.

THE BUDDING BUREAUCRATS

Although by 1961 the policy of localization of staff in industry
and in the Civil Service was fairly well accepted, at least in principle, in East Africa, Africanization of the very high posts had not
advanced very far. Top management in nearly all Companies
operating in East Africa was still in the hands of non-Africans,
expatriate and local. Thus, these men were, in actual fact, occupying 'upper middle' and 'lower upper' posts—intermediate between top management, on the one hand, and clerks and shop-

floor foremen, on the other. They were 'budding bureaucrats' in the sense that they had 'put forth the tender leaves of hope' that, with the speeding up of Africanization and all things being equal, they would soon 'blossom and bear their blushing honours (of top management) thick upon them'. Indeed, two or three of them have since been appointed to Directorships.

Statuses

Two held full managerial posts—one, of Personnel Manager in a non-Oil Company; the other, of Public Relations Officer in an Oil Company. The criterion of managerial status used in the study was whether or not the person had a seat on the Board of Management. The rest were in various executive grades; and the criterion used in the study was whether or not the person had a right to facilities and amenities for non-African executives in the Company, such as, cloakrooms, lockers, toilets, refreshments, etc. But then these posts, though high and novel for Africans in East Africa, were in fact mainly *advisory* to top management. Non-African top management tried to understand its African employees, in a changing political climate, through these men. This was possible for a number of reasons deriving from the following descriptive characteristics of the men in point.

(*a*) Their experience in private industry had a range of 1 to 8 years, an arithmetic mean of 3·4 years, and a mode of nearly 4 years. They were no novices.

(*b*) Fifteen of them were married and had children; only two of these were aged 25 to 29 years, the rest were 30 and over. The twelve single men were relatively young, with five aged 20 to 24; the rest, 25 to 29. But then more than half these single men had one or more dependants to support. Thus, the group as a whole was not unused to status-role obligations and responsibilities.

(*c*) All but one of the twenty-seven had at least completed secondary schooling, i.e. twelve years of education, as the following tally shows:

Below Sec. School	Sec. School only	University Graduate	University Post-Graduate	Total
1	16	8	2	27

(*d*) Only eight had had no previous jobs; the other nineteen had had from one to six previous jobs either in the same or other employing agencies. One possible implication of this high mobility, especially of those without university education, is that they had a fairly varied knowledge and experience of the employment situation to be able to appreciate the problems of the African industrial worker.

(*e*) Sixteen (all but two without college education) had worked their way to executive and managerial positions *from within* the Companies for which they were working. The rest (all but one with college education) had worked their way *from without*—moving almost directly from higher education to higher positions of responsibility. Thus, this group of budding bureaucrats combined, albeit in different individuals, a stock of practical knowledge gained from within and a stock of theoretical knowledge gained from outside the Companies for which they worked. There is involved here the question of differential adjustment of the two sections of this group—'the insiders' and 'the outsiders'.

An important factor in the adjustment of an individual to his status-role is the kinds of contacts and relationships he has with the occupants of relevant status-roles, especially if the latter are racio-ethnically different. And such contacts and relationships are not likely to be independent of the more generalized inter-communal attitudes, stereotypes, and prejudices.

Contacts and Relations

In general, these African bureaucrats had more frequent contacts with Europeans, during and outside working hours, than with Asians whom they met only occasionally and more casually in trading shops. Within industrial bureaucracy, Europeans generally occupy the top managerial posts, and the Africans have to consult with them from time to time before final decisions can be made by them. Asians tend to occupy positions parallel to those occupied by the African bureaucrats, hence there is a reduced need to consult with them on any matter of importance beyond routine requirements for communication. Also, it is not far-fetched to suggest a measure of 'subdued rivalry' between African and Asian bureaucrats in parallel bureaucratic status-roles.

Formal relations between these Africans and their European colleagues were also much better than with their Asian colleagues, despite the mounting anti-colonialist sentiments in the generalized African community. The explanation lies in the fact that these Africans did not view Europeans as a monolithic group, as the following comment shows:

> On the whole, Europeans here fall into three groups: (a) There are those who believe that nothing good can come out of an African whether he is a Christian or has a B.A. degree—this is the idea that nothing good can come out of Nazareth. (b) There are those who believe that nothing bad can come out of an African—these are the fanatical so-called African-lovers and extremist missionaries. (c) Then there are those who say that 'After all, Africans are human just like ourselves.'

Contrast this attitude with the following towards Asians:

> With Asians I do not know how much of their cordiality is a put-up job. They must be aware of the inevitability of African ascendancy in East Africa. There is therefore an enforced genuineness. They cannot afford to adopt negative attitudes towards us now. Theirs is what I may call a 'compulsive cordiality'.

It is clear that these attitudes are drawn from the wider African community rather than acquired within industry itself. But then experience in industry itself tends to reinforce these attitudes and to invest them with a rationale which has an air of objectivity about it, as the following case shows.

In response to the question: 'Whom would you rather have (*a*) as a colleague, (*b*) as your immediate superior—an African, a European, or an Asian—to work in close collaboration with you on your present job in the Company?' there was an overwhelming choice of a European colleague or superior—with very few choices of an African and of an Asian, in that diminishing order. Why?

> Europeans are efficient. One can learn more from them than under the others.
> I would prefer Europeans to either an African or an Asian. Europeans reason throughout. Asians backbite you quite a lot. They will try to undermine you with top management for fear that you may displace them with

increasing Africanization. Of course, Africans can be pretty nasty too. Some that I know I wouldn't work under them for anything.

Such attitudes raise the question of the future of the Asians under conditions of such distrust and suspicion when the policy of Africanization is fully put into effect. It seems clear that a radical re-orientation is imperative on both sides if the two communities must co-exist both in industry and commerce and in the open society. On the other hand, now that the European has ceded political power and prestige to the African his position is likely to be much more secure in East Africa than ever before, as long as it is based on claims of technical competence rather than on exaggerated ascriptive self-conceptions.

STATUS-ROLE ADJUSTMENT

Asked the question: 'If, at the time you left schooling and started working, you had been offered a scholarship to study further, would you have accepted it?' eighteen out of the twenty-seven men said that they would have accepted such a scholarship. Only a third were undecided; but then these were the men who had had three or four years of college education. Thus, it should be recognized that two-thirds of the men in question started working mainly because they had no chance of furthering their education.

Closely related to this is the fact that only twelve of the respondents thought that, if they had been given scholarships to study further, they would have studied for the kind of jobs they were doing, i.e. business management; one was undecided, but the rest said that they would definitely not have studied business management. Contrasting with these observations was the fact that as many as twenty felt that if they were given a chance to change their jobs for others in the *same* Companies and at the *same* salaries they would be unwilling to change; the others were either willing to change or were undecided. Related to this, is the fact that ten felt that they were likely to stay with their Companies for another one to five years; ten, for another five to ten years; and of the remainder, four said that they were likely to stay on for ten to twenty years, while three intended to stay on to retiring age.

It should be noted that, at the time of this study, political independence, both for Uganda and Tanganyika, was close at hand, and even that of Kenya did not appear too far off. These men, therefore, felt that if they stayed where they were, acquiring useful experience in administration, the speeding up of Africanization might bring greater opportunities to them. Thus, not one of them said he was contemplating leaving his Company immediately. Add to this the fact that, until recently, salary scales in private industry have been higher than in the Civil Service—and in some cases this is still so.

Asked what kind of Company they would rather be in if they were to choose all over again, nine said they would choose to stay with their present Companies; six would choose to start their own private enterprises; four would prefer to join Statal or para-Statal Companies; while the remaining eight would choose the Civil Service. It is significant that all eight who would choose to stay with their present Companies were 'insiders' whose practical knowledge was restricted to the kinds of jobs they were doing, while the generalized theoretical knowledge of the 'outsiders' allowed them greater elasticity in their aspirations.

However, pending Independence and Africanization in the Civil Service, ten felt that, considering everything, their Companies were giving them a 'very good chance' to show what they could do; fourteen felt that they were being given a 'fairly good chance'; and of the remaining three, two said they were being given 'not much of a chance', while the third felt that his Company gave him 'no chance at all'. The latter has since joined a para-Statal Company.

Regarding promotion chances, nine said there was a 'very good chance' for an African manager/executive with ability to be promoted in their Companies. This is in agreement with the feeling that private industry gave 'very good' or 'fairly good' chances, in the main, for these men to prove their worth. Another nine felt that the chances of promotion were 'fifty–fifty'; and of the remainder, seven saw 'fairly good' chances of promotion; one saw only a 'poor chance', and the last 'no chance at all'.

Once more, the reader is reminded that the men with college education were the more impatient and critical; but as these were in the minority, it may be concluded that these budding bureaucrats, as a group, felt that their Companies were giving them good opportunities to prove themselves; and that private industry offered them fair to very good chances of promotion if they measured up to the status-role expectations and challenges of industrial bureaucracy. Indeed, political independence and the subsequent strivings for economic independence would unveil more and wider vistas of achievement to these men and other members of the educated elite of Uganda and of East Africa.

We must now turn to the more detailed problems of adjustment experienced by these budding bureaucrats.

Accoutrements of Status

When comparing themselves with their Asian colleagues, most of these men expressed satisfaction with Company housing and pay. Just over a third were satisfied with leave, while about seven-tenths were satisfied with gratuities. Of those dissatisfied with leave arrangements, one remarked that: 'Asians in my Company are entitled to two months' leave in every four years or £100 in lieu of leave. There is no such arrangement for us.' Such a situation can hardly lead to amicable official and race relations.

On the other hand, these men were 'very dissatisfied' when they compared themselves with European colleagues in regard to the above accoutrements of managerial and executive status. Over half of the respondents were dissatisfied with their housing; over three-quarters, with pay; and just under nine-tenths of them, with leave and gratuities. One reported that:

European quarters are fully furnished by the Company; we get only partly furnished quarters with hard furniture only. The house itself is satisfactory.

Another observed that:

Locally recruited Europeans are entitled to four months' leave in four years with passage paid by the Company. I know of one European who recently went to England *for the first time in his life* on the scheme. If so, why not African Company employees?

It may be noted that the attitudes of these men to the accoutrements of their status are a clear case of reference-behaviour.

Perceived Motive for Status Conferment

Well over half the twenty-seven men felt that their appointments were regarded by their superiors as contracts necessary to their Companies mainly on grounds of political expediency.

That it was political expediency is clear from the fact that during the first six months after my appointment, there was nothing for me to do in the Company. I was doing all sorts of odd jobs. My appointment was mere political window-dressing. (This man has since resigned from the Company.)

However, about a fifth felt that they were appointed mainly on economic or business grounds:

I joined the Company when political pressure towards Africanization was non-existent. Industry took the first step towards Africanization for purely economic reasons. Even now there are still more university graduates in industry and commerce than in the Civil Service.

But the predominant view was that these appointments had been made for political reasons. The reader is reminded that the Europeans were regarded, as shown above, as 'unwilling partners' who, willy-nilly, had to fall into line with the present political developments in East Africa.

Perceived Attitudes of European Management towards African Managers

Having contended that the original motive in the appointments had been mainly political expediency, seven-tenths of these men conceded that European top management needed African managers and executives to mediate between European management, on the one hand, and the African worker and consumer, on the other. This is a clearly problematic role as the following respondents clearly analyse it:

(*a*) I have only one superior—the General Manager. My Company cannot think of a non-African Public Relations Officer. They know that an African is the only chap who can deal with Africans production-wise. They are also scared of making a wrong move political-wise. When the Sudan became independent, my Company localized its personnel automatically, leaving only finance in European hands. Economy-wise too they know that the better their P.R.O.'s the better, e.g., the sales.

(*b*) The senior European management wants the African manager to advise them. The junior European manager thinks he knows the African mind. But the appointment of an African manager is the decision of senior management. Senior management cannot trust the junior European manager to handle the Africans. But the position of the junior European manager is such that, seeing that the appointment of the African manager is given from above, he will now have to look at the African manager as the interpreter of the African mind, (which he thinks he knows), for fear that his boss will turn upon him and ask, 'Did you check this with the African manager?'

In such a situation it may be expected that the junior European manager resents the African manager, but he also needs him for making his suggestions more acceptable to senior management and for cover in case his suggestions lead to unfortunate results. For, he can always say, 'but I checked this with the African manager', who then takes off part of the blame from the junior European manager. Also, under the Africanization policy, the junior European manager may be expected to view the African manager as a potential competitor for the higher managerial posts, but accept him because he can serve as a scapegoat when things go wrong. The African manager, on the other hand, finds his upward mobility threatened by the presence of the junior European manager. Thus, both sides look at each other with concealed resentment, and co-operation may be expected sometimes to be formal and compulsive. But as no social organization can long survive on this basis, the question of the moral or value commitment of these African bureaucrats to the ethos of private industrial enterprise becomes crucial.

IDEOLOGICAL VALUE-COMMITMENT

This problem was investigated through items selected from the final version of the P.E.C. Scale used by Adorno *et al.*, in *The Authoritarian Personality*, with necessary adaptations. The sole interest was in the *distribution* of favourable and unfavourable *responses* to the items and not in personality-typology. So that the elaborately explicit assumptions and interpretations of the conservative–liberal continuum on which the scale was based and the scathing methodological criticisms that have been made of the scale by, *inter alia*, Shils, Hyman, and Sheatsley in Merton's *et al.* (eds), *Continuities in Social Research*, may be regarded as somewhat beside the point. It was also found to be methodologically necessary to investigate, with the same items, a non-bureaucratic elite *control* group. For this purpose, the same items were administered to a class of sociology students at Makerere. The two distributions are shown below:

Distribution of Responses of Kampala African Bureaucrats and of Makerere African Sociology Students to an Adapted Form of the P.E.C. Scale

	Individualistic Value Responses		Collectivistic Value Responses		Total
	Number	%	Number	%	
Bureaucrats	110	37·03	187	62·97	297
Students	89	44·06	113	55·94	202

It will be noted that the difference in the distribution of individualistic and collectivistic responses within the group of bureaucrats was significant at the 0·001 level ($x^2 = 19·96$), and the group as a whole showed a highly collectivistic orientation. The difference in the same distribution for students ($x^2 = 2·84$) was not significant, i.e. the students showed no decisive commitment to either type of values. The overall difference between the two groups was highly significant ($x^2 = 22·80$) at the 0·001 level. The pronounced commitment of the bureaucrats to collectivistic values may be regarded as consonant with socialistic thinking in the contemporary African elite circles, although it may hardly be regarded as conducive to optimum adjustment to a bureaucratic set-up based on individualistic values. There is clearly involved here the familiar *mechanism of segregation* of the spheres of relevance of the two types of values. And it would be presumptuous to see in this situation any element of real or felt conflict of values. The apparent 'ambivalence' of the students, with a slight bias towards collectivistic values, may be expected during this formative period in their world-perspectives.

CONCLUSION

In conclusion, the following points may be worth noting:

1. That these African elites showed very little planning of their careers; but, having joined private enterprise, were ready to stay where they were, biding any better opportunities elsewhere.

2. That, in terms of their descriptive characteristics, they were not altogether unsuited for the status-roles they were occupying —with about a third who had college education clearly in line for greater calls to the service of their country.

3. That, in the meantime, their attitudes towards their colleagues, especially Asians, left much to be desired from men of their educational level—a factor which may or may not have seriously affected their role-performances.

4. That there was a strong *political* component in their perception of their status-roles, the distribution of the accoutrements of status, the motivations of their employers, and the attitudes of their employers towards them.

5. That their ideological value commitments seemed to derive more from the ethos of the wider African social organization than from that of the bureaucratic organizations for which they worked. They were 'in' but not 'of' these Companies.

Résumé

LES ÉLITES AFRICAINES DANS LA BUREAUCRATIE INDUSTRIELLE

Il y avait en 1961 environ 27 Africains nommés aux emplois exécutifs et directoriaux dans l'industrie du secteur privé à Kampala, Uganda. Ceux ci réprésentaient 'la nouvelle élite' dans l'histoire de la bureaucratie industrielle de Kampala, car jusqu'à alors ces deux rangs d'occupation avaient été consacrés presqu' entièrement au personnel éuropéen ou asiatique. Or, ce discours traite surtout de l'adaptation de cette petite élite africaine à une bureaucratie industrielle qui leur est étrangère dans sa structure et qui fonction aussi bien que par la composition racio-ethnique de son personnel d'auparavant.

Les Nouveaux Bureaucrates. Ces hommes remplissaient les fonctions intermédiaires, entre la direction d'une part et les employés de bureau et les chefs d'atelier ('shop-floor foremen') de l'autre. Deux d'entre eux remplissaient les fonctions pleinement directoriales et les autres avaient les places exécutives. Leurs fonctions, hautes et nouvelles pour les Africains, étaient, en effet, consultatives. La Direction essayait de comprendre ses employés africains dans un nouveau cadre politique par moyen de ces hommes. Ils avaient été bien préparés à ce rôle: (*a*) L'étendue de leur expérience dans l'industrie du secteur privé était d'une à huit ans avec une moyenne de quatre ans; (*b*) 15 d'entre eux avaient au moins 30 ans, et étaient mariés et résponsables, tandis que 12 étaient de jeunes célibataires énergétiques de 20 à 29 ans; (*c*) Il n'y avait qu'un seul qui n'avait pas fait le lycée et 10 avaient fait l'université; (*d*) 8 n'avaient pas été employés auparavant, mais les autres avaient eu d'une jusqu'à 6 places, ou dans la même compagnie ou dans les compagnies diverses, et 16 s'étaient élevés dans la compagnie pour laquelle ils travaillaient en 1961. Les autres étaient parvenus aux hautes fonctions de résponsabilité presqu' immédiatement après avoir terminé leurs études supérieures. Il y avait, donc, dans le groupe, une combinaison de pratique gagnée dans la compagnie et de théorie acquise dehors.

Les Rélations. Le genre de rélations qu'on a avec ceux qui sont du même rang social mais d'une race diverse est un facteur important dans le 'status–role–adjustment'. Il y a des rélations plus fréquentes et plus amicales entre les informateurs et leurs collègues européens qu'avec leurs collègues asiatiques. On a tiré d'une communauté africaine plus large les attitudes exprimées, mais les remarques suivantes tirées de l'ambiance industrielle semblent les renforcer; 'Les Européens sont habiles; on peut mieux apprendre d'eux que des autres'; ou bien: 'Les Européens sont raisonables. Les Asiatiques sont de mauvaises langues; ils disent du mal de vous à la Direction, parcequ'ils ont peur que vous les remplaciez à cause de l'Africanisation.'

Le 'Status – Rôle – Adjustment'. Au début de leurs carrières industrielles, la plupart de ces informateurs auraient accepté les bourses pour continuer leurs études, si on les leur avait offertes, mais il n'y avait que 12 qui auraient étudié l'administration commerciale. Il n'y avait que quelques uns, cependant, qui voulaient changer d'emploi ou quitter leurs compagnies tout de suite. Ils croyaient que, s'ils restaient sur place afin de gagner plus de pratique administrative, ils auraient de meilleures opportunités après l'Indépendance, quand l'Africanisation irait plus vite. Ils trouvaient, entre temps, 'd'assez bonnes' ou même 'de très bonnes' opportunités d'avancement dans l'industrie en comparaison de celles du service gouvernementale à cette époque.

I. Les Accoutrements de Statut: Ils exprimaient leurs opinions de leur traitement dans la compagnie et ils étaient, pour la plupart, assez contents de leurs conditions en comparaison de celles de leurs collègues asiatiques mais 'pas contents du tout' en se comparant à leurs collègues européens.

II. Les Motifs d'Action et les Attitudes: Plus de la moitié des informateurs croyaient qu'à l'avis de la Direction leurs nominations étaient nécessaires au point de vue politique, mais 70 pour cent croyaient que la Direction européenne avait besoin des sous-directeurs africains pour agir en médiateur entre la Direction européenne et les ouvriers et les clients africains. On a remarqué un certain dépit entre le sous-directeur ou exécutif africain et le jeune sous-directeur européen qu'on peut voir dans l'observation suivante:

'La Direction veut avoir des conseils du sous-directeur africain. Le sous-directeur européen croit comprendre la mentalité africaine. . . . La Direction ne le croit pas capable de traiter les Africains. Alors le sous-directeur européen doit maintenant considérer son collègue africain comme interprète de la mentalité africaine—qu'il croit comprendre lui-même—sinon, son patron lui demandera 'Avez-vous verifié cela avec le sous-directeur africain?' Le sous-directeur européen ressent, donc, un dépit de son collègue africain dont il a, au même temps, besoin pour rendre agréables ses propositions à la Direction et pour lui servir de bouc émissaire quand les choses ne vont pas bien. Le sous-directeur le voit, lui, comme une menace potentielle à son avancement.

L'Engagement aux valeurs Idéologiques. On a investigué le
dégré d'engagement de ces bureaucrates africains aux valeurs
individuelles associées, en générale, avec l'entreprise privée, par
moyen d'une adaptation de la 'P.E.C. Scale' dont Adorno se
servit dans *The Authoritarian Personality*. Une classe d'étudiants
de sociologie à Makerere, une élite non-bureaucratique, constituait le groupe de contrôle. On a trouvé le groupe de bureaucrates africains beaucoup plus orienté vers les valeurs collectivistes
que le groupe de contrôle. Les étudiants ne montrèrent pas un
dégré d'engagement significatif, au point de vue statistique,
($x^2 = 2\cdot84$) à aucun des deux genres de valeurs. Leur 'ambivalence' s'accorda avec leurs années de développement. Le collec-
tivisme des bureaucrates semblent se dégager de l'esprit d'une
communauté africaine plus large, plutôt que des organisations
bureaucratiques pour lesquelles ils travaillaient. Ils étaient dans
ces compagnies mais ils n'en faisaient pas partie.

X. L'ÉMERGENCE DE CADRES DE BASE AFRICAINS DANS L'INDUSTRIE

A. HAUSER

Depuis que des industries ont été introduites en Afrique il s'est posé le problème de l'encadrement de la main d'œuvre par du personnel local. Il a fallu trouver des chefs susceptibles de diriger —ou tout au moins de surveiller—des équipes de travailleurs dans des travaux non coutumiers. Ce problème a longtemps été résolu empiriquement, et plus ou moins heureusement. Sous la pression des circonstances, du fait que la formation professionnelle des Africains s'améliorait et que l'on commençait à devoir tenir compte des prix de revient, en particulier de celui du personnel expatrié, on est venu peu à peu à considérer que certains postes d'agents d'encadrement, exigeant un minimum d'autorité et de sens des responsabilités, pourraient être tenus par des Africains et depuis un assez grand nombre d'années on trouve çà et là des agents de maîtrise africains dans les entreprises industrielles. Mais ce n'est guère que depuis l'après-guerre que l'on a commencé à prévoir, à plus ou moins long terme, le remplacement progressif des Européens par des Africains dans l'encadrement des travailleurs de l'industrie. A la suite de l'accession de nombreux territoires à l'indépendance politique tous les employeurs européens ont dû prendre ce problème en considération.

Au début de cette année j'ai fait une courte enquête auprès de représentants africains des cadres de base des industries manufacturières de la région de Dakar. J'ai choisi cette branche d'activité car elle m'est familière du fait que j'y ai enquêté à plusieurs reprises depuis 1953. C'est, d'autre part, une de celles où se posent avec acuité les problèmes d'encadrement. Elle a, enfin, une certaine importance dans la vie économique du Sénégal: le service des statistiques de la main d'œuvre fait état de 14.000 travailleurs employés dans les industries manufacturières en Février 1962, sur 72.000 salariés—à l'exclusion des agents de la fonction publique—Le seule région de Dakar en emploie 12.000 sur 45.000 salariés. Les industries de transformation traitent des produits locaux ou des produits importés, bruts ou semi-ouvrés; l'industrie la plus importante est celle des corps gras, à cause de la production locale d'arachide qui avoisine en général un million de tonnes par an: mais d'autres industries se sont développées: textiles, confection et chaussure, industries alimentaires, industries du bois, industries chimiques, fabrication de matériaux de construction. Il existe d'autre part quelques importants ateliers de mécanique générale et des chantiers maritimes.

L'expression de cadre de base que j'emploie dans cette communication désigne la catégorie des agents d'encadrement qui se trouvent à un niveau intermédiaire entre celui des chefs d'équipe et celui des cadres moyens. Ce sont, d'une manière plus précise, les travailleurs classés dans la maîtrise, entre le deuxième et le cinquième échelon. Ce peuvent être des Européens ou des Africains. Dans les services de la production et de l'entretien, où mon enquête a porté, les cadres de base ont des fonctions de chef de quart, de contremaître, de chef d'atelier ou d'adjoint à ces trois postes. Actuellement tous les chefs d'équipe, la plupart des chefs de quart et un certain nombre de contremaîtres sont des Africains dans les industries manufacturières. Les postes de cadre au sens strict, c'est à dire de cadre moyen ou supérieur, sont beaucoup plus rarement tenus par des Africains.

Le service des statistiques de la main d'œuvre donne les précisions suivantes sur les industries manufacturières, en Février 1962:

Direction, cadres, ingénieurs:[1]	africains	25 —	0,18%
	européens	280 —	1,97%
Agents de maîtrise, techniciens:[1]	africains	320 —	2,26%
	européens	546 —	3,85%
Ouvriers:	africains	6.705 —	47,24%
	européens[2]	26 —	0,18%
Manœuvres:	africains	4.150 —	29,24%
Apprentis:	africains	927 —	6,53%
	européens	30 —	0,21%
Employés:	africains	919 —	6,48%
	européens[3]	264 —	1,86%
	Total:	14.192 —	100,00%

[1] Un certain nombre de cadres et d'agents de maîtrise sont employés dans des services administratifs ou compatables.

[2] On ne trouve d'ouvriers européens que dans les industries qui démarrent et ont un besoin immédiat de spécialistes qu'on n'a pas encore eu le temps de former sur place.

[3] Les employés européens sont pour la plupart des femmes recrutées sur place.

Q

En 1959 j'ai effectué une enquête sur l'absentéisme auprès de 2.600 travailleurs représentant l'ensemble de la main d'œuvre africaine permanente des services de production et d'entretien de huit unités industrielles: deux huileries, deux usines de textiles une cimenterie, une fabrique de chaussures, deux ateliers de mécanique générale. La majeure partie des 35 agents de maîtrise africains avaient été promus dans la maîtrise pour des considérations extra-professionnelles; un seul était classé au deuxième échelon. Actuellement, dans ces mêmes établissements, où l'effectif de la main d'œuvre s'élève à 2.800 travailleurs, la répartition des cadres de base africains des services de production et d'entretien est la suivante:[4]

agent de maîtrise 2è échelon:	46
3è échelon:	11
4è échelon:	6
Total:	63

Les postes du cinquième et dernier échelon des agents de maîtrise—correspondant à la fonction de chef d'atelier—sont encore tenus par des Européens, qui occupent aussi des postes des 2è, 3è, et 4è échelons. Mais il est difficile de faire une comparaison statistique des agents de maîtrise européens et africains car ils n'appartiennent pas nécessairement à la même convention collective. D'autre part la plupart des Européens ont un rôle de formateurs, ou sont polyvalents, ce qui leur donne droit à un surclassement ou un sursalaire. On peut seulement signaler que, pour les huit établissements, le nombre total des agents européens d'encadrement des services de production et d'entretien s'élève à 109 agents de maîtrise et 23 cadres. Deux postes de cadre moyen sont tenus par des Africains; 37 pour cent des cadres de base et 8 pour cent des cadres moyens et supérieurs sont africains.

En 1959 j'ai effectué, en complément de mon enquête sur l'absentéisme, une enquête par questionnaire auprès d'un échantillon de 447 travailleurs, avec l'aide de cinq enquêteurs. J'ai utilisé

---

[4] Dans les industries textiles les contremaîtres du 1è et 2è échelon ont été considérés respectivement comme agents demaîtrise du 2è et 3è échelon; les contre-maître-chefs ont été assimilés au 4è échelon car ils n'assument pas encore pleinement les fonctions de chef d'atelier.

avec les cadres de base ce même questionnaire; il comporte deux parties; la première donne des informations relatives à l'instruction, à la vie professionnelle, familiale et sociale et aux conditions de vie; la deuxième fournit des données sur les attitudes à l'égard de la vie traditionnelle ou industrielle et du travail. De plus j'ai eu avec chaque enquêté un entretien libre centré sur les problèmes posés par le commandement qu'il exerce. Il faut une heure et demie en moyenne pour faire passer un questionnaire et je les ai remplis au domicile des enquêtés ou dans mon bureau, s'ils le préféraient, mais pas à l'usine où je me contentais d'expliquer le but de l'enquête et de prendre rendez-vous avec chacun. Dans un cas seulement aucune suite n'a été donnée à deux rendez-vous successifs. J'ai choisi presque tous mes enquêtés dans les établissements où j'avais déjà enquêté en 1959 et j'ai pu les mettre facilement en confiance en leur donnant une version abrégée de mon rapport d'enquête sur l'absentéisme. J'avais déjà interrogé en 1959 26 agents de maîtrise dont 19 sont actuellement des cadres de base des mêmes établissements.

Ma brève enquête a porté sur 18 individus; c'est un trop petit nombre pour que je puisse en dégager des conclusions statistiques, comme je l'ai fait pour mon enquête de 1959 qui portait sur 447 travailleurs. Aussi vais-je présenter les résultats sous forme comparative avec ceux de l'enquête de 1959. D'autre part j'ai commencé une enquête sur les cadres africains (ingénieurs et techniciens supérieurs) occupant des postes dans toutes les branches d'activité—sauf l'administration générale—et je mentionnerai, le cas échéant, les quelques informations que j'ai déjà pu obtenir sur cette catégorie de travailleurs—qui peuvent être des employeurs.

CARACTÈRES DES CADRES DE BASE

Les cadres de base interrogés sont jeunes dans l'ensemble la moitié d'entre eux ayant moins de trente ans; presque tous sont nés en milieu urbain, et leurs parents dans les trois quarts des cas, aussi bien la mère que le père. Or l'étude de l'échantillon de 1959 a montré que l'âge et le lieu de naissance sont deux des principaux facteurs de différenciation des travailleurs: les conditions de vie et d'emploi, les attitudes à l'égard de la vie traditionnelle et de la vie industrielle ne sont pas les mêmes chez les travailleurs jeunes et âgés d'une part, d'origine rurale et urbaine d'autre part. S'il en est ainsi c'est avant tout parce que deux variables importantes et liées entre elles ont surtout fait sentir leur action chez les jeunes et en milieu urbain: l'instruction et la formation professionnelle.

Presque tous les cadre de base interrogés ont fait des études primaires complètes. Là s'est arrêtée leur instruction générale. Elle est bien supérieure à celle des travailleurs et même des agents de maîtrise de l'échantillon de 1959, dont 65 et 15 pour cent respectivement étaient illettrés, mais évidemment inférieure à celle des cadres moyens, qui ont au moins achevé le premier cycle des études secondaires.

Presque tous les cadres de base interrogés ont fréquenté un centre d'apprentissage. L'échantillon de 1959 donne 3 pour cent de travailleurs et 23 pour cent d'agents de maîtrise ayant fréquenté un centre d'apprentissage. Les cadres moyens sont passés par un établissement d'enseignement technique d'un niveau correspondant au moins au deuxième cycle des études secondaires.

Les cadres de base interrogés, qui sont presque tous fils de salariés, mais rarement fils de salariés de l'industrie, ont commencé leur carrière industrielle, dans la proportion de 50 pour cent, comme ouvriers professionnels dans un atelier de mécanique générale, attenant ou non à une entreprise; ils ont ensuite été promus dans la maîtrise.

Les salaires mensuels des cadres de base varient de 35.000 à 65.000 francs CFA environ; aussi leurs conditions de vie sont elles nettement supérieures à celles des autres travailleurs. Rares sont ceux logés par l'entreprise, cependant la grande majorité d'entre eux vivent dans des logements en matériau durable (ciment) dont la moitié sont propriétaires, avec un certain confort: l'électricité, fréquemment l'eau courante et un minimum d'installation sanitaire. Quelques-uns d'entre eux ont même d'autres biens immeubles. 27 pour cent des travailleurs de l'enquête de 1959 vivaient dans des logements en 'dur'.

Les cadres de base interrogés sont pour la plupart mariés, très peu ont plus d'une épouse; leurs charges sont lourdes malgré tout: à la charge entière de l'épouse et des enfants s'ajoutent dans un grand nombre de cas des charges partielles sinon entières de parents âgés, de frères et de sœurs d'un au moins des conjoints, trop jeunes les uns pour travailler, les autres pour se marier. Les cadres moyens et supérieurs, qui sont logés par l'entreprise, hébergent moins de personnes, semble-t-il, que les cadres de base; mais ils ont à supporter des dépenses de 'prestige' en faveur d'amis ou de parents éloignés dont le total est élevé.

Les cadres de base interrogés sont dans la moitié des cas issus de père et de mère de groupes ethniques différents, dans un cas de religion différente. Leur épouse est aussi fréquemment d'un autre groupe ethnique que du même groupe ethnique, parfois d'une autre religion.[5] 10 pour cent seulement des travailleurs mariés de l'échantillon de 1959 avaient des épouses d'un autre groupe ethnique.

Ces unions interethniques—la plupart d'ailleurs concernant des groupes ethniques voisins—ont peut-être contribué à l'adoption par les cadres de base de certaines des attitudes précisées ci-dessous, qui semblent cependant surtout en relation avec le degré d'urbanisation et d'instruction. Une autre raison en sera donnée à la fin de cette communication.

A l'égard des coutumes matrimoniales, les cadres de base apparaissent comme plus modernistes que les autres travailleurs. Bien que presque tous soient musulmans peu d'entre eux souhaitent avoir plus d'une épouse. Pour les autres travailleurs, même chez ceux nés en milieu urbain et chez ceux ceux qui sont jeunes, il se dégage une majorité favorable à la polygamie. D'autre part les cadres de base cherchent à se libérer de l'emprise de leur famille dans le choix d'une épouse et surtout ils cherchent à se libérer—encore plus que les autres travailleurs—de l'emprise de leur belle-famille, qui exige actuellement une importante dot, du moins au Sénégal Central. Ils sont encore plus favorables au mariage interethnique que les autres travailleurs mais ils rejettent presque autant que les autres l'idée d'une union intercaste, soit

---

[5] Les enfants sont toujours du groupe ethnique et de la religion du père.

qu'elle leur apparaisse contraire à l'ordre social (contre la religion m'a dit l'un d'eux) soit qu'ils craignent l'opposition absolue de leur famille dans les quelques cas où ils ne manifestent pas de répugnance personnelle.[6]

A l'égard de l'éducation des femmes les cadres de base sont plus libéraux que les autres travailleurs, dont 23 pour cent n'acceptent pas d'envoyer leurs filles à l'école. Aucun des cadres de base interrogés ne s'y oppose et presque aucun ne s'oppose à ce qu'elles apprennent un métier. Cependant très peu de cadres de base interrogés ont une femme instruite.

La vie sociale des cadres de base présente des différences avec celle des autres travailleurs: on observe un élargissement des relations interethniques et fort peu de cadres de base limitent leurs fréquentations à l'intérieur des groupes ethniques, ce qui est le cas d'un travailleur sur deux. La moitié des cadres de base interrogés ont déclaré avoir des camarades à l'entreprise, mais seulement parmi les autres agents de maîtrise: il est, en effet, exclu qu'ils fréquentent des ouvriers, comme certains l'ont dit explicitement. Une bonne partie des loisirs sont absorbés dans ces relations. Les distractions semblent exclusivement d'origine occidentale, qu'elles soient sportives ou culturelles, alors qu'on trouve à peu près autant de travailleurs ayant des distractions purement africaines (lutte notamment) que de travailleurs ayant des distractions purement occidentales.

En ce qui concerne les associations, les cadres de base se comportent comme les autres travailleurs vis-à-vis de celles qui se réfèrent à des valeurs traditionnelles: c'est ainsi qu'un certain nombre d'entre eux appartiennent à des associations ethniques ou religieuses. Je n'ai entendu aucun agent de maîtrise déclarer ne pas avoir d'activité religieuse: tous sont pratiquants et jeûnent si c'est prescrit; certains participent à des lectures, des chants, la plupart à des pélerinage. Pour trouver dans l'industrie des individus qui subordonnent leurs pratiques religieuse aux impératifs de leur activité professionnelle, il faut atteindre le niveau des cadres moyens ou même supérieurs. Ce n'est qu'à ce niveau que

---

[6] Les sociétés sénégalaises sont en effet presque toutes des sociétés à castes.

l'on peut aussi trouver des travailleurs qui n'ont aucune pratique religieuse par suite d'une prise de position personnelle vis-à-vis d'une religion concrète.[7]

La majorité des cadres de base interrogés font partie d'une association sportive (ou en ont fait partie) et quelques-uns d'entre eux font même partie d'une association à caractère culturel. Les autres travailleurs font beaucoup moins fréquemment partie d'associations sportives et presque aucun n'appartient à une association culturelle. D'autre part un certain nombre de travailleurs participent à une association à caractère économique ou ethnico-économique comme la 'tontine' où chacun reçoit à tour de rôle une partie du salaire des autres. Aucun des cadres de base n'éprouve le besoin de participer à une telle association; cela s'explique par l'importance relative de leur propre salaire. Mais il apparaît chez eux une autre sorte d'association: au type association d'anciens élèves, qui groupe ceux d'entre eux ayant suivi des cours de technique de commandement ou d'animateurs de formation: ces associations permettent aux anciens stagiaires de rester en relation et de bénéficier mutuellement des connaissances qu'ils peuvent acquérir par la suite.

Très peu de cadres de base participent à la vie politique du pays, alors qu'une importante minorité de travailleurs étaient membres d'un parti en 1959. D'autre part la grande majorité des travailleurs appartiennent à un syndicat, alors que la moitié seulement des cadres de base interrogés sont syndiqués; mais ils n'ont pas de syndicats distincts des ouvriers, ce qui ne signifie pas qu'ils approuvent toujours les positions prises par la fraction ouvrière des syndicats; ils ont évidemment leurs propres délégués du personnel à l'intérieur de l'entreprise.

Chez les cadres moyens et supérieurs (ingénieurs et techniciens) de toutes les branches d'activité, sauf l'administration générale, existe, depuis quelques années déjà, une association, qui s'étend aussi à d'autres Etats d'Afrique francophone. Ses membres, groupés en commission, font diverses études techniques ou économiques qu'ils communiquent aux pouvoirs publics, de façon

[7] Dans l'enquête de 1959 8 pour cent des travailleurs déclaraient n'avoir aucune activité religieuse mais il s'agissait plutôt d'un manque d'assiduité.

à leur faire connaître des déficiences éventuelles. L'association peut même intervenir plus directement auprès des pouvoirs publics lorsqu'elle croit devoir les conseiller. Il n'existe pas de syndicat de cadres africains au Sénégal; le besoin ne s'en fait pas sentir. Ces cadres éprouvent une certaine désaffection pour l'administration publique; la plupart ne veulent pas s'engager vis-à-vis de la politique générale des dirigeants de l'État: ni en faveur de cette politique, ni dans une opposition ouverte.

Les cadres de base interrogés envisagent tous un avenir dans l'industrie et la plupart semblent aimer vraiment leur métier. Cependant certains d'entre eux avouent être gênés par le fait que l'employeur et beaucoup d'agents d'encadrement sont européens. D'où l'ambiguïté de l'attitude des cadres de base envers les travailleurs; ils peuvent en venir à ne pas prendre de sanctions à l'égard d'un travailleur ayant commis une faute, et ne pas en référer à leur supérieur, mais agir uniquement par persuasion, de façon à maintenir la solidarité africaine, selon leur propre expression; ils peuvent aussi adopter une attitude réprobatrice vis-à-vis d'une action syndicale et ne pas s'associer à une grève. Leur promotion a pu susciter des jalousies. Vis-à-vis des chefs d'équipe et des délégués du personnel ouvrier ils se trouvent parfois dans une situation embarrassante et certains d'entre eux tiennent compte des réactions éventuelles d'anciens camarades ou des syndicats. Pour les cadres moyens et supérieurs, qui n'ont jamais eu les mêmes contacts avec les autres travailleurs, ces problèmes ne se posent pas

Les cadres de base africains ont sous leurs ordres un nombre variable de travailleurs, selon l'industrie et le service auxquels ils appartiennent. Ce nombre dépasse toujours la dizaine et parfois la centaine. Ils éprouvent des difficultés dans le commandement, ou en ont éprouvé à leurs débuts, du fait qu'ils sont relativement jeunes et—dans certains cas—que les travailleurs qu'ils dirigent sont d'un autre groupe ethnique. Du point de vue de la caste ils sont presque tous du groupe des hommes libres, ce qui est préférable pour leur autorité. Je n'en ai connu que deux de caste inférieure, agents de maîtrise depuis 1959. Les cadres de base d'origine noble déclarent qu'ils se font facilement obéir des travailleurs de leur groupe ethnique. La religion ne pose pas de problème particulier pour les rares cadres de base catholiques.

Avec les agents d'encadrement européens le dialogue des cadres de base africains n'est pas toujours facile non plus. On ne peut dire que ceux-ci soient mis en place hâtivement dans l'industrie. Cependant il est évident que les employeurs sont obligés de tenir compte du contexte politique, économique et technique actuel. Les agents européens, qui ne voient évidemment pas tous favorablement leur éviction progressive, ont tendance à se référer à une situation européenne, où le niveau d'instruction et de formation professionnelle des agents de maîtrise et des cadres est dans l'ensemble plus élevé, où le milieu humain et physique est différent, et ils expriment à l'égard des cadres de base africains qu'ils supervisent des exigences disproportionnées avec les connaissances générales et techniques que ceux-ci ont eu jusqu'à présent la possibilité d'acquérir à l'école ou à l'atelier. Et ils sont loin d'être tous des éducateurs. Aussi certains employeurs commencent-ils à recourir à des méthodes de formation fonctionnelle, sur le plan de l'entreprise, de tous leurs cadres et agents de maîtrise, européens et africains.

Il semble, dans la conjoncture actuelle, que les cadres de base, moyens et supérieurs engagés dans la vie industrielle, qui bénéficient d'un statut social supérieur à celui des autres travailleurs de l'industrie, éprouvent une certaine satisfaction de la situation à laquelle ils sont parvenus mais ne cherchent pas à prendre part à la direction des affaires du pays. Ils n'en constituent pas moins un élite par l'influence indirecte qu'ils peuvent exercer parce que leurs qualités et leur comportement sont imitables (Nadel, 1956). Il ne s'agit évidemment pas des compétences particulières de cette élite spécialisée mais, d'une part, des qualités plus générales acquises dans l'exercice de la profession, et, d'autre part, de manières d'agir dans toutes les situations et de penser dans tous les domaines.

L'utilisation des techniques européennes de domination de la matière contraint les cadres, beaucoup plus que les autres travailleurs, à une discipline dans le travail et une maîtrise de soi bien supérieures à celles qu'exige la vie courante, même en milieu extra-coutumier. Dans la pratique de l'industrie ils acquièrent aussi un sens accru de la responsabilité individuelle et de l'efficacité, ils apprennent à prévoir, et accepter, les obligations qui découlent de leurs fonctions.

Au niveau des cadres, la vie professionnelle est beaucoup moins indépendante de la vie domestique qu'au niveau des autres travailleurs. Aussi les cadres se rendent-ils compte que certaines coutumes sont incompatibles avec le style de vie qu'ils sont nécessairement amenés à adopter pour être en état physique et moral d'exercer leur métier. C'est une des raisons pour lesquelles ils attachent de l'importance aux conditions de logement, ils cherchent à simplifier la vie familiale et à réduire l'autorité des ascendants, ils sont favorables à la promotion de la femme et comprennent que si l'éducation africaine convient à la vie traditionnelle, les valeurs et les habitudes qu'elle confère à l'individu ne facilitent pas son incorporation à la vie industrielle. Ils ne veulent pas pour autant rompre avec leur environnement socio–culturel.

Les cadres de l'industrie, comme les autres élites, 'sont en mesure de faciliter l'évolution de la société et d'assurer la diffusion d'idées nouvelles' (Nadel, 1956, p. 424). Leur conduite et leurs opinions sont susceptibles d'être acceptées comme modèle, au moins par les éléments jeunes de la population ouvrière et même urbaine tout entière. Cette élite est encore très restreinte, mais elle se développe d'année en année et l'aménagement de la vie africaine auquel elle est en train de procéder pour concilier les impératifs techniques et les obligations sociales ne manquera pas d'influencer l'ensemble de la communauté.

On a souvent souligné la tendance statique des civilisations des pays en voie de développement, insisté sur l'orientation non matérielle du dynamisme interne des sociétés non industrialisées, fait ressortir d'autre part qu'au processus d'industrialisation est sous-jacente une philosophie au moins implicite du progrès technique dont la seule culture occidentale a suscité l'éclosion. L'émergence de cadres africains dans l'industrie montre que ces antinomies ne sont pas insurmontables.

BIBLIOGRAPHY

Nadel, S. F.
(1956) 'La Notion d'élite Sociale.' *Bulletin International des Sciences Sociales*
Tome 8, pp. 419–31.

Summary

THE EMERGENCE OF A CADRE OF AFRICAN SUPERVISORY STAFF IN INDUSTRY

A short inquiry was conducted in the Dakar area among African representatives of the basic supervisory staff of the manufacturing industries—that is to say, supervisors at an intermediate level between the 'boss boys' and the higher-grade technicians. In general, they serve as shift bosses or foremen; 37 per cent of the basic supervisory staff and 8 per cent of the higher-grade technicians and engineers are Africans. The results of this inquiry are compared with those of an inquiry conducted in 1959 among labourers and artisans; in the last part of the paper reference is also made to the first results of an inquiry in progress on higher-grade technicians and engineers.

The supervisors interviewed were mostly young; nearly all were born in an urban environment and could therefore complete primary studies and go to a trade school. Half of them began their industrial careers as qualified workers in a general mechanical workshop before being promoted to the supervisory staff. Their monthly wages range from about 35,000 to 65,000 francs CFA (£50–£90) and their living conditions, and notably their housing, are clearly of a higher standard than those of other workers. Most of them are married; very few have more than one wife, nor are they on the whole in favour of polygamy, though nearly all are Moslems. Their attitude towards marriage appears generally more modern than that of the workers, whether to free themselves from the ascendancy of their family in the choice of a wife, or from their wife's family in the imposition of dowry. However, if they are more in favour than other workers of inter-ethnic marriage they reject the idea of inter-caste union. The supervisors are more tolerant towards the education of women than are other workers; they have the same attitude as these towards associations involving traditional ethnic or religious values to which some of them belong, but participate to a greater extent in sport and cultural associations and in inter-ethnic relations. A new type of technical association, consisting of those who underwent supervision courses, has appeared. Few supervisors take part in the political life of the country, but an important minority of workers are party members. Lastly, only half of the supervisors interviewed belong to a trade union, while the great majority of workers do.

It seems that the basic and higher-grade supervisors, who benefit from a superior social status, are to a certain extent satisfied with the position to which they have attained, but make no effort to participate in the affairs of the country. They nevertheless form an elite because of the indirect influence they can exercise, since their qualities and behaviour can be imitated.

The utilization of European techniques demands from the supervisors a greater degree of discipline and self-control than is required by everyday life; they also acquire an increased sense of individual responsibility and efficiency, learning to anticipate and accept the duties which proceed from their office. The supervisors are much less detached from domestic life than other workers, for they recognize that certain habits are incompatible with the style of life they must of necessity adopt in order to be in a fit physical and moral state to carry on their trade. This is one reason why they attach importance to living conditions; they attempt to simplify family life and to reduce the authority of the older generation; they are in favour of improving the status of women and are aware that while African education is compatible with traditional life, the values and habits that it inculcates in the individual do not facilitate his incorporation into industrial life. Yet they do not wish to go so far as to break away from the socio-cultural environment.

The behaviour and opinions of the industrial supervisors, like the other elites, are susceptible to acceptance as patterns, at least by the younger elements of the working and even the whole urban population. This elite is still restricted, but it is developing from year to year, and the changes in African life, through which it is in process of uniting technical imperatives and social obligations, will not fail to influence the entire community.

Emphasis has often been laid on the static tendency of the civilizations of under-developed countries and the non-material orientation of the internal dynamism of non-industrialized societies. Underlying the process of industrialization is an implied philosophy of technical progress to which western culture alone has given birth. The emergence of African supervisors in industry shows that these differences are not irreconcilable.

XI. LES FEMMES COMMERÇANTES AU DÉTAIL SUR LES MARCHÉS DAKAROIS

D. VAN DER VAEREN-AGUESSY

LE GROUPE SOCIAL ÉTUDIÉ

Revendeurs et revendeuses au détail sur les marchés urbains sénégalais, forment un groupe social que l'on peut considérer comme une classe sociale en formation. En effet, ils forment un groupement de fait assez homogène du point de vue de la situation personnelle des individus qui le composent, et ils ont conscience d'appartenir à une catégorie sociale déterminée. Ils commencent à s'organiser et à règlementer l'accès d'autres individus à leur groupe.

Dans ce contexte, nous accorderons notre attention spécialement aux femmes, car elles forment dans la plupart des cas, la majorité des commerçants au détail sur les marchés.

Elles occupent 60 pour cent de cet emploi à Dakar en 1959, 66 pour cent à Brazzaville-Bacongo en 1962, 83 pour cent à Lagos en 1960 et 85 pour cent à Accra en 1959 (chiffres cités par Mme Comhaire-Sylvain d'après des approximations basées sur le nombre des emplacements réservés aux femmes sur les marchés).

Groupement de fait partiellement organisé

Les vendeuses africaines sur les marchés constituent un groupement social de fait; ses membres y participent à postériori, sans l'avoir voulu au préalable. C'est-à-dire qu'une nouvelle vendeuse ne sollicite pas des autres l'autorisation de s'installer comme telle. Mais la recherche d'un gain monétaire, d'un moyen de subsistance, la conduit à exercer ce 'métier', et elle en éprouve une sorte de solidarité avec toutes celles qui se trouvent dans la même situation.

Ce groupement est 'ouvert' quant à son mode d'accès, puisqu'il n'y a pas de conditions très particulières à remplir pour se déclarer vendeur-détaillant à Dakar. C'est l'habitude et le succès remporté auprès des consommateurs qui intègrent la nouvelle venue sur le marché. Le service de la Municipalité qui a la charge de la police des marchés, en principe, ne fait le plus souvent qu'inscrire dans ses régistres cette décision de fait, ou qu'intervenir en cas de litiges au sujet d'une même place.

Apparemment anarchique, mais en réalité partiellement organisé, ce groupement est formé d'individus qui poursuivent un même but économique et c'est ce qui fait son unité. Il s'agit de fournir aux femmes africaines illettrées, à certaines du moins, un moyen de subsistance, en assurant le morcellement des divers produits alimentaires en unités de consommation directement accessibles à la bourse de l'africain moyen et la distribution des biens périssables d'utilité immédiate produits au Sénégal, en particulier les fruits du maraîchage et de la pêche.

Ce groupement est apparemment anarchique, avons-nous dit, car il ne règne pas sur les marchés sénégalais un ordre rigoureux. On y trouve les mêmes denrées en plusieurs endroits. Et cependant, le marché obéit à une organisation interne suffisamment respectée pour qu'elle influence le fonctionnement du marché et la bonne entente entre les vendeurs. Cette organisation interne se manifeste par des horaires d'ouverture, la règlementation des places de vente, une certaine hiérarchie entre les divers groupes de vendeurs. En effet, il y a un responsable des vendeurs et vendeuses, élu par l'ensemble du groupe. Les femmes élisent, elles aussi, une responsable générale, mais celle-ci est également soumise à l'autorité du responsable général des vendeurs. C'est là une organisation efficace, qui résout la plupart des difficultés qui s'élèvent entre vendeurs ou vendeuses. Ceux-ci sont groupés sur le marché à peu près par catégorie de produits vendus, et chaque rangée possède son chef de file. Celui-ci est choisi un peu arbitrairement pour la sympathie qu'il inspire, parfois aussi à cause de son âge ou de son ancienneté sur le marché.

Ainsi sommes nous en présence d'un groupe social qui a conscience de son entité et est décidé à s'organiser pour défendre des intérêts communs. Au sein de ce groupe, les femmes représentent la majorité même si, dans la hiérarchie de l'organisation interne, elles dépendent d'un responsable masculin. Leur situation n'est pas négligeable, indépendemment de leurs revenus parfois assez maigres (au Sénégal), car elles s'estiment heureuses d'avoir un métier même lorsqu'il est peu rentable, alors que la plupart de leurs congénères ne peuvent en exercer aucun-sans parler de l'indépendance que cette activité leur donne au sein de leur ménage et de leur famille.

Groupement homogène de par sa constitution, d'après l'origine, le degré d'urbanisation et les motivations de l'activité

Le groupe des vendeuses sur les marchés est homogène de par sa constitution; ceci est important pour que les individus qui le composent aient conscience d'appartenir à un groupe donné. Une enquete menée a Dakar l'an dernier auprès des vendeuses au détail sur les marchés dakarois, nous a permis de constater que les zones rurales constituent leur milieu d'origine le plus fréquent: 66 pour cent d'entre elles en proviennent. Les individus émigrent parce que la campagne est très pauvre ou parce que le centre urbain proche joue le rôle de pôle d'attraction, et ceci se comprend bien pour une ville comme Dakar.

Mis à part le lieu d'origine, l'âge au moment de la migration, la durée du sejour au bieu de destination et les causes du déplacement sont autant de variables qui rapprochent les individus qui composent un groupe social.

L'âge moyen des vendeuses se situe aux environs de 45 ans à Dakar, de 30 a 39 ans pour l'ensemble du Sénégal (cf. recensement 1961–62). Une faible proportion des vendeuses sont itinérantes (4 pour cent). Presque toutes appartiennent à une même catégorie de population, la population domiciliée. Elles résident de façon permanente, et depuis plus de 10 ans en moyenne, dans la ville. Cela contribue également à en faire un groupe homogène.

Quant aux causes de leur déplacement, elles se résument dans le besoin d'un revenu monétaire, complémentaire ou non de celui du mari, en vue d'ameliorer le niveau de vie familial ou d'acquerir plus d'indépendance personnelle. Ce besoin naît de la migration, car la monnaie est en milieu urbain, le seul moyen d'obtenir des biens de consommation courante.

Niveau de revenu

La grande majorité des individus de la population étudiée on un revenu journalier net de 200 a 500 Frs. CFA, soit environ 70.000 a 180.000 Frs. par an (ou encore 250 livres). Pour cette classe de commerçantes, la limite supérieure de revenu se situe aux environs de 3.000 a 4.000 Frs. par jour, soit 1.080.000 a 1.440.000 Frs. CFA (ou 1,400 a 2,000 Livres) par an. Cependant, au cours de notre enquête, plusieurs indices nous ont laissé supposer que les vendeuses sousestiment leurs recettes ou bien qu'elles avaient déjà, avant de répondre à nos questions, déduit de leur gain quotidien déclaré certaines dépenses habituelles.

Les caractéristiques que nous venon d'envisager rapidement font des vendeuses sur les marchés un groupe social en formation. Elles representent, avec leurs collègues masculins exerçant le même métier, une partie nouvelle du prolétariat urbain qui ne cesse de se développer avec l'accroissement de la population dakaroise. Masse inconsistante et inorganisée jusqu'alors, elles commencent à prendre conscience de leurs importance et participent de plus en plus aux mouvements d'opinion politique, et elles seront bientôt à même d'exposer aux autorités responsables de ce secteur de la vie économique leurs revendications et leurs aspirations. Déjà plus personne n'ignore l'importance de cette catégorie de femmes dans les circuits de distributions, au Ghana, au Nigeria, au Dahomey ou au Togo par exemple.

LEUR SYSTÈME D'ORGANISATION ET LEURS MOYENS DE DÉFENSE

Nous en avons enregistré deux: le 'Nath', association semitraditionelle, et le Syndicat des Petits Commerçants et Artisans du Sénégal (A.P.C.A.S.), plus moderne.

Voyons d'un peu plus près l'une et l'autre association.

Le 'Nath' est une association d'épargne groupant plusieurs vendeurs d'un même marché et d'un même produit. Il mérite notre attention non seulement à cause des sommes de monnaie dont il permet à chaque vendeuse de disposer en une seule fois,

R

mais surtout en tant que mode d'organisation économique et social: il constitue un moyen de répondre, à partir de schémas traditionnels, aux problèmes économiques modernes posés par la vie en ville. Le problème essentiel pour les commerçantes est de posséder en une fois un revenu monétaire leur permettant de faire face à des depenses plus importantes que celles necessitées par la subsistance quotidienne. Inconnu en milieu rural, disent les femmes interrogées, le 'Nath' apparaît en milieu urbain sous la pression de l'individualisme et des impératifs économiques. Il constitue l'une des formes les plus simples de groupement à fondement économique. On retrouve ce genre d'organisation dans de nombreuses autres villes noires; G. Balandier en mentionne de semblables à Poto-Poto, quarter africain de Brazzaville.

Le 'Nath' groupe un nombre variable de vendeuses d'un même produit, 5 à 60 personnes. Chaque membre de 'Nath' verse quotidiennement à la présidente de l'association le montant fixé par l'ensemble du groupe (50 a 100 Frs.). Chaque jour, l'une des participantes perçoit la totalité des sommes ainsi épargnées, et ceci chacune à son tour. Cependent, lorsque l'une d'elles se trouve en difficulté ou doit faire face immédiatement à une dépense imprévue, elle peut percevoir, avec l'accord de l'ensemble du groupe, le total des sommes recueillies en dehors de son tour, ou deux fois successivement. Elle devra rembourser le trop perçu lorsque sa situation financière sera meilleure. D'autres fois encore, le produit de la collecte n'est pas alloué quotidiennement, mais confié à la présidente qui, au bout de la quinzaine ou du mois, selon la périodicité décidée pour le 'Nath', le remet à celle dont c'est le tour. Lorsque le 'Nath' a une périodicité journalière, les associées bénéficient d'une somme d'autant plus grande qu'elles sont plus nombreuses. Entre deux tours au profit de la même personne, il s'écoule un nombre de jours égal au nombres des participantes.

La choix de la présidente responsable du 'Nath' est basé sur des critères traditionnel; ce choix dépend du crédit qu'on lui accorde, de son origine sociale, de son âge, de son ancienneté sur le marché, de la sympathie qu'elle inspire. C'est en général une vendeuse influente, donnant des garanties de probité et d'équité, et ayant un répondant financier suffisant. Sa tâche est de déterminer la périodicite des versements et de diriger l'attribution des sommes collectées. Elle est élue pour une durée indéterminée par l'ensemble des participantes.

On voit ici comment se mêlent les éléments traditionnels et modernes. La répartition du 'Nath' semble rationnelle et démocratique, mais l'élection de la responsable ne mérite pas entièrement ces deux qualificatifs, car les critères de choix sont avant tout de caractère social et interpersonnel, plutôt que de caractère économique et fonctionnel.

Cette élection est donc guidée par des références au cadre traditionnel. Ainsi par exemple, la responsable peut être élue parce qu'elle est la 'griote' de plusieurs des membres de l'association. Ce qui veut dire qu'elle leur est liée par une relation de caste. La 'griote' est celle qui est attachée à une plusieurs familles par des liens de dépendance, et qui en retour des avantages matériels ou sociaux dont elle bénéficie, chante les louanges de cette famille et lui rend de multiples services en rapport avec le code de vie sociale.

Comme l'écrit G. Balandier (*Sociologie des Brazzavilles Noires*, pp. 162 et 163), 'alors que les sociétés traditionnelles définissaient d'une manière précise le statut de chacun et déterminaient exactement les rapports avec autrui, ne laissant guère de jeu a l'inclination personnelle, la société urbaine entraîne le recul de telles relations et permet le développement de relations électives. Ce sont là des observations qui peuvent nous paraître particulièrement banales; elles n'en portent pas moins une signification: elles donnent la mesure de la marge de liberté acquise par l'individu qui s'établit en milieu urbain.' Nous ajouterons qu'elles sont également le signe de la transformation des structures sociales et amorcent le passage des groupements de forme traditionnelle à une organisation sociale moderne. Le but essentiel du 'Nath' est de réaliser une somme qui représente un pouvoir d'achat plus élevé que ne le permettent les recettes journalières personnelles et d'imposer, en raison du caractère strict de la discipline, la réalisation d'épargnes, dans des délais relativement courts néanmoins.

Les sommes ainsi réunies atteignent un montant variable.

Elles dépendent évidement du taux de versement quotidien et du nombre de participants. Celui-ci, d'après les cas enregistrés sur l'ensemble des marchés dakarois, tourne autour de quinze à vingt dans la plupart des cas. Pour deux des cas observés, le total des collectes s'élevait à 15.000 Frs. par jour. Ceci represente un 'Nath' déjà important quant au nombre de ses membres (50) et a la cotisation journalière (300 Frs.). Ce sont là, semble-t-il des réalisations exceptionnelles. Généralement le 'Nath' permet aux vendeuses de disposer en une fois de 500 à 1.500 Frs., moins fréquemment de 2.000 à 3.000 Frs. et plus rarement de 4.000 à 6.000 Frs. Il arrive également qu'une même personne participe à deux 'Nath' différents, afin de disposer dans le même delai d'une somme d'argent importante. Certaines portent ainsi leur épargne de 2.500 Frs. en moyenne à 7.000 Frs. tous les 15 à 20 jours.

Le 'Nath' représente une innovation de milieu urbain par rapport au monde traditionnel (rural). Ici il ne s'agit plus d'une communauté liée par la consanguinité, la religion, ou l'ethnie, mais d'une véritable association d'individus autonomes réunis par une même activité commerciale et libres dans le choix des relations qu'ils etablissent les uns avec les autres.

L'entraide sous forme de mise en commun du travail, fréquente à la campagne (aide pour le desherbage d'un champ pas exemple), est remplacée par une association à but purement économique. Mais, sous cette forme nouvelle, subsistent certains traits traditionnels qui favorisent l'adhésion de l'individu. La mise en commun des ressources s'opère sur la base d'une stricte solidarité, d'une garantie mutuelle, obtenue par référence au modèle coutumier, qui favorise la confiance et en est même la condition, et qui engage les associés sans équivoque possible. Les vendeuses restent attachées au modèle culturel que constitue le groupement de solidarité. Mais celui-ci, accomplissant des fonctions entièrement nouvelles, est le lieu de profonds changements internes et sert de cadre à une véritable transformation des structures mentales et sociales. Ce phénomène, né de contacts culturels entre en univers archaique et un monde urbain en voie de modernisation, reste lié au premier sans être complètement intégré dans le second. La femme africaine cristallise cette situation de transition. Toute modification de structure est ressentie par elle d'une manière personnelle, selon qu'elle peut y adhérer ou non, par suite des transformations fondamentales que cela entraîne dans la division du travail, les mentalités, et le degré de liberté de chaque individu au sein du groupement familial. Ainsi s'effectue le passage vers des structures économiques et sociales nouvelles et mieux adaptées aux exigences de la vie urbaine moderne.

La deuxième forme d'association par laquelle le groupe social des vendeuses, groupe social en formation, exprime son autonomie est l'A.P.C.A.S. ou Association des Petits Commerçants et Artisans du Sénégal.

En effet, depuis le 27 Novembre 1961, existe officiellement une association de droit privé, groupant les Petits Commerçants et Artisans du Sénégal. Au moment de notre enquête ils étaient 4,5 — inscrits pour l'agglomération dakaroise y compris Dagoudane-Pikine, importante agglomération satellite de Dakar. Cette organisation concerne l'ensemble des marchés dakarois; chacun de ceux-ci représente une section de cette association, ayant son responsable propre. Le siège social se trouve au marché dit de Sandaga, qui est l'un des plus anciens de Dakar et qui groupe le plus de vendeurs. Le Président Général de l'association, lui-même vendeur à Sandaga depuis plus de 20 ans, assure, avec les autres membres d'un bureau élu, la coordination entre les différentes sections et par là, entre les divers marchés de la ville.

Les membres de l'association souhaitent étendre leur mouvement à tout l'hinterland rural de Dakar, et même aux villes et campagnes de l'intérieur du pays, afin d'établir des liaisons étroites entre les vendeures des zones rurales et ceux des villes, et d'améliorer ainsi l'approvisionnement des marchés.

Le Président Général de l'A.P.C.A.S., dont nous venons de parler, remplit les fonctions de responsable des vendeurs du marché principal, Sandaga. Il possède sur chacun des marchés un homologue élu par l'ensemble des membres de la profession. Il a pour rôle de veiller à la bonne entente sur les marchés et de régler les différends qui pourraient survenir entre vendeurs lorsqu'il n'y a pas de dommage causé aux personnes. Il jouit d'un grand prestige dû, semble-t-il, à son âge et à son ancienneté sur le marché. Il est assisté d'un adjoint, qui est aussi secrétaire général de la section de l'A.P.C.A.S.

Vendeurs et vendeuses au détail sur les marchés dakarois ont choisi le syndicat comme mode d'organisation rationnelle et efficace parceque, vivant en ville, ils s'assimilent aux travailleurs salariés dont les revenus restent bas, aux ouvriers non qualifiés du bâtiment ou de l'industrie pas exemple. Les statuts de leur syndicat, et le rôle que celui-ci est appelé à jouer, sont pour ainsi dire immités des syndicats ouvriers. L'A.P.C.A.S. a pour mission, entre autre, de servir de lien entre les commerçants de cette catégorie et les autorités du lieu, de représenter et de défendre les intérêts des membres de ce syndicat. Nous assistons ici à un phénomène d'assimilation d'un trait culturel moderne par ce monde semi-archaïque que représente dans le milieux urbain dakarois les vendeurs au detail sur les marchés.

Cependant, cette organisation, qui se veut entièrement moderne et démocratique compte parmi ses adhérents une grande majorité d'hommes. Les femmes sont beaucoup plus méfiantes et doutent encore de l'efficacité de ce groupement. Aussi ne s'y joignent-elles que prudemment. D'autre part, elles trouvent normal de s'en remettre aux hommes pour la défense de leurs intérêts communs.

On voit ici que les femmes adhèrent volontiers et en grand nombre à un mode de groupement, semi-traditionnel et semi-moderne comme le 'Nath' dont nous avons parlé précédemment alors qu'elles sont plus réticentes vis-à-vis d'une forme d'organisation pratiquement moderne. C'est de cette manière qu'elles freinent ou accélèrent l'évolution et la création de nouveaux groupes sociaux en milieu urbain.

L'importance, en Afrique, de la participation de la femme aux changements structurels économiques et sociaux, vient de ce que seule son adhésion est une preuve irréfutable de la pénétration et de l'intégration de ces nouveautés aux modes de pensée et au comportement africain. On a pu souvent constater que les changements décidés restaient souvent lettre morte lorsqu'ils ne présentent pour les individus aucune signification personnelle. Ainsi par exemple, et toujours à propos des marchés, les services administratifs ont voulu créer des marchés ruraux hebdomadaires, où les denrées auraient des prix fixés et harmonisés, et où vendeurs et vendeuses ou détail pourraient s'approvisionner en gros. Ceci avait été organise dans l'intérêt même des détaillants, pour leur éviter d'être le plus souvent grugés par les intermédiaires, revendeurs eux-mêmes, qui se chargent de transporter les produits depuis les zones rurales jusqu'a la ville. Les femmes n'ayant pas perçu l'efficacité et la signification de cette amélioration, celle-ci est restée sans effet.

Les cas des commerçantes au détail sur les marchés urbains Sénégalais est ainsi un exemple de la formation de nouveaux groupes sociaux, qui pour s'organiser et défendre leurs intérêts utilisent des schémas de plus en plus moderne. Le marché est à ce point de vue un milieu intéressant à étudier parceque l'archaique y voisine sans cesse avec le moderne, comme nous l'avons vu pour le 'Nath'. Mais déjà nous avons pu enregistrer de nombreux indices de la transformation des structures économiques, sociales, mentales, des habitudes de vie, qui tendent à favoriser le developpement de cités tout à fait modernes, avec les avantages et les inconvénients que cela comporte.

Summary

WOMEN TRADERS IN DAKAR MARKETS

Retail traders in the town markets of Senegal form a social group which may be regarded as a class in the making. In this paper particular attention will be paid to women, who generally form the majority of retail market traders (60 per cent in Senegal). A study of the characteristics of this emergent social group, with its system of organization and means of defence, will show how the African woman encourages or hinders the formation of new social classes.

This group is already in existence and is partially organized. Market women working in the same conditions are united by the search for financial gain. This group, unconditionally open to all, is made up of individuals who are pursuing the same economic end. The apparent confusion of the markets nevertheless conceals an internal organization regulated by timetables, the fixing of selling places, and a certain hierarchy among the different groups of traders. The group is thus aware of its unity and organizes itself to defend its common interests.

Within this new social class women are in the majority, although in the internal hierarchy they are sometimes subordinate to a man. This group is homogeneous by reason of its constitution, its origin, the degree of urbanization, and the motivation of the market women. The majority of these women (66 per cent) come from the rural areas. They nearly all belong to the resident population. They are about 45 years old in Dakar (30 to 39 in Senegal). On average they have lived in the town for more than ten years. The need for money and the desire for greater personal independence were the reasons for their move. Their average income is about £250 a year, rising to £1,400 or £2,000. These figures are approximate, since the traders do not keep strict accounts. With this income they form a new section of the urban proletariat which is growing up in all African towns.

There are two forms of association for this new social group: the semi-traditional 'Nath' association, and the more modern Syndicat der Petits Commerçants et Artisans du Sénégal (A.P.C.A.S.).

'Nath' is a savings association comprising several traders in the same product on the same market. The total subscriptions of the group are allocated to each of the members in turn. The woman responsible for the division is chosen by traditional and modern criteria of personal suitability: age, credit-worthiness, personality, and rank.

The A.P.C.A.S. has been legally recognized since November 1961. Women are less attracted to this type of group because it breaks with traditional methods and does not include any traditional elements in its organization. African women encourage or resist this movement according to their attitude to modernization and progress.

Women traders on African markets, and particularly those in Senegalese towns, thus illustrate the formation of new social groups which make use of increasingly modern forms to organize and defend themselves.

XII. ASPECTS OF OCCUPATIONAL PRESTIGE IN A PLURAL SOCIETY

J. C. MITCHELL

Social status, if it is to operate as a factor in social interaction in a large-scale society, must be patent. Thus, invisible wealth must be converted into conspicuous symbols of status, and social origins expressed in manners, accent of speech, bearing, and in the general style of life. Of the various indicators of status one of the most easily observable and clearly recognized is the occupation that a person follows.

In western societies the occupation, because of its close relationship with social status, is of particular significance in the study of social stratification. Hence in American and British society, for example, it is usually possible to make a reasonable guess at a man's social standing if his occupation is known. Warner made use of this fact in his studies of social stratification of American communities by giving occupation the highest weighting of all the items he used in his Index of Status Characteristics (Warner, Meeker and Eells, 1960, pp. 176–85). Similarly, Glass (1954, p. 6) argued that occupation reflects the combined influences of a number of factors linked with social status and suggested that occupation might be used as an initial index of social status in Britain. More generally, an empirical examination by means of factor analysis of nineteen possible indicators of socio–economic status revealed two underlying factors, one of which was closely related to type of house and residential area and the other to occupational prestige (Kahl and Davis, 1955).

The evaluation of the social standing or 'prestige' of occupations in these societies, therefore, has provided a relatively simple and direct means of assessing the otherwise latent nature of social stratification and of measuring changes in it. Occupational prestige studies consequently have been common in the United States since 1925, but interest in them was renewed following two important studies conducted almost simultaneously in the United States and Great Britain in the late 'forties. In 1947 the National Opinion Research Center conducted a survey among 2,900 interviewees in order to secure information on the social grading of ninety occupations (North and Hatt, 1950). At about the same time Hall and Jones conducted a similar survey concerning thirty occupations in an English sample (Hall and Jones, 1950). As a result of the interest created by these two studies there was a rapid extension in the next decade of studies of this sort to a number of Commonwealth and Western European countries and also to some countries with somewhat different cultural backgrounds, such as the Phillipines, India, and Java (for references see Mitchell, 1964a).

For practical reasons it is much more difficult to conduct studies of this sort in countries where the general level of literacy is low (Mitchell, 1964a). There have been, therefore, few studies of occupational prestige in Africa. In 1953 Mlle Xydias, a member of the International African Institute research team working in Stanleyville, conducted a series of occupational prestige studies in different groups using from twelve to twenty-eight occupations (Xydias, 1956). In 1954 Epstein and I conducted an occupational prestige study in Lusaka, Northern Rhodesia, using thirty-two occupations (Mitchell and Epstein, 1959). There has been a subsequent study in Zambia, partial findings of which have been published (Mitchell, 1964a), and another in Southern Rhodesia, some results of which are used in this analysis. There have been other studies in Africa, but these are unpublished, and therefore not available for use in this paper.

The interpretation of the results of these studies in Africa involves special problems. Some difficulties arise from the method used to arrive at the rank order of the occupations, but these are inherent in all studies using these techniques and are not peculiar to studies in Africa. But other difficulties arise on the nature of the system of social stratification which the prestige ranking of the occupation is assumed to reflect, and this in turn involves a consideration of the social structure as a whole, of which the social stratification is only a feature. In any set of occupational prestige ratings obtained in circumstances such as generally exist in Africa the effects of these two sources of ambiguity appear simultaneously. Our analysis, therefore, must try to separate the purely mechanical sources of ambiguity from those arising from the underlying social system which is the real focus of our interest.

DIFFICULTIES ARISING FROM THE METHODS OF STUDY

In the earlier studies attempts were made to arrange the entire set of occupations into one rank order. This proved to demand an amount of patience and goodwill on the part of the respondents that most do not possess. Simpler procedures have therefore gained favour. The most common technique in recent studies has been to ask respondents to grade every occupation against a five-point prestige scale ranging from 'very high prestige' at the one end to 'very low prestige' at the other. Usually the respondent has been asked to complete a short questionnaire about his own personal characteristics at the same time.

The gradings of any occupation usually show some scatter in most, if not all, the five prestige categories, with a concentration in one particular category. If every category is given a numerical value, then it is simple to compute a mean rating for every occupation and to use this score to arrange the occupations in a single prestige hierarchy.

It is obvious that the categories 'very high prestige', 'high prestige', etc., are not absolute and that two respondents may differ in their judgement of whether any particular occupation rates as, say, 'high prestige', or 'neither high nor low prestige'. If we are interested in the rank order of occupations this uncertainty of absolute prestige is unimportant, provided the respondents arrange occupations in higher or lower prestige categories consistently in relation to other occupations. For example, it does not matter whether a respondent rates the occupation of Medical Officer as possessing 'very high prestige' or 'high prestige', provided that he rates lower-ranking occupations in lower prestige categories than these. What is really important is the difference in grading of the occupations rather than the specific category in which they are placed. It can be shown simply that the difference in mean rating of two occupations is the mean of the differences in the ratings of the two occupations (Mitchell, 1964b). Therefore the mean rating may be used to arrange occupations in a rank order of social grading. The difficulty arising from the lack of objective criteria of prestige may therefore be ignored.

However, if we give arbitrary weights to the prestige categories to enable mean rating to be computed and so make a general ranking of occupations possible, we thereby impute a prestige distance between categories. It is common, for example, to give the highest prestige category a weight of one, the next lowest two, and so on down to the weight of five for the lowest. This assumes that the prestige distance between the 'very high prestige' category and the 'high prestige' category is the same as the distance, say, between the 'low prestige' category and the 'very low prestige' category. Once again this does not matter much, provided we are interested only in the ranking of occupations. If, however, we wish to compare the ratings given to an occupation by one group with the ratings given to the same occupation by another group we need to take into account the possibility that the overall rating of one group is consistently higher or lower than that of the other.

We can overcome this difficulty by apportioning weights to every prestige category for every group of respondents so that the mean of the aggregate of all ratings of all occupations is the same. This can be done simply by adjusting the values of the categories on the assumption that the aggregate of all ratings is normally distributed (Yaukey, 1955).

The way in which a ranking of occupations can be arrived at is illustrated in Table 1. This refers to a rating of occupations of Africans in Rhodesia by 1,485 African secondary schoolchildren. The weights used to compute the mean ratings according to which the occupations have been ranked, adjust the mean of the aggregate of all ratings to 2·0.

It is quite clear from this tabulation that the occupations arrange themselves in an order in which a pattern occurs which is similar to that to be expected in European and American studies.

Table 1

Prestige Ratings of Occupations
(1,230 Boys and 255 Girls at Secondary Schools)

Prestige Rating

Occupations	Very high	High	Not High or low	Low	Very low	Total	Don't know	Mean rating	S.D.
Weights	(0·59)	(1·54)	(2·21)	(2·80)	(3·60)				
	i	ii	iii	iv	v	vi	vii	viii	ix
Lawyer	1,228	147	45	18	15	1,453	32	0·79	0·53
School Inspector	1,144	253	40	16	13	1,466	19	0·85	0·54
Sec. Schl Teacher	1,009	426	36	7	3	1,481	4	0·92	0·51
Medical Officer	914	434	100	10	18	1,476	9	1·03	0·63
Headmaster	797	567	87	12	7	1,470	15	1·08	0·58
Priest	822	439	150	34	16	1,461	24	1·13	0·68
Afr. Min. of Rel.	776	491	153	33	20	1,473	12	1·17	0·69
Senior Clerk	610	720	124	22	2	1,478	7	1·23	0·58
Sergeant in Army	595	549	206	64	48	1,462	23	1·37	0·78
Radio Mechanic	501	618	296	41	3	1,459	26	1·39	0·66
Radio Announcer	483	683	271	27	11	1,475	10	1·39	0·64
Bus Owner	462	687	254	46	18	1,467	18	1·42	0·67
Afr. Police Insp.	528	611	218	55	58	1,470	15	1·43	0·78
Newspaper Editor	475	619	247	66	37	1,444	41	1·45	0·74
Medical Orderly	385	719	310	47	7	1,468	17	1·48	0·63
Afr. Welfare Officer	364	644	292	64	13	1,377	108	1·51	0·67
Hlth. Demonstrator	392	689	300	62	35	1,478	7	1·53	0·70
Typist	330	741	338	54	7	1,470	15	1·54	0·62
Primary Sch. Tchr.	327	751	318	63	16	1,475	10	1·55	0·64
Trade Union Br. Sec.	310	593	313	63	27	1,306	179	1·58	0·69
Garage Mechanic	326	647	397	83	14	1,467	18	1·60	0·67
Laboratory Asst.	263	651	373	65	19	1,371	114	1·63	0·65
Preacher	336	583	426	84	34	1,463	22	1·64	0·72
Carpenter	164	568	591	104	28	1,455	30	1·84	0·62
African Constable	238	548	414	145	117	1,462	23	1·86	0·81
Reporter	156	552	518	140	70	1,436	49	1·90	0·70
Bus Driver	156	468	650	159	27	1,460	25	1·91	0·64
Storekeeper	142	480	638	174	33	1,467	18	1·94	0·64
Taxi Driver	123	456	698	153	38	1,468	17	1·96	0·62
Diviner	292	306	407	210	225	1,440	45	2·04	0·97
Foreman	105	457	524	263	112	1,461	24	2·10	0·72
Painter	80	327	723	294	42	1,466	19	2·13	0·60
Plumber	137	366	531	274	134	1,442	43	2·13	0·77
Lorry Driver	79	341	699	285	62	1,466	19	2·14	0·62
Lift Operator	81	304	552	293	119	1,349	136	2·21	0·71
Office Messenger	60	257	668	371	99	1,455	30	2·27	0·63
Nat. Com. Messenger	94	309	517	334	209	1,463	22	2·30	0·78
Shoe Maker	49	185	713	411	100	1,458	27	2·33	0·60
Bricklayer	78	244	524	364	252	1,462	23	2·40	0·77
Station Boy (Rlys.)	48	192	562	443	201	1,446	39	2·44	0·68
Bus Conductor	30	152	630	472	179	1,463	22	2·47	0·62

Table 1—continued

Prestige Ratings of Occupations
(1,230 Boys and 255 Girls at Secondary Schools)

Occupations	Very high	High	Not High or low	Low	Very low	Total	Don't know	Mean rating	S.D.
Weights	(0·59)	(1·54)	(2·21)	(2·80)	(3·60)				
	i	ii	iii	iv	v	vi	vii	viii	ix
Domestic Servant	53	193	471	444	295	1,456	29	2·52	0·74
Market Seller	18	112	612	484	244	1,470	15	2·56	0·61
Petrol Pump Boy	26	99	494	573	252	1,444	41	2·61	0·62
Hotel Waiter	23	104	463	595	277	1,462	23	2·64	0·63
Cook	58	92	394	534	383	1,461	24	2·68	0·73
Pedlar	16	60	420	434	377	1,307	178	2·76	0·65
Newspaper Boy	35	67	348	574	445	1,469	16	2·79	0·68
Road Repairer	87	91	206	305	790	1,479	6	2·94	0·87
Tea Boy	26	50	230	585	571	1,462	23	2·94	0·65
Wood Cutter	20	50	249	506	639	1,464	21	2·98	0·66
Lorry Boy	18	42	255	506	656	1,477	8	2·99	0·64
Garden Boy	40	52	164	414	801	1,471	14	3·07	0·71
Dagga Boy	29	51	154	342	898	1,474	11	3·14	0·68
Sweeper of San. Lanes	34	41	137	268	970	1,450	35	3·19	0·68
Scavenger	73	38	65	98	1,166	1,440	45	3·27	0·77

The top positions in the list are occupied by the professional and higher white-collar occupations. These are followed by a mixed group including skilled and semi-skilled, supervisory and lower-grade white-collar occupations. At the lower end of the scale are the unskilled occupations. The strong presumption must be that the underlying set of norms and values in terms of which these occupations have been rated is similar to that of industrialized countries all over the world. By analysing the data in more detail, however, we are able to make certain deductions about the influence of the social background of the respondents on the way they perceive the social standing of particular occupations, and also about features of the system of social stratification characteristic of 'plural' societies such as that found in Rhodesia.

THE SOURCES OF VARIABILITY IN PRESTIGE RATINGS

A detailed analysis might begin by examining the variability of prestige ratings. While the rank order of occupations derived from the ratings yields useful information as such, a study of the variation in the ratings throws additional light on some aspects of social stratification. This variability may be traced to five basic causes.

(*a*) It may arise out of erroneous rating of occupations by respondents. The variability arising from this source can be expected to be distributed randomly around the mean and to be constant in all occupations.

(*b*) Because the prestige categories are not in any sense absolute, the variability may be due to the fact that respondents use different, albeit consistent, rating scales. Thus, if some respondents use only high prestige categories and others only low, then the overall result will be that the ratings in all occupations will be scattered.

(*c*) It may arise because the occupation is defined too vaguely and means different things to different respondents; e.g. is a 'road repairer' the labourer who wields the pick and shovel or is he the engineer who directs activities in repairing roads?

(*d*) Variability may arise because respondents with particular social backgrounds may perceive the prestige system in a special way. The scatter in responses therefore will reflect the social heterogeneity of the respondents rather than the variability in the ratings of the occupations.

(*e*) Variability may arise because different respondents emphasize disparate but nevertheless component aspects of prestige. This reflects the uncertainty in the concept of general prestige.

From a sociological point of view the variability in the ratings of occupations of the last two types is of particular interest.

DIFFERENT VIEWS OF PRESTIGE SYSTEMS

If we tabulate the prestige ratings of occupations made by respondents with differing social characteristics we note that the mean ratings of occupations vary. The overall ratings of two groups may be compared effectively by computing the regression equation relating to two series of mean ratings and by assessing expected ratings obtained from the equation against the observed mean ratings and comparing the difference with the standard error of estimate. I have used this technique, for example, to show that the prestige of the African policeman had fallen in relation to other occupations in Northern Rhodesia between 1954 and 1959 (Mitchell, 1964a).

But the difficulty in most social research is that several factors usually operate simultaneously. Some technique is needed therefore which measures the effect of one factor singly while the others are held constant. Such a technique is a factorial arrangement of characteristics which we anticipate may affect the rating of occupations. A method used by Keyfitz to analyse the effect of six factors on family size in Canada (1959) provides a suitable model.

In so far as occupational prestige is concerned we may illustrate the method by considering the effect on the mean rating of occupations of the following five factors;

(i) High education (i.e. nine years of schooling and over) against low education (i.e. eight years and under).

(ii) Mother with high education (i.e. six years and over) against mother with low education (five years and under).

(iii) Father with high education (i.e. six years and over) against father with low education (five years and under).

(iv) Father in high-ranking occupation (professional, white-collar, or supervisory) against father in low-ranking occupation (unskilled and domestic).

(v) Long residence in town (five years and over) against short residence in town (four years and under).

For simplicity each of these factors has been divided into two parts as near as possible to the median point of its distribution. It is now possible to classify all respondents into categories showing various combinations of these characteristics. Each category may

s

be appropriately designated by a pattern of plus and minus signs. For example, a person with a pattern of (+ + + + +) would be better educated than the average, have a mother and father with relatively high education, have a father in a high-ranking occupation, and have lived in town for a relatively long period. Persons with a pattern of (+ − + − +), on the other hand, would be better educated than the average, have a mother with relatively poor education, a father with relatively high education, in a low-ranking occupation, and would have lived in town for a relatively long period. There are thirty-two of these patterns possible. To illustrate the method of analysis we may consider the way in which respondents with different patterns of social characteristics rated the occupation of 'Diviner'. Table 2 sets out the number of persons in every pattern of characteristics together with the mean rating they gave to the Diviner. In this Table a set of weights which shifts the mean rating of all occupations to 2 has been computed for every pattern of characteristics. These weights have been used to compute the mean ratings.

It is now possible to consider the effects of any one factor on the mean rating of the Diviner while holding the other factors constant. For example, we note that the mean rating of the 139 respondents with the pattern (+ + + + +) was 2·025. To hold the first four factors constant and allow the fifth to vary we must compare the mean rating with that of the seventy-four respondents with the pattern of characteristics (+ + + + −). This we find is 1·940. We may conclude therefore that in this case the effect of the longer urban residence (the fifth factor) is to increase the mean rating of the Diviner (i.e. to lower his prestige rating) by 0·085 (i.e. 2·025−1·940). There are sixteen such comparisons possible and we are able to compute from them the average effect of longer than median residence in town on the mean prestige rating. The mean ratings, however, are based on widely differing numbers of respondents. We must weight the differences in accordance with the number of respondents concerned. We do this by computing the sum of the reciprocals of the numbers involved. We are now able to test whether the differences due to any one factor are greater than could be expected

Table 2

Distribution and Mean Rating of Diviner for Groups with Different Social Characteristics

A	B	C	D	E	Prestige Ratings					Total	Mean rating	Sum of squares
					1	2	3	4	5			
+	+	+	+	+	20	33	50	19	17	139	2·025	100·06
+	+	+	+	−	18	15	15	16	10	74	1·940	75·37
+	+	+	−	+	26	23	32	11	18	110	1·928	109·00
+	+	+	−	−	13	10	20	11	13	67	2·109	65·72
+	+	−	+	+	1	—	3	—	1	5	2·280	5·10
+	+	−	+	−	—	—	—	—	2	2	3·190	0·00
+	+	−	−	+	4	6	4	1	3	18	1·983	17·73
+	+	−	−	−	1	2	1	2	2	8	2·221	8·57
+	−	+	+	+	7	6	9	7	5	34	2·042	33·05
+	−	+	+	−	8	9	10	3	4	34	1·921	26·83
+	−	+	−	+	13	11	16	12	7	59	1·982	54·90
+	−	+	−	−	13	14	26	9	8	70	2·007	55·44
+	−	−	+	+	7	4	3	2	7	23	2·059	32·33
+	−	−	+	−	4	1	2	3	2	12	2·072	15·77
+	−	−	−	+	14	12	24	8	10	68	1·990	63·17
+	−	−	−	−	21	25	32	17	14	109	2·010	97·12
−	+	+	+	+	—	4	9	1	3	17	2·395	7·43
−	+	+	+	−	10	3	6	4	7	30	2·051	40·57
−	+	+	−	+	3	3	7	7	2	22	2·191	16·09
−	+	+	−	−	14	9	17	7	6	53	1·977	51·73
−	+	−	+	+	—	—	—	—	1	1	3·570	0·00
−	+	−	+	−	1	—	—	—	2	3	2·837	2·25
−	+	−	−	+	1	—	1	1	—	3	1·807	2·56
−	+	−	−	−	2	—	1	4	1	8	2·318	8·07
−	−	+	+	+	—	1	2	1	1	5	2·524	2·81
−	−	+	+	−	3	6	9	4	3	25	2·060	18·58
−	−	+	−	+	1	1	4	2	4	12	2·503	9·24
−	−	+	−	−	17	11	15	7	17	67	2·200	82·55
−	−	−	+	+	1	—	1	—	2	4	2·435	5·63
−	−	−	+	−	4	5	4	1	3	17	2·120	19·28
−	−	−	−	+	3	2	4	2	5	16	2·242	19·41
−	−	−	−	−	22	39	33	19	19	132	2·108	119·14
					252	255	360	181	199	1,247*		1,165·50

A = Educational level (+ = 9 years schooling and over, − = 8 years schooling and under)

B = Mother's Education (+ = 6 years schooling and over, − = 5 years schooling and under)

C = Father's Education (+ = 6 years schooling and over, − = 5 years schooling and under)

D = Father's Occupation (+ = Professional, white-collar or skilled occupation, − = Unskilled and domestic)

E = Length of Town Res. (+ = 5 years and over in town, − = 4 years and under in town).

* All respondents for whom full details of personal characteristics were not available have been excluded from this table.

by chance. These values are set out in Table 3. This table shows that the higher education level of the respondent and that of his father tend to raise the prestige rating of the 'Diviner'. The

Table 3

Effects of Different Factors on the Mean Prestige Rating of the Diviner

Factor	Weighted average difference in Mean Rating	Equivalent number of observations (N)	Estimated Standard Error $\sqrt{0.9593/N}$	$t = \dfrac{\text{col 1}}{\text{col 3}}$
1. Educ. level	−0·152	240·71	0·062	2·45
2. Mother's Educ.	−0·003	216·26	0·066	0·04
3. Father's Educ.	−0·029	203·11	0·069	0·42
4. Father's Occup.	+0·032	245·80	0·061	0·52
5. Length Resid. in Town	+0·034	256·88	0·061	0·56

father's high-ranking occupation and longer residence in town tend to depress the rating of the 'Diviner'. These effects, however, except for that due to the educational level of the respondents, were small and might easily have arisen on a chance basis.

The interactances of the factors were also small and insignificant.

From an analysis of this sort of all fifty-six occupations in Table 1 we ought to be able to determine those occupations for which ratings are affected by the five factors we have chosen to examine, and in what way these factors affect the ratings. We may conclude from findings of this sort that people with specific social backgrounds have different perceptions of the prestige system against which occupations are rated. In other words, we may argue that occupational prestige has many facets, some of which figure more prominently for people with one kind of social background than for people with another.

FACETS OF OCCUPATIONAL PRESTIGE

In so far as the social grading of occupations is concerned, these different facets manifest themselves as differing 'criteria' against which the occupations may be judged. An overall ranking of occupations in a single prestige hierarchy assumes a general prestige system. This may be related to 'rewards'. Hatt does this when he writes: 'Those studies which attempt to describe occupational prestige actually attempt a synthesis of the total reward system' (Hatt 1950, p. 55). Moser and Hall (1954, p. 46) referring to an English study argue: 'A social ranking of occupations cannot be made simply in terms of a single criterion such as income, working conditions, responsibility, educational standards, or any other single characteristic . . . social status involves associational prestige and allied matters.'

We cannot be sure, however, that respondents give the same weight to the different factors in overall occupational prestige, particularly if the prestige factors operate in directions opposite to one another. Consider, for example, the position of an African policeman in a country which is governed by a European minority. On the criteria of education and income his rating among Africans is probably fairly high. Yet, on the other hand, he is expected to uphold laws, some directed against African political expression, which have been promulgated by the politically dominant minority. The social standing of the policeman, therefore, may be assessed against two somewhat discrepant standards: the one in terms of his membership of an African community, the other in terms of his representing an alien political power. We cannot be sure *a priori* which of these criteria any respondent is using in his grading. (See Mitchell and Epstein 1959; Mitchell, 1964a.)

If some respondents rank an occupation unfavourably against one criterion and others rank it favourably against another, the scatter of the ratings as a whole in the five categories of prestige is likely to be wide. This degree of scatter may be measured by the standard deviation of the ratings. In Table 1 the six occupations showing the highest standard deviation were:

Occupations	Standard deviation
Diviner	0·97
Road Repairer	0·87
African Constable	0·81
Sergeant in the Army	0·78
Police Inspector	0·78
Nat. Com. Messenger	0·78

The scatter of ratings of the Road Repairer suggests that the occupation is too vaguely defined for assessments to agree closely. The Road Repairer appears to have been interpreted by a majority as the labourer who works on the road, and by a minority as the foreman in charge of a gang of labourers mending the road.

Four of the remaining occupations—African Constable, Army Sergeant, Police Inspector, and Native Commissioner's Messenger—are of an authority-bearing type, which in Southern Rhodesia involves a political component in the prestige rating which conflicts with the rating on other criteria. The Diviner, on the other hand, is probably assessed by some respondents in terms of a 'traditionalist' criterion, against which he is highly rated, while others probably view the occupation of 'Diviner' from a modernist point of view which tends to denigrate his status.

SOCIAL STRATIFICATION IN A PLURAL SOCIETY

These features of the ranking of occupations and their variabilities have significance in terms of the overall system of stratification at present operating in Southern Rhodesia. Here, as Epstein and I argued earlier (1959), a European minority which is dominant socially, economically, and politically over the African—and other—sections of the community has been responsible for instituting an economic structure into which Africans have been drawn in restricted occupational capacities. The evaluation of these occupations is on the same basis as in occupational prestige studies in America, Australasia, Great Britain, and other Western European countries. This leads to a similar general ordering of occupations.

The Europeans, who, as in all 'colonial' type societies, have come to occupy superior positions *vis-à-vis* Africans in nearly all aspects of social life are in fact 'exemplars' in respect of stratification of African communities. They have introduced the norms and values which underpin the industrial system and represent these values to Africans. Occupations are graded in terms of these norms and values and reflect the general system of status evaluation.

At the same time evaluations based on other factors, themselves related to the 'plural' nature of Rhodesian society, may enter into the grading of an occupation. Data regarding this general grading in terms of 'European' and 'traditional' evaluations will be revealed when the results of the analysis of the factorial arrangement of the five factors on occupational ratings become available. These five factors have been chosen because they would appear *a priori* to distinguish those who might have a 'European', from those who have a 'traditional', viewpoint as regards occupational grading by virtue of education, home background, or contact with urban industrial conditions.[1]

The rating of the 'Diviner' may be seen as the result of evaluation in terms of disparate value systems associated with the two main culturally dissimilar groups that constitute Southern Rhodesian society. The same divided standard of evaluation may show itself also in the scatter of the ratings. The scattered ratings of occupations which bear political authority similarly may be explained in terms of the political opposition between the two major groups.

These observations have been stimulated by the findings in a study on occupational prestige. No one would argue that it would be possible to draw far-reaching conclusions about the system of social stratification in Rhodesia from the results of a ranking of occupations alone. Occupational prestige studies, however, may provide valuable supplementary data to back up, or to refute, existing analyses of social stratification.

BIBLIOGRAPHY

Glass, D.
(1954) *Social Mobility in Britain*, London, Routledge & Kegan Paul: pp. 29-50.
Hall, J., and Jones, C.
(1950) 'Social grading of occupations.' *British Journal of Sociology*, vol. 1, pp. 3-55.

[1] In fact, the analysis presented as an example showed that the status of the Diviner *rises* as the education of the respondents rises. There may be several explanations of this, one of which is that because of nationalist sentiment, which is stronger among more highly educated respondents, certain features of 'traditional' society are now highly evaluated.

Hatt, P. K.
  (1950) 'Occupation and social stratification.' *American Journal of Sociology*, vol. 55, pp. 533–43.
Kahl, I. A., and Davis, J. A.
  (1955) 'A comparison of indexes of socio-economic status.' *American Sociological Review*, vol. 20, pp. 317–25.
Keyfitz, N.
  (1953) 'A factorial arrangement of comparisons of family size.' *American Journal of Sociology*, vol. 58, pp. 470–80.
Mitchell, J. C.
  (1964a) 'Occupational prestige and the social system: a problem in comparative sociology.' *International Journal of Comparative Sociology*, vol. 5, no. 1: pp. 76–90.
  (1964b) 'The differences in an English and an American rating of the prestige of occupations: a reconsideration of Montague and Pustilnik's study.' *British Journal of Sociology*, vol. 15, pp. 166–73.
Mitchell, J. C., and Epstein, A. L.
  (1959) 'Occupational Prestige and Social Status among Urban Africans in Northern Rhodesia.' *Africa*, vol. 29, pp. 22–40.
Moser, C. A., and Hall, J. R.
  (1954) 'The social grading of occupations', in Glass, D. (ed.), *Social Mobility in Britain*. London, Routledge & Kegan Paul, pp. 29–50.
North, N. N., and Hatt, P.
  (1954) 'Jobs and occupations: a popular evaluation', in Bendix, R., and Lipset, S. M. (eds.), *Class, Status and Power*, London, Routledge & Kegan Paul, pp. 411–26
Warner, W. L., Meeker, M., and Eells, K.
  (1960) *Social Class in America: The Evaluation of Status*. New York.
Xydias, N.
  (1956) 'Prestige of Occupations', in Forde, D. (ed.), *Social Implications of Industrialization and Urbanization in Africa South of the Sahara* (Tensions and Technology), UNESCO: pp. 458–69.
Yaukey, D.
  (1955) 'A metric measurement of occupational status.' *Sociology and Social Research*, vol. 29, pp. 317–23.

Résumé

LES ASPECTS DE PRESTIGE DE MÉTIER DANS UNE SOCIÉTÉ HÉTÉROGÈNE

En Afrique on ne fait que depuis peu les études, courantes en Europe et aux États Unis, sur le prestige de métier. L'interprétation des résultats de ces études présente des difficultés qui se dégagent des méthodes employées pour ranger les métiers aussi bien que de la nature du système social dans lequel ils se trouvent.

On peut établir une gamme des rangs de métier en estimant d'abord les métiers individuels et puis les transformant en nombre de points par le 'five-point-scale'. Ces résultats montrent, cependant, des variations qui pourraient être dues aux erreurs dans l'estimation des métiers, aux gammes différentes employées par les informateurs, aux vagues définitions de métier, aux milieux variés des informateurs, à l'insistance sur les aspects différents de prestige.

Le sociologue s'intéresse à la variation due au milieu social des informateurs et aux divers aspects de prestige.

On peut estimer cette première variation par une 'analyse de variation' qui montre, quand on l'applique au métier de Devin, par exemple, que l'éducation de l'informateur est le facteur le plus important de ceux qui influencent les estimations.

On peut analyser les différents aspects de prestige en étudiant le dégré d'accord dans les estimations par les déviations normales, ce qui suggère que quelques métiers, tel que celui de Devin, peuvent être éstimé selon les critères divers, par exemple, le traditionalisme et le modernisme.

On peut interpréter ces résultats sous les termes de la société hétérogène du Rhodésie du Sud où cette étude a été faite.

XIII. SOCIAL NETWORKS OF FARMERS AMONG THE PLATEAU TONGA OF ZAMBIA

A. D. JONES

INTRODUCTION

This paper is concerned with an emerging 'tribal elite'. Although the material presented here was collected as part of a study of human communications among the Plateau Tonga, it does, I think, throw some light on the character of a new and emerging agricultural elite. A general description is given of the economic position of these farmers, from which springs their influence. This is followed by discussion of their networks of interpersonal relationships, which are seen to differ in some respects from the traditional pattern more commonly found among the Plateau Tonga.

The majority of Tonga are involved in cash farming to some extent. Maize is the main cash crop. Groundnuts, sun hemp, velvet beans, cotton, and a number of other commodities are also raised for sale. Cattle, pigs, and poultry are sold, and incomes are also made from various business activities, the most notable of which is burnt-brick making. The commercial, or elite, farmers are easily identified from the rest. To begin with the Tonga have a name for them: *mulimi simpindi*, 'a farmer for profit'. There seems to be good agreement in any particular area as to who the commercial farmers are.

The area of study was approximately ten miles by ten. It contains upward of 600 male cultivators, of whom fifteen are recognized locally as commercial farmers. They can be distinguished from the other farmers and cultivators in a number of ways. Their resources, in terms of land, machinery, implements, and labour force are high, and so is their income. A casual observer will be struck by the costly capital equipment owned by these farmers. All but three own at least one of the following (the figures in brackets give the total owned by the fifteen): maize mill (4), saw mill (1), motor vehicle (6), tractor (3), wind pump (1), store (4), bakery (1), petrol pump (1).[1] The rest of the population in the area has two maize mills, both owned by old men who made money selling cattle in the 1940s. They own none of the other items, although it is possible that there are some buildings which the owners would call a store, but which are used only as sleeping quarters for children.

A casual observer would also be struck by the homesteads of the commercial farmers. Four of them live apart from their neighbours at distances of more than half a mile. The density of homesteads in areas not under the plough or reserved for grazing probably prevents more from building isolated homesteads. Their separation from neighbours is expressed by fencing off the homestead area. All but one have tree or barbed-wire fences. I was only able to count another fifteen such fences in the rest of the population.

This general description of the commercial farmers could be added to and amplified in various ways which might be of importance in understanding their social position. It is included here, however, only as a background against which to present material on some aspects of the inter-personal relationships which seem to mark them off from the non-commercial farmers.

The Concept of Network

The tribal life of Africa has been examined using a theoretical structure based on kinship networks. Many aspects of social behaviour have been understood in terms of the rules and obligations relating to lineage. The individual's relationships with others are largely determined by these principles. In many urban societies, and even in some tribal societies, the pattern of personal relationships is less dominated by kinship principles and in some cases they appear to have very little significance at all. Yet each individual is part of a network of inter personal relationships which vary according to his social status and position. The

[1] The petrol pump is owned by an Ndebele in a small settlement of aliens bordering the area of study. I have included him in the study, as many Tonga look upon him as being a Tonga, as indeed they tend to look upon any alien resident of long standing.

examination of such networks, although it is unlikely that they can be related to a set of underlying determinants such as a lineage, seems a fruitful way of investigating social change in Africa, particularly in the urban context, but also in some non-urban areas.

The network concept has been implied in a number of instances. Southall (1961) and Pons (1961) are two examples. Mayer (1961, 1962), Bott (1957), Barnes (1954), and Epstein (1961) have used the concept explicitly, although they have each put it to different use. Mayer's work offers an example of how it can be used to understand social change in Africa. He shows how the networks of certain migrants to town act to prevent their forming essentially urban-based relationships and 'incapsulate' them in a system which is orientated towards the rural areas. The other writers demonstrate the variety of applications to which the concept can be applied in understanding, for instance, class structure and the formation of values in a community. More work needs to be done on network studies before a system of assessing their operation can be drawn up into some sort of framework or typology.

My intention here is merely to show differences in the content and operation of the personal networks of commercial farmers when compared with non-commercial farmers.

THE NON-COMMERCIAL FARMERS

The Plateau Tonga follow a matrilineal system of descent and traditionally lived in a stateless society (Colson, 1958, 1962). Until the coming of European rule there were no hierarchies o status or control. There were no positions based on office or rank with the exception of rain-shrine keepers, who exercised a small influence on this account. Each person was bound into a network of relationships with neighbours and with some people who lived farther afield. These relationships were underpinned in many cases by a kinship system. Other, non-kinship relationships existed, being based, for instance, on a loose and unorganized age-grouping or on the loan of cattle.

There was a considerable element of contract in these relationships, even in the case of kin. Elizabeth Colson (1958, p. 20) states what is probably the basic Tonga formulation: 'those who help one another in a particular fashion are relatives, and those who do not so help one another are to be considered unrelated'.

These relationships still dominate the non-commercial farmers. The fact that a genealogical link exists may or may not be used as a basis for striking up a relationship. A number of these links may be putative. There are also links which operate as if they were links of kinship, but where no genealogical link is imputed beyond the use of kinship terms in forms of address. A wide variation seems to exist in relationships of this type. At one extreme the relationship can amount to a kinship link in everything but name, at the other the link can amount to little more than respect or loose friendship, in which kinship terms are used in address. Each relationship carries with it an implied agreement over mutual obligations. By accepting or rejecting a greater or lesser number of obligations the nature of the link can be changed over time.

The network of such links affects a wide range of social action such as residence, marriage, and inheritance. It also affects the day-to-day obligations of help and assistance in disputes and in the domestic labour unit. An obligation may be avoided on a number of occasions with the only result that the link is weakened. If a weakening is to the advantage of the individual he will accept the situation, if not he will try to accept more obligations in order to strengthen it.

The different types of kinship and non-kinship links, if entered into, carry their own specific obligations and rights which are sanctioned by custom. A sister's son, for instance, inherits from his uncle, whereas his own son does not. In day-to-day farming and domestic activities all links can carry the same weight of obligations. A nephew, son, or brother can be called upon for his labour, and the reciprocal obligation in terms of supplying material needs can be the same in all cases. The nature of these day-to-day obligations typify, I suggest, the network of relationships of the non-commercial farmers. These obligations show a recognition of a difference in status which gives one man a degree of dominance over another. This dominance can vary in different cases and can change over time, becoming almost total dependence in some cases or, ultimately, being broken off altogether. Mannoni (1956) seems to have this in mind when he describes the personality of certain Malagasies as affected by a tendency to form strongly dependent relationships. Among the Tonga the precedence of accepted obligations determines the degree of dominance and dependence at any one time. In a dependent position decisions over housing, food, clothes, and other material things are made by another, dominant, person. So, to a large extent, are decisions affecting relationships with other people. In short, a dependent person has decisions concerning a wide range of his social needs and activities made for him, in return for which he is obliged to perform manual services.

The following example is given of part of a non-commercial farmer's network. It shows some kin- and non-kin-based links and the types of behaviour which, I suggest, reflect the principle of dependence operating in these links.

The example shows the relationships between eight men, who live in a half mile square, with one man, A, who is accepted as the *mupati*, the big man, or in my terminology the most dominant individual at the centre of the network. All nine have their own homesteads.

B is a younger brother of A. In 1961 he returned after twenty-three years in South Africa. In 1957 he sent A £17 with which to buy cattle for him. On returning he gave A £19 and became completely dependent on him, e.g. he lived in A's homestead, was fed by A and received clothes, soap, cigarettes, and other small needs from A. In return he helped A to plough and to do other work appropriate for a man. He also ran messages and made visits to the township 20 miles away to shop on A's behalf. After one year B accepted A's advice about a wife. A negotiated with the wife's relatives and provided the marriage payment, two beasts of his own and two from B's money. A then gave B a 3-acre garden and suggested a site on which to build him a homestead. A recruited other dependants to help build the homestead, and when B was installed gave him two ploughing oxen, a cow, a plough, £5, and either two or three bags of maize. B kraals his cattle with A, and continues to depend on A for small items such as thatching twine, salt, and the loan of implements. He is still dependent, but is becoming less so. In return, A can call on B to help him, and did so in November 1963, when he needed assistance in ploughing.

C is another younger brother of A. Eleven years ago C ceased being a school teacher. Already married, he built a homestead next to A's and became dependent on A in a similar way to B. He was fed, clothed, given land and oxen, and loaned implements. In return, A called on C's labour. C is now independent of A, although a tacit recognition of dependence still exists. A has negotiated disputes for C, and when A had trouble transporting manure C volunteered to help and spent four days doing the job for A without any immediate or obvious reward. C says he is an independent man because he has a cattle kraal, but that A is the *mupati*. C has acquired one dependant, J, and if he moves, taking J with him, he might then be free of any dependent relationship and have one dominant relationship to his credit.

D is unrelated to A or anyone in the group. He is also an ex-teacher. He built a homestead some four hundred yards from A, receiving the same help as C. Over the last four years he appears to have severed his relationship with A, returning the oxen he had borrowed, receiving nothing from A, and giving nothing in return. He apparently used to greet A on occasion as 'uncle', but has now ceased to do this and uses a term which means 'friend'. A calls D *mwiiyi*, or 'teacher', but it is possible he always did this. D's position has been strengthened by having his mother and a sister and, temporarily, two young nephews move into his homestead. In the last year he has begun a close relationship with F.

E and F are also unrelated to anyone in the group. In the past they have been dependent on A for cattle, implements, and for negotiating personal interests. They are now independent of A. One year ago, however, F's wife ran away. He began eating at D's homestead and shows signs of becoming dependent on him, seeking advice and assistance. D acted as a go-between for F with his wife's relatives. In return, F helped build a house for D's nephews, and on one occasion was sent on a long journey by D to look for cattle which had strayed.

G and H are both nephews, by different sisters, of A. In the past they have both lived in A's homestead. They both received land from A and help with marriage payment. They still receive gifts of maize. In return they help A to plough and H, especially, acts as a general help in male activities when called upon.

J is distantly related to A on the mother's side and is called nephew. He is, however, completely looked after by C, for whom he herds and does odd jobs when called upon to do so. During the last year J has been looking for land and C has not given him any. He constantly talks about moving elsewhere, and presumably anyone who offered to keep him and to give him land would also receive his labour in favour of C. H, who has done petty trading with J and is the same age as well as being distantly related, has asked A to give J land, who, as yet, has declined, presumably in order not to offend C.

I offer these few examples of the types of relationship which exist in a non-commercial farmers' network primarily, I hope, to show how the recognition of a relationship can occur between two people based on a number of kinship or other ties. Once recognized, the relationship requires the acceptance of a type of dependence and dominance in material and social activities. Each person mentioned is, of course, part of a still wider network of relationships based on kin and other ties and carrying their own specific weight of mutual obligation.

THE COMMERCIAL FARMERS

The commercial farmers do not have the same pattern of relationships with other homesteaders as the non-commercial farmers. In addition, they have relationships which operate in a way which is not found at all among the non-commercial farmers.

As might be expected, the commercial farmers are not dependent on any other head of a homestead. Being wealthy, they are in a position to have a considerable number of homesteads dependent on them. An individual who wants to form a link of mutual obligation with a richer man would be attaching himself to a relatively high source of wealth if he entered into such a relationship with a commercial farmer. These links, however, require acceptance on both sides to set them up. The commercial farmers do not have as many dependent homesteaders as their resources would allow. This seems to suggest that it is the commercial farmers themselves who do not allow such relationships to develop, presumably because it is not sufficiently to their advantage.

I am lacking full information on two of the commercial farmers on this point. Of the remaining 13, however, 8 have no dependent homesteaders, 2 have 1 each, 2 have 2 each, and 1 has 3. It seems that out of this small sample about half the commerical farmers do not have a relationship which their wealth would allow them and which exists, either in a dominant or dependent form, for most non-commercial farmers.

A commercial farmer can reach this position and maintain it because of the contract nature of relationships existing in Tonga society. He can minimize the obligations to those who are intent on realizing a kin relationship without arousing hostility or gaining the reputation of being miserly. All he is required to do to prevent a relationship from developing is to make the occasional gift when it is demanded. Providing he does not consistently offer help or make demands in return for gifts, the relationship cannot develop. From the economic point of view the value of a dependent homesteader to the commercial farmer does not offset the expense of maintaining the relationship. The commercial farmer requires a labour unit over which he has a high degree of control from day to day. The labour of a dependent homesteader does not give him this.

Although the commercial farmer does not form a large number of relationships with other homesteaders, he does maintain relationships with a large number of people who live in his homestead. These are relationships where the dominance and dependence principle operates in a way similar to the relationships typical of the non-commercial farmers. The commercial farmers have more wives, averaging more than three each, and a greater number of adult men, sons, nephews, and other kin and non-kin living in their homesteads. The focus of the commercial farmer's dependent relationships is in his own homestead. This serves his economic need for a labour supply. In return, he supplies food and personal needs and, when the time comes, material assistance for the marriage and the setting up of an independent homestead for his ex-dependants.

The commercial farmers also have a greater number of formal employees than the non-commercial farmers. They are employed for a longer period of time and on explicit agreement with regard to the amount of food and pay to be received for a specified amount of work. Some non-commercial farmers do have the services of, say, a thatcher, and pay him a set price to do a roof at his own speed, but he will usually receive some meals on a casual basis while he is working.

There are also some types of relationship which are unique to the commercial farmer.

All but one of the commercial farmers have relationships with European farmers. Although non-commercial farmers do have some relationships with European farmers, usually as ex-employees, those relationships are not as fully entered into. The commercial farmers tend to receive and reciprocate hospitality, receiving tea and biscuits on their visits to Europeans and inviting Europeans to weddings and on one occasion to a 'housewarming'. Whereas the non-commercial farmers hope to beg and

T

to receive help, the commercial farmer makes a point of paying for anything he receives and acknowledges advice by a return of services when he can give them. Thus, one commercial farmer who had received advice from a European farmer on maize production, and who had been entertained on a number of occasions, on hearing that the European was having trouble with firewood delivered a lorry load and refused any payment. Another has helped to negotiate disputes between employer and employees. Another made a special trip to visit a European farmer who was sick and took him a basket of mangoes.

Commercial transactions with European farmers show a different pattern for the Tonga commercial farmer. He will often go, cap in hand, to buy something and leave it at that. I have never heard of a case of blatant begging following such a transaction. On the other hand, six non-commercial farmers who have begun to rear pigs have attempted to beg for medicine for them. In all cases the begging was unsuccessful, and on paying for the medicine they attempted to beg for something else—salt, a piglet, and in one case, a pile of old sacks. The commercial farmer has his eye open to the possibility of receiving gifts, but will not openly beg for them. The same pattern seems to exist for loans. It is not uncommon for an ex-employee who has become a non-commercial farmer to beg for a loan of a few pounds from his European employer. The only request for a loan by a commercial farmer which I know of was for a largish sum to pay off the debt on a tractor. In this case the individual offered to place cattle on the European's land as a security.

The commercial farmer, while accepting tacitly a lower status than the European farmers, strikes up relationships in which this is minimized. The non-commercial farmer does the reverse, emphasizing lower status by begging and readily accepting gifts without reciprocating them. Mannoni (1956) has used similar examples as a demonstration of attempts to set up a dependence relationship with Europeans.

Another type of relationship which marks off the commercial from the non-commercial farmer is the 'disciple' or 'pupil' relationship. This exists in an obvious and recognized form for four of the farmers. There are elements of it among some of the others. One of the four 'disciples' is a half brother of the farmer, one is brother of a junior wife, and the other two are unrelated. In all cases the disciple is ten or more years younger, gregarious and popular, a non-commercial farmer who aspires to become a commercial farmer. All live within a mile of the commercial farmer with whom they have a relationship. In two cases the pupil was once an employee. These relationships can be termed friendships, being in some ways similar to the relationships which exist between European farmer and commercial Tonga farmer. The disciple acquires knowledge and advice from the farmer. In return, the farmer hears any gossip about himself from his disciple. In addition, the disciple acts as a sort of information and public relations agent. He saves the farmer from time-consuming questioning about farm methods, which the disciple will answer at length and perhaps with a better understanding of the real nature of a particular non-commercial farmer's problems. He also presents an image of the farmer as a good man presenting no threat to the non-commercial farmer and offering a means to learn how to become wealthy. This relationship is clearly of advantage to the farmer in maintaining good relationships with non-commercial farmers. Among some of the others paid employees tend to fill this function, though the man still remains an employee.

The 'disciple' relationship is not a dependence relationship. The commercial farmer is not expected to assist the disciple in material ways, although he will often share luxuries, especially bought food, with him. The disciple does not expect to have to perform jobs in return, although he may well offer his assistance on the more interesting or technical farm practices, such as injecting pigs or using a new planter.

The following is an example of the network of a commercial farmer, M.

M has four wives all of whom live in his own homestead. In addition, he has three unmarried adults living in the homestead; a son, a daughter, and the son of a deceased brother. There are also a number of young children by his wives. He feeds, clothes, houses, and sees to the material needs of this group, which forms his labour unit. In addition, he hired in 1963, four employees from distant homesteads to make bricks on a piece-work wage basis.

M visits a European farmer N, with whom he is on friendly terms. He consults N on farming matters, notably on maize production. He has given N advice on buying pigs from certain non-commercial farmers in the area.

M has no dependent homesteads round him, but he does have important relationships with some of the people who live near by. He makes gifts of food to his widowed mother. He sometimes visits an unrelated man on whom he was once partially dependent, but they have ceased to exchange more than small gifts. Another old man on whom M was also once partially dependent commands his respect. This is shown in the form of address, when the term for father is most often used. M makes no demands on the activities of these three and, beyond receiving small gifts, they receive no substantial benefits from him, with the possible exception of the mother.

M has a relationship with a younger, unrelated man, O, whom he calls 'friend' or, using in English, 'brother'. O has his own homestead, but is partially dependent on his own father. His relationship with M is of the disciple type. He visits M frequently when the conversation often turns to farming. He is often offered food at M's homestead and has taken an interest in mechanical work, especially the use of a cotton sprayer. Although he may busy himself with a particular machine, it is more by way of interesting himself than of helping M. He does not form part of the labour unit, nor does he receive substantial material support from M.

ELITES AND NEW SOCIAL STRATA

The Tonga commercial farmers belong to a small but significant class of wealthy individuals. Their skill as farmers is sought after by the non-commercial farmers. In this restricted sense they form a new social stratum of an elite nature. They lack, however, many of the characteristics necessary for an elite group. They have not developed institutions of their own. They do not appear to have what Nadel (1956) calls the pre-eminence, the corporate right which is not open to everyone, and the recognition of general superiority operating over an area much wider than one sphere of knowledge or skills.

In order to maintain his position, a commercial farmer must have a different type of inter-personal network. It differs from non-commercial farmers in containing links which are effective in keeping the farmer informed on farm practices and methods. Other links enable him to be in touch with non-commercial farmers without devoting large resources of wealth and time to this end. Other links afford the farmer an efficient labour supply which he can control to meet the more exacting needs of cash farming. This network operates with a lower degree of highly dependent links than exists for the non-commercial farmer.

Among non-commercial farmers the tendency towards highly dependent links does not give a dominant individual an efficient labour supply and can be a drain on his resources. The highly dependent person has the expectancy, sanctioned by custom, of deriving all his material needs directly from the person he is dependent on. In return, he will carry out tasks when he is told to do so. The efficiency and effect of his labour is determined by himself on each occasion. He may fail to meet the exact demands of the person he is working for without any direct and immediate change in the benefits accepted as due to him in return. His rewards are less directly related to the quantity and quality of his labour, being received when his particular needs lead him to make a demand.

The reduction of dependent links is necessary for the commercial farmer. It might also typify the inter-personal relationships of other categories of people, whether they be restricted or more general elites, or new social strata, who have adapted to an industrial, bureaucratic, or commercial setting.

BIBLIOGRAPHY

Barnes, J. A.
(1954) 'Class and committees in a Norwegian island parish.' *Human Relations*, vol. 8, pp. 39–58.
Bott, E.
(1957) *Family and Social Networks*, London.
Colson, E.
(1958) *Marriage and the Family among the Plateau Tonga of Northern Rhodesia*, Manchester.
(1962) *The Plateau Tonga*, Manchester.
Epstein, A. L.
(1961) 'The network of urban social organization.' *Rhodes–Livingstone Institute Journal*, no. 29, pp. 29–62.
Mannoni, O.
(1956) *Prospero and Caliban*, London.
Mayer, P.
(1961) *Townsmen or Tribesmen*, Cape Town.
(1962) 'Migrancy and the study of Africans in towns.' *American Anthropologist*, vol. 64, pp. 576–91.
Nadel, S. F.
(1956) 'The concept of social elites.' *International Social Science Bulletin*, vol. 8, pp. 413–24.

Pons, V. G.
  (1961) 'Two small groups in Avenue 21', in Southall, A. W. (ed.), *Social Change in Modern Africa*, London, pp. 205–16.
Southall, A. W.
  (1961) 'Kinship, friendship and the network of relations in Kisenji, Kampala', in Southall, A. W. (ed.), *Social Change in Modern Africa*, London, pp. 217–29.

Résumé

LES RÉSEAUX DES RELATIONS SOCIALES DES FERMIERS PARMI LES PLATEAU TONGA À LA ZAMBIE

Ce discours traite de la position sociale des fermiers commerçants parmi les Plateau Tonga de la Zambie. On peut distinguer ces fermiers selon les moyens suivants; il y a un mot dans la langue Tonga qui les décrit et dans toute région particulière il paraît qu'on reconnaisse sans difficulté les gens qui appartiennent à cette classe. Ils ont des fonds capitaux et des rentes supérieurs aux autres fermiers. Ils ont une tendance d'établir leurs fermes clôturées loin des autres fermiers.

Il y a une analyse des deux réseaux de rélations inter-personnelles pour les fermiers commerçants et pour les fermiers non-commerçants. Il y a des références à l'œuvre de Barnes et à celle de Bott qui se servirent de cette méthode et à Southall et à Pons qui s'en servirent par implication, aussi bien qu'aux deux auteurs Epstein et Mayer qui s'en servirent explicitement dans leurs études en Afrique.

On montre les réseaux des fermiers non-commerçants par un exemple, dans le cadre d'une structure sociale matrilinéaire et 'sans état'. Il y a un élément de contrat dans ces relations mais, une fois établies, elles agissent selon les droits et les obligations soutenus par les coutumes de parenté et d'autres liens. Chaque fermier non-commerçant fait partie d'un réseau qui le lie aux chefs d'autres fermes. Ces relations contiennent un fort élément de différentiation de statut où la dominance d'un homme et la dépendance d'un autre entrent en jeu. Il y a des références à Mannoni sur ce point là.

Les fermiers commerçants n'ont pas autant de rapports avec les chefs des autres fermes. Quoique leur richesse leur permettrait de dominer sur un nombre de chefs des fermes aux alentours et de les faire travailler pour eux, ils ne le font pas. Ils aiment mieux dépendre du travail des employés ou des habitants de leurs propres domaines. Le centre du réseau des relations sociales du fermier commerçant se trouve dans sa propre ferme. Il y a, à part ça, des relations amicales avec les fermiers européens, et dans certains cas, un rapport 'professeur-élève' avec un autre fermier Tonga.

On constate que la dominance d'un fermier sur les autres épuise ses biens et ne lui rende que peu de compensation sous la forme d'une source de travail. La dominance oblige qu'on s'occupe des besoins très variés du dépendant, ce qui exige une perte de temps et d'argent. Il n'est pas possible de contrôler le travail d'un fermier dépendant d'une façon convenable aux exigences de l'agriculture commerciale.

Le fermier commerçant ne doit avoir que peu de relations inter-personnelles où il y a une tendance à une association de dépend-ance. Cette nécessité pourrait être caractéristique aussi du réseau des relations d'autres genres de Tonga qui se sont adaptés à un milieu industriel, bureaucratique, ou commercial.

Les fermiers commerçants ne constituent une élite que dans le sens borné du mot. Ils font partie d'un groupe plus riche que les autres, et qui possède certaines techniques d'agriculture, mais ils montrent une tendance, en commun avec les élites plus évoluées, à ne pas avoir les associations de dépendance.

XIV. THE TRIBAL ELITE AND THE TRANSKEIAN ELECTIONS OF 1963

PHILIP MAYER

THE TRANSKEI

This paper is concerned with some problems of a tribal elite in a plural society, notably the problem of its relation to derived power. The setting is the Transkei, well known today as the scene of the first Bantustan experiment launched by the South African Government. Before this the Transkei had long been South Africa's largest continuous area set aside for African occupation, first as Native Reserve land and subsequently as a Bantu Area. It is roughly the size of Switzerland, is almost entirely rural, and has a population of about one and a half million Africans, all of them Xhosa speakers. There are also about sixteen thousand whites (traders, professionals, etc.), mostly concentrated in the few small towns.

The main contention of the paper is as follows. In what are called modern democratic societies, two complementary tendencies can usually be seen to operate: groups that become elite will tend to attract some political power, and groups that have political power will tend to attract some elite status. In South Africa, as a plural society, however, neither process has been able to operate as regards African elite groups. Hence a divorce has occurred between power and elite status—something which I regard as typical for the situation of the African in this country, and possibly for other dominated groups in some other plural societies.

The theme is illustrated here from a time of crucial importance in the political history of the Transkei. Early in 1963 the parliament of the South African Republic passed the Transkeian Constitution Act (No. 48), following the lines of a draft constitution which had been accepted some months earlier by the Transkeian Territorial Authority. (The Authority was successor to the Transkeian Territories General Council—see below.) The first elections under the new constitution were held on 20 September 1963. It was during the election period that I collected most of the field material for this paper.[1]

On the face of things it may seem remarkable that a tribal elite should still be of significance in South Africa—the most industrialized country south of the Sahara and the one with the longest history of westernization and urbanization. South Africa has more city-dwelling Africans than any other country (if we are thinking of modern western-style cities) and its modern African elite is impressive both in numbers and in sophistication. The decisive criterion of an elite is that it embodies highest common values; here, if anywhere in Africa, the shift towards western values might well have deglamourized the old-style tribal leaders. It must first be explained why this has not been altogether the case in the Transkei.

Hereditary chieftainship was traditionally the central political institution of all the Transkeian peoples. During a century and more of contact with whites, many Transkeians turned first to whites and then to westernized Africans as their new elite, with a proportionate disregard for the chiefly class, who remained largely uneducated. But another part of the population took a different line, refusing to value positively anything that was associated directly or indirectly with the white man. These conservative, culture-proud, and nationalistic pagan Africans are locally known as 'reds' or 'red blanket people'. Today it may be estimated that nearly half of the Transkeian population is still red.[2]

[1] When collecting material I was fortunate in having the help of Mr. Percy Qayiso, B.A., himself a Transkei-born African and my research assistant at Rhodes University. My thanks are also due to the many informed Transkeians, in different parts of the territory and with different political outlooks, who helped with material.

Professor Gwendolen M. Carter (now at Northwestern University) had asked me to make notes on current developments in connexion with her forthcoming study of the Transkei. A small fraction (only) of the material collected on her behalf has been utilized in this paper, with her kind permission.

[2] For an account of the Red Xhosa and especially their opposition to the 'School' Xhosa (as the other half are called) see Mayer, 1961, chapter 2.

The territories were annexed by a white government towards the end of the last century (1879–94). The hereditary chiefs were not deposed but lost most of their administrative and judicial powers to white magistrates. The Transkei was administered under a system of direct rule. Chiefs were still entitled to hear civil cases according to native law, but appeals lay to the white magistrate's court. Moreover, the Department of Native Affairs of the Union Government (as it then was) appointed headmen for each Location (rural administrative unit, with populations ranging from perhaps a few hundred to a few thousand). This drastically curtailed what remained of chiefly prerogative. With all this, however, many of the Transkeian chiefs—to different degrees in different areas—managed somehow to continue playing administrative and judicial roles, more or less *sub rosa*. In the eyes of their red followers they had the legitimacy which the newer authorities could not have.

The official system of local government was completed by a structure of District Councils. Instituted in 1894, these were federated in 1931 into a United Transkeian Territories General Council (more familiarly known as 'the Bunga'). This Council was largely confined to discussing and expressing opinion on matters affecting the local population. It had thirty *ex-officio* members (twenty-seven white magistrates plus three Paramount Chiefs, of Thembuland, Pondoland East and Pondoland West), and an elected majority, seventy-eight strong. In spite of its restricted powers, membership in it lent an African prestige among his own people. But, apart from the three Paramounts, not many chiefs took part in it. The reasons why they did not offer themselves for election can be surmised: the Bunga was regarded as a white-dominated 'talking shop' in which the educated were the best qualified to take part.[3]

Considering their sixty years of official discouragement and curtailment of power, it is the more remarkable how much prestige some Transkeian chiefs retained in the eyes of their uneducated followers and even of some of the better educated. The

---

[3] Cf. A. L. Epstein's analysis of elections to office in trade unions, etc., on the Rhodesian Copperbelt (Epstein, 1958).

fact must be seen in the context of black–white relations. Chiefs even without power served as a symbol of the indigenous tribal world as against the white-controlled world. Their authority, however restricted, had value as the only authority *not* derived from whites. It appeared as something quite different from the authority of the headmen, who, people said, 'are only government servants'. While some educated Transkeians saw chieftainship as outdated, others remained not far behind the uneducated reds in sentimental attachment to it. Permanent migration to town was apt to undermine this attitude; the red people even today often express their disapproval of permanent urbanization by saying that 'town people have no regard for the chiefs'.

A major change occurred in the 1950s. The system of local government in the reserves (including the Transkei) was changed from one of direct rule to one of indirect rule. Henceforth local administration was to be based on the tribal authorities headed by the chiefs. This resuscitation of chiefly power was embodied in the Bantu Authorities Act of 1951. It threw into relief a new issue, which leads to the heart of the present subject.

APARTHEID POLICIES

The white government's new attitude to chiefly power is easily explained in terms of Nationalist Party ideology (the Party has been in power from 1948 till the present), but also in terms of power politics. While some Transkeians saw chieftaincy as a symbol of non-involvement in the white-dominated world, many whites were equally in favour of it as a symbol of non-competition.

The official Nationalist ideology of cultural pluralism requires that every section of the South African population should 'develop according to its own culture and traditions'. And 'Bantu culture' is seen as requiring chieftainship, while western governmental institutions belong exclusively to 'white culture'. But beneath these ideological considerations one can discern a political equation. Chieftainship is a particularistic governmental institution; it is by definition limited to the tribe, and can therefore never bring whites under black control. Strong tribal chiefs are a threat only to tribesmen. By contrast, participation by Africans in the white governmental institutions—which are universalistic in principle —would constitute competition on fairly equal terms, and expose whites directly to the possibility of black control. To this extent government support of chieftainship is an endorsement of the paternalistic as against the competitive scheme of race relations (to borrow terms from P. van den Berghe, 1958).

In this light we may interpret the fact that as world opinion requires South Africa to give more political rights to her African population, the government's choice has been to build up a separate governmental system based on chiefs, rather than to allow any Africans—even the most highly qualified of the modern elite—to participate in white governmental institutions. Both the system known as Bantu Authorities and the subsequent Bantustan policy, now inaugurated in the Transkei, are fruits of this philosophy. They have brought the tribal chiefs out of relative obscurity and invested them with more power than they had enjoyed for some generations. But in doing so they have exposed the chiefs themselves to a considerable dilemma.

In the South African situation legalized power could flow only from the white government; but whatever flows from the white government has been *ipso facto* resented by most, if not all, of the African population. Any African group that accepted delegated power would to this extent cease to embody the common values, which means it would cease being elite. Hence the dilemma, and the paradox that the African craving for autonomy *vis-à-vis* whites seemed to have been better satisfied by chiefs who were mere symbols than it now was by chiefs who received 'real power' at last. New power was interpreted as new weakness. In this particularly aggravated intercalary situation[4] the chiefs seemed to the people to be turning into stooges of government, rather than into masters of the people.

The question arises, then, whether the new policies (Bantu

[4] For the term 'intercalary' cf. Mitchell (1956), p. 16.

Authorities and now Bantustan) have breathed new life into the tribal elite, or have sealed its fate with a kiss of death.[5]

To those who assume that a political ruling class is *ipso facto* a kind of elite, the first alternative will seem the obvious answer. But this assumption is, I think, a confused and confusing one. It has been convincingly exposed by Nadel, some of whose arguments I should like to recall. True elite influence (as Nadel, 1956, points out) is indirect influence. It does not command obedience, it elicits imitation. A class or group can govern, can be politically dominant, without having any of this quality. Or it may have this quality only for one section in a plural society, meanwhile remaining for other sections a remote and meaningless super-elite. There are instances of governing elites of course, but such groups do not come into power *because* they are elites (i.e. embody common values). On the contrary—they become elites because their government has been successful and popular. Their elite quality is a spill-over.

PLURAL ELITES

Before the question can be discussed in detail it is necessary to describe briefly the plurality of elites in South Africa—a feature perhaps even more marked here than it has been in many African colonial territories. To begin with, the status of whites as elites is more ambiguous here. Of course, the white section in South Africa is not just an administrative and managerial stratum whose class spectrum starts where that of black people leaves off. It is a settled population three million strong, and its class spectrum far overlaps the black one; many South African whites are much below many South African Africans in the scales of education, occupation, wealth, and sophistication.

[5] I am aware that the problem as just stated already begs certain questions. For instance, the statement that most Africans tend to resent whatever flows from government can be neither substantiated nor disproved without much more intensive fieldwork, oriented both qualitatively and quantitatively. Some of this work could perhaps not be carried out at all in present South African conditions. Further, much too little research has been published on the aspirations of African elite groups in South Africa.

The educated, 'westernized' African elite in South African cities shares many values with the whites. But it is exposed to a two-way pull—a choice, in any given situation, between two reference groups: it may align with the middle class, which transcends colour lines, or alternatively, with its own colour group, which transcends class lines. Further, there is good reason why neither this African elite nor the white elite has ever been able to serve as an *overall* elite, i.e. one recognized as such by all Africans. The reason was given above: not all Africans have accepted white-derived values as their own, and some have opposed them almost fanatically. Nowadays an African who rises high in the scale of western or middle-class sophistication may command the respect even of some tribal conservatives, but it is the respect accorded to an outsider.

For Transkeians, as for other Africans in South Africa, the rather deep division between town and country is another factor working against the recognition of a common elite. Western-style towns in South Africa are many and old-established; town-dwelling Africans have developed social patterns and values of their own. These urban patterns remain meaningless for many rural Africans, and vice versa. Although the Transkei itself is predominantly rural, and includes no major city, many thousands of city-dwellers outside its limits are counted as Transkeian citizens under the new constitution, and had voting rights in the elections we shall be considering.

As regards the Transkeian elections three different African elite groups could be seen as possible contenders: a modern urban elite, a modern rural elite, and the old-style tribal elite, which, of course, is rural too. By modern-type rural elite I mean such people as African teachers, lawyers, ministers of religion, traders, who have lived only briefly or not at all in a city. Such people are often better able to support themselves in the rural areas than are their less-educated fellows, who mostly have to sell their unskilled labour in the towns.

The modern-type rural elite, in the Transkei, have been spared the worst experiences of South African race relations. The life around them is an almost all-black life, and relations with the few whites in the small towns have been fairly easy. The new urban elite, on the other hand, are thrown up against whites *en masse*, and undergo all the painful impact of a rigorous discriminatory system. They are a pariah elite *par excellence*—elite to their own group, pariah to those very whites whose values they have principally absorbed. Not surprisingly, the trend to political radicalism has been largely in the towns, and a predominant number of African political leaders has been drawn from the urban elite.

To return to the tribal elite, which is our main concern. I would define this as comprising chiefs, and to varying degrees headmen and councillors, as well as their families and close associates There are sixty-four recognized chieftainships in the Transkei.

S. G. Ngcobo, writing in 1956, states that 'the high social position of chiefs, particularly those of the hereditary line, is acknowledged or respected by all sections of the African population. The marriage of a chief or his visit to a mission station or an urban centre becomes an important social event attended by Christian, educated, urbanized as well as red-blanketed Africans.' The Transkei has long had this reputation as an area of high respect for chiefs. Today, however, I would say that the reputation is true of some Transkeian districts but not others. In at least two out of the nine (Fingoland and Umzimkulu) chiefs clearly have had no elite status for some time—at least not *qua* chiefs.

Some members of the tribal elite also belong to one or another new elite. This can conveniently be illustrated by the two leading figures in the elections—Chiefs Kaiser Matanzima (now chief minister of the Transkei) and Victor Poto. Matanzima is a university graduate, a lawyer, and a 'man of the world'. Poto belongs rather with the rural modern elite, having secondary but not university education and much experience in Transkeian local government. The emphasis in his case has been more on local roots and local patriotism. There are other chiefs who stand outside the school and urban ranking systems altogether: dignified but tribal figures. And then there are some members of chiefly families who hold incongruously low places in those ranking systems—men of little education earning their livings perhaps as ordinary labourers in some town.

I have already mentioned that during the 1950s the government began building up chiefly power while continuing to withhold power from the new elites and particularly the urban new élite. It suppressed several African political parties and associations: it also refused during these years to meet or negotiate with modern elite leaders on any political level at all, and paralysed many of them by banning orders or imprisonment. Meanwhile the Bantu Authorities' policy was giving the chiefs an appreciable increase of power, judicial and executive. Tribal Councils were appointed for them and also so-called 'ambassadors' to the town-dwelling population. Considerable efforts were made to track down the legitimate heirs to chieftaincies.

The Bantu Authorities' policy also gave the chiefs fairly substantial salaries, regarded as compensating for the revenues they no longer derived from their peoples. The intention was that they should once again become men of substance whose will would be respected and whose patronage would be courted. While this showed signs of working out in some areas, in others it was a dismal failure. Complaints about chiefs' injustice, corruptibility, the high bribes one now had to offer instead of the modest customary gifts, were heard on all sides. So far it was a weakening not a strengthening of their position; whatever they gained in power and wealth, they had more than lost in influence and prestige.

From many field notes collected in the Ciskei and Transkei, and also in an urban area, before the scheme was fully in operation, I am impressed by the number of ordinary people who seem to have foreseen this. 'Chiefs will become despised by their own people', 'they will lose their reputations', were frequent comments. 'When chiefs are paid by the government [said one red man] it is sure to be bad. They will be the yes-men of the Europeans, and they will be harsh to us because they have the European government on their side.' Or as a school man put it: 'Traditionally the chiefs got cattle and other things from their own people. But now, since they are to receive salaries, they are too independent of us, so they will be the government's most active servants in oppressing us. A dog like its master.'

The salaried government chief anywhere is the prototype of the uncomfortable status which Mitchell and others call inter-calary,[6] but the difficulties of an intercalary position are likely to be accentuated in proportion to the intensity of opposition be-tween the two social sections concerned. In the case we are considering, the opposition was scarcely relieved by any of the cross-cutting cleavages which in some other countries have helped to make the position of the government chief somewhat less invidious.

Small wonder, then, that this time was notable for the numbers of violent physical attacks on chiefs and headmen. Secret move-ments known as 'Makuluspan', 'Congo', and 'Poqo' were blamed. Records of the T.T.A. show chiefs repeatedly requesting to be given guards and firearms.[7] The violence expressed people's resentment at chiefs' support of government-sponsored agri-cultural betterment schemes, and sometimes at their alleged extortions.

As Chief Victor Poto has put it: 'Under the Bantu Authorities people felt that the government was determined to use the chiefs and ignore the people. Thus militant groups were formed like Ikongo and Poqo, and people began to lose their lives.'[8]

THE TRANSKEI CONSTITUTION

It is against this background that one has to consider attitudes in the Transkei towards the proposed new constitution, which was steered through a recess committee of the Transkeian Territorial Authority, and then through the T.T.A. itself, in the first months of 1962. Though views were sharply divided, again many people foresaw further new difficulties and role conflicts for the chiefs. No paragraph caused a stormier debate than paragraph 24, which proposed that the new legislative assembly should be composed

---

[6] Cf. note 1 above, page 290.

[7] Cf. for instance *Transkeian Territorial Authority Proceedings*.

[8] Election speech in the Transkei (1961, pp. 70 f.; 1963, p. 37).

of sixty-four chiefs and forty-five elected members. It was variously argued that the elected element should be increased, the chiefly element reduced, or the chiefs removed to a second chamber. Some speakers who were not chiefs brought up the principle of popular representation. 'The people must be given a chance in this government ... because after all the greater numbers are those of the people.' And some stressed the superior claims of the new elite to be the people's legislators, compared with the chiefs: 'I would like to say that there are a number of people more intelligent than chiefs.'[9] But many dwelt on the advantage to the chiefs themselves of not being a majority in the assembly, and the role conflicts to which they would be exposed there. Among those who spoke to this effect were chiefs themselves. The kinds of role conflict envisaged included the following:

1. Intercalary conflict, caused by having to mediate the commands of an irresistible government to an unwilling people. 'The people will have the impression that whatever oppression they suffer is due to the chiefs.' There would arise an 'enmity which would result in the destruction of our chiefs'. 'By virtue of my being a chief, how can I oppose anything that springs from the government?'

2. Conflict between the role of chief as an ascribed status and the role of legislator in a modern-type assembly: 'What we are trying to set up now requires men of intelligence and learning. If we close the door against such people this parliament will not be a success and that will have an adverse reflection on the very chiefs.'

3. Conflict between the chief's role as authority in his own tribe and his role as legislator in the assembly: 'Our Bantu commissioners ... have never been in parliament. According to this new procedure the chiefs have to make the laws and at the same time administer those laws.'

4. Conflict between the chief's dignity and the role of either spokesman or debater: 'The people we [the chiefs] should have

[9] All quotations in this section are from the official record of the debate in the T.T.A. 2–3 May 1962. Transkeian Territorial Authority Proceedings, Umtata, 1963.

sent here are our sons, to represent us and discuss the laws for our country. Then they should come and report back to us. . . . Ordinary people should be in the majority and should . . . report their deliberations to us.' I may add that an almost ritualized aloofness from all debate and discussion is one of the traditions of chieftainship in the Transkei. Traditionally the chief speaks little, never argues, only listens and then announces his decision, often through a spokesman rather than directly.

Nevertheless, after a day and a half of hot discussion (including several requests for more time) all the amendments were either withdrawn or defeated and paragraph 24 was passed in the T.T.A. by the enormous majority of 70 to 3. I shall not take it on myself to comment on the claim of some participants that this vote reflected official pressures put on members.

ELECTIONS

In the elections held under the new constitution in September 1963, although many town-dwellers were entitled to vote, the urban elite did not come forward as candidates. They were partly unable and partly unwilling. Emergency regulations, in force throughout the elections, meant that those who had been associated with banned parties or leaders might be running considerable risks. And on grounds of principle, too, the more politically conscious townspeople were inclined to shun the elections altogether, along with the whole Bantustan policy, as a kind of fraud: an imposition of 'separate and inferior', not 'separate but equal'.

Accordingly, of the 180 candidates who stood for the forty-five seats in the nine electoral districts, most were either tribal elite (headmen, councillors, or family connexions of chiefs, etc.) or else modern-type rural elite (retired teachers, ex-members of the Territorial Authority, traders, etc.). The chiefs were sure of an *ex-officio* majority in the new assembly, anyway, but they might have seen the elections as an opportunity for a straight fight with the rural modern elite—the first time such a prize of power had been offered for competition: and if this was their attitude they might have sought to sway voters in their own districts towards the candidates of tribal-elite type. As it was, this did not happen, or not to any extent. The reason—I would say—was that the issue between tribal and modern elite was quickly dwarfed by the much graver one of the chiefs' own role conflict.

The issue of the chiefs' role conflict soon became the overt focus of the elections. This was made clear with the emergence of Chief Victor Poto as rival for the office of Chief Minister, against the Government favourite, Chief K. D. Matanzima. Although the rivalry of these two very different men might be analysed in terms of personal leadership, and perhaps of local tribal loyalties (for Poto was Paramount Chief of Pondoland West and Matanzima of the Emigrant Tembu), it was formalized as a battle between their two different interpretations of the chief's role.

Poto's platform offered to preserve the chiefs as the Transkeian aristocracy. They would sit in a second chamber and leave the dust of politics largely to elected legislators. Matanzima's platform offered to entrench the chiefs as the permanent majority in a single-chamber assembly, using all the power they could get from the white government, regardless of possible damage to their aristocratic dignity or elite status. These were both logical but opposite solutions in the situation where white-derived power was apparently impossible to combine with elite status.

Eventually most of the election candidates declared themselves, openly or implicitly, as standing behind either Poto or Matanzima, My material on both candidates and electors shows Poto emerging as a symbol of the 'good chief' and Matanzima of the 'bad chief'. Tribal conservatives invested the Poto image with many time-honoured qualities of the good traditional chief, but he also had something that appealed to conservatives and others alike—he stood for an apparently less close relation with the white government. Thus, he stood as well for the good government chief, the one who, in the intercalary situation, sides with his own people. Conversely, Matanzima seemed to stand for the bad traditional chief (lacking traditional qualities) but also for the bad government chief (hand in glove with government). Somewhat paradoxically, for all the emphasis he laid on preserving the chieftainship, his own strength was in another role—the role of modern-type politician and administrator.

Poto—people said—like a good traditional chief, always listens to his people; he lets even critical views be expressed. Matanzima is ruthless to anyone who dares disagree with him. Poto never needs to use force, Matanzima depends on it. 'If Poto had been chief minister', as one voter said when it was all over, 'there would have been no need to give him a police guard—he stands for the people'; 'he goes anywhere in public without protection'; Matanzima is always seen with a guard and is known to be able to command police assistance at short notice. Poto—so the phrase often ran—'acts like a true prince', 'shows his royal blood in every gesture'; Matanzima's nicknames were 'Bossboy', 'Hitler', 'Verwoerd', or more simply 'tyrant'. Innumerable stories circulated about Matanzima's alleged brutality to his own people—opponents said to have been molested, kicked, even blinded or beaten to death by his henchmen, huts burnt, families evicted from their land. How many of the stories were authentic or unexaggerated I cannot say, but there is little doubt that Matanzima had been used to rule his own people with a rod of iron, and the accounts of his warmest admirers have represented him as a strong man with a good deal of ruthlessness. So much for the bad traditional chief; Matanzima would stand also for the bad government chief—the one who has drunk too deep of white power, because he was known to have earned government favour by his previous able support of the official policies. *Inter alia*, he had done more perhaps than any other one man to get the new draft constitution through the Transkeian Territorial Assembly.

As I have emphasized, most Transkeians and no doubt most Africans in the Republic place a high value on an 'autonomous' attitude *vis-à-vis* whites. Matanzima and Poto both had strong views on autonomy, but they interpreted it differently, and thus interpreted differently also the intercalary situation.

Matanzima's position is that Africans must satisfy their desire for autonomy as the white government itself proposes, on the lines of apartheid or 'separate freedom' as government spokesmen like to call it. His conversion to this view seems none the less genuine for being expressed as a philosophy of rebuff. 'White people,' he is quoted as having said, 'do not want to live with us, so I say with all emphasis "Away with them". Why should we run after people who literally hate us?' True to his own principles, Matanzima pointedly refused an invitation to eat at a local 'white' hotel during the elections, and drove away regardless of pleas that he change his mind. With equal dramatic effect he was seen to turn on a young white policeman who had tried to prevent him from entering a polling station; the white district sergeant had to come out and follow him with apologies. Such little incidents impressed the people by showing Matanzima as a man whom whites also fear.

Poto's autonomous stand is not against whites as such, but is rather in terms of achieving a satisfactory and non-subordinate relation to them. He belongs to an older generation, one that could still benefit from close contact with white missionaries. 'At a very tender age,' says his election manifesto, 'I became the ward of, and member of the family of, the Rev. E. J. Barrett of the Methodist Church, and thence continuously remained under his religious teaching and influence.' Poto's stand during the elections was 'multi-racial' in so far as he proposed that the Transkei should welcome any non-Africans who might wish to stay and work there under an African Government. Matanzima's line was a black Transkei, a point he has made clearer still since coming into office.

The multi-racial stand taken by Poto did not necessarily align the fiercest anti-whites against him; to some people its charm was simply that it contradicted the official government line. One man was overheard to say that, 'Poto is speaking truly when he says that whites ought to stay in the Transkei. Yes, they ought to stay, so that they may be ruled by black people and we may have our revenge.' Conversely, Matanzima's all-black Transkei policy did not necessarily draw the fiercest black nationalists, for it was widely interpreted as simply the relaying of the government's own message by the government's chosen instrument.

Of the two alternatives of achieving 'autonomy' in relation to the whites, the multi-racial one sold better during the elections.

This was partly because Poto seemed so obviously the man with greater independence. 'How can Matanzima want to do without the Europeans, if he is depending on them for his very life?' But, above all, separate development is the government policy. 'I support multi-racialism wholeheartedly,' wrote a candidate from the Maluti region in his manifesto, 'and oppose separate development as much as I do that thing—apartheid—which is brooding over my soul like a nightmare.' Poto tried to impart his own spirit of independence to his chiefly colleagues. 'Personally, I don't fear the government,' he told them, 'because it is not my God. If your chieftainship was given to you by God, what is there to fear? Vote with no fear of being victimized. It is just a threat.'

In Poto's eyes the destiny of the chiefs was to become a true elite, rather than a power group as such. 'The two houses of parliament,' he said, 'are an attempt to save the chiefs from a dangerous position. We want them to stay clear of the conflicts and tribulations of the lower house, where there will be hot verbal exchanges. Let them take their position of dignity in the upper house.' Time and again he spoke as an arch-aristocrat: 'I am the son of the Pondo Royal House,' begins his manifesto, and it continues with a detailed account of his family's close alliances by marriage with the Tembu Royal House, the Baca Royal House, the Hlubi chiefs, the Paramount Chief of Zululand. At a meeting at Butterworth he was heard to say, 'I came out of the womb so that I should be a chief.' 'Knowing my background,' runs another utterance, 'you will not doubt me when I tell you that I shall perpetuate the institution of chieftainship in the Transkei till my dying day.'

THE ROLES OF CHIEFS

In the circumstances, all elements of the population seemed ready to fit themselves into a contest waged in terms of the good and the bad chief. Nowhere was there a major clash between the tribal and educated elite. What was typical were the various forms of alliances between them in the various districts; and the tendency of the older educated elite to support Matanzima, while the younger paradoxically rallied behind the older less-educated Poto.

To give just a brief outline:

(*a*) Gcgaleka land is a backward, strongly tribal region. Here the uneducated Paramount Chief would or could give no lead, but the councillors took over and the tribal elite was in full control. Most candidates and many of those elected were headmen, some of the chiefly clan (Tshawe). The younger men respected their elders' claim to office: mainly older men were elected. Nearly all later joined the Matanzima camp.

(*b*) In Quakeni, Paramount Chief Botha was ostensibly uncommitted. A clear division arose between a party connected with the 'great place' (largely men put forward by the district chiefs) and a 'people's' party (putting forward youngish, educated men, some with links in the city and/or A.N.C. background). The latter supported Poto.

(*c*) In Nyanda, Poto's own district, all elements, old and young, educated and illiterate, rallied behind the Paramount Chief.

(*d*) In Dalinyebo, likewise, the district of Chief Sabata, Poto's principal supporter, the peasants were willing to vote for the candidates put forward by their chief. These included men of the educated rural elite, notably Guzana, a lawyer and now Poto's main lieutenant.

(*e*) In Emigrant Tembuland, Matanzima's district, the list of candidates known to be supported by the chief was accepted by the great majority of the largely illiterate electorate. The chief's candidates included his brother, a lawyer like himself, and an elderly ex-teacher who holds a degree. But this did not secure him the support of the younger educated voters. In the least 'red' area of Emigrant Tembuland Matanzima's candidates met with considerable opposition.

(*f*) In Fingoland the tribal elite is weak and chiefs do not play the same prominent part. Here a battle arose between older and younger people. The older men who had affiliations with the tribal elite were for Matanzima, the younger for Poto.

(*g*) Emboland, too, is a 'progressive' area, where the chiefs are no longer powerful. Here the chiefs had for some time relied on councillors and advisors drawn from the modern elite. At election time the councillors and the educated elite agreed in support of Poto.

Thus, we see that there were all kinds of combinations of the tribal and the educated elite, but that there were a few areas like Fingoland where the educated elite took the initiative. In most regions the chiefs and headmen were in command of the situation.

The elections over, the assembly of the sixty-four chiefs and forty-five elected members met in October and voted Matanzima into the position of chief minister by a narrow margin, after some last-minute changes of mind. Though the meeting was secret, it seems clear that it was the vote of the chiefs, not the elected members, that brought Matanzima in. Many observers have read in this the simple logic of the intercalary situation—that chiefs were more afraid of government pressure than elected members, or that they were actually put under pressure during the adjournment which preceded the final voting. Another possible reading would be that since power, after all, attracts, few chiefs were strong-minded enough to resist the lure when the moment came.

One interpretation which would not be justified, however, is that their doubts about the role conflict had been set at rest. Even a pro-Matanzima chief (from Fingoland) had been heard to voice anxieties about sitting in one chamber with his people's elected representatives. 'Though we are representing the same people we might find that our policies are different.' But it was expressed still more dramatically by another chief who at the last minute had switched over to vote for Matanzima. Surprised at the still militant spirit of the Poto camp, he began to understand the dilemma: 'I will kill myself as soon as I come home,' he is quoted as having said, 'I can't face the people after what I have done.'

However, during the first months after Matanzima's election as chief minister a great majority of chiefs seemed to have accepted the *fait accompli*. Some who had previously been Poto supporters crossed the floor to Matanzima, and by and large there was little sign of any serious opposition to him by any solid party of chiefs in the Assembly. Two factors were probably at work. Many chiefs, as had been predicted, were doubtless finding it impossible in open debate to come out against anything the government wanted, as channelled to them through the government-approved chief minister. And secondly, the power now put into their hands—limited though it appears in the total context of the South African state—may have genuinely begun to fascinate them, as being 'real power' at last, and worth everything it could cost them in popularity or elite status among their own people. Both would be natural reactions in a situation of extreme intercalary pressure.

It is another question how the modern elite, and the Transkeian people in general, have reacted to the choice declared by the chiefs. We have seen that in rejecting the Poto solution the chiefs rejected the opportunity of climbing down gracefully, of translating the chief's ancient dignity and elite prestige—though not his ancient power—into terms compatible with the demands of modern politics. The Poto solution (one would think) would have conveniently allowed for the important sociological ambivalence to which Epstein has drawn attention—the fact that people may have the highest regard for tribal leaders as an elite, and the greatest willingness to be guided by them in purely internal matters, and yet prefer another, non-tribal type of representation when it comes to involvement in external relations or participation in non-tribal institutions. Poto's solution would therefore have seemed a way to come to terms with all elements at the same time: with the reds who desired to be ruled by chiefs, with the educated who wished to be represented by democratic methods, and with the modern elite leaders who wanted more political scope. The fact that Poto regards himself as an ally of the educated and the modern elites, to whom no doubt the long-term political future belongs, appears from speeches he has made, including some that stress his concern for urban opinion as well as opinion in the Transkei itself.

The Matanzima line, on the other hand, has seemed a bitter pill for all three—for the reds (who dislike seeing their chiefs dependent on white power) as well as for the educated and the modern elite, who are now to be 'kept in their places' politically speaking, and made to come to terms with a basically tribal-oriented constitution. Yet Matanzima (in my opinion) could still succeed in reconciling all these elements—as well as in retaining the support of the chiefs—on one condition: that he manages to project an image of autonomy. Power attracts, but not if it looks like a by-product of puppet dependence on whites. If Matanzima should manage to present himself as a man so strong that the pressure of the whites behind him can be overlooked, then he may in time reverse the trend whereby governing chiefs could not be prestige chiefs at the same time.

CONCLUSION

Thus, the factor to which sociological analysis of this political problem must return first, last, and all the time is the nature of the plural society.

M. G. Smith (1959) has proposed that while the plural society is characterized by its plurality of institutions (it is these that define the separate culture sections), nevertheless there is one set of institutions in which plurality cannot be tolerated by the dominant section: the institutions of government. To preserve the structure of the society, the dominant section must insist on its own institutions monopolizing this particular field. It seems to me that there are a number of alternative ways of applying this interesting analytic principle to the South African plural society. In recent years—as I have been showing—the white-dominant section in South Africa has not insisted on a monopoly of governmental institutions. It has indeed gone out of its way to devise a separate set of governmental institutions for the African section; a set in which tribal chiefs will also function as modern parliamentarians and legislators. But what the white government has been consciously buying at this price is the ability to go on monopolizing its own governmental institutions. These now share the field with the other set, but within their own field they are not to be shared by anyone else—they are participated in by whites alone.

This arrangement is intended to satisfy at the same time the whites' desire for supremacy and the Africans' desire for autonomy; but any arrangement aimed at reconciling such opposites must, one would think, have a strong inherent instability. The ends of white supremacy (it would seem) are best served by a Transkei that is self-governing but never independent; while in the long run probably nothing short of full independence could really satisfy Transkeian aspirations to autonomy. Obviously the question of what powers the Transkeian authorities can be allowed to wield will continue to bristle with difficulties for this reason; so far the limitations of these powers are what have caused many Africans to see the whole Bantustan policy as an empty fraud.

Should the inherent instability lead to independence as the logical end, we would have a model for the ending of the plural society by fission, by the extrusion of one of its sections: the one society will have become two societies. On the other hand, if instability were to cause the abandonment of the Bantustan policy the reversion to a single set of governmental institutions, and the opportunity for all sections to participate in these, then we would have a model of the plural society ending in a different way—not by ceasing to be one society but by ceasing to be plural. This issue—one may say—is the one ultimately reflected by the dilemma of the Transkeian tribal elite. By becoming governing chiefs they seem to move one step on the road to the extrusion solution; by stepping down in favour of a more 'western democratic' system they might have moved a step towards ending the plurality of institutions.

POSTSCRIPT

In the fifteen months since this paper was written (in December 1963) the line of analysis has been largely confirmed.

1. *Chiefs' Support for Matanzima as the* Fait Accompli; *Elected Members Prefer Poto*

Two political parties have been formed, with the two key figures as leaders: Matanzima's National Independence Party and Poto's Democratic Party. Figures of voting in the assembly indicate that Poto's party, although the opposition party, can generally count on the support of more than two-thirds of the elected members (31 as against 14). But three-quarters of the chiefs (48 as against 16) generally support Matanzima's party.

A few chiefs have crossed over to Poto. (Cf. especially Chief Diko of Eastern Pondoland, who crossed the floor dramatically during a sitting of the assembly.) But as a few elected members have crossed over to the ruling party—attracted by the offer of official positions—the government majority has not diminished; in fact, it has slightly increased.

2. *Increased Recognition of Chiefs' Dilemma*

The dilemma of the chiefs' position has become increasingly a subject of public controversy. For example, at a mass meeting in the Transkei the chairman of the Democratic Party predicted that 'Chiefs who went to the legislative assembly just because they were chiefs, and did not represent the views of the people, would lose the aura of chieftainship which surrounded the traditional leaders' (Knowledge Guzana at a mass meeting of the Democratic Party at Engcobo, Transkei). The ruling party also shows increased sensitivity on this subject. Thus, in a debate in the assembly Chief Minister Matanzima accused the opposition of wanting to abolish chieftainship. He turned on the elected members, saying that they had been elected to support the chiefs. This was greeted with a chorus of 'No, no!'

3. *Two Ways to End the Plural Society*

The National Independence Party openly aims at the ending of the plural society by a process of fission. Its programme speaks of development by gradual stages towards greater self-determination, 'culminating in eventual independence' (paragraph 2). The Democratic Party, on the other hand, aims at 'the continued retention of the Transkei as part of the Republic of South Africa' (paragraph 2 of the constitution of the Democratic Party). The ending of pluralism would be via 'non-racialism'—'the development of a non-racial loyalty to the government of the Republic of South Africa' (ibid.).

4. Ruling Chiefs versus Elite Chiefs

The Democratic Party includes among its objectives 'democratic government', 'government of the people for the people and by the people'; for chieftainship it claims no more than that 'the institution of the traditional chieftainship should be maintained and perpetuated' (paragraph 2). But according to paragraph 3 of the 'programme of principles' of the National Independent Party 'chieftainship is the traditional form of authority among the Bantu of the Transkei' and therefore 'forms the framework of political structure'; the party is pledged not only to 'preserve the office of chieftainship' but also to preserve 'the chiefs' automatic membership of the Transkei Legislative Assembly'.

BIBLIOGRAPHY

Epstein, A. L.
 (1958) *Politics in an Urban African Community*, Manchester.
Mayer, P.
 (1961) *Townsmen or Tribesmen*, London.
Mitchell, J. C.
 (1956) *The Kalela Dance*, Rhodes–Livingstone Paper, No. 27.
Nadel, S. F.
 (1956) 'The concept of social elites.' *International Social Science Bulletin*, vol. 8, pp. 413–24.
Smith, M. G.
 (1959) 'Social and cultural pluralism.' *Annals of the New York Academy of Science*, vol. 83, pp. 763–85.
van den Berghe, Pierre L.
 (1958) 'The dynamics of racial prejudice: an ideal type dichotomy', *Social Forces*, 37, pp. 138–41.

Résumé

L'ÉLITE TRIBALE ET LES ELECTIONS AU TRANSKEI EN 1963

Cette communication concerne les problèmes d'une élite tribale dans une société plurale. Normalement, le pouvoir politique et la condition d'élite sont en corrélation, mais on remarque en Afrique du Sud une séparation entre les deux. La situation au Transkei, le premier Bantustan, est examinée ici en se référant particulièrement aux élections qui eurent lieu en 1963 pour la nouvelle assemblée législative du territoire.

Un phénomène remarquable en Afrique du Sud—le plus industrialisé de tous les états africains—est le prestige élevé qui continue à être accordé à l'élite tribale. Ceci est en corrélation avec les différences de valeurs frappantes entre les sections de 'l'école' et du 'rouge' de la population Xhosa—la première section épousant les façons occidentales et la seconde rejetant positivement quoi que ce soit étant directement ou indirectement en rapport avec l'homme blanc. Les chefs de tribu conservèrent leur office sous l'administration du gouvernement sud-africain, bien que leur pouvoir ait été très réduit; pourtant toute perte de prestige découlant de leur perte de pouvoir fut compensée par leur rôle de symbôles de la société tribale indigène contre un monde contrôlé par les blancs. L'autorité du chef tenait sa valeur de ce qu'elle ne dérivait pas des dirigeants blancs. Quand, après des décades d'administration directe, l'administration locale des réserves africaines devint indirecte, le pouvoir des chefs fut rehaussé. Ceci eut d'importantes implications dans l'élection que nous étudions ici.

La politique du gouvernement sud-africain a été de construire un système gouvernemental distinct pour la population africaine, ayant les chefs de tribu à sa base. Ainsi l'élite instruite africaine est incapable de concurrencer les blancs dans les sphères politiques; les blancs favorisent la dévolution du pouvoir aux chefs puisque ces derniers ne pourront jamais exercer leur autorité en dehors de leurs territoires ou sur la population blanche. Ce pouvoir accru ainsi donné aux chefs augmentent leur dilemme. Jusqu'alors, le prestige leur avait été accordé parce qu'ils représentaient des institutions et valeurs indigènes; maintenant qu'un pouvoir accru leur vient des blancs, leur prestige est-il rehaussé ou diminué? Continueront-ils à exercer cette influence indirecte habituellement associée avec le rang d'élite?

Il existe une pluralité d'élites africaines. Car l'élite occidentalisée instruite n'est pas à même de servir d'élite pour une large proportion de la population. La division entre les africains des villes et les ruraux inhibe aussi la reconnaissance d'une élite commune. En ce qui concerne les élections du Transkei, on pouvait distinguer ces élites—une élite urbaine moderne, une élite moderne rurale (composée d'enseignants, ministres du culte, etc.) et l'élite tribale (ainsi que rurale). L'élite urbaine est naturellement la plus radicale; les élites rurales ont la moindre expérience de la discrimination de couleur. L'élite tribale consiste principalement en des chefs et leur entourage—bien que tous les chefs ne sauraient aujourd'hui être classés parmi l'élite. Certains chefs, notamment les deux concurrents principaux dans l'élection ont des positions dans l'élite moderne—Chef Kaiser Matanzima, un avocat, et Chef Poto, ayant reçu une instruction secondaire et ayant beaucoup d'expérience du gouvernement local du Transkei.

La place des chefs de tribu dans la législation proposée du Transkei donna lieu à beaucoup de débats. On argua que le prestige du chef en souffrirait s'il devenait un médiateur entre son peuple et le gouvernement blanc; en tant que titulaire d'un statut attribué, il serait incapable de maîtriser les techniques gouvernementales modernes; un conflit existe entre le rôle du chef vis-à-vis son peuple et son rôle de législateur dans l'assemblée; le prestige du chef souffrirait au travers des procédures dans la salle des débats—le rôle traditionnel du chef étant de parler peu, ne jamais discuter et d'annoncer les décisions d'une manière indirecte. Cependant, il fut décidé que la nouvelle assemblée législative consisterait en 64 chefs et 45 membres élus.

Les contestants des sièges électoraux venaient principalement de l'élite moderne rurale et de l'élite tribale. Pourtant l'épreuve n'évolua pas en une lutte entre ces deux groupes, mais en une bataille entre deux interprétations différentes du rôle du chef dans la nouvelle assemblée. La tribune du Chef Poto offrit de préserver les chefs en une aristocratie à l'écart dans une seconde chambre; Chef Matanzima chercha à retrancher les chefs en une majorité permanente dans une assemblée unique, utilisant n'importe quel pouvoir qu'ils pourraient obtenir du gouvernement blanc. Ces deux théories étaient considérées comme des solutions au problème de la combinaison du pouvoir dérivé des blancs avec le rang d'élite. Poto fut identifié avec le 'bon chef tribal', Matanzima avec le 'mauvais chef'. Pourtant de dernier fut considéré comme celui qui recherchait l'indépendance, tandis que Poto, orienté vers les missions, pensait encore en termes de coopération sur des bases égalitaires. Ces thèmes furent développés tout au long. L'élite instruite plus agée tendait à appuyer Matanzima, tandis que paradoxalement, l'élite instruite jeune avait tendance à favoriser le plus âgé et moins bien instruit Poto. La majorité des représentants élus à l'assemblée législative suivent Poto, tandis que les chefs appuient Matanzima, lui donnant une majorité générale et la direction. Pourtant, cette victoire des chefs a intensifié le vieux conflit dans lequel ils se trouvent. Les chefs peuvent encore être à même de maintenir leur statut d'élite si leur chef, Matanzima, projète une image de son autonomie envers le gouvernement blanc duquel il détient sa position actuelle.

XV. CLASS CONSCIOUSNESS AND CLASS SOLIDARITY IN THE NEW ETHIOPIAN ELITES

DONALD N. LEVINE

Unique on the African continent, Ethiopia's traditional elites represent indigenous institutions and customs that have a history of close on two thousand years. Their authority is buttressed by a written tradition which, though largely foreign in origin, has been thoroughly Ethiopianized in character and has in the past been a primary repository of Ethiopian national sentiment. Their power was never compromised by subordination to European rulers until 1936, and then but briefly and partially. Traditionality has thus far been disturbed to a relatively slight extent in this land; for example, the proportion of Ethiopians attending secular schools is lower than any country on the continent except South-West Africa.

Viewed from afar, Ethiopian society might seem ripe for the emergence of an energetic new social class, oriented in opposition to these traditional elites, and animated by a concern for secular development, technical innovation, and rationalization of government. The basis for such a class would appear to have been laid by the education of a small but conspicuous number of Ethiopians in modern secular schools and universities at home and abroad, a number which in 1962 probably exceeded 6,000, about 1,000 of whom held a Bachelor's Degree or higher. Indeed, if one were to credit the words of a small minority of the foreign-educated Ethiopians, a situation of class conflict might be said to obtain between this growing group of modern-educated, 'middle-class' nationalists, and the class of traditionalist notables associated with the *ancien régime*.

To make such a statement is to use pre-fabricated concepts imported from the European experience rather than to attend to the realities of Ethiopian social life. While the emergence of a stratum of modern-educated Ethiopians has been accompanied by a certain development of 'class consciousness', based on their common historic position and aspirations and their opposition to the traditionalistic elites, neither they nor their alleged antagonists form a solidary class in any politically relevent sense of the term. In analysing this phenomenon, the present paper will discuss briefly the traditionalist secular elites, and then examine at greater length the modern-educated elite.

THE MONARCHY AND THE OLD NOBILITY

The emperor has always stood at the pinnacle of the Ethiopian stratification system. His position is legitimated by notions of divine monarchy which ante-date the conversion to Christianity (fourth century); by legends which present him as the sole legitimate successor to the kings of Israel and bearer of the Christian mission; and by the charisma of his anointment by the *abuna* (archbishop) traditionally imported from the Coptic Patriarchate at Alexandria. The awe and esteem accorded the emperor have not been accompanied by a pattern of unswerving loyalty to him, however. Adherence to the emperor's desires has largely been due to personal ambitions or the proximity of his traditionally mobile camp, and opposition to him, including outright rebellion, has not been uncommon in Ethiopian history. This has been so because the imperial power, while theoretically absolute, has historically been limited to a considerable extent by the primitive state of technology, the forbidding geography of the highlands, and the partial autonomy of the nobility and the clergy.

The old nobility in Ethiopian society may be defined as including all those individuals who possess high secular status and bear some honorific title. They may be divided into three categories: a 'royal nobility', consisting of relatives of the Emperor; a 'national nobility', consisting of high dignitaries at the imperial court and governors of large provinces; and a 'local nobility', consisting of district chiefs and judges, or even wealthy landowners commanding considerable deference. For present purposes these may be treated as members of a single status group, often referred to by the Amharic term *makuannent*. One might also divide them according to the nature of their honorific titles: military titles, the most prestigious; the titles of civil officials; and the titles of court dignitaries. But such a categorization is misleading in so far as it implies functional differentiation, for the nobility like the emperor performed highly diffuse roles which involved a variety of military, administrative, judicial, and ceremonial functions.

Vis-à-vis commoners, members of the old nobility regarded themselves as superior as well as privileged people. They regarded their titles and offices as personal rewards, to be used chiefly for purposes of self-aggrandizement. They created and maintained a distinct gentry sub-culture, which stressed the virtues of dignity, sobriety, and gentility.

While sharing these and other characteristics, members of the Ethiopian old nobility did not form a closed social class akin to the pre-industrial aristocracies of Europe. They were oriented vertically, to their respective superiors and retainers, far more than horizontally to one another. They attained no sense of corporate identity nor solidarity of interest, but sought rather each to outdo the other in perpetual competition for imperial favour. In addition, the legal basis for an hereditary aristocracy was missing, in that honorific titles, while held for life, could not be passed down from father to son. It was thus possible for men of lowly origin, even slaves, to rise to the highest powers and honours in the land.

Recruitment to the nobility was based on two quite different factors: appointment from above, and support from below. Theoretically the emperor was the source of all secular rank in the society, and in practice he could often take back offices and lands as quickly as he bestowed them. But a quasi-hereditary nobility did in fact exist, owing to the tendency of high appointees to establish families which attained local eminence, consolidated wealth, attracted military retainers, and passed on various political advantages, if not titles, to their sons. Such men were regarded as natural rulers by the local populace, and the emperor could never totally ignore their ascriptive claims to high rank. Thus, while the nobles never acted in concert in behalf of their interests as a class, Ethiopian history involved a continual oscillation between the assertion of imperial privilege and the assertion of claims by presumptive nobles who came from noted families and built up large personal followings.

The task of eliminating the partial autonomy of the nobility *vis-à-vis* the emperor has been one of the more conspicuous accomplishments of His Imperial Majesty Haile Selassie I. It was begun as soon as he came to power and successfully concluded by the late forties. He did this by replacing regional personal armies of the nobles by a substantial national standing army under his control; by replacing the traditional system of tax-farming by nobles with a centralized fiscal system under the Ministry of Finance; and by depriving the nobility of a number of their customary prerogatives. He further disarmed a number of the more prominent nobles of the day by appointing them to the Senate. Those nobles who remain in the provinces now play a much smaller role in the national political life, and are somewhat embittered against the newer elites emanating from Addis Ababa. Even so, they continue to comport themselves in the genteel manner of the old nobility, and remain, in the eyes of the provincial populace, the only fully legitimate secular elite.

THE 'NEW NOBILITY'

While curbing the independent power of the traditional elites, Haile Selassie was careful to prevent others from acquiring the authority they once had. Owing to his centralization of power in Addis Ababa, however, a new group of men have come to the fore at the national level. For want of a better term they may be referred to as the 'new nobility': 'new' because of their development of an urban style of life, and because their influence as an elite is directed chiefly to the modernizing infra-structure, and 'nobility' because of their perpetuation of the hierarchical image of a superior and privileged status group. The core of this group consists of government officials with the ranks of minister. Connected with them socially are a small number of urban plutocrats who have made their fortunes since the war in import–export trade and real estate.

The high status of these men rests on their possession of political influence, measured partly by the strength of their personal followings but primarily by how close they are to the Emperor, and on the Westernized style of life made possible by wealth acquired through political office, rents, and commerce. Their ascendance as an elite group may be located roughly in the decade after 1945, the year in which the failure of a revolt in Tigre Province marked the end of attempts to assert provincial claims inspired by allegiance to members of the old nobility. Their growing power during this decade was based on a rapid expansion of the governmental bureaucracy, strengthening of the national military forces, and economic advance due largely to the favourable world coffee market.

The members of the new nobility have been recruited from three different types of background. Some of them have been members of the old nobility who were absorbed into the new machinery of state built up by the Emperor. Another group consists of commoners who have risen to high position because of outstanding personal loyalty to the Emperor, especially prior to and during the time of his exile. A third group consists of those who were educated abroad before the Italian Occupation, and whose technical competence has made them invaluable in carrying out the functions of modern administration. In recent years a few Ethiopians of commoner background who studied abroad since the war have acceded to the top levels of leadership.

Members of this ruling elite have exerted intermittent influence over the Emperor, by providing him with privileged information and by offering their opinions on policy questions. But they have lacked power to effectuate decisions on their own, alone or as a group. Haile Selassie has maintained his power over them and forestalled coalescences of interest through a variety of techniques: *shum-shir*, a frequent reshuffling of offices, makes it difficult for officials to build up stable allegiences and keeps them anxious to remain in his good graces; *daj tenat*, the traditional custom which requires all officials to pay their homage at the court periodically and the related protocol of periodically ranking them according to how they stand in his favour; an extensive system of formal surveillance; and such punishments as arbitrary fines and house arrests.

The mentality of this new nobility has thus been marked by a constant anxiety geared to the Emperor's shifting policies and favouritisms. While they are conscious of themselves as a ruling elite, distinct both from the old nobility and the younger educated Ethiopians, their social relations follow the traditional pattern: they look for recognition from above and supporters from below, and regard one another chiefly as competitors and rivals for imperial favour.

THE MILITARY ELITE

The transfer of military functions from the old nobility to a large professional standing army has given rise to what should be regarded as an elite group in its own right. Ethiopian officers enjoy the deference their countrymen have always paid towards men of war, and have achieved some prominence in the national life from their efforts during the Italian campaign and, more recently, from their performance in United Nations missions and in defending the Somali border.

Except for the fact that they tend to be somewhat more anxious to modernize the country than are members of the new nobility, the higher military officers are sociologically quite similar to their civilian counterparts. Their styles of life are not very different. While dissatisfaction over income on the part of non-commissioned military personnel has been a source of tension during the past decade, the perquisites of higher officers compare favourably with those higher civilian officials. They receive substantial salaries, as well as free housing, cars, and male servants. A number of them have received personal gifts directly from the throne. There is, furthermore, a good deal of friendly intercourse between the two groups. Army officers are in many cases related to civilian officials. Military men have in several instances been assigned to civilian posts in the Government. While the military carry on much of their social life among themselves, they also enjoy a good deal of interaction with civilians of high status at parties, dances, weddings, and funerals.

Like the new nobility, moreover, the military officers do not form a cohesive group with common interests and ambitions. The one group which did develop a high degree of solidarity, *esprit*, and common political goals—the Officers Corps of the Imperial Bodyguard—was dissolved in the wake of its defeat in the 1960 rebellion. The military men have been checked and balanced in much the same way as have the new nobility, and are held together by little more than the formal structure of the security forces.

ETHIOPIA'S 'INTELLIGENTSIA'

The existence of a nascent counter-elite may be dated around 1955, the year of the Jubilee Celebration of the twenty-fifth anniversary of the Emperor's Coronation. This was a lavishly contrived affair which, occurring at about the time that the first sizeable group of post-war college students had returned from abroad, accentuated in their minds a sense of estrangement from the *ancien régime*. Although the intellectual interests and activities of this counter-elite are as yet rather meagre, they may, for want of a better term, be identified as an intelligentsia, inasmuch as their defining characteristic is the possession of what is still very rare in Ethiopia—modern education at least at the secondary level—and their function is that of bearers of modern culture in the traditional Ethiopian society.

Compared with the rest of Ethiopian society, the members of this intelligentsia share a number of characteristics which may be said to distinguish them as a social class: similar amounts and sources of income, standard of living, patterns of association, and cultural orientations. Their income falls in a range of Eth. $250–650 per month, and is in the great majority of cases derived solely from salaries paid by the Government. This contrasts with the ministerial elite, on the one hand, who earn $1,000–$2,000 in salary and usually supplement this with considerable income from rents, bribes, and at times diversion of government funds; and with such groups as the old nobility in the provinces, who as district governors earn $100, plus rents, bribes, and produce from their lands, or policemen, labourers, and servants in the

cities, who earn $15–$30 a month. The modern-educated
associate with one another, and with resident Europeans, far more
than with other Europeans. They maintain humble residences,
scattered all over the city, but place great store on owning fine
European clothes, automobiles, and radios.

Above all, they have assimilated a basic core of modern ideas,
skills, and values which sets them apart from all other segments of
Ethiopian society. They see their modern values compromised and
their aspirations blocked by the members of the 'new nobility',
whom they charge with excessive intrigue, 'corruption', and
nepotism, and whom they blame for lack of desire or courage to
promote the country's modernization. The masses of the people
they regard, on the other hand, with mixed feelings: partly with
sympathy and appreciation, idealizing the 'wisdom' of the
peasantry and identifying with them as oppressed and under-
privileged; partly with condescension and disdain, regarding them
as little better than ignorant savages, who must be forcibly
manipulated for some time to come if Ethiopia is to advance.
This ambivalence is related to a conception that they have of their
role in the country's future: that of a cadre of technical and
administrative experts who will transform the country overnight
for the benefit of the people, but as the acknowledged new masters
of the people. At the same time it should be noted that the
intelligentsia, by virtue of their prolonged isolation from the
traditional peasantry and their identification with the world of
modernity, have very little direct and realistic understanding of
the actualities of peasant existence.

Despite the many life conditions and values which members of
the modern-educated class have in common, one of the most
conspicuous and problematic features of this class is its high
degree of atomization. They have been assimilated to the traditional status system far more than they have attained a solidary
stance in opposition to it. This atomization was particularly
evident prior to the 1960 rebellion. Not only were there no formal
associations to which Ethiopian intelligentsia belonged, let alone
a political party (except for a Ministry-sponsored Teachers'
Association which existed largely on paper). Even friendship

groups were rare and tenuous. One frequently heard the complaint: 'I cannot even trust my best friend.' Two or three conspiratorial groups existed, but they did not function effectively or over a long period.

Since 1960 some changes have occurred. On the one hand, some formal associations have been established—notably, a Medical Association, an Engineers' Association, and an Ethiopian College Teachers' Association. On the other hand, a number of informal associations have sprouted. These are groups of friends bound by a variety of ties—kinship, ethnic identity, common study abroad, professional interests. Perhaps the most important basis of these groups are friendships which were formed during the crucial years of secondary-school attendance. For the most part they do not carry out activities or formal functions, but serve simply as a forum within which anything can be said without fear of recrimination. A member of one of these groups has written:

> Ethiopia and its ills are widely discussed and talked about by a great many educated Ethiopians, the so-called elite. But years of talking, of throwing words at the administration, of vaguely talking about rights and reform has proved to be meaningless. There is only the talk over a glass of whiskey or after some beers; otherwise nothing constructive. In the past two years or so a group of us have been attempting to give this discontent some meaning, some purpose. To date it has mainly limited itself to what one may term 'natural associations' between friends. More than anything else it is our aim to create an atmosphere of trust between suspicious and frightened young (people) who share the same ideas.

Such efforts towards solidarity have so far amounted to little. A climate of suspiciousness persists and blocks effective group activity. So do habits of passivity and unfamiliarity with disciplined co-ordination; members of associations and informal groups continue to come late to appointments or fail to remember meetings all together. The desire to accomplish is subverted by a failure of nerve and low morale, rationalized by the statement that nothing significant *can* be accomplished so long as the present régime remains in power. Lack of solidarity in the modern-educated class persists, above all, because it is the natural outcome of fairly deep-seated sociological factors.

SOURCES OF DISUNITY AMONG THE INTELLIGENTSIA

The high degree of disunity among the Ethiopian intelligentsia may be attributed primarily to the influence of four factors: the diversity of their educational experience, the diversity of their class and ethnic backgrounds, the influence of individualistic patterns from traditional Amhara culture, and the practices and policies of the Government.

Educational Differences

Ethiopia's modern educational system reflects the pluralism of metropolitan traditions which have been represented there. Different secondary schools have been administered, respectively, by groups of Americans, British, Canadian Jesuits, French, and Swedes. Graduates of these schools have thus been estranged from one another to some extent by virtue of the different external traditions which have coloured their school experience and with which they have in some measure identified.

This diversity has been compounded in the case of those who studied abroad. While the modal tendency for Ethiopians studying abroad has been to attend schools in the United States, Canada, and England, substantial numbers of them have been trained in Egypt, France, West Germany, India, Israel, Italy, Lebanon, and Sweden; and smaller numbers have been trained in such diverse countries as Mexico, Greece, Turkey, Uganda, Yugoslavia, and several others. This diversity inhibits solidarity by inhibiting communication among those who have studied in radically different foreign cultures. Their models for the modern component of language are different, as are their images of modern society and their sentimental associations regarding the lands of their alma mater. It also promotes disunity in that status differences among the intelligentsia are based largely on the extent and quality of education acquired, and this is measured in part in terms of the country which one has attended. In the mid-fifties competition along these lines was particularly keen between those who were educated in England and the United States; and the issue lingers, generating status differences between those who have studied in high-prestige and low-prestige countries, whichever these may be at a given period.

The distinction between Ethiopians who have studied and those who have received all their training at home, the 'Returnees' and the 'Locals'—in the past few years the West African term 'Been-to's' has been introduced into Amharic to refer to the former—provides another basis of disunity among the modern-educated. Antagonism along these lines was particularly prominent around 1957. It has since subsided, largely because the market value of a foreign degree has diminished with the return of greater numbers from abroad and the graduation of many students from Ethiopia's colleges; but the difference remains as a basis of status differences and different life situations and styles which impede communication between the two groups.

Ethnic and Class Differences

Traditional prejudices, resentments, and rivalries among members of Ethiopia's different ethnic groups have diminished but not disappeared among modern-educated Ethiopians. The principal ethnic groups involved are the Amhara, Tigre, and Galla, the former oriented in terms of a feeling of superiority, the latter two oriented in terms of resentment concerning Amhara political dominance and style. While these attitudes tend to be subordinated to nationalist orientations during the course of higher education, they re-emerge in the course of competition for jobs and prestige in the modernizing sector. At times they amount to no more than a source of jests and harmless banter, at times they lead to more serious accusations and recriminations.

Differences of socio-economic status likewise introduce strains in the relations among the modern-educated Ethiopians. Sons of notables tend to feel that they are entitled to the best positions, and are resentful when someone from a poor and unknown family surges ahead of them in the competition for good positions. Conversely, those of commoner background believe that no matter how qualified they may be, they have no chance to compete with the more privileged children of the highest families.

The situation has been summed up by one American-trained Ethiopian educator as follows:

> Though they are educated, are modern, and seek the welfare of the majority of the people, etc., yet, in some strange way, their ethnic, religious, or cultural and even class differences seem to linger and are bound to show up in a critical situation. This stimulates subdued feelings of suspicion of one another's motives.

Traditional Amhara Behaviour Patterns

Ethiopian behaviour at the national level is governed primarily by the culture of the Amhara, who also constitute a majority of the modern-educated population. The primary thrust of their culture is to oppose fraternal solidarity, both at the communal level and in interpersonal relations. This phenomenon has been examined at length elsewhere in connexion with an examination of Amhara 'individualism' (Levine, 1965, ch. 7). The results of that analysis which bear on the present discussion may be summarized here briefly as follows.

Both in their subjective dispositions and their patterns of social organization, the Amhara place far more importance on personal interests than on collective concerns. They have virtually no conception of a civil community; the word 'community' can scarcely be rendered in idiomatic Amharic. In their personal relations, coloured though they are by patterns of hospitality, sociability, and respect, the primary dispositions are self-assertion, dissensus, and distrust.

Consistent with this type of subjective orientation, the organization of Amhara society does not rely to a significant extent on co-operative arrangements or the machinery of consensus. Nor does it involve, on the basis of either a division of labour or the sharing of diffuse obligations, the traditional performance of numerous functions on behalf of territorial communities or other collectivities.

The axes of cohesion in traditional Amhara society are for the most part *vertical*. They take the form of chains of relations between superiors and subordinates. Relations among status equals have been ordered either in terms of conflict or competition, or else respect, but have rarely provided a basis for solidary action or corporate consciousness.

Thus, unlike the educated elites of many other African societies who, however much divided by ethnic or other differences, may yet be inspired by a communalistic or fraternal ethos deriving from the traditional cultures of their childhood, the modern-educated elite in Ethiopia lives under the influence of a traditional culture which stresses independence, self-assertion, and a patriarchal ethos.

Government Influence

A final factor affecting the divisiveness of the intelligentsia is the interest of the monarchy and new nobility in preventing the development of an active class solidarity among them. For the reasons given above, they have been able to do this without resorting to terrorist or rigid coercive policies. Their primary tactic has been to turn the thoughts of the intelligentsia upward, to the sources of income, power, and prestige. Where possible, they have sought to win the attachment of the modern-educated, and to make this vertical relation a basis for accomplishing whatever goals the latter have.

In so far as the intelligentsia have chosen to remain aloof from such attachments, the development of consensus among them and capacities for solidary action has been rendered difficult by the Government's policy of discouraging formal associations and free speech. Voluntary associations have either been forbidden or else have been infiltrated by informers. Even in friendship groups, numerous informal networks of informers as well as official security systems inhibit the intelligentsia from speaking their minds and developing them through open exchange with others.

As a result of the Government's interest in fragmenting the ranks of the intelligentsia, their own deeply ingrained habits of distrust and independence, and the divisive aspects of their educational, class, and ethnic backgrounds, the modern-educated Ethiopians have not moved beyond a consciousness of kind to a posture of class solidarity and social cohesion. Their social adaptation has taken the form that has always characterized the traditional Amhara order—an order defined in terms of highly differentiated status hierarchies, but never organized into stratified groups having a clear sense of corporate identity and marked by solidarity of interests.

CONCLUSION

In conclusion, I might suggest a few aspects in which the modern-educated Ethiopian elite contrasts with the educated elite in most of the colonial and ex-colonial African nations.

1. The presence of European elites in the colonial countries created a strong stimulus for educated Africans to emulate them, to achieve their standard of living and education, and so to replace them. The absence of such an alien elite in Ethiopia has left the educated Ethiopians with less incentive and favoured their passive acquiescence to the traditional order.

2. Inspired by the variety of organizations and clubs created by European colonists, other Africans have themselves organized numerous kinds of associations—religious, political, professional, youth, and so on. Modern-educated Ethiopians had virtually no associations of this sort prior to 1961, and even now the few which have been formed are not taken very seriously.

3. While a few mission schools have been operating in Ethiopia for many years, they are almost invisible compared to the government-operated schools; in further contrast to the situation in colonial countries.

4. Finally, it might be mentioned that in many other African countries, especially West Africa, women have exerted a good deal of leadership in government and in commerce, while in Ethiopia the relatively suppressed status of the woman has not yet been significantly altered.

BIBLIOGRAPHY

Levine, Donald N.
(1965) *Wax and Gold: Tradition and Innovation in Ethiopian Culture*, Chicago.

Résumé

LA CONSCIENCE DE CLASSE ET LA SOLIDARITÉ DE CLASSE DANS LA NOUVELLE ÉLITE ÉTHIOPIENNE

Le développement d'une strate d'Éthiopiens d'éducation moderne dans une société dont les élites traditionnelles n'ont jamais été boulversées par les puissances étrangères, semblerait, à l'avis de quelques observateurs, avoir produit une situation de conflit social, organisé selon les règles de classe, mais une analyse plus exacte montre que cela n'a pas été le cas.

Pour arriver à un haut rang séculier dans la société traditionnelle de l'Éthiopie il fallait avoir la faveur de l'Empereur et le soutien local. Il y a été dans l'histoire de l'Éthiopie une oscillation continue entre les privilèges de l'Empereur et les revendications des droits des nobles qui appartenaient aux familles importantes avec de larges partis personnels. L'ancienne noblesse, cependant, n'agitaient de concert selon les intérêts de leur classe: ils n'achevaient aucune identité collective, aucune solidarité d'intérêt, mais ils luttaient continuellement, l'un contre l'autre, pour la faveur de l'Empereur.

L'Empereur actuel a éliminé définitivement l'autonomie traditionnelle des membres importants de l'ancienne noblesse. Au même temps il a établi de nouveaux offices de pouvoir et de prestige dans le gouvernement centralisé à Addis Ababa. Tandis que les membres de cette 'nouvelle noblesse' sont conscients d'être une élite règnante, distincte de l'ancienne noblesse aussi bien que des plus jeunes Éthiopiens instruits, leurs rapports sociaux suivent le modèle traditionnel. Ils cherchent, avant tout, la reconnaissance d'en haut et le soutien d'en bas, et se sont regardés l'un l'autre comme des concurrents et des rivaux à la faveur impériale.

Les plus jeunes Éthiopiens instruits constituent une 'contra-élite' qui rencontre la nouvelle noblesse aux certains points, mais en est pour la plupart distincte. Ils comprennent environ 6,000 Éthiopiens qui, en 1962, terminèrent leurs études secondaires et 1,000 d'entre eux obtinrent le B.A. ou une qualification supérieure.

Les membres de cette 'intelligentsia' ont plusieurs caractéristiques en commun qui les distinguent comme classe sociale; les salaires, les sources de rente, le niveau de vie, les relations, les orientations culturelles. Ils ont assimilé une base d'idées, de techniques, de valeurs modernes qui les distinguent de tout autre segment de la société éthiopienne.

Malgré les similarités de vie et de valeurs qui leur ont donné une certaine conscience de classe, les membres de cette 'intelligentsia' ne constitue point une classe unie et solidaire. Un haut dégré d'atomisation est, en effet, une des caractéristiques les plus évidentes et les plus problèmatiques de cette classe. Le désaccord entre les membres de l'intelligentsia semble se dégager de 4 sources principales:

1. Les différences d'éducation, dues aux différences de personnel et d'orientation dans les écoles secondaires, la diversité des pays étrangers où les Éthiopiens ont fait leurs études, la distinction entre ceux qui ont fait leurs études en Éthiopie et ceux qui les ont faites à l'étranger.

2. Les différences ethniques et de classe de leurs familles.

3. Les modèles traditionnels de comportement chez les Amhara. La tradition dominante en Éthiopie, celle des Amhara, insiste sur l'indépendance, l'affirmation de soi-même, l'esprit patriarcal, plutôt que sur l'unité, la solidarité, l'esprit fraternel ou collectif.

4. Les principes et les pratiques du gouvernement qui tendent à diviser plutôt qu'à unifier.

Comme résultat de ces facteurs, l'adaptation sociale des Éthiopiens qui ont reçu une éducation moderne a suivie le modèle caractéristique du rang dans la tradition Amhara; c'est à dire les hiérarchies de statut, nettement distinguées, mais jamais organisées en groupes stratifiés avec un sens bien défini d'identité collective et une solidarité d'intérêts.

XVI. CLASS CONSCIOUSNESS AMONG THE YORUBA

P. C. LLOYD

The western-educated Yoruba elite of Western Nigeria are a small group; they have a highly distinctive style of life; they enjoy great economic privileges in the state. Most leading members were educated in Britain and many participated in left-wing political parties. Yet, in their descriptions and analyses of the social stratification of their society the vocabulary of 'class' is conspicuously absent. This paper suggests some reasons for the non-egalitarian classlessness perceived by the Yoruba; it postulates, furthermore, that the development of this elite and the class-less perception of society is an important factor in the development of the one-party state—a development which itself promotes an image of a classless society.

THE ELITE DEFINED

In the context of this paper I use the term elite to denote those men and women who have received a substantial western education and are (almost in consequence) relatively wealthy. They are a national elite—well over half their members reside in Ibadan. Excluded by definition are wealthy but illiterate or semi-literate traders, traditionally orientated and often prominent within the towns of their birth. Marginal to the group are the educated obas and chiefs, men of affluence but slight influence outside their own towns. The elite are thus the bureaucrats, the secondary-school teachers and university lecturers, and the politicians (Lloyd, n.d.).

This elite forms a very homogenous group. Its members have received a uniform style of education in a small number of Nigerian secondary schools and overseas—predominantly British—universities. Most are salary earners on scales which, whether in the civil service, public corporations, or educational bodies, are substantially uniform. The salaries are high; for in stepping into places vacated by the expatriates, Nigerians have assumed the remuneration and privileges of the offices. Thus, a university graduate commences to earn at a salary of £750 per annum and may rise to £3,000 per annum. In contrast, a daily paid unskilled labourer earns £75 per annum; the mean income per head in Western Nigeria is £30 per annum.

The style of life is uniform. The elite usually live in houses built and partly furnished by the employer. The range of soft furnishings and decoration reflects the limited choice offered by local Ibadan shops. Among the elite one may detect a variety in the pattern of family relationships, ranging between a traditional pattern, in which the wife is to a large extent economically independent of her husband, a Victorian pattern, with an authoritarian father and greater emphasis on the individual, and an egalitarian pattern, with an emphasis on shared roles and responsibilities between husband and wife. These three patterns seem to correlate with the family background of the couples, and with their own style of life (Lloyd, n.d.).

The size of the elite has grown most rapidly within the past decade as the Western Region first gained internal independence in 1957, followed by national independence in 1960. Vast programmes of social services have created new offices. The elite are thus a group of young people. For those who graduated from university in the early 1950s promotion has been extremely rapid; of the graduates living in Ibadan, 40 per cent have fathers who did not complete (or perhaps even start) primary education and only 25 per cent have fathers with post-primary education. In the former category are some sons of wealthy farmers, traders, and chiefs, but many of the men come from very humble houses.

Intermarriage between men and women from different ethnic groups within Yoruba country increases with education. The elite is thus becoming a more cosmopolitan group. Close friendships exist mainly with persons of similar economic and educational status, a majority of these friendships antedated the marriages of those concerned. Half the friendships were with persons of other Yoruba ethnic groups. There seem, however, to be relatively few associations with an exclusive elite membership. The social life of the elite seems to be based on a high degree of interaction between close friends and family members.

As Barbara Lloyd's paper shows, the elite are most anxious that their children should attain the same status as themselves; the children's success will depend mostly on their educational achievement, and their parents' efforts are thus directed to ensuring their entry to a good secondary school and university.

ELITE PRIVILEGES

Professor Bauer has written (1964):

> The economic policies pursued in many African territories, notably those under British rule, over the last twenty years or so, have created tightly controlled economies in which people's lives and activities and the alternatives open to them (outside subsistence production) . . . are largely determined by the government. They include the establishment of state trading monopolies; extensive licensing of industrial and commercial activities; and the setting up of many government owned and operated enterprises . . . These policies have created the framework of ready-made totalitarian states for the incoming governments. . . . Above all, these policies have greatly increased the prizes of political power and the intensity of the struggle for them.

Through the administrative infra-structure of government and through the public corporations, the Nigerian politicians and bureaucrats control a large sector of the nation's economy. Very few of the elite are managers of their own businesses. Many are executives in the large expatriate trading enterprises, such as the United Africa Company. However, in the recently developed local industries the managerial and technical staff is, as yet, predominantly expatriate. In the absence of a local bourgeosie, the elite, as a social group, is highly dependent on the Government— the locus of political power.

The elite is highly remunerated for its services. Salary scales outside the civil service tend to follow those set by the Government. The Western Region Government, like others in the Federation, has refused to lower civil service salaries for fear of alienating the bureaucracy. Furthermore, it has retained most of the colonial service privileges and perquisites—loans for car purchase at low interest rates, a monthly allowance for running the car, subsidized housing for its senior officers. Rates of income tax are relatively low, and in the opinion of Orewa (1962, ch. 8), insufficiently progressive; he argues that taxation should be increased to reduce the consumption of imported luxuries among the elite.

Education is heavily subsidized by the Government. Primary-school education is almost free (parents pay for books and uniforms). Boarding and tuition fees in secondary grammar schools amount to about £75 per annum irrespective of the quality of the school; the real costs of education in the better schools are two or three times this figure. Thus, although admission to these schools is by competitive examination, it is in fact restricted to those with the financial means. Similarly, the fees charged by the Universities in Nigeria (about £150 per annum) amount to one-eighth of the cost of the education provided. In competing for entrance to the better secondary schools and universities, the children of the elite have the advantages of a home life which stresses academic achievement, of private education and coaching, and of attendance at primary schools of the highest quality.

The elite are thus a group, distinguished from the masses by their high incomes and acceptance of a largely westernized style of life. The privileges of high salaries, additional perquisites, low taxation, and subsidized education are maintained by the Government, in which so many of the elite serve. Why, then, are they not regarded, by themselves or others, as an upper social class?

FACTORS PROMOTING CLASSLESSNESS

Traditional Yoruba Views of Stratification

Great differences in wealth, in political power, and in prestige existed within traditional Yoruba society. Furthermore, achievement of high status was open to all freeborn. Chieftaincy titles rotated between lineage segments, and men could not be succeeded directly by their own sons. The most wealthy traders frequently had humble beginnings. Wealth was demonstrated largely in the number of one's wives; and the division of one's estate into as many equal shares as there were wives with issue ensured the fragmentation of large estates and the prevention of inherited fortunes. High prestige was accorded to wealth and political office, and there was considerable striving and competition for such statuses.

Yoruba attitudes are reflected in their own terminology. *Akuse* is a term of abuse for the man whose poverty stems from his laziness. The *mekunu* is the humble, decent person; the term is used of oneself in modesty. The *borokini* is the moderately wealthy person with a steady income. The high status terms reflect, in varying degrees, wealth, honour, or prestige (being of good character and upholding the values of society) and generosity. *Gbajumo* denotes the popular and generous giver; *oloro*, the man whose wealth lies more in property than in ready cash; *olola*, the man of highest character, wealth, too, being implied here. Achievement of such statuses is largely pre-destined, though one's destiny or fate can be modified for the better by service of one's tutelary deities, or for the worse by witches and evil spirits. Again, one's own character, an element not pre-determined but the product of one's responsibility, may affect one's fate.

Significant here is the emphasis on adherence to the values of the whole society, generosity being one of these. For many, the achievement of high status depends on the support of one's fellows—as in election to a chieftaincy title, the growth of a trader's customers. Although the rich man certainly enjoys to the full the benefit of his wealth, both material and non-material advantages accrue to his supporters—his descent group members, other kin, and his followers.

Those designated by such terms as *olola*, *oloro*, *gbajumo* do not form a social group in their towns. They stand, individually, at the apices of groups consisting of kin and followers, with whom is most of their interaction. Common interests do not bind the prestigious in distinction from, or opposition to, the masses.

Such an image of Yoruba society continues to exist today, even to some extent among the elite. The vernacular terms cited are used for those in modern statuses. The flamboyant politician is *gbajumo*. The senior civil servant is described as wealthy but not as having honour or generosity; the term 'senior service' denotes a style of life rather than social approval. This conception of the structure of society is not compatible with a horizontal stratification of society.

Tribalism and Patronage

'Tribalism', one of the evils cited of contemporary Nigerian society, is, according to most commentators, on the increase. This opprobrious term has several usages; in spite of the growing cosmopolitan nature of the elite, most individuals retain strong ties with the towns of their birth. Their parents and less-educated siblings still live at home. Here they plan to retire, and thus they currently invest their savings in an imposing house. Ibadan does not seem to offer to the elderly such prestigious positions as they might hold in their own towns. The elite are expected to participate in the local branches of the 'Progressive Unions' of their towns; most of them, and especially the older members, do so. A political career depends on strong popular support in one's home area.

Colonial administrators ruled all parts of Nigeria with reasonable impartiality. Universal suffrage has led to fears by the minority in any political unit that the majority will exercise its power to its exclusive advantage. Ethnic hostilities have been aroused at every level as each group tries to gain a greater share of the new social services. To assuage such fears, and to reward the electorate for their support, social services are distributed with ostensible fairness. Other rewards, such as ministerial offices, are also so distributed—with the result that more than half the members of the governing party are ministers. Recipients of ministerial office—and of its high salary and numerous perquisites—must in turn reward those who, by their campaigning, helped them to office. Government control of customary courts, of contracting firms and the like enables the politicians to distribute patronage. The symbols of regional and national unity tend not to be flags, anthems, a picturesque governor, parliament buildings, but a set of ministers, each identified with a particular town or ethnic group.

There seems to be an increasing tendency for aspirants for

promotion in bureaucracies to manipulate ethnic loyalties; they seek the patronage of a highly placed official from their own group; they suggest that their own group is receiving an insufficient share of well-paid posts; when they fail to achieve the desired office they claim that the selectors have favoured their own group, possibly accepting higher bribes from them.

The establishment of universal suffrage in a society where the electorate is largely semi-literate, with loyalties to the town transcending those to the state, leads to increased ethnicity at the higher political levels and among the elite. Such ethnicity inhibits the horizontal stratification of the nation.

The Self-image of the Elite

The achievement of political independence created the new elite; to the elite now falls the task of developing the country economically from its poverty.

At the local level the politicians perform an interpretative function between the traditional and modern society. At the national level their aim is to bring the welfare state to the masses. 'Freedom for all and life more abundant' is the Action Group slogan. All southern Nigerian political parties claim to be socialist —the democratic socialism of the Action Group, the pragmatic socialism of the N.C.N.C. The most publicized activities of governments are their provision of free primary education, more hospitals, better water supplies. Economic development is but a means to these ends. Little difference thus exists between the political principles of each of the main southern Nigerian parties; the rival parties cannot each appeal convincingly to different strata of the society.

Not only do the elite see their role as the material improvement of the entire population but they also regard themselves as the spearhead of cultural unity. Ethnic loyalties are a centrifugal force threatening the unity of the state which supports the elite. The elite has thus encouraged such associations as the Egbe Omo Oduduwa which engendered pan-Yoruba sentiments and sought to make these transcend loyalties to constituent ethnic groups. For many reasons the educated Yoruba identifies himself with the historical past of his own society—but generally it is a past from which conflict and local differences have been excluded. The sentiments of unity produced by such movements are, however, strongest among the elite themselves and are an important factor in considering their cohesion as a social group.

The self-image of the Yoruba elite as the leaders of the masses in the political, economic, and cultural spheres is easily sustained in the particular situation of past-colonial Africa, where the politicians have attained power through the ballot box and where most of the elite have risen from among the masses. But this is, moreover, an image of society generally fostered by privileged groups in most countries. As Ossowski writes (1963, p. 154):

> From the viewpoint of the interests of privileged and ruling groups the utility of presenting one's own society in terms of a non-egalitarian classless society is apparent. In the world of today, both in the *bourgeois* democracies and the people's democracies, such a presentation affords no bases for group solidarity amongst the under-privileged; it inclines them to endeavour to improve their fortunes, and to seek upward social mobility by means of personal effort and their own industry, and not by collective action.

The Lack of Solidarity Among the Masses

The Yoruba are still a peasant society. Only 5 per cent of adult males are in wage employment, and slightly more are probably living away from the towns of their birth. The remainder—farmers and self-employed craftsmen and traders—live in their lineage compounds. Traditional loyalties to kin and other local groups remain paramount; national or even provincial groupings based on agricultural or craft interests do not exist.

Factory workers, local government employees, school teachers, and the like have their trade unions. These, however, tend to be inefficiently organized. Their members look to their ethnic associations for most forms of social security. Several trade-union leaders have a certain charismatic appeal to their members and can effectively exploit local grievances by strike action; they seem incapable, however, of constructive criticism of the structure of their society. In the early 1950s the N.C.N.C. in conducting election campaigns in Lagos, described itself as the party of the proletariat; such claims are no longer made, and there is no close identification of the unions with any one political party. In the 1960 Action Group manifesto defining 'democratic socialism' classes were described as representing economic interests, the classes being: the self-employed masses, the urban workers, and the senior employees of the state and public corporations. It seems unlikely that this analysis made much popular impact. The victorious N.N.D.P. makes its strongest appeals to Yoruba unity.

The clerks and teachers, the skilled and semi-skilled factory workers are a junior elite. Their wages are not high, but they are regular. The labour turnover in the factories is very low, so prized are the jobs. The efforts of primary-school teachers and clerks to pass G.C.E. examinations are well known; more surprising is the finding that almost half the workers in one Lagos factory were studying after working hours.[1] The example of those numerous members of the contemporary elite who went to overseas universities in their early thirties, or even later, inspires men to continue to strive for academic achievement long after the completion of formal schooling.

Thus, the social category which one would expect to provide the most local and organized opposition to the elite and criticism of their privileges, consists instead of men who aspire to enter the ranks of the elite and who have high hopes of eventually succeeding. The elite is their reference group. Furthermore, when they fail they are likely to ascribe this to witchcraft by their own kin, or to their competitors' more effective use of bribery and patronage; they are less likely to criticize the structure of society.

These four factors account, at least in part, for the classless image of Yoruba society held by all strata. But the situation is not static. Annually the size of the elite appears to grow, but the gap between its wealth and that of the masses does not diminish. The social services, together with prestige buildings, have been paid for from savings in the sterling balances. Currently, taxes are difficult to collect (for the politicians have too little popular appeal) and foreign loans are fewer than expected. As future government revenues provide fewer social services, the image of the elite as parasitic upon society may well develop among the

[1] D. Seibel, University of Ibadan, personal communication.

masses. Educational expansion is resulting in the flow to the major towns of thousands of school-leavers, unemployed in the sense that they cannot find the type of job to which they believe their schooling to entitle them. Over a longer period the elite will become a quasi-hereditary group through its control and manipulation of the higher educational system.

THE ELITE AND THE ONE-PARTY STATE

The role of the elite in the trend towards one-party states in Africa has not been stressed by political scientists. Yet the existence of this group, with its substantial privileges, depends directly on the stability and integrity of the new state; it, above all, has a vested interest in the protection given by the state. Other factors, too, are, of course, important. When politicians are among the wealthiest men in the society, and when most of them would earn considerably less in any other employment open to their qualifications and talents, they will cling tenaciously to office. It is widely felt, too, that rivalry between parties with almost identical policies and programmes is an impediment to economic development.

Fear dominates much of the politician's thinking. The recent *coups d'état* in Africa have demonstrated that a régime may be changed by a small handful of organized and armed men. Elections often show that the voter is still thinking more in terms of a candidate's personality than of party and will suddenly transfer his loyalties. The example of the breakdown of administration in the Congo stands threateningly.

One response of the politicians is to seek closer control of all possible centres of 'subversive' thought—the civil service or the universities—to the point of influencing promotions and appointments therein. The corollary is that the ambitious man may try to rise in rank by impugning his competitor's loyalty to the government. Such is government control of bureaucracies and schools that a man dismissed from one post on (usually disguised) political grounds finds equivalent employment most difficult to obtain.

The members of the elite are anxious for their future as individuals and as a group. If the economy stagnates but the universities continue to train increasing numbers of graduates, competition within the elite will intensify. Appointments and promotions will seem to be made according to patronage rather than merit. The unemployed graduates will join the growing numbers of discontented literates who oppose the privileges of the elite. Political parties are already emerging which do not merely criticize the corruption of those wielding power but call for a radical change in the structure of society. Thus, Dr. 'Tunji Otegbeye's Socialist Workers' and Farmers' Party adopts a Marxist terminology of class conflict describing itself as the party of the 'labouring classes, workers, farmers, intellectuals, petty traders, artisans and the have-nots of Nigerian society' against the 'rich upper classes, feudalists, compradore bourgeousie (which) protect the interests of foreign investors, monopolies and exploiters'. Yet, there seems to be little knowledge of the writings of Trotsky, Djilas (1957), or, nearer home, Fanon (1963), all of whom have trenchantly attacked the elite in similarly revolutionary situations.

These fears must be seen against a background of apathy among the better educated members of the elite. Disillusion exists with the failure of political independence to produce marked economic progress. The learned and accepted western values of bureaucratic efficiency and achievement by academic merit are increasingly negated by corruption and patronage. Rapid Nigerianization is apt to set older men above younger ones with a superior training. The response is to emphasize past academic achievements, to be over-concerned with relative rankings, to evade decision-making and initiative but to carry out bureaucratic procedures with exactitude; and, above all, to maintain the *status quo*.

The elite fears that a sudden change of political leadership may produce chaos. Thus the government may be attacked, through the press, for its bad roads, for the failure of electricity supplies, but on issues of freedom of speech, academic freedom, the accuracy of the census, the opposition seems (to an outsider) surprisingly feeble. One dare not rock the boat so that it capsizes and all sink. Again, as the politicians increasingly control the bureaucracies through patronage, numbers of elite fear the defeat of their own sponsors. A one-party state (either *de facto* or *de jure*) promises the security and stability that the elite seek.

A further attraction of a strong government without effective opposition is that its decisions will be based less upon political expediency, more on national bureaucratic procedures or economic considerations. The short period of rule by administrators in Western Nigeria in 1962 demonstrated this to many civil servants.

The elite thus fosters the development of the one-party state in spite of its avowed fidelity to western parliamentary democracy and its concomitants. Such a development accords well with its own image of the classlessness of Yoruba society.

In Western Nigeria the leading politicians and bureaucrats have such similar social and educational backgrounds that the usual opposition between these groups is minimized.

In the single-party state the classlessness of society is emphasized, becoming an official doctrine. The role of the elite in providing national leadership is maintained. Upward social mobility is open to all, primarily through academic achievement, though qualified by loyalty to the state. As patronage increases, men are grouped according to their individual sponsors and benefactors.

The stability of such a system will ultimately depend on the degree to which the masses can be satisfied by tangible improvements in their standards of living and by a demonstrable degree of upward social mobility. An expanding economy will provide these opportunities; a recession in development will reduce them and will reinforce the tendency for the elite to become an almost closed group.

BIBLIOGRAPHY

Bauer, P. T.
   (1964) Letter to *The Times*, quoted in 'Matchet's Diary', *West Africa*, no. 2432, 11 January 1964, p. 37.
Djilas, Milovan.
   (1957) *The New Class*, London.

Fanon, Franz

   (1963) *The Damned*, Paris. (Translation by Constance Farrington of *Les Damnés de la Terre*.)

Lloyd, P. C.

   (n.d.) 'The elite of Ibadan', in Mabogunje, A., Awe, B., and Lloyd, P. C. (eds.), *City of Ibadan* (forthcoming).

Orewa, G. O.

   (1962) *Taxation in Western Nigeria*, Ibadan.

Ossowski, S.

   (1963) *Class Structure in the Social Consciousness*, London.

Résumé

LA CONSCIENCE DE CLASSE CHEZ LES YORUBA

Le vocabulaire de classe est manifestement absent chez l'élite Yoruba; il y a dans sa place une notion d'une société non-égalitaire mais sans classe. Dans ce discours on suggère des raisons pour le développement de cette notion.

L'élite d'éducation occidentale constitue un groupe homogène. Ils gagnent, pour la plupart, de bons salaires dans la bureaucratie. Leur mode de vie est uniforme et nettement opposée à celle des masses. L'élite s'est développée plus rapidement pendant la dernière décade. L'élite est un groupe privilégié. Leurs salaires comprennent beaucoup d'avantages subsidiaires et l'enseignement secondaire et universitaire—achevé plus fréquemment par les enfants de l'élite que par les enfants des masses—est subventionné par le gouvernement.

L'élite est donc un groupe tellement distinct qu'on attendrait qu'ils soient considérés et par eux-mêmes et par autrui comme une classe d'haut rang social dans la société. Il y a, cependant, plusieurs facteurs qui favorisent l'idéologie d'un groupe sans classe.

En premier lieu, selon la notion traditionnelle de la stratification sociale chez les Yoruba, on trouvait l'homme riche et de prestige à la tête d'un groupe de parents et de suivants. Ces hommes élites ne constituent point un groupe social en eux-mêmes. Une telle idée de la structure sociale est irréconciliable avec celle d'une stratification horizontale.

En second lieu, la loyauté à la région natale est devenue, récemment, plus manifeste à cause de plus vives craintes que les avantages de l'indépendance politique ou le développement économique soient distribuées selon la tribu ou le patronage.

En troisième lieu, l'élite se voit comme l'agence la plus importante dans le développement de l'économie et l'unité culturelle du pays.

En quatrième lieu, les masses appartiennent à une société paysanne qui ne peuvent pas attaquer les privilèges ou le pouvoir de l'élite. Ceux qui pourraient remplir les fonctions des 'leaders' —les artisans ou les employés de bureau—sont des membres aspirants de l'élite.

On suggère, finalement que dans une situation pareille à celle des Yoruba, l'élite favorise inconsciemment le développement d'un gouvernement unitaire afin de sauvegarder sa propre position privilégiée dans l'état.

XVII. THE CONCEPT OF ELITES AND THEIR FORMATION IN UGANDA

A. W. SOUTHALL

THE USAGE OF THE CONCEPT

There is no doubt that elite is a most convenient shorthand word in discussion. Its imprecise yet vivid connotation often suffices when it would be tedious to have to spell out every time that one is referring, for example, to persons of superior education, wealth, status, and influence. Its very vagueness has been counted an advantage in dealing with those formative aspects of social behaviour which fall outside more precise categories. Yet most writers have held that some awareness of itself, and even control of entry to itself, is an essential aspect of an elite (Nadel, 1956).

Granted that elites must either form the top layers of society, or of certain sectors or institutions within it, or at least must aim at doing so, it is not clear how elite behaviour, or elite groups (since if they control entry they must to some extent be groups), as partially organized influential individuals, differ from the aggregate of persons playing dominant roles in those institutions which have most power or influence in society or the relevant sector of it. 'They are in command of the major hierarchies and organizations of modern society. They rule the big corporations. They run the machinery of the state and claim its prerogatives. They direct the military establishment. They occupy the strategic command posts of the social structure, in which are now centred the effective means of the power and the wealth and the celebrity which they enjoy' (Mills, 1957; p. 4). If we can say that a society is highly centralized, then its elite certainly must be, or at least it must have a central elite, as well as various subordinate, sectional, local, or peripheral elites. On the other hand, in African and under-developed countries the total elite is essentially pluralistic, but if we take an African elite, ethnically speaking, it is likely to be centralized in the sense of being small and closely knit at the top, though there may be many subordinate or local elites of great importance in their own sphere.

While African elites were only would-be elites in still colonial societies, they remained very flexible and open, easy of access to visiting political scientists. When they became established and had established jobs to do, sheer reasons of efficiency compelled them to define their limits, close their ranks, and restrict access to themselves as persons.

If we pick out the relevant institutions of power and influence, perhaps certain political parties, schools, universities, clubs, trades unions, banks, and various organizations of big business, have we empirically described an elite? Or is the elite essentially a more informal network of relationships between pre-eminent persons in these institutions and hence cutting right across them? 'The leading men in each of the three domains of power, the warlords, the corporation chieftains, the political directorate—tend to come together, to form the power elite of America' (Mills, 1957; p. 9).

If an elite is self-aware, self-perpetuating, and able to control entry, how can it fail to become institutionalized? In that case is it still an elite? If so, the term then describes only a certain collection of institutions. There is the further point that, in a very slowly changing society, it would seem impossible for an elite not to approximate almost identically with certain definite institutions, and hence appear analytically somewhat redundant. We obviously have to distinguish clearly between elite individuals, the extent to which they are organized, and the wider institutions to which they belong, without whose members, staffs, or followers they could not remain elite. For example, when we think of the British Public Schools endeavouring to restrict the entry of unsuitable new boys or new schools we really mean headmasters or housemasters individually controlling the entry of boys, according to a ruling set of values, or headmasters in their collective organization controlling the recognition of new schools, with the general moral support and acquiescence of their masters, boards of governors, boys, and parents. With established elites we think

z

essentially of roles which represent, control, and manage institutions. The question is how far elites consist of the incumbents of such institutionalized roles.

Is it accepted that the presence of elites presupposes a certain pace of change? If they merely circulated, without accompanying change of structure, they would again inevitably be institutionalized, perhaps rather like the political parties in a two-party democracy. Or does elite refer essentially to the growing edge of social activity, to that which at any one time is not yet institutionalized (although it inevitably will be if successful), to those with influence but not yet power or legitimate authority? In this case we precisely exclude the already established, who have often been taken to constitute the elite.

There may, however, be certain categories of people who are permanently or at least for long periods denied access to the formal institutions of authority yet possess the qualifications for influence. This is almost the opposite of the establishment. Obvious instances of this in many societies have been the influence of women, of Jews and Nonconformists during recent centuries in England, of Asians in East Africa today, in West Africa perhaps the Syrians and Lebanese, and indeed the whole European influence in the new African states. In these cases it is undoubtedly meaningful to speak of the feminine elite, the Jewish or Nonconformist elite, and other minority elites such as Asians in East Africa and Europeans in the new states of the less-developed world. The case of women raises the interesting question of the importance of expressive activity in elite behaviour. But to follow this line of argument too far is surely to arrive at an elite quite unrecognizable to common sense. It is an unresolved dilemma that the more we endeavour to delineate the contours of an elite as a continuing body with some awareness and ability to control entry, the more we approximate to certain definite institutions and tend to render the elite concept redundant. While, on the other hand, the more we concentrate on the areas of influence which the Establishment attempts to exclude by deliberate discrimination, the more we tend to exclude those very persons who are usually most in mind when elites are considered.

Another kind of growing edge, or area of informal influence, which can be conceived in the abstract, consists of the informal or even clandestine acts of influence on the part of powerful individuals, much or most of whose influence may be exerted through quite formal acts of authority within definitely institutionalized structures. But this again would be to give elites a very new definition in terms not of a more or less discernible body of individuals but of a particular abstract sector of their activity.

Expressive elite activity is usually concerned with maintenance through emotive symbols and finds its greatest contrast in the manipulation of power behind the scenes to initiate change, which is self-rewarding and eschews publicity. Both are equally important, and the same individuals can indulge in both on different occasions. 'While Oxbridge dons dress up in flat caps and rich robes to give honorary degrees and mumble Latin compliments to each other—all duly reported and photograped in *The Times*—their future is being settled by nineteen men in mufti, from a shabby office in Belgrave Square' (Sampson, 1962; pp. 213–14). But not altogether, for it is uncertain whether the University Grants Committee is a rich nephew subsidizing distressed uncles, or a rich uncle on whom young nephews can lean. The mumbling of Latin at the famous contest of Macmillan and Franks for the Oxford chancellorship was not so ineffective, but 'a curious illustration of how, at a time when the country desperately needed to increase the prestige of Redbrick universities, the whole energies of Oxford men, from the cabinet downwards, were devoted to perpetuating the overblown Oxford myth' (Sampson, 1962; p. 217). Myths have force, and expressive activity can be instrumentally effective. Questions of expressive elite activity demonstrated in public, on the one hand, and manipulation of power behind the scenes, on the other, the relative influence of university scholars and politicians and the interchange of role-playing by them in both political and non-political institutions, are highly relevant to the study of elites in modern African states.

Perhaps a precise definition of elite is neither possible nor desirable, the value of the concept being to call attention to those dynamic aspects of power and influence which are liable to elude formal analysis. It has little to offer in the analysis of very slowly changing societies, but as fairly rapid social change is becoming characteristic of the whole of humanity, this need not disconcert us. The elite, then, includes the people of the Establishment and includes their acts within the formal structures of authority. But since the latter should be catered for by institutional analysis, elite studies should particularly stress the areas of influence which lie outside this sphere, whether they belong to individuals who are deliberately excluded, or who are just in process of becoming established, or whether they are the informal acts of Established individuals, lying outside their formal roles. However, the assumption that the formal structures of authority are adequately cared for by institutional analysis may miss another aspect which could be fundamental to elites, although it does not so far seem to have been brought out very clearly in theoretical discussion. That is the extent to which the structures of authority and influence are tied together by the pervasive multiple role playing of key or nodal individuals who thus straddle them. Although in principle this should be revealed by structural analysis, in practice frequently it is not. It can be very effectively dealt with by role analysis in terms of role sets and sequences (Merton, 1957; Southall, 1959). Beyond this interlocking of roles there are, of course, likely to be informal networks of relationships serving similar purposes. Finally, we may note that this process of multiple role playing for purposes of power and influence occurs at a number of different levels and sectors of society, all of which can be seen in this sense as part of the context of the elite process.

While the main framework of relevant theory has been explored by Lasswell, Lazarsfeld, Nadel, and many other writers, professional field studies of elites are few and unimpressive compared with popular, concrete works like that of Anthony Sampson. *Anatomy of Britain* brings out the multiple-role-playing quality of the elite all the way through, and pin points it in a number of diagrams, tables, and even genealogies. It would be good if any anthropologist in Africa could do so well.

A practical question is how far it is justifiable to study African elites outside political parties and governments. Many students are now doing this and being strongly encouraged to do so for the very good reason that the top political elites have been worked to death as informants. But if new African societies are as highly politicized as many scholars say, a non-political elite is Hamlet without the Prince. Counting the number of people with so much education or income is necessary but most unsatisfying. In my view, the biggest contribution which social anthropologists can make is to ensure that elites are studied in their local, subordinate, and sectional as well as their central forms and in their becoming as well as their Establishment, concentrating most on their multiple-role-playing networks, which will, of course, have to include the political.

RELEVANT ASPECTS OF ELITES IN THE AFRICAN CONTEXT

In what follows we shall have in mind three main aspects of the concept of elite: its meaning and its structural and cultural dimensions. In Africa and probably in general it is more useful to envisage elites as dynamic and flexible categories rather than as groups; as groups in process of becoming rather than as actually achieving corporate definition. In the kaleidoscope of multifarious activity whereby influence is exerted, authority exercised, power manipulated, whether in relation to the whole society or any functional, institutional, or local section of it, there is always the attempt on the part of those engaged in these seductive activities to consolidate their positions; a process which would lead to the precipitation of an increasingly clear-cut category of persons, more and more aware of one another and likely to crystallize eventually into a simple or multiple corporate form, or at least a class or estate, were it not for the fact that some are always failing to maintain themselves in their enviable positions and others are succeeding in breaking into them. The more stable or unchanging the effect of external forces upon the society, and the level of its resources, depending upon its economy and technology, the nearer its elites are likely to come to crystallization at the corporate level. But when external forces threaten disruption, or when economic and technological development is rapid, elites are likely to remain for ever in the process of becoming, as their personnel, their aspirations, their appropriate behaviour, and the system which they manipulate continually change. The ideological counterpart is the Open Society. The New Nations of Africa are for the most part open societies composed of a number of relatively closed traditional enclaves at various stages of integration.

Although an elite taken as a whole is a dynamic category rather than a group, it is likely to include those who occupy predominant positions of power and authority, but cannot exclusively be defined in terms of formal positions and roles or the institutions of which they are a part. It may have a more stable core of persons occupying such formal positions, though such occupants may themselves change, with a growing edge of persons in less-defined positions, who may either build new corporate groups to support them or break into those which already exist. In any case, an elite is not seen as a set of formal positions and their occupants but as a vaguely defined aggregate of people with certain similarities of behaviour, which provide a model for imitation by likely aspirants and for admiration or ambivalence among those at greater social distance who can at best imitate such models in compensatory ritual.

In any extensive empirical inquiry the study of who influences whom becomes so time consuming that inevitably recourse is had to other criteria, often theoretically unsatisfactory. It may be assumed that persons of a certain education or wealth, or in certain formal positions, are influential, or some sample of informants is questioned as to whom they regard as important, and the most popular responses are taken.

While the elite concept may refer to the dynamic aspect of leadership and influence in any kind of status system, it is of limited value in traditional or aristocratic societies where such processes are most nearly confined to formal and stable roles in a clear-cut corporate structure. It is therefore of little relevance in this respect to the more isolated African rural communities or to those states, such as Ethiopia, where traditional structure remains strongest and still successful in incorporating and internalizing change. The emergence of elites is not properly to be regarded as an aspect of westernization but of the changing emphasis towards achieved status and an open society. Even in largely traditional contexts the elite concept is useful in exploring the adaptation of traditional leaders and status groups to new contexts and techniques of influence.

In traditional contexts there may be a further relevance on the cultural dimension at which elite can be taken to refer to those who carry to the highest plane of excellence the central values of the culture. These may indeed be the most influential also, but clearly the perspective is different and the coincidence with channels of influence and networks of social relationships not necessarily so complete. This perspective is less applicable to societies of pluralistic and polyethnic composition and cultural tradition where indeed an integrated cultural focus may be lacking for some time. We should therefore expect cultural elites to be most discernible in states where there is a single dominant cultural tradition, such as Ethiopia or Burundi and perhaps Dahomey, Basutoland, Bechuanaland, and Swaziland. The same may be true of a number of federal or near-federal components, such as Yoruba, Ibo, and Hausa in Nigeria, or Buganda and other traditional Kingdoms in Uganda. Where there is a multiplicity of cultural traditions of tribal background in the state, there is less chance of maintenance at a recognizably elite level, since the present exponents are liable to fall outside the mainstream of the new national life. In these contexts it is rather the new social and intellectual elite who strive to fulfil a cultural function, in questing after new formulae of integration, in terms of the African personality, *négritude*, African socialism, Ujamaa, and the like (e.g. Senghor, 1964; Mphahlele, 1962; Burke, 1964).

CENTRAL AND SUBSIDIARY ELITES IN UGANDA

I shall endeavour to illustrate these various aspects of the elite concept from work done in East Africa. Today Uganda and the whole of East Africa is obviously in transition. The cliché that political but not economic independence has been won is a reasonable first approximation. There are only one or two expatriate permanent secretaries left. In April 1964 the expatriate Inspector General of Police in Uganda became chief police adviser for the last half year of his service, his executive position being taken by an Acholi. This is the common pattern everywhere. Earlier in the year the expatriate Chairman of the Uganda Development Corporation was joined by a Ugandan understudy previously an economics lecturer in Makerere University College, as Joint Chairman to take over later. Another Makerere lecturer—one of the most promising creative writers in East Africa—became the first Ugandan chairman of the Uganda Electricity Board, which is one of the country's largest and most important parastatal bodies. Any European left in an executive position feels rather exposed. When two of the three colleges in the University of East Africa had African principals the white principal of the third began to feel it was time to go. An expatriate archbishop began to think of withdrawing soon after quite irresponsible criticism was levelled at him by a youth movement. In both these cases the Africans in the institutions most concerned wanted to keep the persons involved. During 1964 the Chief Justice of Uganda and the President of the Court of Appeal for Eastern Africa were Nigerians, the Attorney General of Buganda was a Sinhalese, and there were more Asian and European than African magistrates. With this kind of exceptions, the main institutions of government, religion, and education were either firmly in the hands of the Africans of Uganda or were rapidly coming under their control. As elsewhere, and for similar reasons the University retains the highest proportion of expatriates, though from plans already made, the situation will be different in five years' time.

As expatriates vacate executive roles their place is taken by a new model army of expatriate advisers, so that the foreign element is little if at all reduced in numbers. Its members are far more unstable, rarely staying more than two years. Being thus uncommitted, they may often be more adaptable and less prejudiced than their predecessors. Despite their technical competence, they do not have time to get to know the country or the people very profoundly, and much of their social life remains as isolated as before.

Industry and commerce remain highly expatriate, despite many schemes of training and encouragement to African business and the taking on of prominent and wealthy Africans as directors, personnel managers, or public relations advisers. A significant part of the white commercial elite can be seen most evenings in the Kampala Club. Most middle-scale private business remains in Asian hands. Yet half the cotton-ginning industry has passed from many Asian and a few European firms to African co-operatives in the last ten years, and there are also many wealthy African coffee curers.

Many Europeans and Asians with large business interests and sometimes idle capital inevitably woo suitable Africans for what the Minister of Commerce and Industry himself recently referred to as window dressing. It is a happy combination of intelligent self-interest. Africans and expatriates can largely choose what scope to give their egocentric relationships with one another. But certainly there are many friendly, warm, and even intimate relationships of this kind, while both parties to the game know very well that quite different and apparently contradictory public sentiments will frequently have to be expressed in categorical or structural contexts.

In other words, Uganda is still a highly pluralistic society, and its complexities in this respect would take a very long time to describe except in a highly impressionistic way. The incumbents of key roles in certain major institutions do constitute an elite as in other societies. But although they are in no way segregated from one another, they are often deeply set apart in beliefs, values and upbringing, in the languages they are accustomed to speak, in family life and kinship obligations, and in informal social relationships. I do not mention differences in wealth and education here, because if they alone were crucial they could easily be overcome for the elite few. But the Africans must belong fully to the wider local social system which surrounds and entrammels them, whereas many expatriates have to some extent left such entanglements for the time being elsewhere.

The process whereby local institutions are woven together and integrated or manipulated into a foundation for the national elite is one of the most interesting features of the social situation in Africa. I shall give some brief illustrations from recent work in this field. Despite the racial or ethnic pluralism of the elite, with its consequent ambivalences of political and economic power, its parallelisms and ambiguities of prestige and social influence, the African members of it undeniably have considerable common ground underlying their political divisions. The former tribal areas remain to some extent as local bases for differences of interest as local and national concerns diverge somewhat in any state. But the central African elite, educated, English-speaking, urban for much of its time, is subjected to many other new pressures, and is therefore no longer chiefly dominated by those which are local and ethnic. But it is only by the central elite that the latter can be successfully transcended. The intercalary structure between local and central groups and interests is therefore important.

In the metropolitan city of Kampala the various groups of different tribal derivation do seem to react differently, and it would be interesting to discover how far the factors revealed here could be generalized elsewhere. Stated in fairly concrete form they seem to be:

1. The traditional structure of the tribe.
2. Its size.
3. Its distance from the town.
4. Its numbers in town.
5. The residential distribution of its members in the town.
6. The intensity and length of their urban residence.
7. Their socio-economic structure in the town.
8. Their orientation of interest as between various types of occupation.
9. Their adult sex ratio.

Greater Kampala may be divided into three distinctive social zones. The first is central Kampala, containing the main shopping, business, and government premises and the official and private residences, formerly occupied almost exclusively by Europeans and Asians, with their African domestic servants in quarters behind; but now also by African ministers of the central government, senior civil servants, business executives, and some professionals. This is the area of the top elite.

The second zone is Mengo Municipality, administered quite separately from the City of Kampala and still the capital and headquarters of Buganda Kingdom and Ganda culture and aspirations. People of all races live there, but Africans are an overwhelming majority. Living there implies tolerance or at least acquiescense towards Ganda institutions, if not active desire to be assimilated into and promote them (Southall, 1956).

The third zone is East Kampala, administered by the City Council and a predominantly African area in which both official housing estates and small-scale private building have developed since the Second World War. Like the whole city of Kampala, it is a kind of extra-territorial enclave in Buganda, no longer because mainly occupied by foreigners from Europe and Asia, but because its African population has no commitment to Buganda, and is largely beyond its control, having allegiance rather to the State of Uganda, or even Kenya, from which many immigrants come. It is consequently in this zone particularly that the accommodation between local and national interests, leadership and elites can be observed.[1]

The largest and most impressively organized tribal groups are the Luo and Luyia. Both of these come from Kenya, but this is not the relevant factor. Both are traditionally organized at home in localized, polysegmentary lineages. Their urban organization is at three main levels: that of some major lineage segment, often popularly referred to as clan, that of the sub-tribe (called tribe by Evans-Pritchard, 1959), and that of the tribe. The lineage associations are the most numerous, the smallest, the most ephemeral, the most intimate and important at the personal or egocentric level. They are formed by persons of relatively low

---

[1] For much of this material I am indebted to Dr. D. J. Parkin, whose detailed and intensive research in this area will carry our knowledge of such situations a definite step forward.

education, wealth, and skill to meet immediate problems of personal welfare and security.

Persons of somewhat higher general status organize the sub-tribal associations. They put correspondingly less emphasis on meeting immediate personal problems and more on recreation and general uplift. Indeed, their major activity has been running soccer matches and championships. Most of these leaders have somewhat more economic independence than the leaders of lineage associations, but some of the latter have managed to play a leadership role in both lineage and sub-tribe associations by devoting a great deal of time and energy to each. One is reminded a little of the soccer and rugger clubs which have a 'home-boy' basis in Langa (Wilson and Mafeje, 1963).

The unions which supposedly represent the whole Luo and Luyia peoples in Kampala are run by more important people. They are concerned with community rather than individual welfare activities: establishing and administering schools and nurseries, organizing concerts and dances, making financial collections for either tribal or national causes. Sometimes the social distance between these leaders and the bulk of the tribes' urban population is so great as to bring about an estrangement between the two.

These pyramidally organized associations undoubtedly reflect the traditional segmentary structure of the Luo and Luyia in a selective yet genetic sense. In the case of the Luyia the sub-tribes were each of them traditionally autonomous tribal polities. Their new sense of overall unity and tribal identification was a product of attempts at integration by the early British colonial administration and of their own new aspirations and realizations of the modern utility of larger scale and numerical strength which developed during the inter-war period.

The ramifications of leadership and functional differentiation at the three levels of these modern, urban, ethnic associations are delicate. The Luo Union tried and failed to monopolize all the subsidiary Luo sub-tribal and lineage associations as integrated branches of itself. The functional differentiation is clear, though there is some overlap. The clientele at all three levels is potentially the same. Effective participation is most frequent at the lowest and least at the highest level. Many of those who attend the occasional mass meetings of the Luo Union are potential members both of the sub-tribal and lineage associations. Members of lineage associations would concede some legitimacy to the leaders of the Luo Union as spokesmen of all the Luo in town, but they would not concede their right to restrict the operations of lineage associations. We cannot deal here with the other dimension of relations between large tribal associations such as these with their home areas and with Luo and Luyia organizations in Nairobi, Mombasa, and other East African towns.

Looked at in the wider perspective of informal civic organization and leadership three somewhat different levels may be perceived, and have been described by Parkin as civic/political, tribal, and locality. Such roles as city councillor or political party branch officer belong to the first. All levels of tribally based organization belong to the second, and tenants' associations, debating societies, Y.M.C.A. local branches, and political party sub-branches belong to the third. Everyone has his ascriptive ethnic or tribal status already as a basis for participation in urban ethnic relationships, whereas the locality and civic-political levels are new and non-traditional dimensions of achievement-oriented activity. It seems that from the point of view both of institution building and of individual careers the resources of the former often, if not usually, provide the foundations for the latter, however much those are formally defined as transcending ethnic considerations.

Some energetic persons can achieve leadership in both lineage and sub-tribal associations, but hardly in the tribal union as well. Just as tribal union leaders are in some danger of estrangement from the bulk of their fellow tribesmen, so they have the possibility of using their tribal leadership role as a spring board for the achievement of civic or political leadership. One who succeeds here will almost inevitably lose some of his close personal touch with ordinary tribal association members and will attract criticism accordingly. As long as he forges ahead he can discount this somewhat, but since most of these leadership roles depend on the popular vote, it is most important to avoid a reputation for pride, which is very damaging and about which people are highly sensitive.

A number of other segmentary societies are represented in Kampala by fewer numbers than the Luo or Luyia and have only two levels of organization, that of the whole tribe and of the lineage, sub-tribe, or small locality. Among the Uganda Lango local lineages are branches of a few very large and very widely dispersed clans, most of which are common to them, the Teso and several other Nilo-Hamitic-speaking peoples. Accordingly, the Lango only have two levels of organization in Kampala. The Acholi, northern neighbours of the Lango, are also segmentary, but their local lineage segments were clustered round a number of hereditary lines of chiefs, whose traditional political powers were embryonic, though their ritual sanctions were great. The sub-branches of the Acholi Association in Kampala seem to represent these lineage clusters in Acholi chiefdoms, or domains, as Girling (1960) calls them. Although the Acholi are actually somewhat more numerous in the housing estates of East Kampala than the Luyia, the latter were doubtless already accustomed to three-tiered associations in Nairobi, where their numbers are much larger and a similar associational structure exists.

The Banyankole–Banyakigezi Association is an interesting case about which unfortunately less is known. The exact nature of the descent group structure of the Kiga of Kigezi remains somewhat uncertain, although it seems to be based on localized poly-segmentary lineages. Thus far we should expect them to be prone to urban association formation. However, their Banyankole neighbours clearly belong to a stratified and centralized society. But the Banyankole in this association almost certainly belong to the traditionally subordinate caste of Iru, not to the superior Hima. The Iru of Ankole have a great deal in common with the Kiga, so that on the common boundary between Ankole and Kigezi there is no real hard-and-fast line between them. The same is true of the Hutu of Ndorwa in Rwanda, who are similar to the Kiga of Ndorwa in Kigezi. This evidently intermediate type of association of the Banyankole–Banyakigezi has no sub-branches at all. A further factor is that the vast majority of Kiga and Ankole working in and around Kampala belong to the lowest socio-economic strata and form one of the most fluctuating and unstable elements in the urban population. Many of them live very frugally in grass huts on the urban fringes, saving money to meet their target and return home. Such people are not good material for association formation.

Peoples like the Nyoro, Toro, and Soga, all coming from centralized social systems which had hereditary chiefs or kings, have never formed successful urban associations, although they are present in large numbers. The hypothesis, which cannot be taken as proved, but is certainly worth further testing, is that ordinary folk who are accustomed to centralized political systems, such as those of the Interlacustrine Kingdoms, tend to take the major organizational framework of society for granted and are not likely to create it for themselves. This is particularly true of the unsophisticated, especially when they are within not too great a distance from their own homes. The more sophisticated or high status persons, having presumably enjoyed a better education, are more likely to transcend tribal interests in town. On the other hand, those who are at a very great distance from home have a special need of mutual support. Thus, the Banyarwanda, though for the most part from a traditionally centralized society, need a mutual aid association in Kampala where they are effectively five or six hundred miles from home, with bad communications and in a foreign state; but their association does not take on a seg-mentary form like those of the Luo, Luyia, Acholi, or Lango. Likewise the Nyasa, who come from an even greater distance, have an association in Kampala for persons from Nyasaland (now Malawi) irrespective of their particular tribe.

The Ganda themselves are in line with the hypothesis, being centralized and without any association, but of course very special considerations apply to them as the locally dominant people.

The Teso also have no urban association. There seem to be a number of reasons for this. They are comparatively few in the East Kampala housing estates, whose conditions seem to en-courage associations. Being fairly prosperous cotton farmers at home, they usually only come to town for relatively attractive and stable jobs, which do not expose them to the kind of need which fosters the Luo lineage associations. Furthermore, although the Teso were traditionally uncentralized, they had an age organization (which always fosters unitary identification, even where specialized political institutions are lacking) until it was smashed by the early Ganda administrators at the beginning of this century. Since then they have lived in extended families, relying more and more on modern local government for the wider framework of order. The better-off Teso in Kampala disapproved of a proposal to form a Teso Association, on the ground that it would represent support for tribalism. Doubtless many high-status Luo and Luyia, or members of other tribes with viable associations, would take the same line if these associations were not in any case indispensable to the less sophisticated, or already well established before tribalism attracted such opprobrium, thus constituting important sources of power and influence which would-be leaders cannot afford to ignore. In fact, the Luo leaders addressed themselves very consciously to this issue, endeavouring to define their association in non-ethnic terms by making the qualification for membership not to be a Luo by birth but to have the welfare of the Luo people at heart. On a similar basis the writer was himself a paid-up member of the Alur tribal association in Kampala.

Segmentary societies, supposedly prone to segmentary associations, do not form them if their numbers are unwarrantably small. Thus, the Alur and Jonam have unitary associations in Kampala. The Lugbara provide an interesting variant (Middleton, 1956). They are about as distant from Kampala as their neighbours the Alur, but are much more numerous in town. They have an association and it does proliferate in branches, but not on the segmentary lineage model so far discussed. Their East Kampala branch includes members from all over Lugbaraland and evidently so does their branch on the big sugar estates between Kampala and Jinja. A *post hoc* interpretation might be that in fact Lugbara traditional lineages are so small and shallow that they would not be likely to provide a suitable basis for associational recruitment in town. These small lineages were knit together into communities by a variety of ancient consanguineal and affinal ties which probably lack the persistent strength and consistency of agnatically articulated patrilineages. Most Kampala Lugbara are of rather slight education and skill, but the members of the association tend to be long-term residents, coming from pockets of Lugbaraland which are so overcrowded that they have no land rights and no incentive to go back. It may therefore be surmised that, having thus become almost permanent Kampala residents, the minutiae of a traditional structure from which they are to a considerable extent cut off retains little importance for them as a basis for urban organization. But the Lugbara are rather isolated and thrown back upon their own resources by the strangeness of their language and culture to all other Uganda peoples (except relatively small groups like the Madi and Lendu, who have few representatives in Kampala). The establishment of local urban branches for all Lugbara irrespective of their place in traditional structure seems quite a logical outcome of these various factors. Many Lugbara who do not belong to the association are even less skilled and tend to be short-term target workers with little urban commitment and still depend on their land and status in Lugbara country. They endeavour to group themselves in Kampala, both residentially and occupationally according to affiliations of kin, clan, wider locality, and county, so that they need no more formal associations for purposes of urban security.

There is a significant clustering of roles round the persons of multiple-role players in these associations. Thus, one man is chairman of his local tenants' association and of his tribal association; another is vice-chairman of the tenants' association, chairman of the political party sub-branch, and an active member of the debating society; a third is secretary of the tenants' association, of the debating society, and assistant secretary of the Y.M.C.A. branch, in addition to being chairman of his tribal association; another is chairman of the Y.M.C.A. branch and assistant secretary both of the debating society and of the tenants' association; another is chairman of the debating society and treasurer both of the Y.M.C.A. branch and of the tenants' association, as well as being secretary of a sub-tribe association, treasurer of a trade

A A

union, and an official in the branch of a Kenya political party; another is vice-chairman of the debating society and secretary both of his tribal association and of a political party sub-branch.

It can be seen that there is here something of a local Establishment, in which roles and persons are interlocked just as closely as they are in merchant banks in the City or in any close-knit committee network. But how far is this due to leaders attracting leadership roles and to the necessity of multiple role playing for leadership dominance or to their deliberate multiplication of such roles? In the South African Housing Estate of Langa, Monica Wilson suggests that Africans are starved of leadership and office, so that rivalries are fostered, associations split, and offices proliferate, providing the wider opportunities for leadership and the prestige of office holding which are sought. It is not clear how far this would be true in other parts of Africa, but certainly in the Kampala tribal associations regular participation often extends little beyond the numbers of actual office holders. This is probably not because these associations are just mutual admiration cliques of leaders in a vacuum. It is that the leaders are both keen on leadership and feel a greater need for the services of the association. The rank and file concede this need, but are only occasionally moved by it sufficiently to participate. Leadership therefore goes to the keenest by default and may appear somewhat hollow much of the time, but it is none the less leadership and enables certain individuals to gain in status and authority.

The most transient workers offer little scope for organization, nor can they themselves aim at leadership in the urban context. The humblest levels of leadership are those of lineage or clan and small tribal associations, which are axiomatically local and ethnic in their horizons. Above this level those who are usually of somewhat better education, longer urban residence, and higher income, as well as possibly possessing personal qualities of leadership, are able to combine ethnic with civic or political leadership to their own advantage. Beyond a certain point they must divest themselves of formal ethnic leadership roles, in order to move higher in civic or political circles, although they can hardly cut off their ethnic roots or dispense with diffuse ethnic support.

Unfortunately systematic data on multiple-role playing in the central elite have not been collected, although the point seems obvious alike from personal experience, observation, conversation, or reading of newspapers. Not only is playing of the right roles in multiple combinations a major mechanism in the achievement of personal power but it is also the means by which the fabric of society is knit together.

The President of Uganda, being Head of State and at the same time Kabaka of Buganda, not only symbolically and expressively but instrumentally transcends in his own person the most dangerous and difficult cleavage in the Uganda State. Similarly, the Prime Minister, coming from Lango, a nilotic people in north Uganda, married a Southern Ganda girl of good family. A Muganda remarked in jubilation 'now we have both the President and the Prime Minister's father-in-law', but in fact interests and powers are very delicately balanced. Those who occupy the foremost roles to which most prestige or power is attached by definition need least buttressing from multiple-role play, but it is those who occupy minor roles and wish to climb who are forced to use this mechanism.

The East African countries are still at a fairly early stage in the transcending of small and separate social systems into national societies. There is continuing doubt as to the level of political and social integration which will be achieved. The social elite as a whole is bound to reflect this situation in its overlapping and segmentary character. Some forces tend towards an integrated East African society, which already has partial institutional expression in the East African Common Services Organization, with its own civil service, its economic agencies, and research services. The University of East Africa gives prestigeful but somewhat precarious expression to the same idea. The East African Academy is one of the most recent and potentially influential upsurges of spontaneous integration by East African intellectuals. But these are very rarefied levels, and the few hundreds of elite persons who move in them are either *déracinés* or must be subject also to many much more local and sectional pressures. Kenya, Tanzania, and Uganda are legally independent.

sovereign states, and each already possesses a far richer national institutional structure than exists between them. While elite behaviour includes much unstructured and dynamic activity which runs far outside the institutional strait-jacket, most elite persons, on the definition implied in this analysis, inevitably do occupy positions in the institutional structure. The dearth of trained man-power ensures that there are very few free-lancers in any elite field, except in their spare time, which for allied reasons is usually very limited for this purpose. Writers, artists, and musicians of elite identification are particularly few, and those with these proclivities almost invariably have to perform primarily as ambassadors, businessmen, bureaucrats, or directors of cultural agencies. Uncertainties in the sphere of social integration and lack of commonly understood and accepted modes of cultural expression are oddly combined with a certain inability to experiment freely resulting from ubiquitous involvement in formal institutional structures. Experiment in the latter there certainly is, but this suggests that, while there is a constant interplay of norm and action, the main determinants may at present arise essentially from the context of social relationships and their evolving structures, rather than from the impact of new ideas upon them. The exception is probably the great idea of Independence which brought these new societies into being. To suggest that the present phase is pragmatist rather than normatist is to re-emphasize the point that elite behaviour is more feasibly studied in its social than its cultural aspect as far as these ethnically composite and pluralist nations are concerned. Greater consensus on cultural values undoubtedly still exists in the sub-cultures of the small traditional units which have now been amalgamated, although these traditional values are becoming more and more inapplicable in all but the most remote and backward areas. Nonetheless, the continued existence of local sub-elites must be recognized, and the major problem of the central elite is that they also belong to these for many purposes and on frequent occasions. The paramount function of the central elite is to mediate between the conflicts and incompatibilities of the local elites, to pass beyond the fringe of present institutional arrangements in devising variations of structure appropriate to changing conditions and eventually providing them with the greater stability, richness, and legitimacy of more integrated cultural norms and values.

BIBLIOGRAPHY

Burke, Fred G.
    (1964) 'Ujamaa', in Friedland, W. H. and Rosberg, C. G. (eds.) *African Social-ism*, Stanford.
Evans-Pritchard, E. E.
    (1949) 'Luo tribes and clans', *Human Problems in British Central Africa*, 9.
Girling, F. K.
    (1960) *The Acholi of Uganda*, London.
Merton, R. K.
    (1957) *Social Theory and Social Structure*, Glencoe.
Middleton, John
    (1965) *The Lugbara of Uganda*, New York.
Mills, C. Wright
    (1957) *The Power Elite*, New York.
Mphahlele, Ezekiel
    (1962) *The African Image*, New York.
Nadel, S. F.
    (1956) 'The concept of social elites', *International Social Science Bulletin*, vol. 8.
Sampson, Anthony
    (1962) *Anatomy of Britain*, London.
Senghor, Léopold Sedar
    (1964) *On African Socialism* (trans. M. Cook), New York.
Southall, A. W.
    (1956) 'Determinants of the social structure of African urban populations', in Forde, D. (ed.), *Social Implications of Industrialisation and Urbanisation in Africa South of the Sahara*, London.
    (1959) 'An operational theory of role', *Human Relations*, 12.
Wilson, M. and Mafeje, A.
    (1963) *Langa: a Study of Social Groups in an African Township*, Cape Town.

Résumé

LE CONCEPT DES ÉLITES ET LEUR FORMATION EN OUGANDA

Les élites consistent en ces personnes qui exercent une influence sur les autres, appellent l'imitation et donnent leur expression aux degrés d'excellence reconnus dans une culture. Certains auteurs soulignent qu'il existe un élément de contrôle d'entrée dans l'élite. S'il en est ainsi, l'élite tend à s'institutionaliser et à devenir difficile à distinguer de la classe établie, ou haute société, ou des titulaires d'un amalgame de rôles influents et conjugués. La différence principale peut résider dans le fait que l'élite se réfère d'une manière plus appropriée aux aspects changeants et dynamiques des situations influentes, spécialement dans le système de classe ouverte d'une société subissant des modifications assez rapides. Elle se réfère spécialement aux zones d'influence croissantes et à ces aspects qui tranchent et s'étendent au delà de l'organisation formelle des rôles dans les institutions. On peut concevoir l'élite comme s'efforçant constamment à accéder à un rang établi, pourtant continuellement transformée par les changements contextuels et personnels des nouveaux venus, tandis que d'autres échouent, les buts et valeurs changeant également. Non seulement est-il utile, aux fins d'investigation, de se rapporter à l'élite du pouvoir, l'élite intellectuelle, esthétique, commerciale, militaire ou professionnelle, mais aussi aux élites minoritaires, élites subordonnées et élites locales.

Il est particulièrement caractéristique des nouvelles nations telles que l'Ouganda, qui consistent en un amalgame moderne d'un grand nombre de petites unités traditionnelles, que la structure de l'élite reflète ce fonds acquis hétéroclite. La nouvelle élite supérieure africaine jouit du contrôle politique, mais l'ancienne élite des expatriés coloniaux a été remplacée par un nombre encore plus grand d'experts, conseillers et techniciens internationaux, en plus de l'accroissement d'une élite diplomatique, nouvelle et influente. Entretemps, les expatriés continuent à dominer l'élite économique, malgré des efforts délibérés pour recruter et promouvoir les africains dans ce domaine.

Il est possible de concevoir un réseau complet de communication et de transfert depuis les différents niveaux d'une élite locale et subordonnée jusqu'à celui de l'élite supérieure centrale. A Kampala-Mengo, la capitale de l'Ouganda, il existe une distinction spatiale et écologique, aussi bien structurelle, entre l'élite supérieure générale, l'élite Ganda de Mengo, et l'élite ethnique de la classe moyenne vivant dans les lotissements. Cette dernière illustre l'un des mécanismes importants par lequel les groupes ethniques locaux et les populations de rang modeste sont liés en une élite supérieure poly-ethnique.

Les associations ethniques se forment à plusieurs niveaux différents sur la base du loyalisme dérivant d'anciens groupements tribals appliqué aux besoins nouveaux. Au niveau le plus bas, les membres d'une même tribu dans une ville forment des mutualités afin de s'aider en cas de maladie, décès et difficultés générales. Ceux jouissant d'un revenu et d'une instruction meilleurs, créent des associations plus récréatives dont ils peuvent considérer les groupes plus humbles comme des filiales, bien qu'en pratique ces derniers soient largement autonomes. A un niveau économique et un rang plus élevés les associations sont formées qui revendiquent la représentation des intérêts particuliers d'un groupe tribal complet. La forme prise par ces organisations et la manière dont elles sont liées entre elles dépendent de l'importance et de la structure traditionnelle de la tribu, son nombre de ressortissants dans la ville, leur répartition démographique, la durée et l'intensité de leur résidence urbaine, la proportion d'hommes et femmes, l'intérêt de leurs occupations et orientation professionnelle et le statut socio-économique urbain. De l'échelon le plus élevé dans la conduite des affaires tribales ou locales, ceux ayant le mieux réussi peuvent s'élever aux échelons les plus bas dans la conduite politique et civique de l'élite centrale poly-ethnique. Il existe une ambivalence inévitable envers les différences ethniques tradition-nelles, puisqu'elles doivent être dépassées pour édifier la nation, pourtant on a recours à elles pour leur appui électoral et com-mercial, tandis qu'elles demeurent la source et le point de mire d'un loyalisme puissant.

L'élite africaine poly-ethnique est à son tour entraînée dans des rapports ambivalents avec les différentes élites d'expatriés dont elle dépend économiquement et technologiquement de plusieurs manières, tandis qu'il existe l'ambiguité supplémentaire sur la mise au point de l'élite, même aux échelons supérieurs, envers l'état d'Ouganda d'une part, et la conception plus largement fédérale de l'Afrique de l'Est d'autre part. Un grand nombre d'institutions dans lesquelles l'élite est occupée expriment égale-ment ce dilemme. Avec de telles diversités et incertitudes, l'élite supérieure est peu intégrée culturellement, malgré les liens étroits que créent des intérêts communs. Il existe un équilibre précaire dépendant du chevauchement des rôles multiples et divergents par les titulaires de postes clés pour combler les fissures latentes. La recherche de nouveaux moyens d'exprimer l'intégration culturelle et en former un lien véritable pour les élites subordonnées, locales ethniques et sectionnelles doit être l'une des tâches majeures de l'élite supérieure.

XVIII. ÉLITES ET FORCES POLITIQUES

P. MERCIER

Le concept d'"élite' est depuis nombre d'années d'emploi très courant dans la littérature africaniste consacrée aux changements sociaux.[1] Il convient cependant de préciser—de façon très sommaire—la signification qui lui sera attribuée ici, et par rapport à quelles préoccupations essentielles elle le sera: il n'est pas assuré que tous les auteurs qui l'ont utilisé[2] trouveraient à s'accorder sur une définition unique de ce concept—la théorie sociologique n'en offre d'ailleurs point qui soit unanimement admise:[3] il en est ainsi, en fin de compte, de la plupart des concepts qui mettent en cause une définition de la société globale et de ses dynamismes d'ensemble.

Les difficultés rencontrées à ce niveau ne peuvent, bien entendu, être détachées de la série des problèmes que pose l'étude des faits de stratification sociale—dans le sens le plus large que peut revêtir ce terme:[4] problèmes généraux, et problèmes spécifiques des sociétés africaines en période coloniale et en période de décolonisation.[5] Les recherches relatives à la stratification sociale dans ces sociétés particulières ont été tardivement entreprises: elles ont été, en définitive, relativement peu nombreuses (Mitchell, 1963): et l'on a, à plusieurs reprises, souligné que l'analyse et l'interprétation de ce phénomène étaient demeurées hésitantes et déficientes (Mercier, 1954). Le retard s'explique assez aisément: les faits de cet ordre ne se sont imposés fortement à l'attention des chercheurs qu'en une certaine phase de l'évolution des sociétés colonisées, celle où la contestation de la domination coloniale commençait à prendre des formes moins dispersées, plus actives

[1] Voir entre autres U.N.E.S.C.O. (1956).
[2] Les auteurs de textes scientifiques n'ayant pas dans tous les cas, il faut bien le reconnaître, donné plus d'importance à l'effort de définition du concept que les auteurs de textes de vulgarisation ou à caractère journalistique.
[3] On sait les problèmes que soulève par exemple la théorie de Pareto.
[4] C'est-à-dire incluant celle du phénomène des classes sociales. Cf., pour une utilisation dans un sens plus restreint, Gurvitch (1964).
[5] En comprenant dans celle-ci les toutes premières années de l'indépendance.

et plus organisées, et ainsi mettait en vedette telles 'catégories sociales' ou tels groupements que les processus de différenciation déclenchés par la colonisation avaient contribué à dégager, et pour un temps au moins à séparer, de l'ensemble de la population.[6] Quant aux déficiences présentées par nombre de ces recherches, les causes principales en ont été plusieurs fois recensées, et il ne convient pas d'y revenir ici (Mercier, 1954). Elles reflétaient d'une part les imprécisions, et les gaucheries, que ne pouvaient éviter des ethnologues travaillant dans un domaine de recherches nouveau, sans qu'aient été suffisamment converties leurs perspectives, sans qu'aient été suffisamment éprouvés les instruments conceptuels qu'ils devaient employer (Beals, 1951); d'autre part la complexité propre à leur objet d'étude: multiplicité des cadres de référence, ambiguïté des statuts et des prestiges, alternances dans les comportements.[7] D'une façon générale, les progrès de la réflexion dans ce domaine ont consisté à examiner les possibilités d'application du concept de 'classe sociale' et à en récuser l'emploi, à cause de ses connotations trop précises[8] En remarquant, pour l'essentiel: d'une part, que la persistance de groupements et de réseaux de relations traditionnels[9] et (au cours de la période coloniale) la commune opposition des colonisés aux colonisateurs, capable en toute situation de crise plus intense de s'actualiser constituaient un frein déterminant à la formation de classes sociales proprement dites (Mercier, 1954; Balandier, 1955); d'autre part, que, si l'on pouvait dire de certaines couches sociales qu'elles préfiguraient des classes ou qu'elles pouvaient être envisagées comme des classes sociales en germe, l'on ne pouvait définir l'ensemble de la société par rapport à un système de classes.[10]

[6] Le problème, essentiel, du conditionnement historique de la recherche en sciences humaines ne peut évidemment être soulevé ici.
[7] Les notions d'ambiguïté et d'alternance ont été remarquablement mises en évidence par Balandier, en particulier dans ses travaux de sociologie urbaine (1955).
[8] Au moins pour ceux, et c'était le cas des chercheurs français, qui refusaient ce que Gurvitch (1964) appelle une conception 'nominaliste et individualiste' des classes sociales ou ce que Gross (1949) appelle un emploi 'qualitatif' (par opposition à un emploi 'substantif') de ce même terme.
[9] Essentiellement de ceux basés sur la parenté et l'ethnie.
[10] Les faits d'hétérogénéité ethnique, de dualité de l'économie, etc., intervenant à ce niveau.

Fallait-il pour autant se replier sur des études de stratification sociale en un sens plus restreint de ce terme, c'est-à-dire sur un effort de catégorisation basé soit sur des caractéristiques objectives —relatives à la situation économique, à la situation professionnelle, au mode de vie, aux choix culturels et aux comportements valorisés —soit sur des caractéristiques d'opinion—concernant pour l'essentiel une évaluation hiérarchisée des prestiges? Certes, on peut ainsi établir une trame de très grande utilité pour une appréciation précise, éventuellement quantifiée, des phénomènes de différenciation qui résultent de l'action combinée des facteurs économiques, culturels, politico-administratifs, etc. Elle apporte, entre autres avantages, la possibilité d'étudier de façon systématique les faits de mobilité sociale.[11] Elle n'en présente pas moins, cependant, une image relativement statique de la société (Mercier, 1954); un tel ensemble de données, aussi riche et détaillé qu'il soit, ne constitue pas, pour l'interprétation des changements affectant la société globale, un instrument suffisant: faute de permettre une appréhension des discontinuités concrètes à l'intérieur de celle-ci,[12] des antagonismes éventuels entre fractions de la population, des tensions multiples caractéristiques de toute société en voie de transformation rapide (Mercier, 1954); faute également de rendre possible une saisie des ambiguïtés que révèlent nombre de statuts et de situations individuels.[13] Un tel effort de classification ne prend toute sa valeur que dans la mesure ou il se fait l'auxiliaire —très efficace (Mercier, 1954)—d'un autre effort, plus important: celui du repérage, par l'observation directe, par l'analyse de séquences d'événements et de situations précises, de groupes plus ou moins permanents, plus ou moins organisés, dont l'existence résulte—de façon directe ou indirecte[14]—de l'ensemble des transformations imposées par la période coloniale, et qui sont capables

[11] C'est, on le sait, l'un des buts essentiels poursuivis par les études se limitant à cet effort de 'catégorisation', et dont les plus typiques sont celles entreprises par des sociologues américains. Cf. entre autres le livre classique de Warner et Lunt (1941).
[12] Problème familier aux ethnologues que cette difficulté de repérer, malgré l'accumulation de données objectives certaines limites entre groupes pourtant clairement ressenties comme telles par les intéressés. Par exemple à propos des groupes ethniques.
[13] Grâce à la coexistence de plusieurs cadres de référence socio-culturels.
[14] Cf. *infra*.

—à des degrés divers—d'influer de façon active[15] sur le devenir de la société. L'analyse des dynamismes fondamentaux que manifeste celle-ci ne peut être abordée si une attention particulière n'est accordée à de tels groupes; la détermination de 'strates' ou de 'catégories' ne peut suffire, quoiqu'elle puisse aider à leur définition.

C'est dans ce sens de groupes ou quasi-groupes porteurs de dynamismes particuliers, susceptibles soit directement soit par le truchement de groupes à fonctions spécialisées (partis politiques, syndicats, associations diverses) qui les expriment en totalité ou en partie, d'infléchir soit de leur propre initiative soit en réponse à l'initiative d'autres groupes l'orientation de l'ensemble de la société, qu'est employé ici le terme d'élites. Elles ont leurs caractéristiques sociales, culturelles, professionnelles, économiques, etc.; elles ont leurs intérêts et leurs aspirations spécifiques, elles sont héritières ou créatrices d'idéologies qui leur sont propres—aspirations et idéologies étant selon les cas plus ou moins clairement exprimées; elles sont à des degrés divers conscientes de leur existence en tant que groupes. Par définition, elles ne constituent pas un système complet, par rapport auquel l'ensemble de la population pourrait être classé, comme il en serait de classes sociales. Elles ne peuvent toujours être situées de façon hiérarchique les unes par rapport aux autres: les enquêtes concernant les prestiges liés aux statuts, aux professions, etc., ne sont pas de ce point de vue entièrement satisfaisantes.[16] Elles se manifestent au niveau des unités à grande échelle de création moderne—territoires, groupes de territoires, puis Etats; constituées, pour l'essentiel,[17] en fonction des transformations apportées par l'histoire récente, elles ne persistent en tant que telles qu'au prix d'une relative imperméabilité aux différenciations et aux clivages traditionnels—par exemple ethniques: l'éventuelle

[15] Ce qui n'exclut pas qu'une telle action puisse revêtir un caractère conservateur.

[16] Comme l'ont fait ressortir, au Sénégal, les comparaisons entre des enquêtes d'opinion, mettant en relief, aussi bien en ville que dans les campagnes, la valorisation des prestiges liés à l'élite de l'instruction, et des comportements révélant l'influence dominante de l'élite religieuse.

[17] Cf. *infra* les remarques à propos des 'élites à base traditionnelle'.

résurgence de ceux-ci peut les remettre en cause en tant que groupements.[18] Les relations entre les élites et la masse de la population sont complexes, et, pour certaines d'entre elles, ambiguës: alternance de phases où elles tendent à n'exprimer que leurs propres intérêts et de phases où elles peuvent l'influencer, la mobiliser en fonction d'objectifs plus généraux.[19] Quant aux relations entre les diverses élites, l'histoire récente les montre fluctuantes; alliances, conflits, compromis, s'y manifestent et y alternent. L'emploi de termes évocateurs de réalités politiques indique déjà à quel niveau il nous semble qu'une part importante de la signification des élites peut être dégagée.

La diversité des élites actuelles ne peut être évoquée ici que par un sec inventaire et de brèves définitions. Celle qui a été l'objet de la plus constante attention est l'*élite de l'instruction* (élite lettrée, élite éduquée, etc.).[20] Elle apparaît comme l'élite par excellence.[21] Elle est caractérisée par une formation intellectuelle de type européen, de niveau modeste jusqu'à la seconde guerre mondiale, plus diversifiée ensuite (Mercier, 1956). Dans une première phase, elle valorise son occidentalisation et prend ses distances par rapport aux cultures africaines, avant de s'efforcer de les ressaisir et de s'y réintégrer (Mercier, 1956). Sa structure professionnelle est d'abord très simple: elle fournit les cadres subalternes des services administratifs—ce sont là les positions les plus recherchées—des compagnies commerciales et des entreprises. Les cadres moyens, les professions libérales, n'apparaîtront que tardivement, sauf en des situations particulières.[22] Économiquement, elle se manifeste comme le groupe qui détient les revenus les plus stables, et une part importante des revenus les plus

[18] La solution pouvant être trouvée dans de multiples compromis, comme le révèle par exemple l'organisation de partis politiques, en principe anti-tribaux et anti-régionalistes; l'exemple de la Côte-d'Ivoire étant de ce point de vue significatif.
[19] Cf. *infra.*
[20] Les indications qui suivent seront exclusivement empruntées aux pays africains d'expression française.
[21] De par sa fonction d'intermédiaire d'abord entre colonisateurs et colonisés, de porte-parole de ceux-ci ensuite, enfin d'héritière du pouvoir et de gestionnaire des nouveaux Etats.
[22] Par exemple celle des 'Quatre communes' du Sénégal, et encore sera-ce un développement modeste avant la deuxième guerre mondiale.

élevés.[23] Définissable d'abord exclusivement comme auxiliaire de la colonisation, elle glissera de la revendication de l'égalité (Mercier, 1956) à celle de l'indépendance, et fournira, après les cadres des partis nationalistes,[24] la couche dirigeante des nouveaux Etats. Des clivages entre-temps l'avaient, de façon parfois confuse, divisée, sur lesquels il conviendra de revenir.[25] L'*élite ouvrière* a moins retenu l'attention. Il est vrai qu'elle est demeurée au cours de la période coloniale, sauf quelques exceptions locales, peu nombreuse; il est vrai aussi que les ouvriers, dans la mesure où ils disposaient d'un minimum d'instruction, tendaient à changer d'emploi et à s'intégrer dans l'élite précédente. Constituant des noyaux relativement stables au sein d'une masse salariée mouvante, les ouvriers ont entrepris très tôt des actions organisées de revendication,[26] avant même de pouvoir former des syndicats proprement dits, où ils se rencontreront avec une part de l'élite de l'instruction.[27] L'*élite de la réussite économique* présente une grande diversité de facies; elle est constituée de planteurs, de commerçants, de transporteurs, d'entrepreneurs, dont le caractère essentiel est de 'rassembler la majeure partie des revenus supérieurs et la totalité des revenus les plus importants (Balandier, 1955). Elle varie considérablement d'un pays à l'autre par sa composition—importance relative des divers types d'activité dominante rurale ou urbaine—par ses perspectives—'traditionalistes' ou 'modernistes'—par la nature des relations qu'elle entretient avec l'élite de l'instruction.[28] Elle est inégalement apte—en fonction surtout de son degré d'homogénéite—à se donner une organisation ou à entreprendre des actions communes. L'*élite à base traditionnelle* pose des problèmes de définition plus délicats; la colonisation a maintenu,[29] en les intégrant dans le système administratif qu'elle

[23] Alignés en partie, après 1946, sur ceux des fonctionnaires français, les traitements des fonctionnaires africains poseront aux gouvernements des pays indépendants de difficiles problèmes, diversement et inégalement résolus.
[24] En un sens large de ce terme. Mercier (1961).   [25] Cf. *infra*.
[26] Par exemple celle des cheminots dès l'entre-deux-guerres. De telles actions, dans le contexte colonial, tendaient à prendre une coloration de contestation politique.   [27] Qui fournit l'essentiel des éléments dirigeants. Cf. Mercier (1961).
[28] La rencontre entre les deux groupes favorisant l'émergence de mouvements politiques nationalistes ou pré-nationalistes. Les cas de la Côte-d'Ivoire est typique à cet égard.
[29] Tout en ne le justifiant pas en doctrine, dans le cas de la colonisation française.

mettait en place, certaines autorités politiques traditionelles: ou
bien elle a, indirectement, favorisé l'émergence d'autres autorités
qui trouvaient aussi leur fondement dans la tradition.[30] Mais la
catégorie sociale ainsi composée ne constitue pas nécessairement
une élite au sens qui a été ici retenu. Elle ne devient telle qu'en
prenant conscience de sa spécificité, de ses intérêts propres et de
la manière dont elle peut utiliser son influence dans la situation
présente, qu'en se donnant une organisation à l'échelle d'un
territoire ou d'un Etat;[31] de toute façon, en dépassant les cadres où
elle était traditionnellement significative.[32] Les quatre groupes
jusqu'ici mentionnés sont repérables aussi bien pendant la période
coloniale que pendant les premières années qui ont suivi l'obtention de l'indépendance: leur importance relative est variable selon
les pays—et chacun d'eux présente de ce point de vue une con-
figuration particulière. Mais il faut noter aussi que l'indépendance
contribue à dégager d'autres types d'élites. L'une au moins est à
signaler, que des événements récents, en plusieurs pays africains,
ont mise en vedette:[33] l'*élite militaire*. Peu nombreuse, relativement homogène,[34] le rôle qu'elle peut éventuellement jouer dans
la vie nationale ne tient pas seulement à ce qu'elle est détentrice
de la force matérielle, mais aussi à ce qu'elle élabore une certaine
idéologie, liée à l'image qu'elle se fait d'elle-même, en tant que
groupe alliant, seul, 'la compétence à la vertu'[35] et assumant avec
le plus d'intensité la conscience nationale.[36]

[30] Ainsi des autorités religieuses bénéficiant de l'élimination des autorités proprement politiques. Cf. Mercier (1956).
[31] On peut rappeler de ce point de vue la création d'un 'syndicat' des chefs
traditionnels en Guinée, d'une association des chefs traditionnels au Dahomey
dans les années qui ont suivi la seconde guerre mondiale.
[32] Ce qui ne va pas sans difficultés et sans contradictions; d'où la fragilité d'une
telle élite.
[33] Par exemple au Togo, au Dahomey, au Gabon, au Congo. Le cas des
mutineries intervenues dans certaines unités militaires en plusieurs pays d'Afrique
Orientale est très différent: ce ne sont pas là les cadres de l'armée qui se dressent
pour la 'sauvegarde de l'unité nationale' et la 'lutte contre la tyrannie'.
[34] Encore faudrait-il distinguer deux générations, au moins dans le cas des pays
d'expression française: celle des anciens officiers de l'armée française, et celle des
jeunes lieutenants qui n'y ont pas servi.
[35] Selon l'expression de G. d'Arboussier.
[36] Voir, entre autres, cette réponse faite à L. Terray au cours de l'enquête qu'il
a conduite dans un groupe d'élèves-officiers, originaires pour la plupart des pays
de l'ancienne Afrique Occidentale Française: 'Je ne tiendrai qu'à faire mon devoir,

Dès qu'apparaît—parfois avant, le plus souvent après la seconde guerre mondiale—la contestation *active, organisée*, et de type moderniste, de la domination coloniale, les groupes qui viennent d'être inventoriés se manifestent comme des forces politiques; soit directement: ainsi l'élite de l'instruction et l'élite ouvrière quand elles forment les cadres des partis et des syndicats; soit indirectement: ainsi l'élite à base traditionnelle quand, spontanément ou sous l'effet des manipulations de l'autorité coloniale, elle constitue un frein, temporairement efficace, au développement et au succès de mouvements politiques radicaux, sans qu'elle se donne nécessairement une organisation à cet effet. Avec l'obtention de l'autonomie interne, puis de l'indépendance, le jeu de ces forces politiques s'étend et se diversifie. Née dans la lutte engagée au cours de la période précédente, une couche dirigeante s'est constituée, qui a pris la relève des gouvernements coloniaux; elle s'est recrutée dans l'élite de l'instruction, mais déjà ne se confond plus entièrement avec elle (Mercier, 1961). Elle n'a au départ nul besoin de justifier la légitimité de sa détention du pouvoir; mais la naissance de nouvelles formes de contestation— de la part d'une jeune élite intellectuelle assurée de sa plus grande compétence et formée à une pensée politique plus radicale, de la part des syndicats rassemblant la bureaucratie subalterne et les ouvriers, etc.—la contraindra peu à peu à le faire et à donner une définition plus précise d'elle-même et de son rôle.[37] Le jeu des diverses forces de contestation est complexe; il est clair que toutes ne visent pas la prise du pouvoir: dans les crises récentes du Congo, du Gabon et du Dahomey, par exemple, les syndicats et l'armée se sont contentés dans une première phase de faire pression sur lui puis, lorsqu'il fut pratiquement tombé entre leurs mains, de s'en dessaisir au profit d'autres membres de la couche politique

---

et que les autres fassent le leur; que les dirigeants ne profitent pas d'abuser de leur autorité sur le peuple; dans ce cas, je me verrais dans l'obligation de passer dans le maquis avec ma troupe et de prendre les mesures de salut public en réprimant terriblement leurs actes.'

[37] D'où entre autres un effort pour préciser la signification de la notion de parti unique que, de façon en apparence paradoxale, des éléments plus jeunes et plus radicaux de l'élite intellectuelle critiqueront à partir de ce moment. Cf. par exemple le débat organisé par *Jeune Afrique* sur ce thème du parti unique de novembre 1963 à janvier 1964.

classique. A l'occasion de telles crises on peut observer de façon privilégiée quelles relations les 'élites' particulières entretiennent les unes avec les autres—conflits et compromis—et comment elles définissent leur place dans la société globale—par rapport aux intérêts ou aux aspirations qui leur sont propres. On peut aussi évaluer leur degré de cohésion: l'unité de certains de ces groupes s'accentue, d'autres connaissent des clivages de plus en plus marqués. Enfin on peut apprécier l'influence qu'ils sont capables d'exercer sur la masse de la population, et qui souvent se révèle de nature très différente selon que l'on envisage les citadins ou les ruraux: ainsi la révolution dahoméenne de 1963 apparaîtra dans les villes comme une victoire des forces syndicales sur une 'bourgeoisie politique' privilégiée et corrompue, dans les campagnes comme une revanche partielle des ethnies du Sud contre celles du Nord qui leur avaient, quelques années plus tôt, imposé leur arbitrage.[38] Il nous paraît souhaitable que soit entreprise une série d'analyses précises des crises politiques survenues au cours des dernières années dans nombre de pays africains: en permettant de saisir les diverses élites en action et en conflit, elles apporteraient un complément indispensable à la description statique que l'on en peut faire.[39]

On ne retiendra ici que quelques cas, concernant l'Afrique d'expression française, qui mériteraient des études plus approfondies, et dont on ne peut donner pour l'instant qu'une vue schématique. Le cas du Sénégal peut être signalé d'abord, où trois crises successives: celle du référendum (1958), celle de la rupture de la Fédération du Mali (1960), celle enfin qui résulta du conflit entre le Président Senghor et le Président Dia (1962), constituent autant de révélateurs quant à la nature et aux possibilités d'intervention des forces politiques organisées ou latentes. La première conclut une période complexe, dont on a ailleurs tenté l'analyse (Mercier, 1961), où se mêlaient des développements politiques propres au Sénégal et des tendances générales à l'Afrique française de l'Ouest. Dans la revendication de type nationaliste, les

[38] Avec la constitution du gouvernement Maga, avant l'indépendance.
[39] Plusieurs chercheurs s'orientent, fort heureusement, vers des études de ce genre (B. Charles, L. Terray, etc.).

syndicats se trouvaient, dans les années 1950, très en flèche par rapport à des partis politiques plus ou moins englués dans la tradition des 'clientèles électorales' des Quatre Communes du Sénégal. Le regroupement des partis jusque là en rivalité, l'intégration à la nouvelle formation politique dominante des jeunes intellectuels théoriciens du 'parti de masse', conduisent à la première prise de position politique en faveur de l'indépendance. La situation semble clarifiée, l'ensemble des élites modernistes paraît se diriger vers un même choix, celui du 'non' au référendum.[40] En fait, un renversement de tendance se produit dans les dernières semaines qui précèdent celui-ci, et le parti dominant, le Bloc Populaire Sénégalais, prend position en faveur du 'oui' et entraîne une adhésion massive de l'électorat. C'est là une situation privilégiée pour l'étude d'une part des clivages qui s'effectuent à l'intérieur de l'élite de l'instruction—selon les générations, selon le degré d'acceptation de la tradition 'assimilationniste', selon le type dominant de formation, politique ou syndicale, selon enfin l'intensité du contact avec l'élite ouvrière—d'autre part de la pesée que peut exercer l'élite à base traditionnelle—il s'agit là des chefs religieux conservateurs—à laquelle en définitive se rallie la direction du parti, que ses 'jeunes Turcs' avaient entraînée plus loin qu'elle ne le souhaitait. La crise de 1960—rupture de la Fédération du Mali—est sans doute moins significative, bien qu'elle mette en scène dans l'ensemble les mêmes protagonistes; l'existence d'un patriotisme sénégalais—ou de sentiments antisoudanais largement diffusés—contribue à la diluer, mais n'efface pas pour autant les tensions fondamentales qui viennent d'être mentionnées (Mercier, 1961). La crise de 1962 se déroule à plusieurs niveaux: conflit entre deux hommes, elle aura pour conséquence l'instauration d'une constitution 'monocéphale', selon l'expression du Président Senghor qui l'emporte dans ce conflit; opposition entre deux conceptions du rôle du parti, entre deux conceptions du développement économique, elle conduira à une réorganisation de celui-là, à une sensible modification des perspectives de celui-ci. Quant au rôle joué par les différents groupes d'influence, elle apparaît en nette continuité avec les

[40] C'est-à-dire le choix de l'indépendance immédiate.

crises précédentes; cependant un nouvel élément se manifeste, l'élite économique, liée au commerce de type colonial et opposée à une socialisation trop précipitée.[41] Ainsi une étude d'ensemble des élites sénégalaises, de leur évolution et de leurs relations doit-elle faire une large part à l'analyse détaillée de cette séquence d'événements ayant qualité de révélateur. Deux autres cas, sensiblement différents, pourraient être l'objet d'études exemplaires. La crise violente connue par le Mali en 1962 révèle l'affrontement entre l'élite de l'instruction, maîtresse du parti unique établi après l'indépendance, et l'élite de la réussite économique, menacée dans ses intérêts essentiels par les restrictions progressivement apportées au libre commerce.[42] La révolution du Dahomey en 1963[43] manifeste les clivages profonds qui sont intervenus au sein de l'élite de l'instruction: ici les syndicats, regroupant la petite bureaucratie, les employés et les ouvriers, trouve immédiatement l'audience des masses[44] et peut aisément exploiter un mouvement, d'abord spontané, dirigé contre les privilèges de la couche dirigeante: elle montre aussi dans quelles conditions les cadres de l'armée peuvent prendre une position d'arbitrage entre les forces politiques en présence.[45] Ce ne sont là que quelques exemples et thèmes de recherche. Il est essentiel que de telles études, au niveau de la sociologie politique, soient multipliées; c'est par l'analyse des situations conflictuelles que les 'élites' en tant que groupes d'influence, groupes de contestation, groupes de pression, peuvent être le plus clairement appréhendées, dans leur évolution, leurs scissions, leurs fusions; et que l'éventuelle apparition de 'classes sociales' au moins embryonnaires peut être le plus sûrement repérée.

[41] Et une première intervention, dans l'hésitation, de l'armée.
[42] C. Meillassoux en a abordé l'analyse au cours d'une recherche conduite à Bamako.
[43] Celle du Congo-Brazzaville, la même année, lui est largement comparable.
[44] Au moins urbaines. Cf. *supra*.
[45] Une première analyse de cette crise dahoméenne est actuellement préparée par L. Terray.

BIBLIOGRAPHY

Balandier, G.
  (1955) *Sociologie des Brazzavilles Noires*, Paris.
Beals, R. L.
  (1951) 'Urbanism, Urbanisation, Acculturation', *American Anthropologist*, 53.
Gross, L.
  (1959) 'The use of the class concept in sociological research', *American Journal of Sociology*, vol. 54.
Gurvitch, G.
  (1964) *Le concept de classes sociales*, Paris.
Mercier, P.
  (1954) 'Aspects des problèmes de stratification sociale dans l'Ouest africain' *Cahiers Internationaux de Sociologie*, tome 17.
  (1956) 'Evolution des élites sénégalaises', in UNESCO, *Bulletin International de Sociologie*, tome 8.
  (1961) 'La vie politique dans les centres urbains du Sénégal', *Cahiers Internationaux de Sociologie*, tome 24.
Mitchell, J. C.
  (1963) 'Theoretical orientations in African urban studies', *American Anthropological Association, Discussion on the Anthropology of Complex Societies*.
U.N.E.S.C.O.
  (1956) 'Les élites africaines', *Bulletin International des Sciences Sociales*, tome 8.
Warner, L., and Lunt, S.
  (1941) *The Social Life of a Modern Community*, New York.

Summary

ELITES AND POLITICAL FORCES

The concept of elite lacks a precise and universally accepted definition; one tends to derive a meaning from the various usages of the word. The problem of definition is bound up with the concept of social stratification—both in general and in particular in its application to African territories in the colonial and post-colonial periods. Few studies of social stratification have been carried out in Africa. This may be readily explained. Ethnographers have been interested in other problems and have lacked the conceptual tools for an analysis of stratification. The conscious use of 'class' terminology has been inhibited by the persistence of traditional relationships and by the opposition between the metropolitan power and the colonial peoples.

Should one therefore rely on a set of objective characteristics—wealth, occupation, style of life, and so on—to describe a population? Such can be used in studies of social differentiation and of social mobility. But they present a static picture of society; they do not describe the tensions which exist in a society experiencing rapid social change. Any analysis of the dynamic processes in a society rests on a study of the development of new social groups rather than on delimitation of strata or categories.

These social groups constitute the elites; with them lies the initiative in processes of change. Each elite has its own social characteristics, its interests and aspirations, its ideologies; to some degree each is conscious of its status in society. The elites do not constitute a complete social system into which the whole population can be grouped. Nor can they be ranked hierarchically. But they are nation-wide, though susceptible to conflicting local and traditional loyalties. The relationship between the elites and the masses is complex and often ambiguous; alternately, the elites pursue their own interests and seek to influence and mobilize the masses. Between the elites themselves the relationship fluctuates.

Five types of elites predominate in African states:

    (a) The highly educated elite—the elite *par excellence*; highly westernized; holds administrative offices; enjoys both high and stable incomes; provides the basic cadres for the nationalist parties.

    (b) The artisan elite—the trained men, organized in trade unions.

    (c) The commercial elite—the entrepreneurs, traders, and planters; its composition varies from one country to another, as does its urban or rural, modern or traditionalist, character.

    (d) The traditional elite—the holders of offices perpetuated under the colonial régime; members of this elite enjoy not nation-wide but only local influence.

    (e) The military elite—small in number and relatively homogeneous; its future importance lies in its control of physical force and its public image of incorruptability.

Either just before or immediately after the Second World War these elites began to be politically active—the educated elite in nationalist political parties, the artisan elite in trade unions. The traditional elite was active in putting a temporary brake on the more radical movements. With political independence a new ruling elite was formed, co-extensive, though not entirely so, with the educated elite. Opposition to this group by a younger elite and by trade unions has forced the ruling elite to define its status in society.

Between these various elites there now exists a complex pattern of competition for power; not all elites, however, seek active power for themselves—some are prepared to act as pressure groups. The outbreaks of conflict or tension in the African states demonstrate this inter-elite competition and the relationship between elites; they illustrate the relationships between the elites and the masses; in studying these conflicts one may evaluate the cohesion among the various elites and the manner in which they are forced to define their position in society.

Some examples are given to illustrate this inter-elite conflict. Senegal suffered three periods of tension. In 1958 the referendum vote took place; this displayed the divisions within the educated elite between those of different generations, those differing in their approach to assimilation, and those in varying degrees of contact with the artisan elite. In 1960 the crisis over the rupture of the Mali Federation showed the same conflicts within the elite, but emphasized in addition the strength of Senegalese patriotism. In the overthrow of President Dia in 1962 the overt issue was the clash between the President and Leopold Senghor. But the underlying issues were the differing concepts of the role of the party and of economic development. The commercial elite were an important factor here in opposing any rapid socialization of the economy.

The same analysis can be repeated in other countries. In Mali in 1962 the conflict lay between the educated elite, controlling the single-party, and the commercial elite. In Dahomey in 1963 the artisan elite found support among the masses in their agitation against the conspicuous affluence of the ruling elite; here the army played a mediating role. The analysis of conflict between the elites is a most necessary element in the study of political processes in the new African States.

INDEX

banks, 343, 360

Bantu, 17, 286, 290, 294, 296, 308; Bantu
Authorities Act, 289; Bantustan, 290,
291, 297, 306

Banyankole, 356

Banyarwanda, 357

barristers, 89, 91

Basutoland, 349

bathrooms, 130

beans, velvet, 272

'Beatrice Cottages', 130, 132

Bechuanaland, 349

Benin, 187

betrothal, 30

bicycles, 201

birth, 193

Boigny, President Houphouet, 36

books, 169, 170, 171, 172

bourgeoisie, 44, 56, 57, 119, 122, 124, 330,
338, 375

Boy Scouts, 37, 169

Brahmins, 50

'Brazilians', 16, 186, 187, 188

Brazzaville–Bacongo, 244, 248

Brew family, 15, 87–100

brick-making, 272, 281

bridewealth, 30

Britain, 5, 203, 257, 268, 321, 328; British,
108, 110, 111, 150–9, 321; *see also*
colonial territories, universities

B.S.A. Company, 126

Buganda, 21, 37, 56, 349, 350, 353; Kabaka
of, 361

'Bunga', 288

bureaucrats, 56, 111, 217–18, 328, 330, 339,
362; bureaucracy, 18, 19, 21, 60, 114,
164, 169, 216–26, 283, 316, 330, 334, 337,
338, 374, 377

burials, 36, 193, 317

Burundi, 349

Busia, Dr., 34

business, 6, 8, 19; management, 220; *see
also* capitalism, commerce, directors,
industry, government corporations, real
estate

Calvinism, 41, 46

Cameroons, 35

Canada, 321; Canadians, 321

Cape Coast, 87–100, 109, 200

capitalism, 41, 42, 105, 174

capitals, 20; national, 5, 28; regional, 5, 28

cars, 1, 11, 12, 39, 111, 129, 131, 133, 134,
164, 166, 167, 201, 317, 319, 330–1

casinos, 37

caste, 235, 236, 238, 249, 356

Catholicism, *see* Roman Catholicism

cattle, 272, 273, 274, 276, 280, 294

cement-works, 232

centralization, 5

ceremonial, *see* traditional ritual

Chagga, 44

Chamber of Commerce, 37

charitable associations, 37, 38

chemical industry, 231

chiefs, 13, 14, 16, 34, 35, 36, 40, 44, 48, 90,
93, 94, 95, 99, 107, 108, 111–12, 113, 192,
193, 201, 288, 289, 290, 293, 294, 295,
296, 298, 299, 303, 304, 305, 307, 308,
313, 328, 329, 356, 357, 373; Chief
Matanzima, 298, 299, 300, 301, 302, 303,
304, 305, 306, 307; Chief Poto, 298, 299,
300, 301, 302, 303, 304, 306, 307; chiefdom, 93, 113, 287, 289; Paramount
Chief, 288, 301, 302; sub-chiefs, 107;
children of, 108

children, 140, 147, 150, 151, 153, 154, 158,
165, 166, 168, 173, 175, 200, 281; child-
bearing, 28; child health, 168; child-
rearing, 24, 43, 163, 167, 175, 179, 180,
209, 210; changed patterns of child-
rearing, 3, 40, 168, 210, 211; of chiefs,
see chiefs; of elite, *see* elite

'Chitepo flats', 130

Christianity, 35, 36, 98, 108, 109, 140, 149,
150, 184, 185, 193, 194, 195, 206, 219,
293, 313; Christian church clubs, 37;
Coptic Christianity, 313; *see also* Calvinism, Methodism, Non-Conformists,
Protestantism, Reformation, Roman
Catholicism, Salvation Army

Ciskei, 294

City Council, 353; city councillor, 355

civil liberties, 59

civil services, 4, 5, 6, 7, 8, 9, 10, 12, 15, 16,
18, 37, 45, 54, 56, 59, 109, 110, 111, 113,
121, 165, 167, 179, 216, 221, 328, 330, 332,
337, 339, 353; colonial, 7, 27, 49, 90, 330

clan, *see* lineage

class, *see* social class

classlessness, 331, 339

clergy, 18, 313

clerical workers, 6, 10, 11, 17, 21, 26, 27, 28,
60, 111, 112, 140, 180, 202, 206, 216, 336

clinics, 129

clothing industry, 231

clubs, 1; *see also* associations, dancing/
drinking clubs

48783

ST. MARY'S COLLEGE OF MARYLAND
ST. MARY'S CITY, MARYLAND